Cultural and Civilisational Links between India and Southeast Asia

Shyam Saran
Editor

Cultural and Civilisational Links between India and Southeast Asia

Historical and Contemporary Dimensions

palgrave
macmillan

Editor
Shyam Saran
Centre for Policy Research
New Delhi, India

Research and Information System
for Developing Countries (RIS)
New Delhi, India

ISBN 978-981-10-7316-8   ISBN 978-981-10-7317-5 (eBook)
https://doi.org/10.1007/978-981-10-7317-5

Library of Congress Control Number: 2018937672

© ASEAN-India Centre at Research and Information System for Developing Countries (RIS) 2018
This work is subject to copyright. All rights are solely and exclusively licensed by the Publisher, whether the whole or part of the material is concerned, specifically the rights of translation, reprinting, reuse of illustrations, recitation, broadcasting, reproduction on microfilms or in any other physical way, and transmission or information storage and retrieval, electronic adaptation, computer software, or by similar or dissimilar methodology now known or hereafter developed.
The use of general descriptive names, registered names, trademarks, service marks, etc. in this publication does not imply, even in the absence of a specific statement, that such names are exempt from the relevant protective laws and regulations and therefore free for general use.
The publisher, the authors, and the editors are safe to assume that the advice and information in this book are believed to be true and accurate at the date of publication. Neither the publisher nor the authors or the editors give a warranty, express or implied, with respect to the material contained herein or for any errors or omissions that may have been made. The publisher remains neutral with regard to jurisdictional claims in published maps and institutional affiliations.

Cover credit: Kreangagirl/Getty Images

Printed on acid-free paper

This Palgrave Macmillan imprint is published by the registered company Springer Nature Singapore Pte Ltd.
The registered company address is: 152 Beach Road, #21-01/04 Gateway East, Singapore 189721, Singapore

सचिव (पूर्व)
SECRETARY (EAST)

विदेश मंत्रालय, नई दिल्ली-110 011
MINISTRY OF EXTERNAL AFFAIRS
NEW DELHI-110 011
Phone : 2301 2760 • Fax : 2379 4139
E-Mail : secyeast@mea.gov.in

FOREWORD

India and Southeast Asia inhabit a shared geographical and cultural space. India's cultural and civilizational linkages with Southeast Asia date back thousands of years. In fact, no other country has such strong links with Southeast Asia as India does, by way of religion, language, culture and civilization.

India's relations with ASEAN have gained momentum, embedded firmly in "culture, commerce and connectivity". Starting as a sectoral partner of ASEAN in 1992, India became a dialogue partner of ASEAN in 1996, a summit-level partner in 2002 and a strategic partner in 2012. On January 25, 2018, India and ASEAN celebrated 25 years of their partnership, at a commemorative summit in New Delhi, with the participation of Heads of State/Government from all the ten countries of ASEAN and India. For the first time, all the ten ASEAN leaders also attended India's Republic Day celebrations on January 26, 2018, in New Delhi, as Guests of Honour.

Our shared cultural linkages help us to understand and confront contemporary challenges. Our leaders recognize that there is a need to deepen ASEAN-India ties, based on our rich cultural affinities. It is also recognized that there is a need to create greater awareness of the linkages between India and ASEAN.

The ASEAN-India Centre (AIC), Research and Information System for Developing Countries (RIS) in collaboration with the Indian Council for Cultural Research (ICCR) and the Ministry of External Affairs (MEA), Government of India, organized an International Conference on "ASEAN-India Cultural Links: Historical and Contemporary Dimensions", which

v

was held at the India Habitat Centre, New Delhi, on July 23–24, 2015. Twenty-four eminent scholars from several parts of the world presented their research papers at this Conference. This book titled *Cultural and Civilisational Links between India and Southeast Asia: Historical and Contemporary Dimensions*, edited by Ambassador Shyam Saran, presents several dimensions of cultural linkages between India and Southeast Asia. It contains research papers, written by eminent scholars on various aspects of historical and cultural relations between India and Southeast Asia, which were presented at the Conference.

As India's engagement with the ASEAN countries moves forward, the socio-cultural linkages between the two regions can be utilized effectively to expand collaboration, beyond the economic and political domains into areas of education, tourism and people-to-people contact. Several new ideas for strengthening our cultural relations emerge in this book.

I congratulate Ambassador Shyam Saran and the AIC in publishing this book for the use of a larger audience. I am confident this book will serve as a valuable reference for researchers and policymakers.

Preeti Saran

Preface

India–Association of Southeast Asian Nations (ASEAN) relations have witnessed remarkable growth in recent years. At the ASEAN–India Commemorative Summit 2012 in New Delhi, the two sides elevated relations to a strategic partnership. The summit welcomed the report of the ASEAN–India Eminent Persons' Group and its vision statement on the future of these relations. In this context, the summit encouraged 'the study, documentation and dissemination of knowledge about civilization along links between ASEAN and India'. India's Act East Policy has imparted fresh momentum to these relations in all their multifarious dimensions, including in the field of arts and culture. ASEAN and India are celebrating twenty-five years of partnership.

The ASEAN–India Centre (AIC) at the Research and Information System for Developing Countries (RIS) in collaboration with the Indian Council for Cultural Relations (ICCR) and the Ministry of External Affairs (MEA), Government of India, organised an international conference 'ASEAN–India Cultural Links: Historical and Contemporary Dimensions' at the India Habitat Centre, New Delhi on 23–24 July 2015. Twenty-four eminent scholars from ASEAN countries, India and several other countries presented original research papers at this conference. They discussed a number of key issues that are relevant to the objective of deepening ASEAN–India cultural relations. These are now presented in a single volume, which will become a valuable reference for scholars and researchers, but will be of interest to the general reader as well.

I would like to record my appreciation of the efforts made by Dr Prabir De and his team at AIC in putting together this volume. I wish to thank the Director General, Dr Sachin Chaturvedi, and other colleagues at RIS for their constant support and cooperation. I wish to thank the President of ICCR, Professor Lokesh Chandra, and its former Director General, Dr Satish C. Mehta, who lent their valuable support to the conference and contributed to its success.

I am also grateful to Ambassador Anil Wadhwa, former Secretary (East), MEA, Government of India; Ambassador Preeti Saran, Present Secretary (East), MEA, Government of India; Ms Pooja Kapur, former Joint Secretary (ASEAN Multilateral), MEA, Government of India; and Mr Anurag Bhushan, the current Joint Secretary (ASEAN Multilateral), MEA, Government of India for their support and cooperation.

This book provides new ideas and suggestions related to deepening ASEAN–India cultural relations. It will be welcomed by all those who have an interest in the rich and remarkable history and contemporary dimensions of India's cultural engagement with its Southeast Asian neighbours.

New Delhi, India   Shyam Saran

Acknowledgements

Cultural and Civilisational Links between India and Southeast Asia: Historical and Contemporary Dimensions has been edited by Ambassador Shyam Saran, former chairman, RIS, with the support of Prof. Prabir De, Coordinator, AIC at RIS, who has also coordinated the ASEAN–India Cultural Links Project under the overall guidance of Ambassador Shyam Saran.

We are grateful to Prof. Sachin Chaturvedi, Director General, RIS for his guidance and encouragement. The publication has immensely benefited from discussions with Ms Malini Saran and Dr Sudha Gopalakrishnan. In particular, we are thankful to Dr Kapila Vatsyayan and Prof. Lokesh Chandra for their contribution, guidance and cooperation. Editorial assistance has been received from Ms Sarah Hasan, Mr Sunando Basu and Ms Sreya Pan.

Every chapter in this volume went through a peer review process. We are thankful to the authors who have extended their fullest support and adhered to deadlines while revising these chapters, despite their busy schedules.

We are grateful to Ambassador Anil Wadhwa, former Secretary (East), MEA, Government of India; Ambassador Preeti Saran, Present Secretary (East), MEA, Government of India; Ms. Pooja Kapur, former Joint Secretary (ASEAN Multilateral), MEA, Government of India; Mr Anurag Bhushan, the current Joint Secretary (ASEAN Multilateral), MEA, Government of India; Col. Sandeep Puri, Director (ASEAN Multilateral), MEA, Government of India; and Mr Abhijit Chakraborty, Deputy

Secretary (ASEAN Multilateral), MEA, Government of India, for their support and cooperation.

In particular, we are thankful to Ambassador Suresh Reddy, Indian Ambassador to ASEAN, for his cooperation. Ms Niharika Gupta and Ms Kiran Wagh extended very useful administrative assistance throughout the project. At Palgrave Macmillan, we are thankful to Dr Sagarika Ghosh and Ms Sandeep Kaur for fast-tracking the project and for extending their cooperation at every stage of publication.

Views expressed in this book are those of the contributors and not those of the Government of India or those of ASEAN countries, RIS, AIC, ASEAN Secretariat, or the Indian Council for Cultural Relations (ICCR). Usual disclaimers apply.

Contents

1 Introduction   1
  Shyam Saran

Part I   Trade and Maritime Links Between South and Southeast Asia   17

2 Early Contacts Between Bali and India   19
  I Wayan Ardika

3 Trans-locality and Mobility across the Bay of Bengal: Nagapattinam in Context   31
  Himanshu Prabha Ray

4 Indian Patterned Cotton Textiles and Trade with the East and Southeast   51
  Lotika Varadarajan

Part II   Continuities and Change   65

5 Indigenous Thought on Indian Traditions in Thailand   67
  Amara Srisuchat

6   Panyupayana: The Emergence of Hindu Polities in the
    Pre-Islamic Philippines   93
    Joefe B. Santarita

7   Indian–Southeast Asian Contacts and Cultural
    Exchanges: Evidence from Vietnam   107
    Le Thi Lien

Part III   Representations of Religions and Rituals   129

8   From Śivaśāsana to Agama Hindu Bali: Tracing the
    Indic Roots of Modern Balinese Hinduism   131
    Andrea Acri

9   Power, Prestige and Possession: Interwoven Legacies of
    Ida Pedanda Istris 'Priestesses' in Balinese Hinduism   151
    Madhu Khanna

Part IV   Textual Traditions and Transmissions   179

10 Transmission of Textual Traditions in South and
    Southeast Asia: A View from India   181
    Sudha Gopalakrishnan

11 The Bhagavad-Gītā Sections of the Old Javanese
    Bhīṣmaparwa, Text-Building and the Formation of the
    State in Pre-modern Indonesia   193
    Thomas M. Hunter

12 The Reworking of Indian Epics in the Hands of
    Javanese and Malay Authors   209
    Ding Choo Ming

13 Camille Bulcke's *Ramakatha-Utpatti aur Vikas*:
    An Important Reference Work for Scholars in the Field
    of Ramayana Studies   225
    Malini Saran and Vinod C. Khanna

Part V   Sacred Geographies and Localisations of Beliefs   239

14   Archaeology as Soft Power in ASEAN–India Cultural Contexts   241
Sachchidanand Sahai

15   Shiva's Land: Understanding the Religious Landscape of Early Southeast Asia   253
John Guy

16   Ancient Architectural Influence Between Bali and Majapahit: Drawing Upon the Affinities with Ancient Indian Architecture and the Way It Is Developed in Bali   275
Ir Nyoman Popo Priyatna Danes

Part VI   Evolving Artistic Expressions: From Tradition to Modernity   291

17   Natyasastraic Links in Cambodia, Thailand and Indonesia   293
Padma Subramanyam

Part VII   Writing Our Own Histories: Changing Methodologies   299

18   An Imperial Divorce: The Division of South and Southeast Asia in the Colonial Discourse of the Nineteenth Century   301
Farish A. Noor

19   Monuments, Motifs, Myths: Architecture and its Transformations in Early India and Southeast Asia   325
Parul Pandya Dhar

Appendix A: Programme of the ASEAN–India Civilizational Links Conference, 23–24 July 2015   347

Appendix B: Keynote Address by Ambassador Anil Wadhwa, Secretary (East), Ministry of External Affairs at the International Conference on 'ASEAN–India Cultural Links: Historical and Contemporary Dimensions' Held at New Delhi on 23 July 2015   351

Appendix C: Inaugural Address by Prof. Lokesh Chandra, President, ICCR at the International Conference on 'ASEAN–India Cultural Links: Historical and Contemporary Dimensions', Held at New Delhi on 23 July 2015   357

Appendix D: Special Address by Prof. Lokesh Chandra, President, ICCR at the International Conference on 'ASEAN–India Cultural Links: Historical and Contemporary Dimensions', Held at New Delhi on 24 July 2015   363

Appendix E: Valedictory Address by Dr Kapila Vatsyayan, Chairperson, IIC-Asia Project at the International Conference on 'ASEAN–India Cultural Links: Historical and Contemporary Dimensions', Held at New Delhi on 24 July 2015   367

NOTES ON CONTRIBUTORS

Andrea Acri EPHE, PSL, Paris, France

I Wayan Ardika Faculty of Letters, Udayana University, Bali, Indonesia

Ir Nyoman Popo Priyatna Danes Scholar and Architect, Bali, Indonesia

Parul Pandya Dhar Department of History, University of Delhi, New Delhi, India

Ding Choo Ming Former Principal Research Fellow, Institute of Malay World & Civilization, National University of Malaysia, Selangor, Malaysia

Sudha Gopalakrishnan Sahapedia, New Delhi, India

John Guy Florence and Herbert Irving Curator of South and Southeast Asian Art, The Metropolitan Museum of Art, New York, NY, USA

Thomas M. Hunter Department of Asian Studies, University of British Columbia, Vancouver, BC, Canada

Madhu Khanna National Museum, New Delhi, India; Centre for the Study of Comparative Religion & Civilisations, Jamia Millia Islamia, New Delhi, India

Vinod C. Khanna Former Ambassador of India to Indonesia, New Delhi, India

Le Thi Lien Institute of Archaeology, Vietnamese Academy of Social Sciences, Hanoi, Vietnam

Farish A. Noor S. Rajaratnam School of International Studies (RSIS), Nanyang Technological University (NTU), Singapore

Himanshu Prabha Ray Distant Worlds Programme, Ludwig Maximilian University, Munich, Germany

Sachchidanand Sahai Preah Vihear National Autimhority, Royal Government of Cambodia, Preah Vihear, Cambodia; UNESCO Expert for the Archaeological Complex of Sambor Prei Kuk, Phnom Penh, Cambodia

Joefe B. Santarita Asian Center, University of the Philippines Diliman, Quezon City, Philippines

Malini Saran Independent Researcher, New Delhi, India

Shyam Saran Centre for Policy Research, New Delhi, India; Research and Information System for Developing Countries (RIS), New Delhi, India

Amara Srisuchat Fine Arts Department, Ministry of Culture, Bangkok, Thailand

Padma Subramanyam Bharata-Ilanimgo Foundation for Asian Culture (BIFAC), Chennai, India

Lotika Varadarajan National Museum, New Delhi, India

LIST OF FIGURES

Fig. 2.1	Rouletted sherds, Arikamedu sherd of type 10, and a complete rouletted ware bowl from Kobak Kendal, West Java. Source: Author's own	20
Fig. 2.2	A sherd of Arikamedu type 18, an inscribed sherd of Kharosthi or Brahmi script and gold beads from Sembiran. Source: Author's own	22
Fig. 2.3	Stupa Pagulingan and Gunung Kawi rock arts. Source: Author's own	23
Fig. 3.1	Archaeological sites along the east coast of India. Source: Author's own (map drawn by Uma Bhattacharya)	37
Fig. 3.2	Bronze Buddha from Nagapattinam now in the Government Museum, Chennai. Source: Author's own	41
Fig. 3.3	Bronze Jambhala and consort from Nagapattinam now in the Government Museum, Chennai. Source: Author's own	42
Fig. 3.4	Sixteenth-century Lokesvara image from Vellipalayam Nagapattinam district now in the Government Museum, Chennai. Source: Author's own	44
Fig. 4.1	Batik. Hair of Bima, Symbolic of Strength. Source: Textil Museum, Jakarta	52
Fig. 4.2	Ramayana panel. *Kalamkari*. Probably South Coromandel. Listed as ceremonial cloth and sacred heirloom (*mawa* or *ma'a*), eighteenth century. Traded to Toraja people, Sulawesi, Indonesia. Source: National Gallery of Australia, Canberra. Gift of Michael and Mary Abbott, 1991	52
Fig. 4.3	*Sarassa*, fragment used in Japanese tea ceremony. Mayeda Collection. Source: Kyoto National Museum, Kyoto, Japan	53

LIST OF FIGURES

Fig. 4.4	*Poleng*, as depicted on wayside shrine. Bali, Indonesia. Source: Author's own	54
Fig. 4.5	Ma'a cloth, Sulawesi. Source: Spertus-Holmgren Collection, New York	57
Fig. 5.1	Bronze drum from Ko Samui, Surat Thani Province, fifth–first century BCE. Source: Author's own	69
Fig. 5.2	Tympanum of the bronze drum from Ko Samui depicting a stylized boat carrying either spirits of the dead or men with bird-like headdresses. Source: Author's own	70
Fig. 5.3	Sanskrit inscription written in Pallava script, sixth century, from Wat Maheyong in Nakhon Si Thammarat Province. Source: Author's own	74
Fig. 5.4	Stone dharmacakra from Nakhon Pathom Province, seventh–eighth century, depicting on its lower segment the personification of god Surya holding a lotus bud in each hand. Source: Author's own	76
Fig. 6.1	Courtesy of K.M. Panikkar. Source: Author's own	94
Fig. 7.1	Google map of Vietnamese and Indian early cultural centers: (a) center of the Jiao Chi realm; (b) center of the Liny–early Champa realm; (c) port-city of the Óc Eo–Funan realm. Source: Google	110
Fig. 7.2	Beads from Lang Vac site, Nghe An province (Photo: Le Thi Lien). Source: Author	113
Fig. 7.3	Beads from Nam Tho Son (Quang Nam province). Source: Author	114
Fig. 7.4	Dau Lady Buddha, Bac Ninh Province. Source: Author	115
Fig. 7.5	Mukhalinga, Óc Eo site, An Giang province. Source: Nguyen Huu Thiet	119
Fig. 9.1	Pedanda Istri Mayun with her husband, Denpasar. Source: Author	155
Fig. 9.2	Ida Pedanda Istri Kania Mas Kajeng in her shrine, Badung. Source: Author	156
Fig. 9.3	Senator, Ida Ayu Agung Mas, Sua Bali. Source: Author	157
Fig. 9.4	Ida Ayu Agung Mas in the ceremonial attire of Pedanda Istri. Source: Author	158
Fig. 9.5	Pedanda Istri Ida Ayu Agung Mas honouring a young priest with a crown. Source: Author	158
Fig. 9.6	Ida Pedanda Istri Kania Mas Kajeng adorned with a crown. Source: Author	165
Fig. 9.7	Balian Metwun, Denpasar. Source: Author	169
Fig. 9.8	Author with two Ida Pedanda Istri, Denpasar, 2009. Source: Author	173

LIST OF FIGURES   xix

Fig. 14.1   Temple N 17, Smiling Face in the Kudu, Ishanapura, Cambodia. One of the salient features of the temple is the kudu or semi-circular arches in which divine and semi-divine figures are placed. This feature also known as chaitya window, is popular both in South and North Indian temples. In this Cambodian example from Ishanapura, one of the several faces smiles in the kudu placed around temple N 17. Source: Author   247

Fig. 14.2   Title: The N 7 Temple in Ishanapura (Cambodia). There are ten octagonal temples in Ishanapura. In the north group of temples only N 7 is octagonal. These temples are octagonal from the base to pinnacle. Top to bottom octagonal brick temples in India are not known. These temples are called flying palaces since on the outer side walls of the temple, palaces are shown being carried by sculpted winged animals. Source: Author   249

Fig. 14.3   Winged animals, horse, garuda and lion shown carrying the octagonal temple as flying palace, Ishanapura, Cambodia. The octagonal temples have been documented from different parts of India, but the motif of winged animals carrying the temple/palace is absent in Indian examples. Source: Author   250

Fig. 15.1   Comb decorated with auspicious emblems (*astamangala*) and *hamsa*. Ivory, Deccan or Andhra Pradesh, *c*, second century CE, excavated Chansen, central Thailand. Source: National Museum, Bangkok   255

Fig. 15.2   Seal impression from an Indian matrix, probably Bihar; clay impression found U Thong, central Thailand, early to mid-sixth century. Source: U Thong National Museum, Suphanburi   256

Fig. 15.3   Rock-cut inscription of Purnavarman, ruler of the kingdom of Tarumanagara, Sunda, west Java, Indonesia, early sixth century (photographed in situ, Ciaruteun River, Ciampea, *c*. 1920). Source: Author   259

Fig. 15.4   Envoy from Langkasuka; detail of *Liang zhgong tu* (Illustrated History of the Liang). Handscroll. Eleventh-century copy of sixth-century original. Source: National Museum of China, Beijing   262

Fig. 15.5   Detail of lintel depicting the *Lingodbhavamurti* myth and a king's consecration, mid-seventh century. Found at Wat Eng Khna, Kampong Thom province, Cambodia. Sandstone. Source: National Museum of Cambodia, Phnom Penh   264

Fig. 15.6   Shiva as an Ascetic, seventh century. Found in Stung Treng province, northeastern Cambodia. Sandstone, h. 164 cm. Source: National Museum of Cambodia, Phnom Penh   266

LIST OF FIGURES

Fig. 15.7	Shiva installed on a lustration pedestal, eighth century. Recovered from temple A4, My Son, Quang Nam province, central Vietnam. Photographed in situ in 1903. Source: Author	267
Fig. 15.8	Ganesha, late seventh–eighth century. Recovered from temple E5, My Son, Quang Nam province, central Vietnam, Sandstone, h. 96 cm. The Museum of Cham Sculpture, Da Nang, Vietnam. Source: Author	268
Fig. 15.9	Tympanum depicting Shiva dancing before his assembled family and royal devotee. My Son, Champa, central Vietnam. Sandstone, h. 143 cm, w. 170 cm. Source: My Son Site Museum, Quang Nam	268
Fig. 15.10	Shiva Natesha, rock cut, Badami, Karanataka, India. Chalukya dynasty, early seventh century. Source: Author	269
Fig. 15.11	Shiva's footprints (*Shivapada*), second half of seventh–eighth century. Found in Stung Treng province, northeastern Cambodia, in 1911. Sandstone, 17 × 32 × 32 cm. Source: National Museum of Cambodia, Phnom Penh	270
Fig. 15.12	Stele with Shaiva Trident, Axe and Vase of Plenty, second half seventh century. Found at Vihar Thom, Kampong Cham province, southeastern Cambodia. Sandstone, h. 102 cm. Source: National Museum of Cambodia, Phnom Penh	271
Fig. 16.1	Expansion of Hinduism in Southeast Asia. Source: www.wikipedia.org	277
Fig. 16.2	Majapahit Empire. Source: www.wikipedia.com	281
Fig. 16.3	Extent of Majapahit Empire in fifteenth centuries. Note: Majapahit was a thalassocracy, extending its territory through maritime trade and dominance. At its height the realm and its diplomatic relations extended as far as Japan and South India. Source: Wijaya (2014)	281
Fig. 16.4	Maospahit temple in Denpasar. Source: Author	285
Fig. 19.1	A view of the brick temples of Campā at Mỹ Sơn, Vietnam. Source: Author	328
Fig. 19.2	Flat-roofed structure, N 17, Sambor Prei Kuk, Cambodia. Source: Author	329
Fig. 19.3	Temple-mountain of Angkor Wat, Cambodia. Source: Author	329
Fig. 19.4	Caṇḍi Arjuna, Dieng Plateau, Central Java, Indonesia. Source: Author	331
Fig. 19.5	Arjuna Ratha, Mamallapuram, Tamil Nadu, India. Source: Author	333
Fig. 19.6	'Flying Palace' on the exterior wall of an octagonal brick temple in the Southern group at Sambor Prei Kuk, Cambodia. Source: Author	335

Fig. 19.7　Drawing of *kāla-makara-toraṇa*, Borobudur, Central Java.
Source: Author　340

Fig. 19.8　Drawing of *prabhāvalī-toraṇa* framing a bronze image of Bodhisattva Avalokiteśvara from Sragen in Central Java.
Source: Author　341

CHAPTER 1

Introduction

Shyam Saran

The Government of India's Act East Policy, which was launched at the East Asia Summit in Myanmar in November 2014, has provided accelerated momentum to engagement with countries of Southeast Asia. The underlining principle of the policy, 'connectivity, culture, and commerce', has placed cultural interactions both in the contemporary period and historically at the forefront of this framework. This reorientation has led to introspection regarding a range of relevant themes, such as changing perspectives in the study and research of cultural interactions across the region in history; the need to expand multilateral conversations among researchers and students regarding the relevance of the past to the present and the future; and to include in the discussion not only the ancient past, but also the more recent past, when most parts of the Association of Southeast Asian Nations (ASEAN) region, with the exception of Thailand, were colonized by European powers.

Chapters in this volume draw on presentations made at the international conference 'ASEAN-India Cultural Links: Historical and Contemporary Dimensions', which was held at the India Habitat Centre, New Delhi, on 23–24 July 2015. The conference was organized by ASEAN–India Centre at the Research and Information System for

S. Saran (✉)
Centre for Policy Research, New Delhi, India

Research and Information System for Developing Countries (RIS),
New Delhi, India

© The Author(s) 2018
S. Saran (ed.), *Cultural and Civilisational Links between India and Southeast Asia*, https://doi.org/10.1007/978-981-10-7317-5_1

Developing Countries in collaboration with the Indian Council for Cultural Relations and the Ministry of External Affairs, Government of India. The conference followed up the Report of the ASEAN–India Eminent Persons Group of 2012, which recommended the inclusion of experts from ASEAN and India, and that researchers should work together on the shared legacy in fields such as archaeology, linguistics, libraries, textiles, fine arts and performing arts. This volume is a step in this direction.

The themes that provide unity to the chapters encompass shifting paradigms of understanding the past, especially with the introduction of new disciplines such as archaeology and art history in the colonial period; religious beliefs and rituals in South and Southeast Asian societies; and travel and maritime cultural contacts. Several issues need further research, especially the mapping of maritime travel and seafaring activity that formed the basis of cross-cultural interactions. In this introductory chapter, we provide a brief overview of secondary writings on the above-mentioned themes that help impart a context to the following chapters. It is important to factor in the beginnings of archaeology in this discussion, and the impact that this had on the study of the ancient past in South and Southeast Asia. In the second section we focus on the religious beliefs and theoretical underpinnings that underwrite the historical study of religion in South and Southeast Asia, while the final section deals with the written word, texts and transmission of knowledge along the maritime routes.

Archaeology and the 'Scientific' Study of the Past: The Beginnings

As discussed by Farish Noor (in this volume), Asia needs to reexamine its pre-colonial past, when it was a contiguous and borderless region. From the region's complex post-colonial legacy, modern states, fixed within identified national boundaries, have emerged—obscuring ancient contiguities. He has argued that since the construction of the nation state was a colonial legacy and artificial to begin with, it can be reconstructed and deconstructed to form new links between the two regions. This process would of course involve critical analysis of developments in archaeology and art history in the colonial period.

Archaeology as a discipline was introduced into South and Southeast Asia during the colonial period, and many of the institutions involved in the practice of archaeology in the ASEAN region were established at this time, such as the Archaeological Survey of India in 1861 soon after the creation of the British Raj in 1858.[1] 'British Burma' came into existence after the defeat of the Burmese king in the Third Burma War (1885–1887). Thus by the late nineteenth century, the British were able to control large parts of South Asia and to keep French commercial influence at bay.[2]

There are several similarities between the British experience in India and the emergence of the Dutch as a territorial power in Java, though Dutch control over the Indonesian archipelago was a slower process and was only completed by the early twentieth century. In the context of Java, the name of Thomas Stamford Raffles (1781–1826) stands out, first as a Malay translator to the Government of India and later in 1811 as the Lieutenant Governor of Java, who was soon promoted as Governor of Bencoolen (now Sumatra) and continued his work until 1824 when Java was ceded to the Dutch. Raffles' *The History of Java*, first published in 1817, remained the standard work until the end of the century and included a chapter on the antiquities and monuments of the region. Borobudur was perhaps the first major monument that drew the attention of the British in Southeast Asia, almost forty-seven years before the French naturalist and explorer Henri Mouhot (1826–1861) brought the ruins of Angkor to the attention of Europe. In 1901, the Dutch government established the Commission in the Netherlands Indies for Archaeological Research in Java and Madura, which was redesignated in 1913 as the Archaeological Service in the Netherlands Indies.

The mid-nineteenth century was also the period when France was looking for chances to expand its trade interests in mainland Southeast Asia, especially with China. In this it saw Vietnam as a springboard, and from the 1860s onwards was able to establish a foothold not only in Vietnam, but also to extend control over Cambodia. In 1863, the Cambodian monarch Norodom agreed to French protection and accepted what the French called their 'civilizing mission'. Even though the King of Siam was able to preserve his autonomy, the European challenge could not be entirely avoided and Thailand had to cede territories that had formed part of the

---

[1] Himanshu Prabha Ray, Archaeology and Empire: Buddhist Monuments in Monsoon Asia, *Indian Economic and Social History Review*, Volume 45, number 3, September 2008: 417–449. Himanshu Prabha Ray, *The Return of the Buddha: Ancient Symbols for a New Nation*, Routledge, London–New York–New Delhi, 2014.

[2] Milton Osborne, *Southeast Asia: An Introductory History*, Allen & Unwin, New South Wales, 2004: 73–75.

country for over a century. Therefore in 1907 Thailand relinquished its control over western Cambodia and Angkor, thus making Cambodia one of France's prized possessions.[3]

In France, the study of Asian religion gained momentum with the establishment and expansion of Musée Guimet in 1889, and the creation of École Coloniale in Paris signified the emergence of a career colonial service. Founded in Saigon on the initiative of the Académie des Inscriptions et Belle-Lettres in 1898, the Mission Archéologique d'Indochine became the École Française d'Extrême-Orient (EFEO) in 1901. At the same time, its seat was transferred to Hanoi. The original tasks of EFEO included archaeological exploration of French Indochina, the conservation of its monuments, the collection of manuscripts and research into the region's linguistic heritage. In 1930 the Buddhist Institute in Cambodia was founded, and the 1860s to 1900 saw French attempts to procure and catalogue Cambodia's Buddhist manuscripts and relics, which were paralleled by indigenous movements to purify and reform Southeast Asian Theravada Buddhism.[4]

In a strange twist of irony, French writings on the archaeology of Southeast Asia were taken up in the 1920s by members of the Greater India Society, set up in Calcutta in their nationalist fervour as they wrote of the cultural conquest of Southeast Asia. Many of the influential thinkers of the society, such as P.C. Bagchi (1898–1956) and Kalidas Nag (1891–1966), had studied in Paris with celebrated Indologists Sylvain Lévi (1863–1935) and Jean Przyluski (1885–1944). Not only did the Director of EFEO George Coedès praise these attempts to rediscover the Indian heritage of colonization, but these interactions between Indian and French scholars of Further India and Greater India continued well into the 1950s.[5]

This theory, termed 'Indianization', was critiqued from the 1960s onwards by several scholars working in Southeast Asia. H.G. Quaritch Wales (1900–1981) was an adviser to King Rama VI and King Rama VII of Siam from 1924 to 1928 and wrote on several aspects of the art history

---

[3] Osborne, *Southeast Asia*, pp. 80–83.

[4] Penny Edwards, Making a Religion of the Nation and its Language: The French Protectorate (1863–1954) and the Dhammakaya, John Marston and Elizabeth Guthrie, eds., *History, Buddhism and New Religious Movements in Cambodia*, University of Hawaii Press, Honolulu, 2004: 63–85.

[5] Susan Bayly, Imagining 'Greater India': French and Indian Visions of Colonialism in the Indic Mode, *Modern Asian Studies*, 38, 2004: 703–744.

of the region as a tool for studying comparative religion. He discussed cultural differences in the art styles of the kingdoms of Southeast Asia and used the term 'local genius' to account for the differences.[6] De Casparis pointed out in 1983 that even such well-known Sanskrit inscriptions as the Kutei inscriptions of eastern Kalimantau of about 400 CE may well 'indicate a truly Indonesian ceremony'. He then substituted 'Indianization' with a pattern of a lasting relationship between the Indian subcontinent and maritime Southeast Asia.[7]

Perhaps the most strident critic of the concept was Oliver W. Wolters (1915–2000), the British historian, academic and author who taught at Cornell University. He put forward the idea of selective 'localization' of Indian cultural elements and emphasized the innovative and dynamic characters of Southeast Asian societies. He argued that

> unless there is convincing evidence to the contrary, Indian materials tended to be fractured and restated and therefore drained of their original significance by a process which I shall refer to as "localization". The materials, be they words, sounds of words, books or artifacts had to be localized in different ways before they could fit into various local complexes of religious, social and political systems and belong to new cultural "wholes" ... Not only did Indian materials have to be localized everywhere, but those which had been originally localized in one part of the region would have to be re-localized before they could belong elsewhere in the same subregion.[8]

Wolters believed that while there was often ubiquitous evidence of foreign elements in Southeast Asia's past, these elements could and should be 'read' as what he termed 'local cultural statements'. In other words, he argued that the Southeast Asian past was like a text which we can read, and that while the language of that text might be Indic or Sinitic, the statements that were made were ultimately local, such as Khmer or Vietnamese. In addition to Wolters, Hermann Kulke has also offered the concept of 'convergence' in between the courts on both sides of the Bay of Bengal, linked by intensive maritime trade relations and being united in a mutual

---

[6] H. G. Quaritch Wales, *The Making of Greater India*, London: B. Quaritch Wales, 1961: 229.

[7] J. G. De Casparis, *India and Maritime Southeast Asia: A Lasting Relationship*, Third Sri Lanka Endowment Fund Lecture, 1983.

[8] O. W. Wolters, *History, Culture, and Region in Southeast Asian Perspectives*, SEAP and ISEAS, Ithaca—Singapore, 1999: 55–56.

process of civilization.⁹ This evolutionary process of early state formation during the first millennium CE was not restricted to Southeast Asia. In many parts of Eastern, Central and Southern India, too, we observe in the same centuries a very similar trajectory of political and socio-economic evolution as in Southeast Asia.

Of these two theories, it is Wolters' 'localization' that finds favour with several contributors to this volume. Dhar, for example, investigates the dynamics of localization of architectural language in the context of seventh-century temples of early India and Southeast Asia. In contrast, Ardika refers to imports such as Indian bronze mirrors and Han pottery found in burials dated as early as the second century CE as status markers in early Balinese society. At this time Bali provides evidence of contacts not only with India, but also mainland Southeast Asia and China. It is some centuries later in the mid-first millennium CE that an Indic model-based state develops on the island. From the eighth to the eleventh century, Bali formed a part of the Buddhist world.

Adding further complexity to the issue, Srisuchat shows how Islam in Thailand has become integrated with practices and beliefs drawing on local animism and deities of Hinduism and Buddhism, not traditionally found in Islam. This is exemplified by the making of a kite by Muslim communities in southern Thailand for the annual ritual ceremony for prediction of rice planting for their community. Another theme that runs through several chapters relates to trade and maritime activity, as will be discussed in the next section. It is generally accepted that maritime contacts between South and South East Asia date to the middle of the first millennium BCE, but there is no clarity on the nature of these contacts or their influence.[10]

---

[9] Hermann Kulke, Indian Colonies, Indianisation or Cultural Convergence? Reflections on the Changing Image of India's Role in Southeast Asia, H. Schulte Nordholt, ed., *Onderzoek in Zuidoost-Azie: Agenda's voor de Jaren negentig*, Leiden: Rijksuniversiteit te Leiden, 1990: 8–32.

[10] H. P. Ray, *The Winds of Change: Buddhism and the Maritime Links of Early South Asia*, New Delhi: Oxford University Press, Chap. 4. Kishor K. Basa, Indian Writings on Early History and Archaeology of Southeast Asia: A Historiographical Analysis, *Journal of the Royal Asiatic Society*, volume 8, part 3, November 1998: 395–410. Bérénice Bellina, Beads, Social Change and Interaction between India and South-east Asia, *Antiquity*, 77, no. 296, June 2003: 285–297.

Travel and Mobility: Shared Religious Values

Travel played a crucial role not only in journeys of rediscovery and diplomacy in the nineteenth century, but also in pilgrimage and visits to sites associated with different religions, such as those linked to the life of the Buddha or with major Sufi saints. At the same time, new sites of devotion also emerged. Bahadur Shah Zafar II, the last Mughal emperor, died in Rangoon in 1862 and his grave has since been revered by local Muslims. The Siamese king Chulalongkorn (Rama V) ascended the throne in October 1868 at the age of eighteen, and is known for sea travels not only to the neighbouring countries of Southeast Asia, but also to India in 1872. Rabindranath Tagore embarked on a sea voyage on 15 July 1927 on the French ship *Amboise* to Java and other countries of Southeast Asia.[11] It was an intellectual pilgrimage, and Tagore's only motive, Bose argues, was 'to collect source materials there for the history of India and to establish a permanent arrangement for research in this field'.[12] Bose stresses Tagore's attempts to highlight the theme of cultural exchange between the two regions and the creativity of the Javanese and other peoples of Southeast Asia in negotiating with Indian cultural forms and products. Tagore was also aware of regional differences in historical developments within India and the fact that relations of the Sriwijaya kingdom (sixth to fourteenth centuries CE) were largely with the Palas of eastern India.[13] Mahatma Gandhi's contribution, on the other hand, requires further research, as he travelled to Burma and addressed meetings in March 1929. How did these travels across the region aid in an understanding of contemporary issues in countries facing the challenges of colonial rule in the nineteenth and twentieth centuries?

In contrast to the somewhat under-researched theme of travel and the colonial experience, there is a relative abundance of secondary literature on trade. Maritime trade has conventionally been viewed as trade in luxury items that is controlled by the state. In the context of ancient Indian history, the emphasis has been on trading networks, which are accepted as having proliferated during certain historical periods and declined thereafter, such as Indo-Roman trade, Arab trade, Chola trade and so on. Few monographs devoted to South and Southeast Asian contacts have appeared

---

[11] Sugata Bose, *A Hundred Horizons*, New Delhi: Permanent Black, 2006: 245.
[12] Bose, *A Hundred Horizons*: 245.
[13] Bose, *A Hundred Horizons*: 259.

in recent years.[14] Following in the footsteps of Oliver Wolters,[15] Kenneth R. Hall underscores the participatory nature of Indian Ocean networks in the ancient period, the agency of local and regional societies, and their reliance on economic and cultural dialogue rather than hegemony and dominance.[16] Hall suggests that itinerant trade became institutionalized in the ninth to thirteenth century CE and that these trade organizations were also involved with trading activity at coastal centres.

A somewhat different approach was adopted by Tansen Sen in his study of Chinese maritime relations with the Tamil coast from 600 to 1400 CE. Sen suggested that by the eighth century Buddhism started to decline in the Indian subcontinent, and that this is reflected in a transformation in maritime networks across the Bay of Bengal as well. By the ninth century China emerged as a centre of Buddhist learning in its own right, with the development of Mount Wutai as a centre of pilgrimage. Relations between China and India underwent a dramatic change in the eighth century from Buddhist-dominated to commerce-centred exchanges in the seventh to fifteenth centuries.[17] The Tang and Song dynasties took greater interest in commercial rather than religious exchanges with the regions to China's south, and as a result trade networks proliferated. Recent writings, especially by Kenneth Hall, have, however, questioned the notion of bilateral Indo-China trade in which 'Southeast Asian societies are portrayed as bystanders, contented agriculturalists who were members of communal

---

[14] D. Devahuti, *India and Ancient Malaya*, Singapore: Eastern Universities Press, 1965. I. C. Glover and P. Bellwood, *Southeast Asia: From Prehistory to History*, London–New York: Routledge Curzon, 2004. K. R. Hall, *Maritime Trade and State Development in Early Southeast Asia*, Honolulu: University of Hawaii Press, 1985. H. Kulke, *Kings and Cults: State Formation and Legitimation in India and Southeast Asia*, New Delhi: Manohar Publishers, 1993. Himanshu Prabha Ray, *The Winds of Change: Buddhism and the Maritime Links of Early South Asia*, New Delhi: Oxford University Press, 1994.

[15] Oliver W. Wolters, *Early Indonesian Commerce: A study of the origins of Śrīvijaya*, Cornell University Press, Cornell, 1967.

[16] Kenneth R. Hall, Local and International Trade and Traders in the Straits of Melaka Region 600–1500, *Journal of the Economic and Social History of the Orient*, 2004, volume 47, 2: 213–260. Kenneth R. Hall, *A History of Early Southeast Asia: Maritime Trade and Societal Development, 100–1500*, Rowman & Littlefield Publishers, Lanham and Plymouth, 2010: 103–134.

[17] Tansen Sen, *Buddhism, Diplomacy, and Trade: The Realignment of Sino-Indian Relations, 600–1400*, University of Hawaii Press, 2003.

agricultural and tribal societies, who were hosts and/or marginal participants in the international trade.'[18]

A recent addition to the historiography on the subject focuses specifically on the eleventh-century naval expedition said to have been despatched against the kingdom of Sriwijaya by the Chola king Rajendra I.[19] The papers in the edited volume titled *Nagapattinam to Suvarnadwipa: Reflections on the Chola Naval Expeditions to Southeast Asia* suggest that the oft-quoted Chola naval expedition is based on a single primary source, the eulogy contained in the inscription of Rajendra I, which is not corroborated by other contemporary sources—especially Chinese sources. Instead contemporary sources refer to an extensive Indian Ocean trading system extending from the Tamil coast to China, and it is this trading system that provides a context to the supposed naval expedition. From the ninth to the mid-fourteenth centuries two of the merchant guilds that dominated economic transactions in south India were the Manigramam and the Ayyavole. Associated with these two merchant guilds were associations of craftsmen such as weavers, basket-makers, potters, leather-workers and so on. These guilds extended the range of their operations beyond the boundaries of the Indian subcontinent into several regions of Southeast Asia. Clusters of Tamil inscriptions have been found on the eastern fringes of the Indian Ocean from Burma to Sumatra.[20]

The expansion of Hinduism, Buddhism, Islam and Christianity helped define the boundaries of this Indian Ocean 'world', creating networks of religious travel and pilgrimage.[21] The history of Buddhism in Cambodia and Vietnam is still inadequately researched. Nevertheless, by the seventh century there are references to visiting teachers from India, including Punyodhana from central India who promulgated Vajrayana Buddhism in

---

[18] Kenneth R. Hall, Local and International Trade and Traders in the Straits of Melaka Region 600–1500, *Journal of the Economic and Social History of the Orient*, 2004, volume 47, 2: 213–260.

[19] Hermann Kulke, K. Kesavapany and Vijay Sakhuja, eds., *Nagapattinam to Suvarnadwipa: Reflections on the Chola Naval Expeditions to Southeast Asia*, Institute of Southeast Asian Studies, Singapore, 2009.

[20] Jan Wisseman Christie, Asian Sea Trade between the Tenth and Thirteenth Centuries and its Impact on the States of Java and Bali, Himanshu Prabha Ray, ed., *Archaeology of Seafaring: The Indian Ocean in the Ancient Period*, Indian Council of Historical Research Monograph Series I, Pragati Publications, New Delhi, 1999: 221–270.

[21] Himanshu Prabha Ray, ed., *Sacred Landscapes in Asia: Shared Traditions, Multiple Histories*, Manohar, 2007. Sachchidanand Sahai, *The Hindu Temple in Southeast Asia*, Indian Institute of Advanced Study and Aryan Books International, New Delhi, 2012.

Champa.[22] From the seventh to the early tenth century there is evidence for the spread of Buddhism in Champa, with links to the religious traditions of Thailand and Java. In the ninth century, Jaya Indravarman II founded a vihara and dedicated the grand temple of Dong-duong, 25 km south-west of My Son to the Bodhisattva Lokesvara Svabhayada and gifted land, slaves, silver, gold and so on. The temple complex was larger than any other religious foundation in Champa, and had relief carvings on the wall depicting narratives from the life of the Buddha.[23]

An inscription dated 902 CE from An Thai in Quang Nam records the consecration of Lokanatha in the vihara of Pramudita lokesvara, and the beneficiary was the monk Nagapuspa, a friend of King Bhadravarman. The next king, Indravarman, confirmed the endowments and exempted the monastery from tax. Another important inscription from the same period comes from Nhan Bieu in the southern part of Quang Tri; it is on four faces of a stele, and records the consecration of a Siva temple and a Buddhist monastery dedicated to Avalokitesvara in honour of their ancestress Princess Lyan Vrddhakula.[24] This inscription is a good example of the Siva Buddha association found in Champa, and has close parallels with the prevailing situation in Java.

In the context of the civilization of Angkor, it is often argued that the capital was the religious and ritual centre of the kingdom, and the emphasis has been on the king who was imbued with divinity. Claude Jacques highlights the essential fact that all the inscriptions, be they in Sanskrit or in the vernacular, were placed in temples or sacred areas and were either concerned directly with the gods or with the administration of the god's properties.[25] There have been several studies on political thought and administrative theory among the Khmer and the structure of the Khmer kingdom and its characterization as a feudal state.[26] Several scholars have

---

[22] D. Snellgrove, ed., *The Image of the Buddha*, Paris, 1978: 155.

[23] Ian Mabbett, Buddhism in Champa, David G. Marr and A. C. Milner, eds., *Southeast Asia in the Ninth to Fourteenth Centuries*, Singapore: Institute of Southeast Asian Studies, 1986: 299–300.

[24] Mabbett, Buddhism in Champa: 302–303.

[25] Claude Jacques, Sources on Economic Activities in Khmer and Cham Lands, David G. Marr and A. C. Milner, eds., *Southeast Asia in the Ninth to Fourteenth Centuries*, Singapore: Institute of Southeast Asian Studies, 1986: 327–334.

[26] Jean Imbert, Histoire des Institutions Khmères, Phnom Penh, 1961; S. Sahai, *Les Institutions Politiques et l'Organisation Administrative du Cambodge Ancien (VI–XIII siècles)*, Paris: EFEO, 1970.

suggested that the brahmanas introduced political treatises in Cambodia and that these largely influenced the Khmers. Chakravarti refers to the recruitment of officials after taking tests (*sarvopadhāśuddha*), and suggests that the administrative system may be regarded as analogous to that in China.[27]

Unfortunately, there have been very few studies that have attempted to locate religious structures in a social context and to analyse their interaction both spatially with other temples and shrines and vertically with a range of communities. The religious affiliations of Khmers rulers are often seen as oscillating between allegiance to Hinduism and Mahayana Buddhism, with Theravada Buddhism appearing somewhat later in the thirteenth century. A study of religious architecture, however, indicates that a Buddhist shrine did not differ markedly from a Hindu temple, and a good example is that of Bat Chum, inaugurated in 953 CE: the Buddhist settlement followed the same architectural pattern as that of others dedicated to Siva or Visnu. Though inscriptions refer to Buddhist monasteries and to a tenth-century hermitage or āśrama dedicated by Yasovarman, none of these have been identified in the archaeological record.[28]

In the final section, it would be useful to take up the theme of writing and the literate cultures that extended across the Ocean.

The Word: Manuscript Cultures Across India and Southeast Asia

The Cambridge anthropologist Jack Goody has argued that writing added an important dimension to the technologies of communication in society. It was especially significant in the politico-legal domain and in the growth of knowledge systems. Historically scholars and pilgrims travelled to the subcontinent in search of manuscripts that enshrined true wisdom. For example, the Chinese pilgrim Xuanzang who travelled to India in the seventh century is said to have taken back with him cartloads of manuscripts. In the late eighteenth and early nineteenth centuries King Bodawphaya of Myanmar invited a brahmana from Varanasi to his court, and also sent

---

[27] Adhir Chakravarti, Some Recent Trends in Old Khmer Studies, *Journal of Ancient Indian History*, XIII, parts 1–2, 1980–1982.

[28] Christophe Pottier, Yasovarman's Buddhist Asrama in Angkor, Pierre Pichard and Francois Lagirarde, eds., *The Buddhist Monastery: A Cross-Cultural Survey*, Paris: EFEO, 2003: 199–208.

missions to India to collect writings in Sanskrit and to Sri Lanka for Pali texts. How did this sharing of traditional knowledge provide meaning to themes of regional and local identity and memory? This is an issue that needs analysis and examination, though a good beginning has been made by the National Museum of Indonesia in its publication titled *Inscribing Identity*.[29]

A majority of the inscriptions found in Southeast Asia are in Sanskrit, though there is evidence of vernacular epigraphs as early as the seventh century CE. Similarly, the generally stated position of scholars working in Southeast Asia is that Indians never colonized Southeast Asia, but the impressive Indic temples constructed after the seventh century could hardly have come into existence without *considerable* Indian knowledge and bodily presence.[30] 'Local rulers chose to adopt Indic gods and language to their own advantage rather than having Hinduism imposed upon them from outside.'[31]

From the sixth century, Sanskrit and Pali inscriptions spread to most regions in Thailand, and the two languages were acknowledged to be official languages of the early states, known as Dvaravati (seventh to eleventh centuries), Sricanasa (seventh to ninth centuries), Srivijaya (eighth to twelfth centuries) and Lavapura or Lopburi (seventh to thirteenth centuries). Between the eighth and twelfth centuries, the wide use of local languages, Mon and Khmer, including Khmer script that records Pali and Sanskrit words and texts on inscriptions found at religious architectural sites and on religious sculptures, suggests adoption of the languages and an opportunity for them to intermingle with the local languages, thereby developing into new terms. The invention of the Thai alphabet in 1292 signalled the end of the use of foreign scripts for writing. In Cambodia, as elsewhere in pre-colonial South and Southeast Asia, written texts were part of a performative tradition of Buddhist practice in which the word and art of listening were both modes of literacy and means of accumulating merit.[32]

---

[29] *Inscribing Identity: The Development of Indonesian Writing Systems*, The National Museum of Indonesia, Jakarta, 2015.
[30] Ian Glover and Peter Bellwood, eds., *Southeast Asia. From Prehistory to History*. London and New York: Routledge Curzon, 2004: 37.
[31] Charles Higham, *The Civilization of Angkor*, London: Weidenfeld & Nicholson, 2001: 9.
[32] Edwards, 'Making a Religion of the Nation and its Language,' p. 68.

'Another example of cultural differences in earlier times is the varying status of the Sanskrit language as the language worthy of being inscribed on something as venerable as stone. The Khmers continued to use Sanskrit into the fourteenth century, and the Chams into the fifteenth, but the Javanese, from the tenth century onward preferred to use their own language.'[33] This is an issue that requires further research.

OUTLINE OF THE BOOK

Part I of the book deliberates on trade and maritime links between South and Southeast Asia. In Chap. 2, I Wayan Ardika, basing his text on recent archaeological researches and findings such as stone figurines and inscriptions, pottery remains and glass beads, suggests that Bali in Indonesia had early contacts with the Indian subcontinent. Several Indian place names such as Nalanda, Varanasi and Amaravati are mentioned in Balinese inscriptions dating from the tenth or eleventh century. However, to establish whether there were direct contacts between ancient Bali and India further research is needed. In Chap. 3, Himanshu Prabha Ray discusses the maritime cultural landscape of the coastal town of Nagapattinam in today's Tamil Nadu, tracing India's cultural contact with Southeast Asia from the eleventh to the twelfth century onwards, based on archaeological and inscriptional data. Lotika Varadarajan proposes in Chap. 4 that many dimensions of mutual relations in the ASEAN region could become clearer through the study of textiles. She looks at the evolving trade dynamics between India and Southeast Asia, the reasons behind the reception of Indian cultural modes and textiles in the region, and the usage to which they were put.

Part II focuses on continuities and change. Based on archaeological and historical evidence found in Thailand, in Chap. 5 Amara Srisuchat argues how Indian traditions expressed through languages, religions and commerce were adapted by indigenous people of Thailand in their way of life and socio-cultural development. Joefe B. Santarita Panyupayana, basing Chap. 6 on historical and anthropological evidence available in the Philippines, seeks to investigate whether the archipelago was once a Hindu polity in the pre-Islamic period of the fourteenth century. In the case of the Philippines, vestiges of the Indian influence in the country, such as the

---

[33] O. W. Wolters, *History, Culture, and Region in Southeast Asian Perspectives*, SEAP and ISEAS, Ithaca–Singapore, 1999: 51.

Ramayana, the use of Sanskrit words, the presence of Hindu-Buddhist artefacts and others are adduced to explore if the country or a part of it was once a Hindu kingdom. Le Thi Lien illustrates in Chap. 7 that ancient Vietnam was a bridge connecting the Indian subcontinent and the farther reaches of archipelagic Southeast and East Asia. It was an intersection point for cultural exchanges and maritime trade. As a result, Le Thi Thien argues, the earliest states of Lin Yi and Funan were enriched with elements of Indian and other Southeast Asian cultures.

Part III focuses on representations of religions and rituals. In Chap. 8, Andrea Acri attempts to provide a fresh perspective on Balinese Hinduism, challenging the accepted view that Balinese religion is not a fully-formed 'religion', but that it is intimately bound with Indian Hinduism. Making use of textual data largely ignored by scholars, and with insights from fieldwork carried out in Bali, modern manifestations of Balinese Hinduism's connection to their pre-modern Śaiva roots in both Java and the Indian subcontinent are traced. Madhu Khanna explores religious lives of Ida Pedandas or priestesses in Bali in Chap. 9. Her chapter investigates their empowered role in the context of modern contemporary discourse in religion, where women are often seen as disempowered and lacking agency.

Part IV presents textual traditions and transmissions. In Chap. 10, Sudha Gopalakrishnan discusses the similar patterns by which textual knowledge was created, organized and disseminated across India, Thailand, Japan and Indonesia. Some of these similarities in manuscript traditions relate to the process of transition from orality to textuality, the evolution of scripts, material used for writing, elements of internal textual organization such as scribal practices and customs such as venerating texts, as well as the existence of vast commentarial literature, all of which show deep connections between India and Southeast Asia.

In Chap. 11, Thomas M. Hunter presents a comparative examination of the Bhagavad-Gītā sections of the Sanskrit *Bhīsmaparva*n and Old Javanese *Bhīsmaparwa*. He is of the view that the transition from Sanskrit to Old Javanese is a matter of text building and the use of language. The Old Javanese Parwa literature can provide us with insights into how a particular form of state and society emerged in the pre-modern world of Southeast Asia. According to Hunter, these insights continue to be valuable today, not only for their historical value, but for their relevance in the processes of cultural interchange and growth that are an essential part of the future of modern South and Southeast Asia.

Ding Choo Ming argues in Chap. 12 that Indian epics depicting Buddhist and Hindu stories are at the root of several literary works in Malaysia and Bali. From these extant works, it is obvious that Malay and Javanese writers and audiences in the early days did not adopt a confrontational approach to Hindu and Buddhist traditions, nor did they accept them in totality. This meant, according to Ding Choo Ming, that the acceptance of stories and ideas from the Indian epics was selective, involving a process of intellectual adaptation and transformation through reworking. In Chap. 13 Malini Saran and Vinod Khanna discuss the importance of Camille Bulcke's scholarly work in Ramayana studies. This text is the most comprehensive to date, not only examining the origins and evolution of the Rama story but also providing a meticulous summary of innumerable Ramakatha or Rama stories composed in multiple languages. Both the authors feel that translating the Ramakatha into English was important since it made the work accessible to non-Hindi speaking scholars in the global domain of Ramayana studies. It could also be of use to those in ASEAN countries working in the fields of literature, ballet and drama, which draw their inspiration from the Ramayana.

Part V deals with sacred geographies and localizations of beliefs. In Chap. 14, Sachchidanand Sahai delves into the two millennia history of cultural exchange between India and Southeast Asia. The cultural linkages were a non-state expression of soft power and pluralism. Southeast Asian nations and India have the same world view, he argues, and more small-scale projects need to be undertaken to explore this. In Chap. 15, John Guy looks at the earliest evidence for a Brahmanical culture in Southeast Asia in the first millennium. There is evidence that these regions were thought as a place infused with Siva's presence by Southeast Asian devotees. This landscape, with its pilgrimage places (tirthas) serving not simply as surrogate locations for the holy lands of India, but rather as an extension of that very religious landscape, indicates deeper religious ties between the two regions.

Popo Danes discusses Balinese architecture as a form of cultural assimilation from Hinduism in Chap. 16. Bali relies on its culture, which includes socio-cultural activities and the architectural form of traditional Balinese architecture inspired by Hinduism, as the main attraction for tourists. An exploration of cultural identity within architecture gives much greater sensitivity to local (built) environment, people and society. Danes also argues that architectural identity is a process, which operates within transforming the (built) environment. Patterns of relationships in the construction of identity and architectural place provide guidance to continue intercultural exchange in order to reconstruct transforming identity.

Part VI deals with evolving artistic expressions, from tradition to modernity. In Chap. 17, Padma Subramanyam presents her field work based on interactions with artistes of Cambodia, Thailand and Indonesia, and the influence of the Natyashastra on dance forms in these regions.

Part VII focuses on writing our own histories. In Chap. 18, Farish A. Noor illustrates how the discursive categories of 'South Asia' and 'Southeast Asia' were imagined by functionaries of the Empire for administrative reasons, and that the 'discovery' of Southeast Asia by the colonial powers severed the long cultural, ethnic and commercial links between the Indian subcontinent and maritime Southeast Asia. In Chap. 19, Parul Pandya Dhar presents the architecture and associated imagery of Indian and Southeast Asian monuments, and the shaping of an architectural language in the region. Interpreting the iconography of these monuments—their underlying concepts, affiliations, diversities and complexities—brings into focus a complex web of cultural interrelationships and yields significant insights into ancient cosmopolitan circuits of exchange. In a larger context, the chapter highlights key issues for a more nuanced understanding of the networks of exchange between India and Southeast Asia, as viewed through the prism of their monumental remains.

In her valedictory address, Kapila Vatsyayan reminds us of the importance of the multivalence of religion and gender in both regions, and suggests that the cultural links between India and Southeast Asia should be viewed as 'influence' and also as acculturation, since the process of cultural osmosis involves plural structures that do not respond to monotheistic solutions. The need of the hour is to expand this collaboration with ASEAN, based on shared histories and culture. It is also vital to highlight the type of research projects, institutions and scholars that need to be encouraged in India and Southeast Asia to further this. Finally, the younger generation has to be engaged in this process in a more systematic way. The narrative of India's cultural interactions with the ASEAN region is an extraordinary story, and remains to be fully explored by those who share this fabled history.

PART I

Trade and Maritime Links Between South and Southeast Asia

CHAPTER 2

Early Contacts Between Bali and India

I Wayan Ardika

INTRODUCTION

Recent archaeological research in Bali has produced significant information concerning the early contacts between Bali and India, Mainland Southeast Asia and China. The discovery of Indian pottery, stone and glass beads, and gold foil eye covers at Sembiran, Pacung and several burial sites such as Gilimanuk, Pangkungliplip and Margatengah suggest early contacts between Bali and India. Sembiran and Pacung in Northeastern Bali, which are close to the village of Julah, could be an ancient port or harbour, and have produced the largest collection of Indian pottery so far in Southeast Asia (Ardika 2013).

Han bronze mirrors were recently discovered at the site of Pangkung Paruk in the northwest of Bali. They are believed to date from the first century CE, that is, during the reign of King Ma Huan from Xin dynasty (Eastern Han), who ruled from 8 to 23 CE (Westerlaken 2011: 13).

The bronze mirrors at Pangkung Paruk were discovered in sarcophagi A and B as burial goods. In addition, Han-style paddle-impressed pottery was found at a depth of 3.1–3.2 m at SBN XIX, in association with other ware and with other ware of possible mainland Southeast Asian origin (Calo et al. 2015: 385).

I. W. Ardika (✉)
Faculty of Letters, Udayana University, Bali, Indonesia

© The Author(s) 2018
S. Saran (ed.), *Cultural and Civilisational Links between India and Southeast Asia*, https://doi.org/10.1007/978-981-10-7317-5_2

The discovery of these artefacts suggests that Bali might have had global contacts from the late second or first century BCE. Contacts between Bali and two cultural centres, namely India and China, might have been stimulated social development to chiefdom and early state formation. The Indian artefacts and bronze mirrors as well as Han pottery might have been functioning as status symbols in Balinese society. The appearance of inscriptions in the late ninth century could be seen as the evidence of early state formation.

ARCHAEOLOGICAL EVIDENCE OF EARLY CONTACTS BETWEEN INDIA AND BALI

Archaeological excavations at Sembiran and Pacung in Northeastern Bali brought a new light to the beginning of contacts between India and Bali. Several Indian rouletted wares, Arikamedu type 10, Arikamedu type 18, Arikamedu type 141 and a sherd with Kharosthi or Brahmi script were discovered, more than 100 Indian sherds, the largest Indian rouletted sherds yet found in Southeast Asia (Ardika 1991; Ardika et al. 1997: 194). A complete rouletted ware bowl has been found at Kobak Kendal in West Java, thought to have been part of the kingdom of Taruma (see Fig. 2.1). It should be noted that rouletted ware sherds were also discovered recently at Batujaya, West Java (Djafar 2010: 97–98, Fig. 3.57).

Rouletted ware was manufactured in India and/or Sri Lanka perhaps between 150 BCE and 200 CE. The earliest rouletted ware probably appeared in Bali and Indonesia in 1–200 CE (Ardika and Bellwood 1991: 229). Some rouletted ware at Sembiran was found in a layer in association with a large black-slipped storage jar tempered with rice husk; this has been dated by accelerator mass spectrometry (AMS) radiocarbon to

Fig. 2.1 Rouletted sherds, Arikamedu sherd of type 10, and a complete rouletted ware bowl from Kobak Kendal, West Java. Source: Author's own

2660+/−100 BP (Ardika and Bellwood 1991). However, recent excavations at Sembiran and Pacung produced an AMS date obtained from charcoal at 2.9–3.0 m depth at SBN XIX as 142 cal BCE–CE 25 (S-ANU 37107). Pacung trench IX, on the other hand, revealed a dense beach cemetery, with more elaborate burial practices, including the use of jar burials and richer burial goods. The sites have produced a cultural sequence starting from the late second century BCE for the burials, to the twelfth century CE, a date represented at 2.2 m depth at Sembiran, just below the ash layer. At 95.4% probability, the bayesian model of eight direct AMS dates from the bones of seven Pacung individuals, and one from charcoal, closely associated with burial XIII, indicates that the burials started between 163 cal BCE and 13 CE and ended between 51 cal BCE and 137 CE (Calo et al. 2015: 381).

X-ray diffraction (XRD) analysis suggests that all have essentially the same minerals, namely quartz with traces of mica, muscovite, potassium feldspar and plagioclase feldspar. Therefore, the XRD results indicate the civilizational links with India (Ardika and Bellwood 1991: 224; Ardika 1991).

Besides, nine samples of rouletted ware (two from Anuradhapura, two from Arikamedu, one from Karaikadu in Tamil Nadu, three from Sembiran and a single sherd from Pacung) went through neutron activation analysis (NAA). The result indicates that all are close in composition, indicating a single manufacturing source. The rouletted sherds form separate clusters in principal components, and facilitate average link cluster analysis from sherds of presumed Balinese manufacture (Ardika and Bellwood 1991: 224).

Apart from rouletted wares, two sherds of Arikamedu type 10 have also been found at Sembiran. This type of pottery outside Arikamedu has also been found at the site of Chandraketugarh in West Bengal and Alangankulam on the Vaigai river in Tamil Nadu (H.P. Ray pers. com.; Ardika and Bellwood 1991: 224). No information is at present available on its occurrence elsewhere.

A sherd of Arikamedu type 18 was also found at Sembiran (Fig. 2.2). The sherd of apparent Arikamedu type 18c was reported from Bukit Tengku Lembu in Northern Malaya (De Sieveking 1962: 29; see Fig. 2a).

An inscribed sherd was found in Sembiran VII. The sherd is black-slipped and the fabric is coarser than that of the rouletted ware, Arikamedu type 10 and type 18. Three characters are clearly visible on the inside

Fig. 2.2 A sherd of Arikamedu type 18, an inscribed sherd of Kharosthi or Brahmi script and gold beads from Sembiran. Source: Author's own

surface of this sherd (see Fig. 2.2). According to Prof. B.N. Mukherjee of Calcutta University, the script is Kharosthi, and his preliminary reading is *te sra vi* (Ardika 1991: 53, Fig. 4.4; see Fig. 2b). He (Mukherjee 1989a, b, 1990a, b) believes that a group of people who used the Kharoshthi script extended their interests from Northwest India to West Bengal, where they became very active as traders from about the last quarter of the first century CE to about the beginning of the fifth century CE. These traders probably conducted maritime commerce with Southeast Asia and reputedly had access to a supply of central Asian horses (Mukherjee 1990a: 2).

Sembiran and Pacung also produced the south Indian coarse dishes, as well as local Indian-style dishes. In Southeast Asia, Indian-style coarse dishes are also known, together with rouletted ware, from Khao Sam Kaeo and Phu Khao Thong in peninsular Thailand and Batujaya in northwestern Java. To date, the total count of fine Indian sherds from Sembiran and Pacung can be conservatively estimated at over 600, with a similar quantity of coarse-fabric sherds of possible Indian manufacture (Calo et al. 2015: 383–384, Fig. 5j).

Beads of glass and stone have been found in several Indonesian sites. Glass beads were discovered in several Indonesian sites including Sembiran, Gilimanuk (Bali), Plawangan (central Java), Leang Bua (Flores) and Pasemah (South Sumatra). The Sembiran beads are similar to south Indian samples in terms of raw materials and were probably manufactured at Arikamedu.

Roman glass has been newly identified in Sembiran (SBN) XIX through chemical data, indicating indirect contact with the Roman world via India, and new compositional data from gold and carnelian artefacts suggest a route from the north Indian subcontinent to Indonesia, via mainland

Southeast Asia. A red bead with grey striation is made of Roman soda natron glass. Moreover, two drawn beads with gold foil analysed as a comparative sample from a cluster of 40 found in a sarcophagus at the site of Pangkung Paruk, to the west of Sembiran, were also made of soda natron glass. These finds constitute the first evidence of Roman materials in a prehistoric context in island Southeast Asia (Calo et al. 2015: 384, 389, Figs. 8d and 8e).

Carnelian and gold beads were also discovered in Sembiran. Several prehistoric sites in Bali including Sembiran, Gilimanuk, Nongan, Margatengah, Pujungan and Ambiarsari produced carnelian beads. They are generally believed to have been imported from India (Fig. 2.3).

Gold foil eye covers have been found in several burial and sarcophagus sites in Bali. These sites include Gilimanuk (burial site), Pangkungliplip and Margatengah (sarcophagus sites). These artefacts were also found at Oton on Panay island in the Philippines and at Santubong in Sarawak (O'Connor and Harrison 1971: 72–73).

It is also interesting to note the result of an analysis of ancient mitochondrial DNA from the human tooth of Pacung III in Northeastern Bali. The tooth sample is generally associated with haplogroup A, which is clearly clustered closest to Indian sequences followed by most Nepalese and Tibetan sequences (i.e. 16240 G. 16261 T) (Lansing et al. 2004: 288–290). AMS radiocarbon analysis of the tooth indicates its age as 2050+/−40 BP) (conventional radiocarbon age 2110+/−40 BP) (Lansing et al. 2004: 288). In addition, preliminary results of Y-chromosome data taken from a sample of 551 modern Balinese men indicate significant prehistoric contacts between India and Bali (Karafet et al. 2005).

On the basis of potteries, beads and DNA analysis, it seems that Indian traders might have visited Sembiran and Pacung on the northeastern coast of Bali around the first century BCE. They brought Indian artefacts such as

Fig. 2.3 Stupa Pagulingan and Gunung Kawi rock arts. Source: Author's own

potteries, glass and stone beads, as well as metal artefacts of gold foil eye covers. These artefacts were mostly found in association with burial goods at several sites in Bali. The beginning of Indian contact with Bali might have stimulated the occurrence of ranked or complex society there: Indian artefacts were utilized as status symbols in Balinese society.

The question arises why Indian traders visited Bali around the first century BCE. This can be answered by understanding the trade system between India and the Roman Empire. Indo-Roman commerce generated a rising demand for exotic and prestigious items of consumption and adornment in the urban civilization of the Mediterranean Basin—that is a 'splendid and trifling' trade in spices, perfumes, precious stones and pearls, silks and muslin, tortoiseshell, ivory and rhinoceros horns, dyes and unguents, ghee, lac and so on (Bellina and Glover 2004: 70). For the demand for exotic products in the West, one needs only to look at the spice trade and particularly at the trade in cloves, the unopened flower buds of eastern Indonesia. Cloves were already known in China in the third century BCE, and were described by Pliny in Rome in the first century CE.

Based on the spice trade, Sembiran and Pacung seem to have been located at a strategic place connecting the eastern and western parts of Indonesia. The beginning of contact between India and Bali was in relation to the spice trade, and it also stimulated the occurrence of a ranked or complex society in Bali.

Early Contacts Between Bali, Mainland Southeast Asia and China

New chemical composition data for glass beads and bracelets excavated in 2012 from a burial context and directly above it at Sembiran and Pacung indicate strong links to Vietnam and, to a lesser extent, elsewhere in mainland Southeast Asia, India and the Roman world. Some 119 out of a total of 759 samples from Sembiran (SBN) XIX, and 33 out of a total of 361 from Pacung (PCN) IX, plus comparative samples from broadly contemporaneous sites in northern Bali, have been analysed using Laser Ablation Inductively Coupled Plasma Mass Spectrometry at the Institut des Recherches sur les Archeomateriaux of the Centre National de la Recherche Scientific (CNRS), Orléans, France.

Of the analysed samples from both Sembiran and Pacung, 80% or more were potash (potassium oxide) glass, compositionally similar to the low-lime potash glass (mKA) which is most strongly associated with Dong son sites, and the moderate-lime, moderate-alumina potash glass (mKCA) associated with Sa Hyunh and Dong Nai sites in Vietnam. Potash silica glass of at least three types was most common in mainland Southeast Asia from the fourth to the second century BCE, although with the occurrence of North Indian high-alumina, high-uranium soda glass at Khao Sam Kaeo and Ban Don Ta Phet (Calo et al. 2015: 388, Fig. 9).

Two volcanic tuff moulds were discovered in Sembiran. One is for a Pejeng drum found in 1989 and the other is for a socketed axe found in 2012. Both were found in the same layer. The first stone mould was carved with geometric motives typical of the decoration on Pejeng type bronze drums (Ardika 1991; Ardika and Bellwood 1991). A similar stone mould is still kept at the Pura Puseh temple at the village of Manuaba, Gianyar.

The second stone mould was excavated in SBN XIX layer 8, which corresponds to the layer where Ardika found the first mould in SBN VII. The conical mould was analysed using portable X-ray fluorescence (XRF), and its surface gave significant readings for copper, tin and lead, exceeding those detected in the associated soil. The conical shape suggests that it would have been used in the lost-wax casting of a socketed bronze axe of Soejono type Vb (Calo et al. 2015: 389–390, Fig. 10).

A selection of bronze burial goods and bronze artefacts SBN XIX layer 8 have been incorporated within the Southeast Asia Lead Isotope Project. All of the Pacung samples and one of the Sembiran socketed point are made of leaded bronze. The results indicate that lead isotope signatures are consistent with the bulk of broadly contemporaneous (500 BCE–200 CE) leaded bronze Southeast Asia Lead Isotope Project database for Cambodia, Thailand and Vietnam. The lead isotope signatures of the points suggest the melting of imported bronze in Bali for local recasting.

An archaeological discovery at Pangkung Paruk, in Northwestern Bali, produced evidence of the earliest contacts between Bali and China. As mentioned in the Introduction, two bronze mirrors were found as burial goods in sarcophagi A and B on the site of Pangkung Paruk, Seririt District, Buleleng Regency during excavations by the Balai Arkeologi Denpasar in 2015. The bronze mirrors probably originated from Xin dynasty (Eastern Han) under King Wang Mang, who ruled from the year 8 to 23 CE (Westerlaken 2011: 13).

It is interesting to note that new evidence of Han-style pottery was found in SBN XIX during the excavation programme in 2012. This pottery was found at a depth of 3.1–3.2 m, in association with other wares of possible mainland Southeast Asian origin (Calo 2009: 385, Fig. 6a).

Archaeological evidence that was discovered at Sembiran and Pacung indicates a revolutionary process involving different types of cultural interaction that led to the formation of Indic-based state in Bali by the first millennium CE.

THE INSCRIPTIONAL DATA

The appearance of archaeological evidence such as gold foil eye covers, Indian rouletted wares and several Arikamedu type potteries, glass and stone beads indicate the beginning of contact between India and Bali. Contacts between India and Bali might have also involved Buddhism and Brahmanical priests.

The epigraphic sources dated from the eighth to eleventh century also indicate a close relationship between Bali and India. The inscription of Bebetin AI, dated to 896 CE indicates that foreign traders (*banyaga*) came to Banwa Bharu to sell their goods (Ardika 1991: 271). The site of Banwa Bharu has not yet been identified; it might be located on the northern coast of Bali.

Bali also produced hundreds of clay stupas which have been found at Pejeng and Blahbatuh villages, Gianyar Regency. The stupas contain certain tiny seals, in pairs, covered up with lumps of clay. The seals are stamped with a well-known recitation of faith, so called *ye-te* formula. Similar clay seals and stupas were also discovered near Borobudur in Central Java (Kempers 1991: 95–96). The texts on seals are in Siddhamatrka script. On the basis of palaeography, the date of the seal is estimated from 800 to 1000 CE (Griffiths 2014: 183; Fig. 12). Two pieces of gold foils, a silver foil bearing a few aksaras and a terracotta tablet bearing *ye dharma* formula were discovered during the preparation for the reconstruction of Pura Pagulingan, at Tampak Siring, Gianyar regency. The foundations of Pura Pagulingan showed an octagonal groundplan.

The appearance of *dharanis* and *mantras* in Bali suggests that the island was an integral part of the ancient Buddhist world. Griffiths (2014: 186) argues that the text used here must have been quite similar to the text that was used in other Buddhist countries.

It is interesting to note that the Balinese inscriptions dated from the late tenth to the eleventh century mentioned several place names in India, such as Waranasi, Nalanda and Amarawati. These place names were associated with a court of justice, high functionaries, the residence of Buddhist priests and the name of a shrine or a sacred place.

The inscription of Sembiran B dated from Saka 873 or 951 CE states III. 2. ... *da dikara di panglapuan di waranasi tuha dara*. It is translated as follows: 'the honourable *Dhikara* (functionary) of the court of justice at Waranasi is Tuha Neko'.

The term Nalanda was first mentioned in the inscription of Serai AII, dated from Saka Baranasi/Waranasi. The inscription of Gobleg, Pura Desa II dated from Saka 905 or 983 CE mentioned Iib.2. ... *da senapati waranasi tuha neko*, ... Translation: 'the high functionary or army commander (*Senapati*) at 915' or 993 CE. The inscription read as follows: Va. 5. ... *mpungku di nalenda dang upadhyaya dhanawan* or 'the Buddhist priest at Nalenda (Nalanda) was Dang Upadhyaya (*honorific* teacher) Dhanawan'. It is interesting to note that Tuha Gato was mentioned as *Senapati* at Waranasi in this inscription. On the basis of the inscription of Gobleg, Pura Desa II, dated from 983 CE, and the inscription of Serai AII, dated from 993 CE, Tuha Neko was replaced by Tuha Gato as *Senapati* (army commander or high functionary) at Waranasi.

The inscription of Bwahan A dated from Saka 916 or 994 CE noted that the Buddhist priest at Nalanda was Dang Upadhyaya Dhanawan and the Buddhist priest at Waranasi was Dangacaryya Sucandra. This inscription indicates that Nalanda and Waranasi were residences of Buddhist priests. In addition, the inscription also mentioned Brahmanical priests (*kasaiwan*) as well as Buddhist priests (*kasoghatan*), court functionaries.

The inscription of Tengkulak A dated from Saka 945 or 1023 CE mentioned the hermitage (*katyagan*) at a Pakerisan river called Amarawati (Ginarsa 1961: 4–8). The Balinese inscriptions indicate that the Indian place names such as Waranasi, Nalanda and Amarawati were transferred to the local place in Bali. These places are associated with the centre of Buddhism in India. Amarawati was the Buddhist-influenced site in the lower Krishna valley under the Mauryas (Ray 1994: 140). However, it is still not clear whether the Balinese might have gone to the Buddhist centres such as Waranasi, Nalanda and Amarawati and other places in India or whether they knew the places. New data from India or Bali are needed for further studies.

Conclusions

The appearance of archaeological evidence such as rouletted wares, Arikamedu-type potteries, an inscribed sherd with Kharosthi or Brahmi script, gold foils eye covers, stone and glass beads in the sites of Sembiran and Pacung in northeastern Bali indicate the beginning of contact between India and Bali during the late second century or the first century BCE.

Contact between India and Bali was associated with the spice trade. Indian traders might come to Bali searching for spices from the Moluccas and sandalwood from East Nusa Tenggara islands, as well as other products from the Indonesian archipelago. Bali seems to have been located on the trade routes connecting the eastern and western parts of Indonesia.

The trade contacts might also have involved the coming of Buddhism and Brahmanism or Hinduism to Bali. The appearance of clay stupas, the seal of *ye te* mantras, dharani as well as several Indian place names such as Waranasi, Nalanda and Amarawati in the Balinese inscriptions support this assumption.

Sanskrit and Pallava script were adopted which stimulated the development of Old Balinese scripts and the Old Balinese language, which were used in the Balinese inscriptions. Social organization based on kingship, Buddhism and Hindu philosophies were adopted and adjusted to the local milieu in Bali. However, local belief systems and traditions still continued to be practised.

References

Ardika, I Wayan. 1991. Archaeological Research in Northeastern Bali, Indonesia. *Dissertation*. Canberra: Australian National University.

———. 2013. Sembiran: An Early Harbour in Bali. In Miksic, John, N. and Goh Geok Yian (eds). *Ancient Harbours in Southeast Asia. The Archaeology of Early Harbours and Evidence of Inter Regional Trade*, pp 21–29. Bangkok: SEAMEO SPAFA, Regional Centre for Archaeology and Fine Arts.

Ardika, I Wayan, and Peter Bellwood. 1991. Sembiran: The Beginnings of Indian Contact with Bali. *Antiquity*, 65: 221–232.

Ardika, I Wayan, Peter Bellwood, I Made Sutaba, and Kade Citha Yuliati. 1997. Sembiran and the First Indian Contacts with Bali: An Update. *Antiquity*, 71: 193–195.

Bellina, Berenice, and Ian Glover. 2004. The Archaeology of Early Contact with India and Mediterranean World, from the Fourth Century BC to the Fourth Century AD. In Glover, Ian and Peter Bellwood (ed) *Southeast Asia from prehistory to history*, pp 68–88. London: RoutledgeCurzon.

Bernet Kempers, August Johan. 1991. *Monumental Bali; Introduction to Balinese Archaeology and Guide to the Monuments*. Singapore: Periplus Editions.
Calo, Ambra. 2009. *The Distribution of Bronze Drums in Early Southeast Asia. Trade Routes and Culture Spheres*. Oxford: BAR International Series 1913.
Calo, Ambra, Bagyo Prasetyo, Peter Bellwood, James W. Lankton, Bernard Gratuze, Thomas Oliver Pryce, Andreas Reinecke, Verena Leusch, Heidrun Schenk, Rachel Wood, Rochtri A. Bawono, I Dewa Kompiang Gede, Ni L.K. Citha Yuliati, Jack Fenner, Christian Reepmeyer, Cristina Castillo & Alison K. Carter. 2015. Sembiran and Pacung on the North Coast of Bali a Strategic Crossroads for Early Trans Asiatic Exchange. *Antiquity* 89, 344: 378–396.
Djafar, Hasan. 2010. *Kompleks Percandian Batujaya. Rekonstruksi Sejarah Kebudayaan Daerah Pantai Utara Jawa Barat*. Bandung: Kiblat Buku Utama, Ecole francais d'Extreme-orient, Pusat Penelitian dan Pengembangan Arkeologi Nasional, 8KITLV-Jakarta.
Ginarsa. 1961. Prasasti Baru Raja Ragajaya. *Bahasa dan Budaya*. Glover, I.C. 1990. 'Ban Don Ta Pet'. Glover, I and E. Glover (eds), Southeast Asia Archaeology 1986, pp 139–83. Oxford: *BAR* International Series 561.
Griffiths, Arlo. 2014. Written Traces of the Buddhist Past: Mantras and Dharais in Indonesian Inscriptions. *Bulletin of the School of Oriental and African Studies*, 77, 1: 137–194.
Karafet, T.M. et al. 2005. Balinese Y-Chromosome Perspective on Peopling of Indonesia: Genetic Contributions from Pre-Neolithic Hunter-Gatherers, Austronesian Farmers and Indian Traders. *Human Biology* 77, 1: 93–113.
Lansing, Sthepen, et al. 2004. An Indian Trader in Ancient Bali? *Antiquity* 78, 300: 287–293.
Mukherjee, B.N. 1989a. 'Decipherment of the Kharoshti-Brahmi script'. *Asiatic Society* XVII, 8: 1–10.
———. 1989b. 'Discovery of Kharoshti inscriptions in West Bengal'. *The Quarterly Review of History Studies* XXIX, 2: 6–14.
———. 1990a. 'A Kharoshti-Brahmi seal-matrix from Oc-Eo (S.E. Asia)'. *Asiatic Society* XIX, 6: 1–4.
———. 1990b. 'A Sealing in the Lopburi Museum (Thailand)'. *Asiatic Society* XIX, 11: 1–2.
O'Connor, S.J., and T. Harrison. 1971. Gold Foil Burial Amulet in Bali, Philippines and Borneo. *JMBRAS* 38, 2: 87–124.
Ray, H.P. 1994. *The Winds of Change: Buddhism and the Maritime Links of Early South Asia*. Delhi: Oxford University Press.
Sieveking, G. De. 1962. The Prehistoric Cemetery at Bukit Tengku Lembu, Perlis. *Federation Museum Journal* 7: 25–54.
Westerlaken, Rodney. 2011. 'Banjar Laba Nangga; A Prehistoric Site in North Bali and Its Interpretation as Cultural Heritage'. M.A. *Thesis*, Leiden University, http://www.rodneywesterlaken.nl/scriptie.pdf. Accessed October 10, 2014.

CHAPTER 3

Trans-locality and Mobility across the Bay of Bengal: Nagapattinam in Context

Himanshu Prabha Ray

INTRODUCTION

The traditionally accepted image of relations between the Association of South East Asian Nations (ASEAN) and India revolves around the spread of religions such as Buddhism and Hinduism and the sharing of knowledge systems, for example the Sanskrit language. In addition to these, two other staples may be added: the Ramayana and its influence across Asia; and trade in Indian textiles across the Indian Ocean. More recently, attention has shifted to historical developments in the region in the nineteenth and early twentieth centuries, as these have a direct bearing on present concerns (Sharma 2013).

A somewhat under-researched theme continues to be the development of new disciplines such as archaeology and art history, which evolved from a European intellectual milieu and were transposed on to the countries of Asia under colonial rule. Thus, the nineteenth and twentieth centuries marked major transformations in an understanding of the past, but more importantly brought it into the public domain. It is significant that these changes be documented and understood as we engage with our neighbours

H. P. Ray (✉)
Distant Worlds Programme, Ludwig Maximilian University, Munich, Germany

© The Author(s) 2018
S. Saran (ed.), *Cultural and Civilisational Links between India and Southeast Asia*, https://doi.org/10.1007/978-981-10-7317-5_3

across the seas. More importantly, common solutions need to be found to problems of preservation and sustainable development, as cities expand and steamroller heritage structures from the past.

Monuments in Asia have generally been studied in terms of architecture and sculpture or with regard to chronology and patronage and more recently within debates of generation of colonial knowledge, but seldom with regard to locations, such as along the coast, cultural plurality indicated by the monuments themselves and historical memory enshrined in them (Ray 2008: 417–449). An important component of the coastal cultural landscape is religious architecture and its interlinkage with travelling groups who moved both across the sea, as well as on routes into the interior.

This chapter suggests that one way of understanding the complex web of interactions of the past is through a deep engagement with markers of maritime cultural regions and the communities that inhabited these spaces. The indicators include archaeological artefacts, as evidence of ancient settlements and routes, architectural edifices and their networks of interaction and of course, continuing boat-building traditions. The larger issue addressed here relates to perspectives through which monuments, especially those located on the coast, are to be understood and made meaningful to contemporary societies, both for an appreciation of their value and also to aid in their preservation for posterity.

Monuments and Memory

A leading historian of Southeast Asia, Oliver Wolters, succinctly stated that the purpose of history and the study of the past could well be an enhancement of self-awareness and a better understanding of the present (Wolters 1994: 1–17). Heritage in this context includes both cultural and natural heritage. Research in several parts of the Indian Ocean has shown a loss of biodiversity, as well as coastal degradation (Ribeiro 2014; Seetah 2014). Unplanned urban expansion along the coasts has meant marginalization of local communities, including those involved in fishing and utilization of marine resources (Chou 2013: 41–66). By focusing on nautical histories, architecture and archaeology, on the central experience of trans-locality of maritime communities and the mapping and remapping of maritime conceptions of space across two millennia, this chapter reorients the reader from the conventional linear imperial construct of maritime history as domination, conflict and control to looking at the reality of constant cultural transfer and transmission within the domain of the Indian Ocean world (Ray 2013: 13–40). The attempt here is to articulate the complex connections built through the mediation of the sea both spatially and chronologically by an examination of coastal architecture on the Tamil coast in the historical period.

Susan Bayly has argued that trans-locality and long-distance pilgrimage and devotional networks have been enduring features of cultural life in South and Southeast Asia for many centuries. The Sufi *pir* (saint) Shahul Hamid of Nagaur in south India, for example, was known among his devotees for travels across time and space. Earth from his shrine at Nagur was taken for the setting up of replica shrines at Penang and Singapore (Bayly 2004: 703–704). Sufism contains inherently trans-regional, trans-national, and trans-ethnic dimensions. In any particular locality there is a wide range of Sufi saints, from major shrines of great antiquity to minor saints with a highly localized clientele; nor is Sufism the only devotional network in South and Southeast Asia, as evident from the sculptural programme at Borobudur in central Java.

BOROBUDUR: ENSHRINING MEMORY OF TRAVEL AND PILGRIMAGE

An important text for the study of pilgrimage in early Buddhism is the *Gaṇḍavyūha*, which forms a part of the *Avataṁsakasūtra*. It dates back in all probability to the early centuries CE and describes the travels of Sudhana who was inspired to travel by the Bodhisattva Manjusri and advised to visit fifty-three 'spiritual friends' in order to learn *bodhicarya* or 'the Bodhisattva practice'. It is not known when and by whom the *Avataṁsakasūtra*, one of the most influential Mahayana *sūtras* was first composed, but it is thought to have issued from different hands in the Indic cultural sphere. Comprehensive renditions of the latter text were made in China in the early fifth and late seventh centuries CE from versions of the text obtained from Khotan (Cleary 1993: 2). It was propagated in at least three different versions all over the Far East, and in the third and last translation the *Gaṇḍavyūha* occurs as an individual text and not as part of the *Avataṁsakasūtra*. An autographed manuscript of the *Gaṇḍavyūha* is said to have been presented to the Chinese emperor in 795 CE by an Orissan king, generally accepted to be a member of the Bhaumakara dynasty. This text and a letter were entrusted to the monk Prajna who was asked to provide a translation into Chinese.

The starting point of Sudhana's journey was Dhanyakara, often identified with Dhanyakataka in Andhra, and the littoral played a significant part in his travels (Fontein 1967: 3). For twelve years, Sudhana travelled through peninsular India; passed through 110 cities and visited the grammarian Megha at Vajrapura, the merchant Muktaka of Vanavasi on the west coast, the monk Saradhvaja at the tip of the continent and the seer Bhishmottaranirghosha in the land of Nalayur on the coast. This was followed by visits to centres such as Samudrapratisthana and Paithan where he met the lay devotee Prabhuta; Bharukaccha or Broach at the mouth of the Narmada on the west coast of India to visit the treasurer Muktasara; Magadha, an ancient kingdom in north India; Kalingavana in the land of Shronaparanta; Dvaravati to see the celestial Mahadeva; and Kapilavastu where the Buddha was born. The text, however, does not contain any details of the centres visited, but is instead full of repetition and descriptions of miracles, together with standard phrases and lengthy discourses.

One of the Buddhist monuments important in this context is that of Borobudur in central Java where the *Gaṇḍavyūha* has been brilliantly sculpted in 460 panels, though there are a number of variations between the sculpted panels and the textual data, and there is 'no clear correlation between the iconography and location of the narrative scenes and the corresponding passages in the text' (Fontein 1967: 125). Borobudur is a unique Javanese monument consisting of a series of terraces of decreasing size that rise above the Kedu plains. Construction at Borobudur probably began in around 760 CE and was completed by about 830 CE (Miksic 1990).

In addition to the *Gaṇḍavyūha* there are several Jataka stories represented on the monument. In the lower register of the walls of the first gallery at Borobudur, a series of four panels illustrate the life of the Bodhisattva as a sea captain and how he and his sailors were shipwrecked on an island inhabited by female ogres. Sea travel is prominently represented in the narratives of Maitrakanyaka: Suparaga Jataka, where the Bodhisattva is born as a navigator who saves the ship from a storm and a monster; and the Kacchapāvadāna, where a giant turtle saves shipwrecked merchants on his back (Bernet-Kempers 1976: 110–119). Besides, the monument at Borobudur is well known for detailed representations of more than ten ships, many of them sea-going vessels. These narratives of travel and pilgrimage across the seas lost their centrality with the development of the so-called 'scientific' disciplines such as archaeology and the search for national histories, but form an important and critical component of any study of travel and trans-locality.

Coastal Monuments: Visual Ordering of the Sailing World

Increasingly, maritime historians are agreed that the history of the seas that unite the ASEAN—India region should be discussed as 'connected history' across porous borders, linked through boat-building traditions, community networks and cultural practices (Satish Chandra and Ray 2013). While the history of maritime trade, trading commodities and ports has received attention and there is a rich secondary literature available on these themes, this is not the case with subjects such as coastal architecture, heritage practices and boat-building traditions.

It is significant that before the construction of coastal facilities, such as docks and ports, sailing ships anchored at some distance from the coast and small boats were used to ferry passengers and cargo to the shore. At the same time, the region also presented special problems for the historian and the archaeologist. On the one hand it provides a profusion of ethnographic data on local traditions of fishing and boat-building, while on the other actual remains of wrecks are rare.

The oldest shipwreck in the region dates to the first century BCE—first century CE and lies off the fishing village of Godavaya on the south coast of Sri Lanka. The ship was transporting a cargo of raw materials, including what appear to be ingots of iron and others of glass, as well as finished stone querns (hand-operated mills) and ceramic bowls, when it sank some time before the first century CE (Carlson and Trethewey 2013: 9–14). Further across the Indian Ocean a somewhat later ninth-century shipwreck of a vessel of possible Indian or Arab origin was found in Indonesian waters. This was located just north of the main town and port of Belitung Island, Tanjung Pandan. A large number of seventh-century Chinese coins and ceramics were recovered from the site, indicating that the ship was travelling on the route from the Persian Gulf to China (Flecker 2000: 199–217). Thus, the data from shipwrecks is gradually adding to our understanding of the cultural milieu of maritime activity in the region.

Other indicators of the deep engagement with the sea include archaeological artefacts, as evidence of ancient settlements and routes, and architectural edifices and their networks of interaction. The larger issue addressed here relates to perspectives through which monuments, especially those located on the coast, are to be understood and made meaningful to contemporary societies, both for an appreciation of their aesthetic value, as also to aid in their preservation for posterity. The attempt in this chapter is to articulate the complex connections built through the mediation of the sea both spatially and chronologically by an examination of coastal architecture.

Recent archaeological research has brought to light several Buddhist sites in coastal Odisha, though the major expansion occurred from the fifth to thirteenth centuries CE, when more than 100 Buddhist sites are known in the region. Nearly 140 Buddhist sites are listed along the Andhra region dating from the second century BCE onwards and the distribution along the coast from Srikakulam in the north to Ramatirtham and Nandalur in the south is quite striking. Of these, thirty Buddhist sites have yielded stone inscriptions that record donations made by a cross-section of the populace to the Buddhist Sangha or community of monks.

An issue that requires consideration at this stage relates to the extent and vigour of the trading network linking eastern India with the Bay of Bengal and evidence for the spread of Buddhism across the ocean. The most interesting of the inscriptions in Sanskrit found in Southeast Asia refer to the setting up of the stone by the mariner Buddhagupta, resident of Raktamrttika, identified with Rajbadidanga in Bengal, on the successful completion of his voyage (Chhabra 1965: 23–24).

There was a shift in maritime networks around the middle of the first millennium CE and pilgrims visiting sites associated with the life of the Buddha formed a major category of travellers. The Chinese pilgrim Faxian arrived overland in India in 399 CE and returned by sea to China in 413–414 CE from Sri Lanka heading towards the northwest tip of Sumatra. The ship was wrecked on the way and perhaps landed in the Andamans. The next phase took Faxian to the northwest of Borneo, where he arrived in 414 CE after ninety days at sea. The pilgrim remained in Borneo for five months and then left for China in mid-414 CE heading towards Canton.

Perhaps the most relevant example for this chapter is the Buddhist monastery at Nagapattinam, which was a major landmark on the Tamil coast from the seventh to the nineteenth centuries CE.

The Vihara at Nagapattinam and Its Cultural Context[1]

The seaside town of Nagapattinam located on the Tamil coast has played an important role in the history of trans-oceanic activity across the Bay of Bengal (Fig. 3.1). The present district of Nagapattinam, which came into

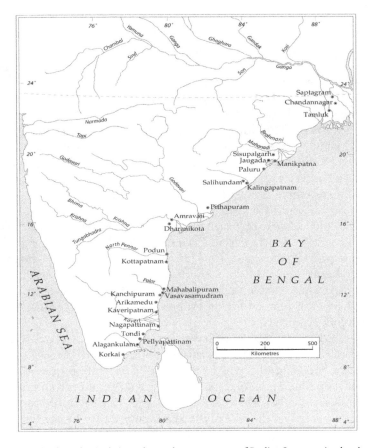

Fig. 3.1 Archaeological sites along the east coast of India. Source: Author's own (map drawn by Uma Bhattacharya)

---

[1] This section was first published as 'A Chinese' Pagoda at Nagapattinam on the Tamil Coast: Revisiting India's Early Maritime Networks'. Lecture by Himanshu Prabha Ray, delivered at India International Centre, New Delhi, on 15 November 2014, and published as *IIC Occasional Publication: 66*.

being in 1991, is known to have been settled as early as the Neolithic period and provides evidence for continued activity well into the present. It was not only an important port and trading settlement, but was also a major sacred centre, as evident from the sixteenth-century dargah, which continues to be a focus of pilgrimage, as also the seventeenth-century basilica of *Our Lady of Good Health* at Velankanni, 10 km from Nagapattinam.

Several seventh-century Tamil saints, such as Saint Thirunavukkarasar (Appar), are known to have compiled devotional couplets in praise of Nagapattinam and its shrines (Seshadri 2009: 107–111). Thirty-one devotional couplets of the seventh-century Tamil saints Appar and Sambandar describe Nagapattinam as a prosperous city with fortified walls and wide roads. Large ships known as *vangam* anchored along the coast, as it was a major centre for onward travel to Sri Lanka and Southeast Asia (Seshadri 2009: 107–108). Tamil tradition also refers to the semi-legendary saint Shahul Hamid of Nagore, whose sixteenth-century shrine is situated a few kilometres to the north of Nagapattinam (Amrith 2013: 88–89). The site had several benefactors, all of whom contributed to structural additions to the shrine, including maraikkayar ship-owners and Nayak rulers, and also the Dutch East India Company (Bayly 1989: 217).

The cultural context of Nagapattinam locates it within a multireligious sacred geography, which preceded and succeeded the establishment of the Buddhist vihara at the site in 1005, rather than a sequential development of Buddhism followed by Hinduism, as often suggested. The Kayarohanaswami temple in Nagapattinam is dedicated to Shiva and is said to have sixth-century origins, though the present structure dates from the eleventh century.

Several eleventh- and twelfth-century inscriptions engraved on the temple walls provide valuable information. In addition to the setting up of the vihara, the King of Srivijaya (identified with Jambi on the island of Sumatra) gave a set of ornaments and jewels to the silver image of Nakaiyalakar (the handsome Lord of Nagapattinam) according to an inscription carved on the wall of the Shiva temple, thereby corroborating a plural sacred landscape at Nagapattinam. A second record refers to donations of several types of lamps by the agent of the King of Srivijaya, while a third mentions donation of gold coins from China for worship of an image of Ardhanarisvara installed on the premises of the temple by the King of Kidar, identified with modern Kedah (Seshadri 2009: 121–125).

About 120 km inland from Nagapattinam on the Kaveri river is the town of Tiruchirappalli with seventh- and eighth-century rock-cut shrines and a rock fort. Inscriptions at the highest parts of the fort date from the third to eleventh century and record names of Jaina ascetics. About a kilometre from the fort is the mosque of Abdullah ibn Muhammad built in the eighth century (Orr 2004: 226). This larger cultural landscape thus provides continuity to engagement of both the coastal and inland communities with the sea. It is important that this maritime orientation is taken into account when discussing the maritime history of coastal centres.

Besides, the multireligious sacred landscape as evident from religious architecture is further corroborated by the textual evidence. In a study of the eleventh-century Tamil–Sanskrit poetic grammar text titled *Viracoliyam*, Anne Monius discusses the wider cultural context of the text, especially its relation to Saiva and Vaisnava devotional literature of the Chola period dating from the mid-ninth to the mid-thirteenth century CE (Monius 2001). The Chola period is marked by 'emergence of new Tamil literary styles and genres, mature and confident in their vision of religious communities both Saiva and Vaisnava … [which portray] Saiva and Vaisnava saints, as calm victors in debate over well-meaning but ignorant Buddhist monks' (Monius 2001: 122). In contrast to this, writings in languages such as Pali of the Theravada monastic tradition depicts south India as a bastion of conservative Buddhist orthopraxy during the Chola period. 'At the same time that Cekkilar imagines in literary Tamil the humble conversion to Saivism of the last remnants of Buddhism in the Tamil-speaking region, Buddhist monks writing in Pali increasingly identify themselves or are identified by others as "Coliya" or "Damila"' (Monius 2001: 123).

The two sets of Leyden copper plates, the Larger Leyden Plate and Smaller Leyden Plates, in Sanskrit and Tamil refer to the establishment of the Cudamanivihara at Nagapattinam at the initiative of the kings of Srivijaya. Construction started during the reign of the Chola king Rajaraja I (985–1016) and was completed under his son and successor Rajendra I (1012–1044). The Smaller Leyden Plates in Tamil refer to nine units of land attached to the Nagapattinam vihara (Schalk 2002: 513–670). The larger plates contain a Sanskrit portion, consisting of 111 lines and a Tamil portion, consisting of 332. The Sanskrit text states that in the twenty-first regnal year the king gave the village of Annaimangalam to the lofty shrine of Buddha in the Chulamanivarma Vihara, which the ruler of Srivijaya and Kataha, Mara Vijayottungavarman of Sailendra family, with the *makara* crest, had erected in the name of his father in the city of Nagappattana. After Rajaraja had passed away, his son Madhurantaka caused a permanent edict to be made for the village granted by his father. It is mentioned that the height of the vihara towered above Kanaka Giri or Mount Meru (Seshadri 2009: 125). Nagapattinam finds mention in the 1467 Kalyani inscription of the Burmese king Dhammaceti. Some Burmese monks who were shipwrecked are said to have visited Nagapattinam and worshipped there (Schalk 2002, volume II: 596).

The Dutch traveller Wouter Schouten visited the Tamil coast in the 1660s and described a brick structure at Nagapattinam that he termed the 'Chinese Pagoda'; an account repeated by a Dutch priest François Valentyn in his 1724 publication. The structure was extant until the nineteenth century. Sir Walter Elliot visited the Chinese Pagoda in 1846 on board the government steamer *Hugh Lindsay*, which travelled down the coast, and described it as a 'four-sided tower of three stories constructed of bricks closely fitted together without cement' (Elliot 1878: 224–227). There was a fort in its vicinity and 'about 1/3 miles NNW from the fort stands the old Black Pagoda, which is one of the most conspicuous objects in approaching this part of the coast'. In spite of local objections, the governor-in-council approved the demolition of the Buddhist monastery on 28 August 1867 by French Jesuits, who had been expelled from Pondicherry and had wanted to construct a college in its place.

During demolition of the monastery at Nagapattinam by the Jesuits in 1856 a large number of Buddhist bronze images were recovered. In a carefully concealed brick chamber five bronze images of the Buddha were found, one of them with a Tamil inscription on the pedestal, which reads: 'Hail Prosperity! The Nayakar [Buddha], who assured the salvation of scholarly Pandits who learnt the Agama [Nikaya]' (Ramachandran 1954: 19–21). Subsequent finds of Buddha images made in 1910 and 1935 were distributed to the museums in Madras and the British Museum respectively. The bronzes may be divided into two broad categories: images of the Buddha (Figs. 3.2 and 3.3) and votive stupas.

In addition to representations of the Buddha, images of Avalokitesvara, Maitreya, Lokesvara, Jambhala (Figure 6), Vasudhara and Tara have also been found, though smaller in number. Some of them carried inscriptions in Tamil on their pedestals dating from the eleventh to thirteenth century. Three categories of inscriptions are common: those containing epithets of the Buddha; inscriptions recording setting up of images by monks and nuns; legends consisting of gifts by lay devotees. The longest and perhaps the most interesting is the two-line legend on the pedestal of a 69.2 cm Buddha image now in the John D. Rockfeller III collection. The 2002 decipherment of the inscription reads as follows:

Fig. 3.2 Bronze Buddha from Nagapattinam now in the Government Museum, Chennai. Source: Author's own

The image of the Lord Buddha is for festival procession (s) at the temple of the Lord Buddha attached to the *akkacālaipperumpaḷḷi* or image house of *Rajendracolapperumpaḷḷi*.

This image of the Lord Buddha has been installed by the venerable Kunākara IV of Ciṟutavūr.

Hail Prosperity! The prefect of artisan manufactories for the merchants of the eighteen countries. (Schalk 2002, volume II: 595)

Thus, the Buddha image was invested with attributes of divinity and was involved in several rituals with close parallels to those associated with Shiva and Vishnu. Two monastic institutions were located at Nagapattinam,

Fig. 3.3 Bronze Jambhala and consort from Nagapattinam now in the Government Museum, Chennai. Source: Author's own

the Cudamanivihara and the *Rajendracolapperumpalli*. The inscriptions from Nagapattinam thus provide evidence for the presence of several monastic orders and gifts by monks and nuns to the Sangha. Pauline Scheurleer suggests that some of the bronze images of the Buddha made in Java in the ninth century used models from Nagapattinam bronzes (Klokke and Scheurleer 1994: 78).

A hoard of forty-five bronzes was found more recently at Sellur village, Kodavasal taluq, Tiruvarur district of Tamilnadu. The images range in height from 7 to 52 cm and include some extraordinary pieces, such as a votive stupa, about 30 cm tall.

> On the base of the stupa, around the four sides, are tales from the Buddha's life. On the one side is Nalagiri, the mad elephant kneeling before the Buddha on hearing his voice, and the Buddha calming it with his hand. On another

side is the Buddha preaching his very first sermon, after his Enlightenment, in the Deer Park of Isipatana, now called Sarnath, near Varanasi. Below him is a Dharma Chakra, flanked by two deer and followers with folded hands. Below this panel is a standing Buddha, with an attendant holding a parasol with a tall stem above the Buddha's head. On another side is the Buddha in Maha Parinirvana, that is after his death. On the fourth side is a seated Buddha, with his right hand in "*bhoomi sparsa*" mudra. On top of this base is the circular "*anda*" and above it is the "*harmika*" or the tiered *vimana*. Lift the *anda* and the *harmika* and, lo and behold, there emerges a tiny seated Buddha.[2]

Another is a 52 cm image of the seated Buddha with musicians playing various instruments around him.

An analysis of the inscriptions on the bronzes shows that many of the epithets associated with notions of divinity and found in contemporary Shaiva and Vaishnava traditions were applied to the Buddha image, indicating considerable interreligious and intercultural communication (Schalk 2002, volume II: 603). Schalk refers to three kinds of Buddhism at Nagapattinam: the first one is evident from bronze pedestal images, which show it to be close to Saivism, so that it is difficult to differentiate between the two (Fig. 3.4).

The second is documented in the twelfth-century text the *Viracoliyam* and its commentary, which propagates a devotional form of Buddhism mediated by the sage Agastya. The third form of Buddhism was that of the acaryas. Very little of this last form survives, except in the form of stone images from several sites along the Tamil coast (Schalk 2002, volume II: 517). How are these wider linkages of Nagapattinam to be assessed? In the next section the wider maritime network is discussed.

The Maritime Network

From the ninth to the mid-fourteenth century several merchant associations dominated economic transactions in peninsular India, such as the Ainurruvar, Manigramam, Nanadesi and the Anjuvannam. Associated with these merchant associations were communities of craftsmen such as weavers, basket-makers, potters and leather-workers. The topographical distribution of the inscriptions is significant and they are clustered in the Dharwad–Bijapur and Mysore localities of Karnataka, while in Tamilnadu

[2] http://www.thehindu.com/features/friday-review/history-andculture/stunning-indicators-of-nagapattinams-buddhist-legacy/article2745233.ece accessed on 3 April 2014.

Fig. 3.4 Sixteenth-century Lokesvara image from Vellipalayam Nagapattinam district now in the Government Museum, Chennai. Source: Author's own

larger numbers are found in Thanjavur, Tiruchirapalli and Madurai districts. Not only did these merchant associations develop powerful economic networks, but they also employed private armies. They donated regularly to temples, which were at times named after them, and also contributed to the construction of tanks (Abraham 1988; Karashima 2002; Kulke et al. 2009).

Information about the organization and functioning of the merchant guilds comes from inscriptions recording donations to temples, and two types of assembly meetings are referred to (Karashima 2009: 135–157). One type, namely *pattana-dharmayam* (Kannada) or *pagudi* (Tamil), meaning shared contribution, records decisions linked to contributions made to the temple; and the second refers to the founding of towns where merchants as well as soldiers lived (*erivira-pattinam*). The *pattana-dharmayam* inscriptions appear in Maharashtra and Karnataka in the twelfth and thirteenth centuries, while they are clustered in Tamilnadu in the thirteenth and fourteenth centuries. Most of the *erivira-pattinam* inscriptions in Tamilnadu come from the eleventh and twelfth centuries, suggesting that at this time the importance of soldiers who guarded the merchants increased greatly. The range of their operations extended well beyond the boundaries of the Indian subcontinent into Southeast Asia.

Several clusters of Tamil inscriptions have been found on the eastern fringes of the Indian Ocean from Burma (Myanmar) to Sumatra. Of the eight mid-ninth- to late thirteenth-century Tamil or part-Tamil language inscriptions so far found in Southeast Asia, one has been found near Pagan in Burma; two just south of the Isthmus of Kra in the Malay peninsula; four in north and west Sumatra; and one on the central coast of China (Christie 1998b: 239–268). The earliest Tamil inscription was found on a hill, about 15 km upstream on the Takuapa river, on the west coast of peninsular Thailand. It was associated with the remains of a small structure and three large stone figures of Shaiva affiliation. The inscription refers to the digging of a tank and a military camp set up for its protection.

There is a temporal gap of almost two centuries between the ninth-century peninsular inscription of Takuapa and the earliest Tamil-language inscription found in Sumatra. This latter inscription dated 1088 was found at the early port site or *pattinam* (as mentioned in the inscription) of Lobo Tuwa, just to the north of Barus on the west coast of the island. This record refers to a tax levied on captains and crew of incoming ships to the settlement on the island. An inscription from the north coast of Sumatra dated to the twelfth century records trading regulations covering losses of goods, the waiving of collection of interest and perhaps of royal fees. The last five of the known Tamil language inscriptions of Southeast and East Asia appear to date to the second half of the thirteenth century. Perhaps the easternmost record is the bilingual Tamil and Chinese language inscription found associated with remains of one of the two Siva temples at Quanzhou in south China. These inscriptions connect merchants' associations operating out of south India with the founding or the endowing of temples or other structures for the use of the resident Indian merchant community.

In the tenth century, local versions of these merchant guilds, termed the *banigrama*, appeared in the north coast ports of both Java and Bali, especially at Julah on the Balinese coast. There are seven Javanese inscriptions dating from 902 to 1053 CE that refer to merchant associations called *banigrama* and to the various tax concessions granted to them. While some foreign merchants may have been included in these groups, these appear largely as indigenous organizations associated with the local economic networks as tax farmers (Christie 1999: 221–270).

The term 'kling' was widely adopted in Indonesia as a blanket term covering all South Asians and in some cases all foreigners. The earliest inscription to contain such a list dates to 883 CE and is from Yogyakarta in central Java. The list includes foreign members of the tax farmer group from Champa, lower Burma and Cambodia or Kmira, as well as Kling, Pandikira, Aryya and Singhala from South Asia. These groups continue to find mention in four eleventh-century inscriptions issued by the rulers of Mataram in central Java, though an additional appears, that of the Drawida, soon to be replaced by the Colika and Karnataka. After the middle of the eleventh century there was a hiatus in inscriptions containing lists of foreign tax farmers, and these reappear in the thirteenth and fourteenth centuries when an important addition is that of China, though Kmir (Khmer) and Champa retain their position (Christie 1998a: 369). The Javanese text *Nagarakertagama* completed in 1365 mentions merchants from Jambudvipa (India), especially from Karnataka and Bengal, from China and various parts of Southeast Asia.

A recent addition to the historiography on the subject that focuses specifically on the eleventh-century naval expedition said to have been despatched against Sriwijaya by the Chola king Rajendra I is the edited volume titled *Nagapattinam to Suvarnadwipa: Reflections on the Chola Naval Expeditions to Southeast Asia* (Kulke et al. 2009). The chapters in this volume suggest that the oft-quoted Chola naval expedition is based on a single primary source, viz. the eulogy contained in the inscription of Rajendra I, which is not corroborated by other contemporary sources, especially Chinese sources. Instead contemporary sources refer to an extensive Indian Ocean trading system extending from the Tamil coast to China, and it is this trading system that provided a context to the supposed naval expedition. In the eleventh century, Nagapattinam was a major outlet for the fertile hinterland along the river Kaveri and acquired pre-eminence amongst the series of towns that dotted the coast from Marakkanam north of Pondicherry to Korkai and Kayal in Tirunelveli district.

CONCLUSIONS

In the final analysis it is evident that narratives of trans-locality, travel and pilgrimage across the seas lost their centrality with the development of 'scientific' disciplines such as archaeology and the search of national histories. The writing of ancient Indian history from a socio-economic perspective in India in the last six decades emphasized trade and urban centres as the prime movers of social change and the movements of brahmanas as legitimizers of political authority in the newly emerging states of the early medieval period. It is important that as maritime history emerges as a discipline in its own right the focus should shift from sequential developments of Buddhism and Hinduism to researching multireligious cultural landscapes across the oceans. Studies on sites such as Nagapattinam become significant, not only as markers of trans-oceanic cultural currents, but also as helping to define local and regional cultural and religious environments.

It is important to locate this shrine in context, both physical and social, in order to unravel the multiple levels at which sacred sites interacted with a diverse range of communities and negotiated between them. Another aspect of the shrine is its horizontal expansion and additions made to it over time to house a variety of functions of interest to this chapter, such as *ghatikāsthāna* or centres of learning, which came to be incorporated in temples, especially in peninsula India, from the eighth and ninth centuries onward.

Eleventh-century inscriptions from the temple in Thirumukkudal, on the banks of the Palar river near Kanchipuram in Tamilnadu, indicate the existence of a Vedic pathsala attached to the temple, and also a medical centre termed *athura saalai* and arrangements for distribution of medicinal herbs. Inscriptions from the Buddhist site of Kanheri near Mumbai and a temple in Gujarat would suggest that this practice may have earlier beginnings. A sixth-century inscription from Kanheri refers to a donation by a vaidya or physician. Three copper plates from central Gujarat dated to the reign of the Huna Toramana (fifth–sixth centuries CE) record gifts made to the temple of Jayaswami or Narayana belonging to the queen mother by the trading community of Vadrapalli. Vadrapalli was probably located 8 km to the west of Sanjeli, and signatories to the donation included traders from Ujjain, Kannauj, Mathura and perhaps Mandasor in central India. A goldsmith constructed a lake near the temple. One of the copper plates states that itinerant mendicants visiting the temple, and also devotees, should be provided with medicines (*bhaisaja*, Ramesh 1973–1975: 175–186). These are aspects which need further research and analysis.

REFERENCES

Abraham, Meera, *Two Medieval Merchant Guilds of South India*, Manohar Publishers, New Delhi, 1988.

Amrith, Sunil S. 2013. Crossing the Bay of Bengal: the Furies of Nature and the Fortunes of Migrants, Harvard University Press.

Bayly, Susan. 1989. *Goddesses and Kings: Muslims and Christians in South Indian Society 1700–1900*, Cambridge University Press.

Bayly, Susan. 2004. Imagining 'Greater India': French and Indian Visions of Colonialism in the Indic Mode, *Modern Asian Studies*, 38, 3: 703–744.

Bernet-Kempers, A. J. *Ageless Borobudur*, Servire, Wassenaar, 1976.

Carlson, Deborah N. and Trethewey, Ken, Exploring the Oldest Shipwreck in the Indian Ocean, *Institute of Nautical Archaeology Quarterly*, volume 40, number 1, Spring 2013: 9–14.

Chhabra, B. Ch. *Expansion of the Indo-Aryan Culture during Pallava Rule*, Munshiram Manoharlal, Delhi, 1965.

Chou, Cynthia, Space, Movement and Place: The Sea Nomads, Satish Chandra and Himanshu Prabha Ray edited, *The Sea, Identity and History: From the Bay of Bengal to the South China Sea*, Manohar, New Delhi, 2013: 41–66.

Christie, Jan Wisseman, Javanese Markets and the Asian Sea Trade Boom of the Tenth to Thirteenth Centuries AD, *Journal of the Economic and Social History of the Orient*, 41, 3, 1998a: 369.

Christie, Jan Wisseman, The medieval Tamil-language inscriptions in Southeast Asia and China, *Journal of Southeast Asian Studies*, 29, 2, September 1998b: 239–268.

Christie, Jan Wisseman, Asian Sea Trade between the Tenth and Thirteenth Centuries and its Impact on the States of Java and Bali, Himanshu Prabha Ray, edited, *Archaeology of Seafaring: The Indian Ocean in the Ancient Period*, ICHR Monograph I, Pragati Publications, New Delhi, 1999: 221–270.

Cleary, Thomas, 1993, *The flower ornament Scripture*, Boston and London: Shambhala.

Elliot, Sir Walter, The Edifice Formerly Known as the Chinese or Jaina Pagoda at Negapatam, *The Indian Antiquary*, vol. 7, 1878: 224–227.
Flecker, Michael, A 9th-century Arab or Indian shipwreck in Indonesian waters, *The International Journal of Nautical Archaeology*, 2000, 29.2: 199–217.
Fontein, Jan, 1967, *The pilgrimage of Sudhana: A study of Gandavyūha illustrations in China, Japan and Java*, The Hague: Mouton.
Karashima, Noboru, edited, *Ancient and Medieval Commercial Activities in the Indian Ocean: Testimony of Inscriptions and Ceramic Sherds*, Taisho University Press, Tokyo, 2002.
Karashima, Noboru, South Indian Merchant Guilds in the Indian Ocean and Southeast Asia, Hermann Kulke, K. Kesavapany and Vijay Sakhuja edited, *Nagapattinam to Suvarnadwipa: Reflections on the Chola Naval Expeditions to Southeast Asia*, Institute of Southeast Asian Studies, Singapore, 2009: 135–157.
Klokke, Marijke J. and Scheurleer, Pauline Lunsingh, edited, *Ancient Indonesian Sculpture*, KITLV Press, Leiden, 1994.
Kulke, Hermann, Kesavapany, K. and Sakhuja, Vijay edited, *Nagapattinam to Suvarnadwipa: Reflections on the Chola Naval Expeditions to Southeast Asia*, Institute of Southeast Asian Studies, Singapore, 2009.
Miksic, John, *Borobudur: Golden Tales of the Buddhas*, Periplus editions, Berkeley – Singapore, 1990.
Monius, Anne E. *Imagining a Place for Buddhism: Literary Culture and Religious Community in Tamil-Speaking south India*, Oxford University Press, Oxford – New York, 2001.
Orr, Leslie C. Gods and Worshippers on South Indian Sacred Ground, James Heitzman & Wolfgang Schenkluhn edited, The World in the year 1000, University of America Press, Lanham, 2004: 225–254.
Ramachandran, T.N. *The Nagapattinam and Other Buddhist Bronzes in the Madras Museum*, Government Press, Madras, 1954
Ramesh, K.V. Three Early Charters from Sanjeli in Gujarat, *Epigraphia Indica*, 40, 1973–1975: 175–186.
Ray, Himanshu Prabha, Archaeology and Empire: Buddhist Monuments in Monsoon Asia, *The Indian Economic and Social History Review*, 45, 3, 2008, pp. 417–449.
Ray, Himanshu Prabha, Introduction: Beyond National Histories, Satish Chandra and Himanshu Prabha Ray edited, *The Sea, Identity and History: From the Bay of Bengal to the South China Sea*, Manohar, New Delhi, 2013: 13–40.
Ribeiro, Edgar E. Legalized Mapping of Heritage of India: Can it be applied to Old Goa? Himanshu Prabha Ray and Manoj Kumar edited, *Indian World Heritage Sites in Context*, National Monuments Authority and Aryan Books International, 2014.
Satish Chandra and Ray, Himanshu Prabha edited, *The Sea, Identity and History: From the Bay of Bengal to the South China Sea*, Manohar Publishers, 2013.

Schalk, Peter edited, *Buddhism among Tamils in Pre-Colonial Tamilakam and Ilam*, Uppsala University, Stockholm, volume II, 2002: 513–670.

Seetah, Krish, Environmental Archaeology in Mauritius, Paper presented at Conference on 'Connecting Continents: Setting an Agenda for A Historical Archaeology of the Indian Ocean World', Stanford Archaeology Center, 6–7 March 2014.

Seshadri, Gokul, New Perspectives on Nagapattinam, Hermann Kulke, K. Kesavapany and Vijay Sakhuja edited, *Nagapattinam to Suvarnadwipa: Reflections on the Chola Naval Expeditions to Southeast Asia*, Institute of Southeast Asian Studies, Singapore, 2009.

Sharma, Anjana, edited, *Civilizational Dialogue: Asian Inter-connections and Cross-cultural Exchanges*, Manohar, New Delhi, 2013.

Wolters, O. W. Southeast Asia as a Southeast Asian Field of Study, *Indonesia*, 58, October 1994: 1–17.

CHAPTER 4

Indian Patterned Cotton Textiles and Trade with the East and Southeast

Lotika Varadarajan

INTRODUCTION

Trade has never taken place in a vacuum, but has occurred as part of a continuum in networking patterns established between sets of trade partners. This is particularly in evidence in the Indian textile trade with East and Southeast Asia of the pre-modern period. The spread of Hinduism and Buddhism in the countries under review, the existence of guilds and a banking system, and the development of a seafaring tradition have all played a role in the network of relations which developed. Specific deities such as Varuṇa were associated with the Sea. Images of Varuṇa and his vehicle, the Makara, are to be found in several Southeast Asian temples including Angkor Wat in Cambodia. The development of the myth of Agastya, fully developed by about 200 CE, shows the spread of the Brahmanical religion from Varanasi to Sangam culture in the south and thereafter to island Southeast Asia (Fig. 4.1).[1] There was also the deity,

---

[1] Lotika Varadarajan, "Indian Seafaring: The Precept and Reality of Kalivarja", in *The Great Circle*, Vol. 5, No. 1, 1983, p. 1.

L. Varadarajan (✉)
National Museum, New Delhi, India

© The Author(s) 2018
S. Saran (ed.), *Cultural and Civilisational Links between India and Southeast Asia*, https://doi.org/10.1007/978-981-10-7317-5_4

Fig. 4.1 Batik. Hair of Bima, Symbolic of Strength. Source: Textil Museum, Jakarta

Fig. 4.2 Ramayana panel. *Kalamkari*. Probably South Coromandel. Listed as ceremonial cloth and sacred heirloom (*mawa* or *ma'a*), eighteenth century. Traded to Toraja people, Sulawesi, Indonesia. Source: National Gallery of Australia, Canberra. Gift of Michael and Mary Abbott, 1991

Brahmā, transferred to Indonesia as Bhatara Guru, around whom an independent mythology developed. Śiva and Viṣṇu also found their adherents and both the Rāmāyaṇa and the Mahābhārata existed in various forms (Figs. 4.2, 4.3, and 4.4). It was not, however, a one-sided relationship. Partners had their own reasons for the acceptance of Indian cultural modes and the usage to which Indian textiles were put.

Fig. 4.3 *Sarassa*, fragment used in Japanese tea ceremony. Mayeda Collection. Source: Kyoto National Museum, Kyoto, Japan

There are numerous references to trade with Eastern and Southeast Asia, both mainland as well as maritime. Before these are taken up it would be well to consider Indian attitudes to the sea and sailing thereon. The ambivalent Indian attitude towards the sea is expressed well in the statement: 'My brother, the great Ocean brings much misery and few joys. Many set sail on it but few return. Never on any account embark on it.'[2] This can be taken as a practical adage rather than an expression of the reality. The *Gautama Dharma Śutra*, placed by P.V. Kane to the period 600–300 BCE states: 'cultivators, traders, herdsmen, money lenders and artisans [have authority to lay down rules] for their respective classes'. In giving his verdict, the king bases his decisions on the views expressed by the community leaders. These injunctions are further stressed in the *Yajñavalkyasmrti* (II. 192) and the *Nāradasmrti* (*Samayasyānapākarma*, I-3). In the first it is stated that the king should guard against breach of distinctive usages and conventions of guilds (of artisans), of traders belong-

---

[2] These words were addressed by Purna to his brother Bharila in the *Pūrṇa Avadāna*. See E. Burnouf, *Introduction à l'histoire du Buddhism Indien*, Paris, 1879, p. 222.

Fig. 4.4 *Poleng*, as depicted on wayside shrine. Bali, Indonesia. Source: Author's own

ing to heretical sects and bands of soldiers. The second prescribes the king to uphold the conventions of heretical sects, of traders, guilds and other groups, and that whatever traditional usages, activities, mode of attendance and means of maintenance were peculiar to them should be permitted to them by the king.[3] The kind of leeway permitted shows how the permeation of Indian influence in East and Southeast Asia could have taken place.

---

[3] G. Buhler, trans., *The Sacred Laws of the Āryas as taught in the schools of Āpastamba, Gautama, Vāsiṣṭha and Baudhāyan*, in *Āpastamba* and *Gautama*, Part I (New Delhi reprint, 1972), p. 220. Gautama, X. 21 and 22; P. V. Kane, *History of the Dharmaśāstra*, Vol. III (Poona, 1946), p. 876. The *Yājñavalkyasmṛti* and the *Nāradasmṛti* are dated by Kane to the periods AD 100–300 and AD 100–140 respectively.

There was a spirit of mutual accommodation and respect which made this possible without, by and large, war and conquest. Brahminical Hinduism has lent itself to absorption over a wide geographical area by peoples of diverse cultural backgrounds, starting with the Indian subcontinent itself with its diverse ecological zones. The fact that the practice of the religion exists at multiple levels from the philosophical to material and from duality to multiplicity has made it possible to draw adherents from many different kinds of backgrounds. This has provided an elasticity which has permitted centralization to coexist with divergence, something that is perceptible in pre-industrial India's relations with her neighbours.

Important and detailed references to the conduct of trade and maritime endeavour are found in texts such as the *Arthaśāstra* and the *Matsya Purāṇa*. Under the heading of functions of the Director of Trade in the *Arthaśāstra* is stated: 'He should establish ... trade ... in many places [for commodities] ... produced in foreign lands. And on the water route he should ascertain the hire for boats, provisions on the journey, price and amount of [his] goods and of the goods in exchange, seasons suited for the voyage, precautions against dangers and regulations at the ports.'[4] The *Matsya Purāṇa* also gives details of the rite of the *Sapta-Sagara Mahadana*, Gift of the Seven Oceans, performed at special wells called *Samudra kupas*. During the Gupta period such wells were considered appropriate places for religious rites performed by those who had successfully returned from voyages. These were also places of worship of the sea god by relatives during the absence of family members. This tradition appears to have waned after the decline of the Gupta power. With regard to Jain settlers overseas, Jains being a premier trading community, the late U.P. Shah demonstrates that while Jain Munis were proscribed from sailing across the waters this proscription was not binding for the Jain laity.[5]

The mythology which developed in the sphere of maritime deities and patron saints reflected the need of those on the high seas, no less than their relatives ashore, to repose their faith in a source which would help them put up with their troubles. It also pointed out how a widening of geographical horizons opened possibilities for transplanting the home culture in other environments. Several stories may be found in the *Jātakas*

---

[4] R. P. Kangle, *The Kautilya Arthaśastra*, Part II (Bombay, 1972), 2.16.4.24, p. 127. Kane assigns the *Arthaśastra* to the period, BC 300 to AD 100.

[5] See U. P. Shah, "Suvarnabhumi men Kalakacarya [in Hindi], in *Vijayavallabhasurismaraka Grantha*, Bombay, 1956.

and *Kathāsaritsāgara* which point to linkages with both West as well as Southeast Asia.[6]

INDIAN TEXTILES: THE RECIPIENTS

An aspect that needs to be borne in mind is that Indian textiles were particularly well suited to the needs of the unstitched garment that was worn throughout Monsoon Asia and the Archipelago until the advent of Islam. Textile exchange can be divided into two periods, the dividing line being placed approximately in the eleventh century CE. The ritual traditions of the Chinese and South Asians extended to extensive usage of textiles, and Indian textiles played a role in this. Textiles bonded different groups of people together particularly in the relationship between superior and subordinates.[7] In the earlier non-Indian records the focus appears to be on textiles as gifts, as these were articles of high prestige. During the tenth and eleventh centuries there was a shift towards the regulation of trade and entrepreneurial pressures came into evidence.[8] The region appears to have had an insatiable appetite for cloth. Despite having highly developed weaving traditions of their own, there was considerable demand for imported textiles, especially from India. The vibrancy of colour achieved in Indian cotton textiles was particularly appreciated. Such fabrics had a formative influence on indigenous societies, both as prestige items that could eventually take on a significant ritual role and as an inspiration for the development of local design.[9]

---

[6] For references to trade in the Jatakas see S. Rajgyor, *Gujarat nu Vahanvatanu Itihasa* [in Gujarati], Ahmedabad, 1976, pp. 26–29. For *Kathāsaritsāgara* [composed AD mid-eleventh century but having its nucleus in the *Bṛhatkathā* composed *c.* 100 BCE], see N. M. Penzer, ed., *Somadeva Ocean of Story* (being C. H. Tawney's translation of *Somadeva's Kathā Sarit Sāgara*), New Delhi, 1968, vol. IV, pp. 191–194, vol. V, pp. 5–14.

[7] http://www.jstor.org/stable/25165206. *Journal of the Economic and Social History of the Orient*, Vol. 50, No. 4, 2007, Gillian Green, Angkor Vogue: Sculpted Evidence of Imported Luxury Textiles in the Courts of Kings and Temples, pp. 441–442; http://www.jstor.org/stable/2743942. *Current Anthropology*, Vol. 33, No. 1, Robert McC. Adams, Anthropological Perspectives on Ancient Trade, p. 151.

[8] Ashmolean – Eastern Art Online, Yousef Jameel Centre for Islamic and Asian Art, Indian Block-Printed Textiles in Egypt, The Newberry Collection in the Ashmolean Museum, Oxford, Vol. 1, Oxford, 1997, Ruth Barnes, *Indian Block-Printed Textiles in Egypt: The Newberry Collection in the Ashmolean Museum*, Oxford, A catalogue of Newberry's block-printed textiles. Chapter on Indian Ocean Textile Trade: India to South-East Asia (no pagination).

[9] http://www.jstor.org/stable/4629611. *Ars Orientalis*, Vol. 34, 2004, Ruth Barnes, Indian Textiles for Island Taste: Gujarati Cloth in Eastern Indonesia, p. 135.

Fig. 4.5 Ma'a cloth, Sulawesi. Source: Spertus-Holmgren Collection, New York

INDIA AND CHINA

Cotton was transferred to China through east Bengal (presently Bangladesh), Assam and Burma to western Yunnan. Zhao Rugua (Chau Ju-Kua), writing in the port of Quanzhou in 1225, records the export of cottons from the Cola state.[10] Although cotton existed in China the finer varieties were imported from India. In about 1380–1460, Ma Huan, who had accompanied Admiral Zeng He on three of his seven expeditions, wrote about the fine fabrics of Bengal (Fig. 4.5), particularly one known

---

[10] http://www.jstor.org/stable/20072045. Accessed: 21-06-2015, *Journal of Southeast Asian Studies*, Vol. 29, No. 2 (Sept., 1998), Jan Wisseman Christie, The Medieval Tamil-Language Inscriptions in Southeast Asia and China, p. 243.

as *pi* cloth which was as fine as starched paper (Dacca *jamdani*?), and also a fine variety purchased at Calicut (Kozhikode).[11]

INDIA AND JAPAN

Indian textiles brought to Japan by the Portuguese fell into the checked and striped variety as well as Indian *sarassa*. *Sarassa* was much prized in the tea ceremony (Fig. 4.6).[12] Such imports were not suitable for Japanese costume, but could be used in the tea ceremony and as an accessory in garments such as sleeve lining, lapel lining and for the *obi*. *Sarassa* could also be used to cover the quilt on the Japanese *futon* and encase temple carts on festive days, as at the Giyon shrine in Kyoto.[13]

INDIA AND THE KHMER COURT

Two kinds of apparel are depicted in Khmer costume. The clothes made from narrow width textiles could be woven locally, but those portrayed on deities and the elite demanded greater width and would have been imported. Indian textiles were predominantly used in finer wear. This may be seen in the many similarities between Indian and Khmer costume, and many textile motifs are also common. The textile ornamentation associated with the *Saudgiri* of Thailand is also to be noted (see Fig. 4.7).[14]

INDIA AND THE JAVANESE COURT

When Islam was introduced to the islands and stitched costume began to be used, it was believed that while native cloths, imbued with value, were not to be cut, it was less hazardous to do so in the case of imported cloth,

---

[11] http://www.jstor.org/stable/20488072. Accessed: 21-06-2015, *Modern Asian Studies* 43, 1, 2009, Stephen F. Dale, Silk Road, Cotton Road or … Indo-Chinese Trade in Pre-European Times, p. 82, 84.

[12] Due to limitation of space, we are forced to ignore Figs. 4.6–4.19. However, these are available from the author on request.

[13] Verbal communication: Professor J. Yoshioko, Kyoto, Ms E. Kuroda, Ethnographic Museum, Osaka.

[14] http://www.jstor.org/stable/3632445. Accessed: 11-07-2015, *Journal of the Economic and Social History of the Orient*, Vol. 43, No. 3 (2000), Gillian Green, Indic Impetus? Innovations in Textile Usage in Angkorian Period Cambodia, pp. 283, 295–296, 300.

particularly of the *sarassa*.¹⁵ The *patola* of Gujarat called *tchinde* in Indonesia as well as the printed and painted cloth from Gujarat and the Coromandel coast, *sarassa*, were important imports particularly after the fifteenth century. The *chhabdi* pattern in *patola* was associated with the Wali Sanga, the nine saints believed to have introduced Islam to Indonesia. The *chhabdi* pattern called *djelamparang* in Java and *dula neggeo* in Roti, along with those having the motifs of the elephant and the tiger, were much prized (Figs. 4.8 and 4.9).¹⁶ Indonesia also had a tradition of double *ikat* practised in Tenganan village, Bali (Figs. 4.10 and 4.11), and this was probably locally developed rather than being derived from the Indian tradition. The humble checked fabric of India could not be duplicated on looms in Indonesia until a mechanism was devised there to ensure even tension between warp and weft. Such material was called *plekat* in Java, doubtless derived from Pulicat from where it was imported. In Bali, where it was called *poleng*, white and black checks were accorded special status (Fig. 4.12) being the attire of Hanuman, Bhima and Ghatotkacha that was also portrayed in *wayang*. Among the Torajas of Sulawesi Indian *sarassa* was invested with ritual meaning (Figs. 4.13 and 4.14).¹⁷ The *tumpal* motif used as an ending in unstitched female garments was developed on the Coromandel coast from samples sent from Thailand (Fig. 4.15). A similar motif is to be noted in the Manastambha, Neminath Basadi, Hiriyangadi and Karnataka (Fig. 4.16). In view of the mid-fourteenth-century dating of this monument and the role of Jains in trade, an introduction of this decorative detail from Khmer-Sukothai Thailand is not ruled out. Not to be forgotten in this context was the *slendang* (Fig. 4.17), a baby carry cloth found in Indonesia no less than in northeastern India.

---

¹⁵ http://www.jstor.org/stable/3632617. *Journal of the Economic and Social History of the Orient*, Vol. 39, No. 2, 1996, Kenneth R. Hall, The Textile Industry in Southeast Asia, 1400–1800, p. 116.

¹⁶ The play of *patola*, is discussed in A. Buhler, E. Fischer, *The Patola of Gujarat*, Vol. I, Basle, 1979, p. 281. However, the technical term, *ikat*, to describe the process is derived from Indonesian, *mengikat*, to tie or bind. http://www.jstor.org/stable/23003922. Accessed: 21-06-2015,*India International Centre Quarterly*, Vol. 21, No. 1. Judith H. Livingston, Ikat Weaves of Indonesia and India: A Comparative Study, p. 155.

¹⁷ See Gauri Parimoo Krishnan, Gujarati in Spirit and Form, an Heirloom Trade Textile found in Sulawasi, Indonesia, pp. 467–482 in Lotika Varadarajan, ed., *Gujarat and the Sea*, Vadodara, 2011.

INDIA AND BURMA

Although much of the data is obtained from Dutch VOC records dating from the seventeenth century, since this pertains to a traditional society formation of taste had an earlier base. There was much demand for the colourfast Indian red cotton yarn which was used to weave much of the locally woven cloth. It would be tempting to assume that such yarn was dyed in south India through the technique which was popularized in Europe as 'turkey red', since it was introduced through Ottoman Turkey. Such yarn was used with indigenous white yarn and filaments of silk to weave high-quality clothes for the royal family and the nobility. In times of plenty ordinary cloth was woven from an admixture of Indian red with local white and blue yarn and was available in different qualities. On festive days, the women dressed in *lungi* made of fine *calmcaris* (*kalamkaris*) or *cattawany* (a striped cloth from Bengal). They wore *chiavonis* (white cotton cloth) with red silk edges on their heads. Several varieties of tightly woven fabrics known as *moorees*, *salempoory* and *sanen* were dyed yellow in Burma and served as robes for monks. Buddhist monks avoided silk as it involved the killing of the moth before the silk yarn could be unwound from the cocoon. In Bengal, fine, loosely woven cotton fabrics such as *mulmul* and *chassen* were ordered specifically for the Burmese trade.[18]

INDIA AND THAILAND

In 1350, Khmer rule was repudiated and the Thai kingdom of Sukothai was established, the period lasting from 1350 to 1770. However, the design repertoire created by the Khmers continued and was further perfected. The National Museum, Bangkok, has a fine collection of cotton textiles made to Thai design and used by the Thai monarchy for royal consumption and to be conferred as gifts to the nobility (Figs. 4.18 and 4.19). When Thai rule was democratized after 1932, an equivalent cheaper block printed repertoire arose in Gujarat, particularly in Pethapur, Gandhinagar district. This category of *sarassa* came to be called *saudagiri*,[19] and it could be freely worn (see Fig. 4.19).

[18] http://www.jstor.org/stable/20072449. Accessed: 21-06-2015. *Journal of Southeast Asian Studies*, Vol. 33, No. 3 (Oct., 2002), Wil O. Dijk, The VOC's Trade in Indian Textiles with Burma, 1634–1680, p. 499, 501.

[19] See Lotika Varadarajan, Textile Traditions—India and the Orient, p. 27, in Carmen Kagal, ed., *Shilpakar*, Bombay, 1982; Lotika Varadarajan, Syncretic Symbolism and Textiles:

WHY INDIAN COTTON TEXTILES?

The predominant Indian loom, the counter balance pit loom, was well suited to serve the needs of cotton textiles, both for home use as well as the export market. Prior to the appearance of the European trading companies in the fifteenth and sixteenth centuries, Indian cloth was a favoured item, enjoying much demand in neighbouring countries as well as overseas. The Persian and Thai markets were the only markets that introduced specific design repertoires. Indian artisans working within the caste system could very well cater to all types of demand, although doubtless the guilds could also guide taste. Dye technology was highly developed. Tanning and mordanting through alum gave a more pleasing array of colours than the use of lime and ash as in Indonesia. The range of colours developed in India for cotton, a cellulose fibre, could vie with those developed in China for silk, an animal fibre. While black and green predominated across the Arabian Sea, red was the preferred colour in Southeast Asia, particularly Indonesia. Shades of red could be developed through skilful variation in mordant; green demanded an admixture of indigo with yellow, while black could be obtained through successive dyeing in the indigo dye bath. It could also be achieved through iron acetate, but the date for this innovation is not known.

The western Indian belt characterized by the use of mud resist comprised printing centres in Gujarat, Rajasthan and Madhya Pradesh. Individual nuclei, each having variations in technique, comprised the Ajrakh printing centres of Kutch (Gujarat) and Barmer (Rajasthan); the ritual cloth *māthājī ne pacheḍī*, which was printed in Ahmedabad, Bagru, Sanganer (Rajasthan) and Rajapur-Deesa (Gujarat), shared a common technique while Bagh and Bhairongarh represent two variants in Madhya Pradesh. Mud and lime resist were well suited to slightly coarsely woven cotton. However, if more delicate work was required wax resist was preferred. Georges Roques, of the French East Indian Company, noted the printing of wax resist in Ahmedabad in 1678.[20] Wax resist was the dominant mode in South India, but it was *kalam* (brush) painted rather than block printed. The practice of block-printed *Kalamkari* in Masulipatam is a nineteenth-century innovation.

Indo-Thai Expressions, pp. 362–372, in Om Prakash, Denys Lombard, eds., *Commerce and Culture in the Bay of Bengal, 1500–1800*, Manohar, Indian Council of Historical Research, New Delhi, 1999.

[20] Details of the manuscript are: La manière de négocier dans les Indes Orientales, Fonds Français, 14,614, Bibliotheque Nationale, Paris.

Technique

There are several stages in cloth printing. These include the initial preparation of the cloth by removal of impurities (washing), smoothening the texture (beating with rod), bleaching by dunging, a natural agent, and preparation of the fibre for enhanced penetration of the mordant. There is no application of the block at this stage. The cloth is then thoroughly washed, preferably in the flowing waters of a river or stream.

The next stage is that of mordanting. Mordant is a chemical substance which enables cotton to absorb and retain certain dyes. Mordants can either be acid or basic (alkaline). Acid mordants are tannin based. The most common source in India is either myrobalam (*Terminalia chebula*) or catechu, *katha* (Hindi) (*Acacia catechu*). Basic mordants are derived from salts of various metals, particularly aluminium, chromium, iron, copper, zinc and tin. Alum is the one most commonly used in India. Alkali from *surti kar* (saltpeter) or *sapan kar* (carbonate of soda) has been used for *al* (*Morinda citrifolia*) dyeing in Berar, but this yields a brownish crimson rather than red. After mordanting, the fabric is boiled in a cauldron along with the dyestuff. The vessel can be of earthenware, copper or iron. In the latter two cases the metal containers themselves contribute an element in the mordanting process, thereby introducing variations in shade and hue.

Other aspects of the dyeing procedure include the use of items such as *jajakku* (*Memecylon edule*) in Tamil Nadu, or *padvas* (*Narigama alta*) in Gujarat, which act as carriers during the dyeing operation. In the case of *al*, on termination of the dying process alum or *dhā* (*Woodfordia floribunda*) is used as a fixing agent.

The process of application of resist is associated with indigo dyeing. The resist is derived from wax, mud or lime. The dye is reconstituted in the vat through a process of fermentation. A cold vat is used. Although indigo blue is a stable colour it tends to rub off. Rubbing fastness can be improved by a final soaking in catechu. The technology of indigo printing had been developed and practised in India long before its introduction to Europe. In 1766, Jean Ryhiner referred to the Indian method of indigo printing with the use of orpiment, sulphur of arsenic, the liquid being further thickened with gum.[21]

---

[21] P. R. Schwartz, Contribution à l'histoire de l'application du bleu d'indigo dans l'indiennage européen, in, Société Industrielle de Mulhouse, *Bulletin Trimestrielle*, No. 11, 1953, p. 64, 66, n.2, 71n.5, 73 n.8, 74 n.16, 76. See also L. Liotard, *Dyes of Indian Growth and Production*, Calcutta, 1881, p. 134.

It was the finesse in dyeing techniques which contributed to the demand for Indian textiles, including those in the double *ikat* category. The form of banking through the system of *hundi* eased the production and supply system while the rich repertoire of Indian Ocean nautical technology facilitated distribution by sea. The arrival of the European East India companies presaged the advent of colonialism and with it the start of the Industrial Revolution. Colonized units now became the hubs of fabrication, with supplies of raw material being used in automated production by the colonial power. The earlier independent status for manufacture through traditional methods was gravely threatened. With the advent of global warming a reexamination of value systems is incumbent on the post-modern world and with it a reappraisal of earlier methods of manufacture and distribution, so rich in human skill and in the conservation of natural resources.

PART II

Continuities and Change

CHAPTER 5

Indigenous Thought on Indian Traditions in Thailand

Amara Srisuchat

INTRODUCTION

The current archaeological evidence in Thailand suggests that many prehistoric and early historic communities already possessed advanced cultural traditions and technology that would have been inherited by the local inhabitants by the time commercial exchanges with overseas merchants began. Since the advent of the Indians into the land of present-day Thailand in the second century BCE, Indian traditions that were expressed through languages, religions and commerce were embraced by indigenous people of Thailand and adapted to their ways of life and socio-cultural development.

In considering the very early history of Thailand within the geographical boundaries of the modern state, the term indigenous people must include people who speak Thai or Tai languages and native people who speak languages from the Mon-Khmer linguistic group, including Malay. From the thirteenth century onwards, or the historic periods of Thailand, the Thai people have belonged to a combination of immigrant groups, such as the Chinese, Indian, Arabian, European or other people who form part of the evolution fabric of Thai culture.

A. Srisuchat (✉)
Fine Arts Department, Ministry of Culture, Bangkok, Thailand

© The Author(s) 2018
S. Saran (ed.), *Cultural and Civilisational Links between India and Southeast Asia*, https://doi.org/10.1007/978-981-10-7317-5_5

Nevertheless, the thoughts of indigenous people about Indian traditions is not discussed seriously in any research. Aspects of indigenous tradition, of Indian tradition and of assimilation of both, as a result of picking and choosing elements of Indian cultures to suit particular needs, and the reason why some Indian traditions were not adopted are discussed sequentially in this chapter. As a result of the study the following findings were obtained.

ASPECTS OF INDIGENOUS KNOWLEDGE AND TRADITION

Archaeological evidence from some known sites in Thailand, such as Non Nok Tha in Khon Kaen Province, Ban Chiang in Udon Thani Province and Pho Lon in Loei Province (2000–300 BCE) suggest that the land of modern Thailand was rich in resource and highly developed culturally, particularly in terms of art and technology. It had been an agricultural society for some time, before learninghe finer points of metalworking, first bronze and then iron, and developing a very sophisticated metallurgical tradition (Charoenwongsa 1989: 47–50). The local people accumulated knowledge handed down by their forefathers, as reflected in the fourth-century BCE site at Ban Don Ta Phet in Kanchanaburi Province, where the bronze vessels, obviously produced by exceptionally skilled craftsmen, are as beautiful to look at as they are difficult to emulate (Glover 1996: 75–79). Perhaps some Indian references to Suvarnabhumi, the Land of Gold, applied to the Southeast Asian region including Thailand, arose from the knowledge that the land was rich in resources of all types, including minerals, which could be easily bought and sold in a large market. It is easy to imagine an endless supply of money (e.g. gold coins) circulating in such a busy commercial centre. It is also possible that gold could be found in this region, that it was good quality and that the technology employed in the manufacture of objects could well have developed as a result of long-standing familiarity with bronze technology which had been developing since prehistoric times (Srisuchat 1996: 239–240).

An indigenous belief in 'life after death' and 'the world beyond the earth' in the early historic period is confirmed by the discovery of a large number of bronze kettle drums, some of which were decorated with pictures of boats carrying either spirits of the dead or men with bird-like headdresses. Drums such as these, dating from the fifth to the first century BCE, were popular in Lower China and Vietnam. They are also found in Lao, Malaysia and Indonesia. The discovery of these drums points towards the theory that contact with the Far East (China) had been established and that foreign traditions were being absorbed from the West prior to India (Fig. 5.1).

The local people may have acquired these drums and brought them into the region for ritual purposes. This was mainly to support religious beliefs that might have entered the area around the same time. Later, the people began to produce their own drums. The recent discovery of a bronze drum from the archaeological excavation at Ban Na Udom site in Mukdahan Province (dating from the fifth century BCE) ought to point towards the hypothesis of local technology for making bronze drums and the belief in and practice of this tradition.

Some early historic communities probably developed by themselves from the agricultural iron age villages, their iron tools making the development of irrigation systems possible. According to several archaeologists, some small figurines of wild and domestic animals and some zoomorphic shapes of pots in association with animal bones of the same kinds, especially, bull, bison and pig, were found alongside burials of the 1500–500 BCE sites, such as Ban Nadi in Khon Kaen Province, Ban Chiang in Udon Thani Province, Non Mak La and Phu Noi in Lopburi Province and Phu Nimit in Saraburi Province. They were made and deposited for ritual purposes, reflecting a belief in the beast power and the 'spirit animal'. It is important to note that a terracotta figurine of a bull with a high hump was found in some archaeological sites of the same period, such as Ban Pong Takhop in Sara Buri

Fig. 5.1 Bronze drum from Ko Samui, Surat Thani Province, fifth–first century BCE. Source: Author's own

Province and Ban Nadi in Khon Kaen Province. It is identifiable as *Bos Indicus*; as the scientific name suggests, the species was imported from India (Fig. 5.2).

The rock art at Phi Ho To cave of Krabi Province (1000–500 BCE) portrayed the wearing of animal skins from a horned beast (bull or ox). This designated guardian spirit of the clan, who appeared in the form of an animal.

The representation of a snake as a painted pattern on pottery of the Ban Chiang site (third century BCE to second century) in Udon Thani Province is regarded as the earliest evidence of the relationship between man and snake. There might be a tradition in which man's progenitor was a snake. Several folktales of the twelfth to thirteenth centuries state that a female progenitor of the Thai people descended from the Great Snake. The tale is probably based on the worship of a snake or indicates that their progenitor had certain favourable or unfavourable experiences with a snake and then ordered that his descendants should respect the whole species. Apart from the snake, there are representations of two amphibians, a crocodile and a turtle, found in several rock paintings, such as at Phu Plara in Uthai

Fig. 5.2 Tympanum of the bronze drum from Ko Samui depicting a stylized boat carrying either spirits of the dead or men with bird-like headdresses. Source: Author's own

Thani Province. Bones of the animals were also found in excavations at some sites in the Dvaravati Kingdom, such as Khit Khin in Saraburi Province and U-thong in Suphanburi Province, dating to the seventh or eighth century. Remarkably, the upper part of some turtles' shells was found to be perforated; this was probably done for ritual purposes.

Some tiny terracotta figures of male genitalia and female vulva that were found at Khao Sam Kaeo site, dating back to the first century BCE or the first century CE, represented the regenerative power of both sexes that was associated with fertility and the tradition of holding an amulet.

According to the folklore and legend of Thai and other ethnic groups in the country, after the big world flood two couples survived, with a brother and a sister receiving a sign from heaven. The sister gave birth to a huge gourd, and when it was opened people of all colours emerged from the gourd. They gathered together in groups of the same colours, and left to settle their own communities in different places (London 2008: 23). One of the groups became the ancestors of the Thai people and others those of other ethnic groups in Southeast Asia.

From the remote past to the present day, the economy of the country has been based on agriculture. Therefore, indigenous people were matrilineal early on. Female images and symbols continued to reappear in various forms throughout the long history of the land, with the fertilizing power of women being a constant belief. The evidence from prehistoric burial sites leads scholars to believe that females at that time were highly respected and equal in status to males. This is exemplified by a female burial discovered during an excavation at Lot Cave in Mae Hong Son Province dating back 13,000 years. The peculiar-shaped pottery-like female Siamese twins showing their sexual organs dating from 1800 BCE and discovered during an excavation at Nong Ratchawat in Suphanburi Province was probably a powerful emblem of fertility and female creativity. The belief that females possessed extraordinary powers continued through the ages and permeated many aspects of Thai culture.

The Thai belief in a mother goddess or mother spirit was associated with life-giving symbols such as earth, water, rice and trees. They believed that nature was controlled by female spirits, and they trusted that by worshipping these spirits they could indirectly influence nature to provide them with a good standard of living and provide protection for themselves, their crops and their animals. Thus, female spirits are believed to be the source of all fertility in nature. The Thai word 'Mae' meaning 'mother' is used as a title of the female spirits of high level, such as Mae Ya Nang

Rua (Mother Goddess of Boat), Mae Phra Thorani (Mother of Earth/ Earth Goddess), Mae Phra Khongkha (Mother of River/River Goddess), Mae Phosop (Mother of Rice Cultivation/Rice Goddess) and Mae Sue (Mother of New-Born Babies/Female Guardian of New Born Babies). These female spirits are considered to protect whatever is related to their names. Mae Sue literally means Mother of Buying; when a baby is born it is believed that Mae Sue comes and buys the baby in order to keep it out of the reach of evil spirits. On the other hand, Mae Sue is also believed to be the cause of illness in children.

There is also Pho Sue, meaning Father of Buying, whose role is the same as Mae Sue's, but is not popular today. The Thai word 'Nang' meaning 'Lady' is used as the title of lower-level female spirits, such as Nang Tani (Lady of Banana Tree), Nang Mai (Lady of Shrub) and Nang Kwak (the Beckoning Lady). Nang Kwak, calling customers to the shop with a raised arm, palm down, is believed to bring good fortune. She has been a popular amulet figure since the eighteenth century and a Nang Kwak diagram or statuette is placed inside a shop to attract customers.

A belief in spirits and ghosts has been common to virtually all people throughout the country. Some Thai inscriptions indicate that this is the case for spirits good and bad, both of this world and of others. Countless spirits are referred to in the Thai language with the general term 'phi'. This first appeared in the 1292 inscription from Sukhothai Kingdom, in which the first Thai alphabet was used and in which there was a paragraph indicating this belief in spirits and ghosts: 'There are mountain streams and there is Phra Kha-phung. This divine spirit [Thai: phi] of the mountain is more powerful than any other spirits in this kingdom.' Later, a 1391 inscription from the same kingdom recorded the belief in Hell and Heaven, when the royal houses were taking an oath of loyalty to each other witnessed by the ancestors and natural spirits. A paragraph said: 'This oath sworn between us, let the witness be all the ancestral spirits of both our houses and the guardian spirits who dwell in water and caves' (Griswold and Nagara 1992: 84). The respected guardians of homes, villages and towns have long been the most obvious inhabitants of Thailand's vastly populous spirit world. It is believed that some of these spirits possess extraordinary supernatural powers that may affect one's life for better or for worse. They live in the land, trees or rocks, and have always been regarded as powerful and needing to be appeased.

Traditionally local communities in Thailand often build a shrine to house spirit guardians. These are carved in the shape of a sima (a temple's demarked stone boundary). The spirit house also serves as a focal point for worshipping and making offerings to the ground and guardian deities.

Indigenous People's Adoption of Indian Traditions

Adoption of Indian Languages and System of Writing

Indian thought that was expressed through Indian languages and literatures was embraced by indigenous people. They adopted the Sanskrit, Pali and Tamil languages to facilitate their commercial transactions with Indian merchants. The oldest evidence of writing that suggests the contact between India and Thailand comes from the ancient port sites in southern Thailand, where a number of inscribed signets or inscribed stone seals have been found. The seals were apparently not produced locally, but were imported from India. Beads or seals made of various types of quartz or gold were carved, as was pottery, using the Brahmi script; they are of the type that may be assigned to the first to third centuries. The languages used are Sanskrit and Tamil (Srisuchat 2011a: 254–256).

Inscribed seals bearing an Indian script and Sanskrit or Tamil languages, from the fifth to seventh centuries, were also found at early port sites on the western and eastern coast of southern Thailand. Being portable objects, they could have been taken there through trading links, and were presumably personal signets used by Indian merchants to seal their document or merchandise (Ray 1989: 42–54). Some signets were used as personal amulets. From the sixth century, the Sanskrit and Pali inscriptions spread to most regions in Thailand, with the two languages were acknowledged to be official languages of the early states known as Dvaravati (seventh to eleventh centuries), Sricanasa (seventh to ninth centuries), Srivijaya (eighth to twelfth centuries) and Lavapura or Lopburi (seventh to thirteenth centuries). The Sanskrit and Pali inscriptions were found at religious sites in various forms. The texts mainly contain historic stories of rulers, people, cities, activities and rituals, including people's beliefs related to Hindu and Buddhist traditions and practices. Sanskrit words or sentences were inscribed on some religious sculptures, especially on the back or the pedestal of the image (Fig. 5.3).

Between the eighth and twelfth centuries, the wide use of the local languages Mon and Khmer, including Khmer script that records Pali and Sanskrit words and texts on inscriptions found at religious sites and on religious sculptures, suggests the adoption of these languages and

Fig. 5.3 Sanskrit inscription written in Pallava script, sixth century, from Wat Maheyong in Nakhon Si Thammarat Province. Source: Author's own

opportunities for them to intermingle with the local languages that would develop into new terms. The invention of the Thai alphabet in 1292 signalled the end of the use of foreign scripts for writing.

Adoption of Indian Religions

Two religious traditions that originated in India, Hinduism and Buddhism, were exported to Thailand. A number of early inscriptions, sculptures and religious ruins bear witness to the adoption and adaption of Indic ideas that fundamentally shaped cultural and social developments Thai kingdoms and states. Archaeological evidence from fourth- to fifth-century sites suggests that early Buddhist states developed in parallel with early Hindu states. However, we do not know the names of these city-states as they were not mentioned in any inscriptions so far found. Early Buddhist and Hindu images were found in sites of this period, an example being the bronze Buddha image in the Amaravati style that was discovered at Sungui Kolok in Narathiwat Province, the stone relief depicting a standing Buddha in the Sarnath style found at Wieng Sa in Suratthani Province, the terracotta relief depicting three standing Buddhist monks holding alms-bowl in the Amaravati style found at U-thong in Suphanburi Province, the stone Ekamukhalinga found at Tha Chana in Suratthani Province, the stone

Shivalinga found at Sri Maha Phot in Prachinburi Province, and the stone images of a four-armed Vishnu found at Ban Na San, at Tha Sala in Nakhon Si Thammarat Province and at Wat Sala Thueng Chaiya in Suratthani Province (Srisuchat 2011b: 96).

From the late sixth century onwards, religious cults and traditions were practised and disseminated throughout the land. The three main kingdoms, the Dvaravati, the Srivijaya and the Lavapura, played an important role in the propagation of Buddhism and Hinduism.

One of the religious objects which was made in the Dvaravati Kingdom is the dharmacakra, the Wheel of the Law, dating back to the seventh or eighth century. This Buddhist symbol, with inscriptions on its spoke or base recording an aphorism from Buddha's teaching in the Pali language, suggests that the Theravada Buddhist faith was firmly established in the kingdom. The Dvaravati stupas' walls were adorned with stories drawn from the Pali Jatakas, stories of the past lives of the Buddha. Nevertheless, the sima or boundary stone for the ordination hall found at Fa Daet Song Yang in Kalasin Province depicts scenes from the Sanskrit Jatakamala, written by Araya Shura. This indicates the adoption of the Mahayana concept by the Dvaravati people. These people had Theravada Buddhism as their principal religion; but they also practised Mahayana Buddhism and adopted the Hindu cult. Apart from the Shivalinga, images of Shiva and Vishnu, images of Surya (Sun god) were found. Their knowledge of the Buddha as descended from the Solar race and Hindu sun god, who is the progenitor of some secular kings, including the Shakya clan of the Buddha, is evident, as confirmed by the finding of some dharmacakras depicting on their lower segments the personification of Surya holding a lotus bud in each hand. The Hindu deified personifications are placed in position as if supporters of the Wheels. The presence of images such as this reinforces the idea that the Dvaravati people developed a concept of Hindu gods which was incorporated into Buddhist tradition (Srisuchat 2010: 113–115) (Fig. 5.4).

Theravada and Mahayana Buddhism prospered in the ancient states of the Śrīvijaya Kingdom on peninsular Thailand, as demonstrated by the quantity of sixth- to twelfth-century statues of Buddha and Bodhisattvas and depiction on Buddhist sealings and miniature stupas. Prominent among the transcendental bodhisattvas are Avalokiteshvara and Maitreya. Other images such as Tara, Prajnaparamita, Jambhala (Kubera), Vajrasattva and Bhaishajyaguru appeared in later periods (Krairiksh 2012: 250–253).

Fig. 5.4 Stone dharmacakra from Nakhon Pathom Province, seventh–eighth century, depicting on its lower segment the personification of god Surya holding a lotus bud in each hand. Source: Author's own

Three inscriptions found in Nakhon Si Thammarat Province, dated sixth to seventh century, provide evidence that people on peninsular Thailand developed a concept of Hindu gods which was incorporated into the Mahayana Buddhist tradition of the Srivijaya Kingdom (Srisuchat 2014a: 20–25).

The Lavapura Kingdom, later known as the Lopburi Kingdom, adopted elements of religious art from India, Khmer (the modern Cambodia) and Cham (the modern Vietnam). A large number of brick and stone sanctuaries, called Prasad (Sanskrit: Prasada) or Prang (Sanskrit: Pranganam) were constructed. The main building of a Prasad has a tower-like shape, which was influenced by Indian shikhara. The decorative parts of a Prasad, especially the lintel and pediment, depict scenes from Hindu myths. A number of religious images found from many sites show the Hindu faith (Shaivism and Vaishnavism) of people in this region. Seventh- to twelfth-century Vaishna icons and Shivalinga reflect the continuity of Hindu faith and practice.

The spread of Vajrayana Buddhism from Nalanda in India influenced artistic production, and people embraced the Tantric Buddhist faith during the eighth to eleventh centuries. During the zenith of the Lavapura Kingdom in the first half of the eleventh century, the main temple of Vajrayana was built at Phimai in Nakhon Ratchasima Province. It is significant that some decorative parts of the temple, apart from the scenes of Buddhist events, depicted scenes from the Ramayana, the Mahabharata, the Hindu epics and the Puranas, the Hindu treatises. This indicates that Hindu traditions were adopted by Vajrayana devotees in the region.

Indigenous Perception of Hindu and Buddhist Spirituality

The Hindu tradition of the early Pashupata Shaivism in the country is known from the recent discovery of four gold Shivalingas dating from the sixth to seventh century in the Pli Muang cave in Nakhon Si Thammarat Province. Situated on the bank of the Tha Wang Phai canal, the mountain was regarded as the representative of the Mount Kailasa, the abode of Lord Shiva, and the canal represented the heavenly river, the Gangas. The sacred nature of the site begins with the mountain close to the holy river. The cave was supposed to be the shrine devoted to the Lord. The brahmins performed a sacred ritual with these gold lingas in the cave in order to allow the souls of dead yogis, who were probably the owners of the gold lingas, to attain the highest state of emancipation and merge into the Supreme Soul (Brahman, in this case Shiva). On the other hand, the lingas were tools of concentration for the mind used during meditation. It is believed that yogis were transformed into lingas by the power of their austerities. Finally, they likely had a solemn wish to promote the site as a Hindu Tirtha, literally a 'sacred spot for Hindu pilgrimage', during their own time and in the future as well.

During the zenith of Pashupata Shaivism in the late eleventh to twelfth centuries, the most notable Hindu temple, called Prasad Phanom Rung and devoted to Lord Shiva, was built on the top of the inactive volcanic mountain in Buriram Province. According to inscriptions found at the temple, the governor of the town became the great ascetic (yogi) of the Pashupata sect and practised the denial of physical or psychological desires so as to obtain his spiritual goal. He became the seer who instructed his son and his disciples about the absolute reality, Brahman. His successor then installed his icon and the gold Shivalinga in the temple.

The Buddhist formula was recognized by indigenous people. A number of Buddhist sealings (votive tablets) and stupas bearing the Pali or Sanskrit inscription, from the sixth to ninth century, focus on the Buddha's teaching or on stanza(s) excerpted from a sutra. Some bear stanzas of causation, also known as 'ye dhamma' or 'ye dharma', a condensed formula of dependent arising. They have been found throughout the country, dating from the late sixth and eighth centuries. The recent discovery of a large number of votive tablets at Khao Nui Cave in Trang Province, southern Thailand, reveals the indigenous tradition of making the cave into a sacred depository and their vision to preserve the Buddha's teaching to the next generation. Some of them are clay sealings with an enthroned Buddha on one side and the verso inscribed with 'Four Truths of the Noble Ones' in Sanskrit. It is a summary of the essence of the Buddha's teachings.

From the thirteenth century the Hindu and Vajrayana traditions were gradually abandoned, but the Theravada Buddhist tradition developed strongly. According to some inscriptions and manuscripts of the Sukhothai and Ayutthaya Kingdoms (early thirteenth to mid-eighteenth century), the Thai people followed the Theravada teaching of egalitarian ideals and impermanence. Thus they rejected a part of Hindu tradition, that is to say the caste system and Lord Buddha as an incarnation of god Vishnu. Despite acceptance by brahmins and Hindu rituals of the royal court, they thought that the Hindu deities did not last forever and were merely protectors of Buddhism and the Buddhists. In this connection, the huge bronze statue of Ishvara (god Shiva) was erected; it was consecrated in 1510 by the governor of the town of Kamphang Phet, to protect animals in the town. An inscription around the statue's base also recorded the governor's activities, including leading Buddhist, Hindu and Tantric revivalism, revitalizing irrigation for rice planting and issuing an edict ordering his subjects not to sell their cattle to members of the Lawa ethnic group (Srisuchat 2014b: 92–100). It is conjectured that Shiva's bull, Nandi, is an animal connected to domestic cattle belonging to the people of the town. With the introduction of irrigation, cattle became increasingly necessary for the planting of rice. To induce his subjects to follow the edict, the governor proclaimed his meritorious policy through the Ishvara image.

Adoption of Indian Technology for Making Commodities

The indigenous knowledge of bronze and tin metallurgy presumes an acquaintance with the sources of the raw material for producing various types of metal, suggesting the possible buying and selling of both raw materials and ready-made products by the time commercial exchanges with Indian merchants began. However, from the third century the Tamil goldsmiths were considered to have some skill in making gold ornaments that would have been inherited by the local inhabitants. This is exemplified by the discovery of an inscribed touchstone of a goldsmith from about the third century. The text reads 'perumpatan kal', meaning 'The stone belonging to the Great (or Senior) Goldsmith' written in the Tamil Brahmi characters in the third century (Ramesh 2002: 225). This distinctive inscribed touchstone belonging to a Tamil goldsmith is considered a special artefact that points to the early presence of Tamil goldsmiths and of the manufacture of gold objects by them in an early community located in Thai territory.

It is evident that glass and semi-precious stone ornaments were local products. They were made for export resulting from the introduction of technology from overseas and its combination with indigenous knowledge. It is surmised that Indian or Middle Eastern technology was introduced and ornaments were made of the materials, especially beads. The evidence for production centres where ornaments were produced for export comes mainly from sites in South and Central Thailand, which were the ancient ports, such as Khao Sam Kaeo in Chumphon Province (first century BCE to first century), Phu Khao Thong in Ranong Province (first century BCE to first century CE), Khun Luk Pat in Krabi Province (first to sixth century) and U-thong in Suphanburi Province (first to eighth century). In this connection, a number of seals bearing Indian scripts that were used to facilitate official trade or the exchange of goods, and other significant finds such as potsherds of roulette ware, were discovered at the above-mentioned sites.

Adoption of Indian Commercial Tradition

It is evident that at some point between the eighth and ninth centuries the Tamil merchants established a merchant community or trade guild that was guarded by troops on the bank of the Takua Pa River in Phangnga Province, where the single Tamil inscription was found. During this time two main ports of the southern peninsula of the Srivijaya Kingdom emerged. They were Mueang Thong Ko Kho Khao at the mouth of the Takua Pa River as the western coast emporium and Laem Pho Payang at the mouth of Phum Riang River in Suratthani Province as the eastern coast emporium. The west–east connections through the trans-peninsular routes were commonly used by people of the hinterland who supplied local products to the two coastal ports. It is the possibility that Indian merchants, especially the Tamils, used the route as well. A Tamil inscription, written in Tamil and Sanskrit and found at Nakhon Si Thammarat Province on the east coast of the Southern peninsula, dating from the eleventh century, is a testimony of this assumption.

Indigenous merchants from the ports played an important role as middlemen trading with Chinese, Indians, Arabs and Persians who desired the local products. Apart from foreign products, such as Chinese ceramics and Islamic glass, locally natural items and glass beads were produced and exported to other countries, whose merchants placed orders with the middlemen at the ports.

From the fourteenth century onwards, the Indian commercial tradition and the capability of Indian merchants had earned the trust of the Thai monarch, having been established over several centuries.

At some point between the fourteenth and the eighteenth century, some Indians were appointed as consuls to the Thai kingdom for an overseas trade mission. When an Indian Muslim consul was appointed a ruler of Singora, the southern city-port of the kingdom, and he fought a war in order to rule independently, the trust was lost.

Assimilation and Blending of Indigenous and Indian Traditions

Loan Words and Literatures

Evidence of early Indian contacts is found in inscriptions where Indian scripts and languages were used. Sanskrit and Pali are not mere languages of religious communication, but are the greatest conveyances for Indian knowledge. Sanskrit and Pali words that preserved in several inscriptions in early states were handed down from generation to generation. Material findings related to the words that do or do not follow their original meaning confirm the Indian influence on social development and its adaptability, but also indigenous perception of the loan words.

The Vedas and mythology of the Puranas and epics, the Ramayana and Mahabharata, not only left their traces in inscriptions, but succeeded in inspiring local people to create art and literature with a broad spectrum of heroic ideals.

Apart from these sources, some Sanskrit works were learned by the indigenous people during the period of the early states; these were the Abhijnanam Shakultalam and the Kumarasambhava of the great poet Kalidasa, and the Kiratarjuniya of Bharavi.

From Buddhist literature, some Mahayana and Theravada works were widely known and were the inspiration for religious work of art. They are the Lalitavistra, Buddhacarita, Jatakamala and Jatakatthakatha. The Thai adoption of the Indian epic reached its zenith in the reign of King Rama I, of the present-day Chakri dynasty, between 1781 and 1809. The king together with his royal poets composed the Ramakien, the Thai version of the Valmiki's Ramayana. The 'khon', a masked drama performed in dance and gesture, has a storyline drawn from the Ramakien. Although the Ramakien and Ramayana followed similar themes, particular heroes and heroines have different characters. For instance, Rama is a man who is sensitive and emotional, while his equivalent Hanuman is flirtatious and a jack-of-all-trades. The Ramakian has been the inspiration for works of art in various forms, such as mural painting and mask-making.

It is the Thai tradition that a set of Khon masks is elaborately made and placed on an altar to represent the teachers of performing arts and music in the ceremony in which respect is paid to them and before performing these activities. The masks normally comprise the heads of Shiva, Vishnu, Brahma, Ganesha, Rama, Bharata, Bharatamuni, Viradha and Pancasikhara. As the names suggest, Indian religious literature has had a lasting influence over the indigenous traditions of performing art and music.

Thai inscriptions and manuscripts from the thirteenth century onwards record Thai terms that are clearly based on Sanskrit and Pali words, running in parallel with the invention of new terms that eventually evolved into Thai expressions used until today.

Although the Thai writing system is based on the Indic script and a large number of the Sanskrit and Pali words are used in the Thai language, the grammars of other languages were not adopted, because they are inconsistent with the indigenous concepts of time and space.

Transforming the Indigenous Spirit to Hindu and Buddhist Deities

The belief in spirits (animism) of indigenous people in the country pre-dates the arrival of Buddhism and Hinduism. Although the arrival of Indian religions did not replace the belief in spirits, it influenced how spirits were worshipped. The indigenous people gradually came to put their faith in Indian deities rather than their local spirits. Some local spirits were transformed into Hindu or Buddhist deities.

The early people adopted Buddhism and Hinduism on the basis of their indigenous belief, which was animism. The indigenous practice of communal fertility with a tradition of worshipping genitals practically merged into that of the worship of Shivalinga.

Chief among the indigenous spirits (Thai: phi) is Thao Wet Suwan, the master of all spirits and described as a yaksha living in heaven. Judging by this information, Thao Wet Suwan is the same as Vessuvanna of the Pali Buddhist canon or Vaishravana or Kubera of the Hindu or Vajrayana gods. He is the divine guardian of the northern quarter, associated with wealth and treasure. The cult of Vaishravana or Kubera may be developed from that of Pancika, the Buddhist protector of the early Indic culture, who was believed to be a yaksha king. His image was found at Tackal near Peshawar in Pakistan, dating from the second century, and his image sitting together with his consort Hariti in the Cave 2 of Ajanta in Maharastra, India, dates from the late fifth century. He is shown holding a bag of riches or a mongoose spewing gems (Huntington 1985: 147). His characteristics and attributes such as this remind us of those of Kubera or Jambhala or, whose epithet is Vaishravana. Images of the god of wealth that were found in Thailand dating from the tenth to twelfth centuries suggest that the god was venerated by both Hindus and Buddhists during that time, before the worshipping cult was replaced by that of Sangkaccay, the belly monk influenced by the Chinese. The indigenous people learned from the Indian myths that the god Vaishravana or Kubera was the master of all the yakshas, nagas (snakes) and wrathful beings, and that he should be venerated to protect the worshipper from awful diseases.

Hariti, the Buddhist protectress of children, has the same role as Mae Sue. Thus, Pho Sue should be compared to Pancika. On the other hand, Pho Sue also merged into the god Vaishravana, and his duty as a guardian who watches over a new-born child was added.

The indigenous people believed that he had a power to cast a certain charm that inflicted smallpox on children (Hoskin 2012: 44).

The assimilation of the indigenous and Hindu beliefs is exemplified by the so-called Pu Khun Chit Khun Chot Inscription (1391) of the Sukhothai Kingdom (thirteenth to fifteenth century), which recorded the belief in hell and heaven. The royal houses of Sukhothai and Nan took an oath of loyalty to each other through the witness of the ancestors and natural spirits (phi), of Hindu and Buddhist gods, including Kubera, Yama and Navagrahas (the Nine Planets), of the heroes of the Indian epics, Ramayana and Mahabharata, such as Rama and Yudhishthira, and of the deities of all heavens from the lowest level to the highest, offering the highest rewards for putting one's faith in the oath Nibbana (Sanskrit: Nirvana) (Srisuchat 2012: 123).

The indigenous people thus adopted the Hindu/Buddhist god or divine guardian to be a spirit in their own tradition. The concept of placing the god above all indigenous spirits suggests the strong influence of the esoteric cult of Hinduism and Buddhism that became embedded in the country's historical states.

Space for Female Spirits and Indian Goddesses

Matrilineal clans of indigenous people were strong at an earlier time, but after adopting the male-dominated religions, Hinduism and Buddhism, from India, they began to exhibit patrilineal tendencies and the role of the female was lessened. At some point between the eighth and twelfth centuries, the Tantric cult was adopted and mixed with the traditional beliefs relating to female nature spirits; thus some female spirits attained a higher level of importance than in any other of the male-dominated regions. In the local view, the female spirits who protected households and natural resources were quite different from the goddesses of the Shakti cult of Hinduism or Vajrayana Buddhism. The female spirits had a personality of their own and were not a consort or a part of a male spirit.

In this connection, there are a large number of representations in art of the Mother Goddess of earth. In a scene from the Buddha's life: his victory over Mara, the Evil One, he points his fingers to the ground to call upon the Earth Goddess to witness his entitlement to attain enlightenment, acquired through innumerable good deeds in past lives. The Earth Goddess then wrung her hair to release the water that the Bodhisattva had poured down on the earth, and the water washed away Mara and his retinue in a flood.

Mae Sue, the local female spirit, changed her role from causing illness to a new-born child to become its protectress. We can compare her to Hariti, and Pho Sue, the local male protector of new-born children, to Pancika, her husband.

Hariti derives from the ancient Indic yakshini cult, and was believed to be a protectress of children after converting to Buddhism. Her story was recorded by Yi-jing, a Chinese pilgrim-monk who visited India in the seventh century. Images of Hariti were found at Sikri and Sahri-Bahlol in Pakistan, dating from the second century (Huntington 1985: 147).

Hariti's story merged into the legend of Mae Sue, who was also influenced by the Hindu Navagrahas, the Nine Planets.

The mural painting at Pho Temple in Bangkok depicts Mae Sue in seven forms, following the characteristics of seven gods of the week. Mae Sue for Tuesday has a head in the form of a buffalo's head, for the buffalo is the vehicle for the god of the dead (Yama) who replaced Mangala, the god of Tuesday. An illustrated manuscript in the National Library, Bangkok, depicts these seven different characteristics of Mae Sue.

It is possible that the Hindu tradition of Sapta-Matikas, meaning the Seven Mothers, came to Thailand. Although no image of the seven motherly forms has been found, a stone sculpture of a female carrying a child on her lap found at Muang Thong Ko Kho Khao site in Takua Pa District, Phangnga Province, the ancient port of the western coast between the ninth and tenth centuries, was probably a sculpture of one of the Seven Mothers. As it was a commercial port, ruins of a shrine that housed Hindu gods, such as Ganesha, were found, as well as the remains of a shrine that housed images of Buddha. The sculpture of the female carrying a child is probably a sculpture of Hariti, a Buddhist mother goddess.

In Indian sculpture the Sapta-Matikas are often depicted in a panel of three or more goddesses, but they can also be depicted separately. They have children either on their laps or standing nearby. Myths related to them narrate that some of these fierce goddesses became the protectors of children. The myth of the Hindu goddesses can be compared with that of Hariti from Buddhism. This probably led to the blending of the myths that was seen in some inscriptions of the Early Western Calukya from the mid-sixth century. According to these inscriptions, the Seven Mothers are the descendants of Hariti (Dalal 2010: 249). On the other hand, the stone sculpture of a female carrying a child on her lap might be the sculpture of Mae Sue, the local female spirit, whose legend is not far from those of Hinduism and Buddhism. In this connection, some terracotta yakshini figurines found in Chansen, a Dvaravati site of the seventh to eighth century CE, are probably representations of Hariti. From the same site, terracotta figurines of a female holding one or three children can be identified with Mae Sue. It was likely used in rituals held to ward off bad luck and served as the protective talisman. The beliefs and rituals handed down from the Dvaravati people to those of the Sukhothai Kingdom are confirmed by a large number of figurines of a headless mother holding a child.

In the name of the female spirit Mae Phra Khongkha (Mother of River/ River Goddess), the Thai word Khongkha comes from Ganga, the Indic goddess of the river Ganga. We do not know the original name of Mother of River. However, it is evident that Ganga appears in a fourteenth-century inscription from the Sukhothai Kingdom. Similarly, a stone statue of a standing female found near the source of the river in the ancient town of Sukhothai, and believed to represent the female progenitor of the Sukhothai kings, was probably Mae Phra Khongkha.

From Indigenous Beasts to Indian Mythical Zoomorphic Creatures

Some auspicious animals and mythical creatures that were adopted from Indian traditions have been a part of religious buildings and palaces, such as elephants, lions (simha), snakes (naga), geese (hamsa), makara, garuda and kinnaras.

The elephant has historically played a pivotal role in the livelihood and customs of the Thai people. After its adoption by Buddhism, the elephant has been highly respected as an auspicious symbol of peace and virtue. It is believed that it has been related to Buddha directly and indirectly. Therefore we have seen a set of elephant sculptures being fixed around the base of a stupa.

Simha or the lion is not a native beast, but the indigenous people likely became accustomed to the animal as lion sculptures are always seen in Buddhist and Hindu temples, especially as guardians of temples or royal buildings.

The four quadrupeds, elephant, bull, horse and lion, have their places in the local cosmology that was adopted from the Indic tradition. In a 1767–1782 Thai illustrated manuscript, Sumaru is the centre of the universe, encircled by a big pond, which flows through the mouths of these four animals before becoming rivers travelling in four directions.

On the basis of Hindu myths, kinnaras are the minor Hindu deities, which have horse bodies and human heads. They are musicians, associated with the gandharvas. They are also mentioned in Buddhist texts (Dalal 2010: 204). Indigenous people in Thailand were not satisfied with the horse bodies of kinnaras, so they created a new form of kinnara: bird body and human head. Furthermore, female kinnara called kinnari were created. It is possible that the Canda-kinnara Jataka of Theravada Buddhism were widely retold in the Dvaravati Kingdom. Some representations were therefore made in accordance with the story of the Jataka, for instance a stucco decoration at the base of a stupa that depicts figures of kinnara and kinnari with bird bodies and human heads.

The oldest lintel of Prasad Khao Noi in Sakaeo Province, dating back to the seventh century, depicts a makara, a mythical sea-creature. Several lintels and pediments or gable boards of Hindu and Buddhist temples depict a makara, often spouting forth another creature or a plant motif from its open mouth. The indigenous people believe that this is a symbol of water, and that the creation of a figure such as this calls for rain.

The indigenous belief in the serpent progenitor, which was considered to be very similar to that of the mythic serpent (naga) of Indian tradition, gradually replaced makara, which represented water. Thai people believe that the duty of naga is to bring water from the sky and ocean to the earth, that is to say the rain, which is needed by an agricultural country such as Thailand. Naga figures have thus been used as a part of religious and palace buildings: the uppermost part points to the sky and the lowest part touches the ground. In the Thai traditional ordination ceremony, a young man who is undergoing training as a Buddhist monk is called Naga.

The figureheads or prows of Thai royal barges from the Ayutthaya to the Bangkok periods mainly feature Indic mythical creatures from Puranas and heroes of the great Indian epic Ramayana. Examples of these are 'Suvarna-hamsa' (gold hamsa), 'Ananta-nagaraja', which features a seven-headed serpent, 'Sugriva who ascended to a throne', which features a crowned monkey, and 'Kapi (monkey) who suppressed the subjects of evil town', which features a figure of Hanuman, the monkey-leader of Rama's troops. One royal barge shows a figure of Vishnu mounted on Garuda in its bow, reflecting the impact of India in Thai tradition and art. The adoption and implementation of the concept of Vishnu's incarnations by Thai royal courts since the mid-fourteenth century has promoted the status of the Thai king as a god. Garuda is the vehicle of the lord; he is always presented holding nagas. According to Indian epics and puranas, garuda and naga are enemies, but both serve Lord Vishnu. Since Garuda, the king of birds, represents the power of sky and light and Naga represents the power of water and darkness, the presence of Vishnu over them denotes his protection of the whole world. This is the reason why the figure is popularly placed at a high level, such as on the pediment of a temple or palace.

Hindu Ritual and Consecration of Indigenous Spirit House

One spirit from the indigenous tradition that was handed down from the remote past to the present is the so-called Phra Phum, which is the guardian spirit of people who live on the land, protecting them against evil spirits. The term Phra Phum means 'Lord of the Land'. No one really knows when the name was adopted. Perhaps Chao Thi, which has the same meaning as Pha Phum, was the native name of the spirit, which is called Phra Phum Chao Thi by some elderly people.

It is thought when a building is constructed on a plot of land; the spirit is disturbed and may leave the land unless provided with a residence of its own. The term San Phra Phum for spirit house comes from a Sanskrit/Pali compound, shala vra bhumi: shal or shala, meaning shrine or residence, vra, auspicious, and bhumi, the earth or place.

This spirit house must be built correctly and should be situated where the shadow of the main building does not fall on it. Furthermore, it must be erected at an auspicious time, and to ensure that everything is correct a brahmin priest is asked to make the necessary arrangements and to perform the required rituals. In some places, such as the spirit house of the former residence of the Prince Successor dating from the eighteenth century, the spirit house is placed on top of an artificial rocky mound, which is a representation of Mount Kailasa, the abode of the Hindu god Shiva. There is a similar structure representing Mount Kailasa in the grounds of the Grand Palace, and this was used in the tonsure or topknot cutting ceremonies for royal princes. This ceremony follows the mythical tonsure of Shiva's son Ganesha on Mount Kailasa (Coleman 1996: 65–66).

The concept of making a shrine for an individual spirit, in the temple or in any venerated spot, probably follows the Hindu concept of the erection of a small shrine for an individual god, to allow worship anywhere. Sometimes an individual spirit shrine or spirit house and a shrine of a Hindu god, especially to Brahma, were erected side by side.

Indigenous Perception of Indian Medical Treatment

The Mahayana idea about the manifestation of the Buddha of medicine, in the form of Bhaishajyaguru, was adopted in the twelfth to thirteenth century. There are many remains of arogyashala (hospitals) housing an image of Bhaishajyaguru built with the rest houses that were erected for the sake of patients and voyagers along the roads from Angkor, the centre of the

Khmer Kingdom, to Phimai, the centre of the Lavapura Kingdom. Although the iconographical treatises of Vajrayana from Nalanda were adopted, images of Bhaishajyaguru were made differently. The indigenous people considered an image of Buddha in meditation, with a myrobolan fruit in his palms and sheltered by Naga's hood, as the same as that of Bhaishajyaguru.

In the long history of the country's early states, the Pashupata yogis propagated the yogic practice, as confirmed by inscriptions and sculptures of temples. The names of local yogis and several Indian yogis or rishis appear in the ancient Thai medical treatment manuscript, such as Agninetra, meaning Eye of Fire (Shiva), Narada and Vasishtha, but the name of Dhanvantari, the Hindu physician of gods, is not referred to. The sculptures of Rishi Dat Ton (Thai term for 'Yogis do yogic exercise') at Pho Temple in Bangkok was made in 1789 and 1832 on the basis of the above-mentioned text. It reflects the role of Yogi/Rishi as a physician to release people from physical suffering with a medical treatment and a mantra. This indicates that the Indian Hathayoga and Mantrayoga were intermingled with the indigenous wisdom of therapeutic treatment in Thailand, and it reflected the survival of Indic yoga in a new form with a new interpretation by Thai people.

Hindu–Buddhist Elements in Locally Muslim Traditions

Islam in Thailand has become integrated with practices and beliefs in the spirit of local animism and the deities of Hinduism and Buddhism, not traditionally found in Islam. This is exemplified by the typical kite that Muslim people in southern Thailand make for the annual ritual ceremony to predict the best time for rice planting in their community. The kite, which shape looks like an anthropomorphic form, is called Devo Mudo, meaning 'Head of gods' or 'Leader of gods'. The term comes from two Sanskrit words: deva (god) for devo and murddhana (head) for mudo. Thus the kite is considered the representative of the god who descended from heaven to earth, and could be back in heaven while the kite is flying, according to the Mayong, the famous Muslim folktale of the region.

A type of Muslim kris (an asymmetrical dagger with distinctive blade-patterning) found in the provinces of Pattani, Yala and Narathiwat in Southern Thailand has the handle or hilt carved to resemble various Hindu gods. The kris' wavy blade symbolizes the movement of the serpent. The term naga is used to describe the shape of the kris' blade. Some have a naga's head curved near the base, with body and tail following the curves of the blade to the tip. According to traditional Muslims in Southern Thailand, the kris contains all the intrinsic elements of nature: water, wind, fire and earth. It is the same tradition of Hinduism and Buddhism that is referred to in both religious treatises.

The rua kolae is the typical fisherman's boat of the Muslims in this area. The boats are painted colourfully with figures of makara, naga and hamsa. It is a testimony of the introduction of mythical animals from Hindu and Buddhist legends to the living art of the Thai Muslims.

Current Trends of Thought about Indian People and Tradition

For a long time, Thai people have called the Indians 'khaek', literally meaning 'guest'. Why do Thai people use this term for the Indians only? The answer is because they think the Indians have come to visit their country over time. Thus, the Indian people have been regarded as special guests who have not only visited the country with empty hands but have brought presents that are of much social worth.

Today, most Thai people think that sacred pilgrimage places in India should be visited once in a lifetime. The number of learners of Sanskrit and Hindi have increased significantly. These languages are regarded as a tool to obtain Indian traditional knowledge about medical treatment, yoga practice and of sacred mantras that can be recited to please Lord Ganesha and Lord Brahma, who will give a boon for what the worshipper prays for.

Conclusion

Indian traditions that came to Thailand from the second century BCE through the commercial exchanges with the indigenous people in what is now Thailand have influenced life, religious belief, ways of writing, creativity of art, economy and political culture in the early communities, which developed into states, countries, kingdoms through the long history of time. However, the indigenous people who owned natural resources and ancestral knowledge which facilitated initiative, creativity and experimentation, thus making up a foundation for the creation of a culture of their own identity, gave rise to a habit of caution in their selection of something new from outside. The great change in indigenous beliefs and traditions was the adoption of Buddhism and Hinduism from India, directly and indirectly. The assimilation of the indigenous and Indian beliefs and traditions has dynamically evolved on the basis of political changes over time. Since the Thai kingdom has been in power over the land since the thirteenth century, the indigenous people have followed Theravada Buddhist practice; nevertheless, primitive animist and Hindu traditions have been embedded in their ways of life. The strong impact of Hindu–Buddhist tradition on Thai Muslims' life is exemplified by their folklore, local ceremony and art. Some Indian traditions have been favoured and adapted by indigenous people rather than those from other outside cultures, for their apparent compatibility with the traditional ways.

Owing to limitations of space, the author has omitted some figures, which can be made available to interested readers on request.

REFERENCES

Charoenwongsa, Pisit. 1989. A Legacy of Ban Chiang. Bangkok: Department of Fine Arts.
Coleman, Shelagh. 1996. The Spirit House at the Bangkok National Museum. In Writing from Asia Treasures Myths and Traditions, ed. Group of the National Museum Volunteers, 64–70. Bangkok: National Museum Volunteers.
Dalal, Roshen. 2010. Hinduism: An Alphabetical Guide. New Delhi: Penquin Book.
Glover, Ian C. 1996. The Southern Silk Road: Archaeological Evidence of Early Trade between India and Southeast Asia. In Ancient Trade and Cultural Contact in Southeast Asia, ed. Amara Srisuchat, 57–94. Bangkok: The Office of the National Culture Commission.
Griswold, A.B. and Na Nagara. 1992. Epigraphic and Historical Studies. Bangkok: The Historical Society under the Royal Patronage of H.R.H. Princess Maha Chakri Sirindhorn.
Hoskin, John. 2012. The Thai World. Bangkok: Asia Books.
Huntington, Susan L. 1985. The Art of Ancient India. New York: John Weatherhill, Inc.
Krairiksh, Piriya. 2012. The Roots of Thai Art. Bangkok: River Books.
London, Ellen. 2008. Thailand Condensed. Singapore: Marshall Cavendish Editions.
Ramesh, K.V. 2002. Reconsidering Cultural Intercourse between India and Southeast Asia: An Epigraphical Report and Appendix 1 Texts and Translations of Indian Inscriptions in Southeast Asia.In Ancient and Medieval Commercial Activities in the Indian Ocean: Testimony of Inscriptions and Ceramic-sherds, ed. Noboru Karashima. Tokyo: Taisho University.

Ray, Himanshu Prabha. 1989. Early Maritime Contacts between South and Southeast Asia. Southeast Asian Studies XX, No. 1: 42–54.

Srisuchat, Amara. 1996. Merchants, Merchandise, Markets: Archaeological Evidence in Thailand concerning Maritime Trade Interaction between Thailand and Other Countries before the 16th Century A.D. In Ancient Trade and Cultural Contact in Southeast Asia, ed. Amara Srisuchat, 237–266. Bangkok: The Office of the National Culture Commission.

———. 2010. Dharmarajadhiraja: Righteous King of Kings. Bangkok: Department of Fine Arts.

———. 2011a. Inscriptions of Early Civilizations in Thailand. In Bujang Valley and Early Civilisation in Southeast Asia, ed. Stephan Chia and Barbara Watson Andaya, 253–282. Pinang: Department of National Heritage, Ministry of Information, Communications and Culture, Malaysia.

Srisuchat, Tharapong. 2011b. Early Buddhist and Hindu Evidence and Civilisations in Thailand" In Bujang Valley and Early Civilisation in Southeast Asia, ed. Stephan Chia and Barbara Watson Andaya, 96–108. Pinang: Department of National Heritage, Ministry of Information, Communications and Culture, Malaysia.

Srisuchat, Amara. 2012. Naming the Buddha: Thai Terms for Images of Thailand. In Enlightened Ways: The Many Streams of Buddhist Art in Thailand, ed. Heidi Tan and Alan Chong, 40 -47. Singapore: Asian Cilisations Museum.

———. 2014a. A Reappraisal of Inscriptions and Icons in Southern Thailand reflecting Religious Perceptions of the Srivijayan People. Paper presented at the International Seminar: Śrīvijaya in the Context of Regional Southeast Asia and South Asia. August 20–25, in Jambi, Indonesia.

———. 2014b. Masterpiece in the Fine Arts Department: Hidden Meanings of Ishvara Image in the Town of Kamphaeng Phet. The Silpakorn Journal Vol. 57 No. 5, 92–100. Bangkok: Department of Fine Arts.

CHAPTER 6

Panyupayana: The Emergence of Hindu Polities in the Pre-Islamic Philippines

Joefe B. Santarita

INTRODUCTION

The precise impact of Indianization in terms of state formation in Southeast Asia has been widely debated in various academic circles both within and outside the region. Although most scholars would no longer accept the arrival of Indian culture as the sole catalyst for the transition of early Southeast Asian polities from prehistoric chiefdoms into kingdoms, there is no denying that Indian concepts of kingship and the religious beliefs and rituals closely linked to them did play a formative role in the process whereby chiefs transformed into rajas and maharajas. Ricklefs and others, however, argue that the Philippines does not seem to have progressed beyond the chiefdom or chieftaincy stage until the arrival of Islam.[1] Whether this observation is either fully or partially correct, the fact remains that those chiefdoms or kingdoms that existed in the pre-Islamic Philippines might have been significantly Hindu-influenced polities.

[1] M. C. Ricklefs et al. *A New History of Southeast Asia* (Hampshire: Palgrave Macmillan, 2010), 66–67.

J. B. Santarita (✉)
Asian Center, University of the Philippines Diliman, Quezon City, Philippines
e-mail: jbsantarita2@up.edu.ph

© The Author(s) 2018
S. Saran (ed.), *Cultural and Civilisational Links between India and Southeast Asia*, https://doi.org/10.1007/978-981-10-7317-5_6

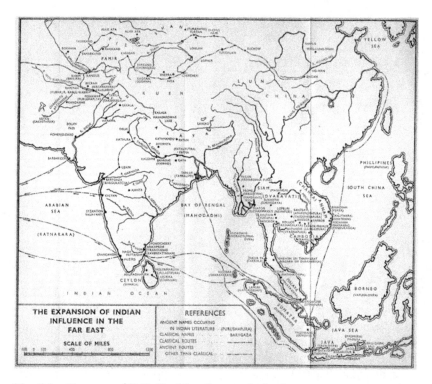

Fig. 6.1 Courtesy of K.M. Panikkar. Source: Author's own

Despite the emerging questions about the presence of Indian kingdoms in the early Philippines, one proof that the archipelago has been on the radar of early Indians, particularly traders and geographers, is the reference they made to these islands as Panyupayana or lands surrounded by water (see Fig. 6.1).[2] In the course of this chapter, the term will be used to refer to the Philippines. This reference, however, should not be misinterpreted as a sign that the Philippines in its early development was completely Indianized. It should be treated instead as a clue that early Indians included

---

[2] The term Panyupayana emanates from the geopolitical orientation of the Indians, which started with the cosmological orientation. This is manifested by the Puranas and other Indian literature, such as Ramayana and Mahabharata. Joefe B. Santarita. "Panyupayana: The Philippines in Ancient India's Geopolitical Orientation". *SEACOM Studies 2* (April 2015): 2.

the area in their geopolitical orientation and that trade existed between these peoples for years, possibly influencing the formation of early polities in the Philippines prior to the advent of Islam.

Additional evidence for these links is reproduced in the *Survey of Indian History* by K.M. Panikkar, where an interesting map of Greater India covering the whole of Southeast Asia is tagged with ancient names occurring in Indian literature.

Using historical and anthropological evidence that is available in the Philippines, this chapter will investigate whether the archipelago was a Hindu polity prior to the Islamization of the fourteenth century. In particular, it will revisit various tangible and intangible manifestations of early Indian influences in the country, as well as consulting numerous studies made by various scholars working on the pre-Islamic Philippines.

EARLY KINGDOMS IN PANYUPAYANA

That Indian-influenced polities were formed in the pre-Islamic Philippines is not a far-fetched assumption. Many kingdoms were established under the Indian influence, as manifested in religion, language and state forms among others. As observed by Higham, the ruling groups as early as the fifth century CE chiefly looked to India for models of kingship and statecraft. The evidence to support the hypothesis that India played a role in the transition from tribal polities to inchoate state forms is available from a number of sites. Carnelian beads from the southeast coast of India have been recovered from sites in the Mekong Delta in Vietnam. Bac Bo in Thailand has yielded gold ornaments and glass beads of Indian origin. Iron daggers, tin slags, bronze drums and glass objects from southern India were found at the Oc Eo site in southern Vietnam.[3] Given these concrete examples, it is proper to survey the polities that existed in Panyupayana long before the advent of Islam. There are a few candidates that can be examined in this chapter, and these include the Rajahnate of Butuan and Cebu.

---

[3] Charles Higham. *Archaeology of Mainland Southeast Asia* (Cambridge: Cambridge University Press, 1987), 16. Also Venkata Raghotham. "The Imperial Cholas and the Indian Ocean: Patterns of Trade and Conquest in the Eleventh and Twelfth Centuries". *Society and Culture: The Asian Heritage* (Quezon City: University of the Philippines Asian Center, 1999).

The Rajahnate of Butuan was to be found in the pre-Islamic/pre-colonial southern Philippines, centred on the present Mindanao city of Butuan. Being at the mouth of the great Agusan river, the area developed into a trading port. Its strategic location was complemented by its rich surroundings, which included abundant game and forest products and most importantly rich deposits of gold. The rajahnate is believed to have had an extensive trade network with China, India, Japan, Indonesia, Persia, Cambodia and others. In fact, Henry Scott even mentions that Butuan was the first Philippine 'state' to establish diplomatic relations with China.[4]

The Indian influences on Butuan were recorded by the Chinese annal Song Shih in about 1001. Although this was intended more to record trade, it serves as important evidence here. The annal states that Butuan was in contact with the Song dynasty in the first century CE, starting with the sending of a Butuan or P'u-tuan tributary mission to the Chinese imperial court in 1001. At this time P'u-tuan is described as a small Hindu country with a Buddhist monarchy in the sea, with a regular connection with Champa and intermittent contact with China under the rajah named Kiling. Casino believes that the name Kiling does not appear to be Visayan but Indian in origin, because Kiling refers to the people of South India.[5]

Rajah Kiling sent an envoy to the court to petition for equal status in court protocol with the Champa representative.[6] The request was denied because of favouritism towards Champa. This treatment changed when Butuan sent a flamboyant representative, Likanhsieh. In the Chinese annal, the Butuan trade mission of 1011 was headed by an official with the name Xi-li-da-sha-zhi, which appears to be a Chinese rendition of the Indianized term Sri Bata Shaja.[7] This official really impressed Chinese Emperor Zhenzong when he presented a memorial engraved on a gold tablet, Bailong, camphor, Moluccan cloves and slaves on the eve of an important ceremonial state sacrifice. These gestures gained China's interest and sealed the diplomatic relations between the two states until their

---

[4] William Henry Scott. *Barangay: Sixteenth Century Philippine Culture and Society* (Quezon City: Ateneo de Manila University Press, 1994), 164.

[5] Eric Casino. "The Balangays of Butuan: Lumad Mindanaoans in China and the Sulu Zone". *Asia Mindanaw: Dialogue of Peace and Development* (2014): 2.

[6] Damon Woods. *The Philippines: A Global Studies Handbook* (California: ABC-CLIO, 2006), 16.

[7] Eric Casino. Indianization of Ancient Mindanao Trade: The Record from Butuan Archaeology. *SEACOM Conference Proceeding*. Iloilo City. 2014. 5.

peak during the Yuan dynasty. Chinese records reveal that the story of the Butuan rajahnate came to an end after Rajah Siagu's suzerainty was subjugated by the Spanish-sponsored colonial expansion of 1521.

The rajahnate of Cebu, on the other hand, existed on the island of Cebu in Central Philippines. The early development of this polity was recorded in oral tradition and the chronicles of Spanish colonizers. According to Visayan folklore, the first rajah was half-Tamil and half-Malay. Originally from Sumatra, Sri Lumay settled in the central part of Panyupayana and on one of the present islands of Visayas. He had several sons, one of them being Sri Bantug who was the father of Rajah Humabon.[8]

Under Humabon, the area became a significant trading port, extensive trading networks developing with Indian, Japanese and Burmese traders. Products made from ivory, leather, precious stones and sugar were brought by Indian and Burmese traders to the area. Japanese merchants, on the other hand, bartered perfumes and glass utensils for native products. It was during Humabon's reign that Lapu-lapu was granted his own domain (Mandawili, present day Mandaue) and Oping island (present day Mactan). In the chronicles, Ferdinand Magellan's unfortunate end at the hands of Lapu-lapu is well documented.[9]

It is interesting to note the extent of Cebu rajahnate's trading network as recorded by Italian chronicler Antonio de Pigafetta. One of his chronicles documents the merchant's warning in the Malay language to Rajah Humabon, in which he was urged to be extra careful in dealing with men who had conquered Calicut, Malacca and all of Greater India.[10]

This warning indirectly tells of the extensive trading contacts of the rajahnate of Cebu, ranging as far as India and Malacca. Mention is made of *kotaraya kita*, which shows that the area was developed as a city (kotaraya) because of its strategic location to sea access and the presence of abundant materials. The glory of the rajahnate, however, was dissolved after Rajah Tupas (cousin and successor of Humabon) was defeated by the Spanish contingent of Miguel Lopez de Legazpi in 1565.[11]

---

[8] Rajahnate of Cebu. Project Gutenberg Self-Publishing Press. Accessed 20 July 2015. http://self.gutenberg.org/articles/rajahnate_of_cebu#cite_note-3.

[9] Emma Blair and James Alexander Robertson. *The Philippine Islands, 1493–1803* (Cleveland, Ohio: A.H. Clark, 1903–1909), 468.

[10] B. A. Skelton. *Antonio Pigafetta*. Nancy-Libri-Philipps-Beinecke-Yale codex. English Translation. 71.

[11] Ricklefs et al. *A New History of Southeast Asia*, 87.

Despite the limited documentation and artefacts available to substantiate the formation of these polities, their existence has generated several assumptions about Indian influences in the Philippines. The formation of these polities, no matter how limited, prior to the coming of Islam and later of the Spanish colonizers allowed for the spread of Indian influences. Along with trading products, Indian ideas, philosophy, languages and other influences also criss-crossed the area. As Sarangani points out, Hinduism did not have much impact in the material (tangible) life of the Filipinos, but its influence was to be found in religion, philosophy and literature.[12]

INFLUENCES

The above-mentioned influences cannot be totally credited to the formation of early Indian polities in Panyupayana. However, it is not impossible that the existence of rajahnates and the presence of Indian traders in the area facilitated the spread of Hindu–Buddhist influence. In fact, Dr. T.H. Pardo de Tavera notes that there is a pronounced Indian element in Philippine society, especially in language. As cited by Prakash,[13] Pardo de Tavera observes that the words that Tagalog borrowed from Sanskrit are those which signify intellectual acts, moral conceptions, emotions, superstitions, names of deities, planets, numerals of high number, some animals, instruments of industry, and related to botany, war, titles and dignitaries, and money.

Considering these unmistakable traces of Indian cultural influence in the archipelago, Pardo de Tavera further observes that:

> It is impossible to believe that the Hindus, if they came only as merchants, however, great their number, would have impressed themselves in such a way as to give to these islanders, the Filipinos, the number and the kind of words, which they did give. These names of dignitaries, of caciques, of high functionaries of the court, of clearly that the warfare, religion, literature,

---

[12] Datumanong Sarangani. *The Islamization of Mindanao: A Study of Islam in the Philippines* (Ph.D. Diss., American University of Beirut, 1971). Cited by Alfred Kroeber. *The Peoples of the Philippines* (New York: American Museum of Natural History, 1919), 31.
[13] Ibid., 119.

industry and agriculture were at one time in the hands of the Hindus and that this race was effectively dominant in the Philippines.[14]

Despite the contradictions between scholars in terms of the diffusion of Indian culture in Southeast Asia and the Philippines, Prakash concludes that the Indians had settled in many parts of the Malay Peninsula and spread their culture there. The people of South India and Ceylon (Sri Lanka) took a prominent part in this progress of migration. From the peninsula, these settlers moved eastwards across the various island groups, carrying not only their pristine culture but also forms of it in which Malayan elements were mixed. Malaya was a necessary springboard for the movement and migration of the Indians and the Ceylonese further eastwards. However, in ancient times the culture of the Indians was the dominant factor in the life of the Filipinos.[15]

These cultural connections between India and the Philippines include the presence of Ramayana in various incarnations, Darangen, Singkil, hundreds of Sanskrit words in Filipino languages and the discoveries of various Hindu–Buddhist artefacts among others.

Foremost is the Philippine version of the Rama story, known as Maharadia Lawana, which was discovered by Dr Juan Francisco in 1968 as a Maranaw narrative. Francisco notes that this version is condensed in comparison with the Indian Ramayana but still contains the major episodes of the latter, such as the winning of Sita, her abduction, the search for Sita and her return. These four episodes as narrated in the Maharadia Lawana correspond to the five kanda (songs or chapters of Ramayana): Balakanda, Aranyakanda, Kiskindhakanda, Sundarakanda and Yuddakanda.[16]

In the Maharadia Lawana story, Rama is Radia Mangadiri, Laksmana is Radia Mangawarna, Sita is Tuwan Potre Malano Tihaia, Kusa/Lava is Laksmana (who in the story assumes the character of Hanuman) and Ravana is Maharadia Lawana. The story is set on the legendary island of Pulu Agama Niog.[17]

---

[14] Ibid., 120. Cited by T. H. Pardo de Tavera, *El Sancrito en la lengua Tagalog*, Paris 1887 and Dhirendra Nath Roy, *The Philippines and India* (Manila: Oriental Printing, 1929).

[15] Santarita, SEACOM Studies, 6.

[16] Juan Francisco. *Sarimanok and the Torogan & Other Essays* (Marawi City: Mindanao State University, 1994), 117.

[17] Pulu means island, Agama village and Niog coconut. Hence, Pulu Agama Niog simply means coconut grove village. Juan Francisco. *From Ayodhya to Pulu Agamaniog* (Quezon City: Asian Center, 1994), 68.

The people of the southern Philippines still observe the darangen as part of their cultural milieu, especially in rural areas. Darangen is thought to echo an Indian term which means 'narrative' or 'story', from the Sanskrit *tarangini*.[18] In the Southern Philippines, it is still customary to invite an onor (singer) to a feast, whether it is for the dead or for any other occasion. The host includes the singing of darangen as part of the activities. If the darangen is sung as Princess Gandingan, the audience has a triple treat: kulintang playing, bayok (antiphonal singing by the two characters) and singkil dancing.[19] In darangen, episodes about the abduction and subsequent recovery of Princess Lawanen are chanted only on special occasions.[20]

It is noteworthy that this pre-Islamic epic consists of seventeen cycles and a total of 72,000 lines. It tells the stories of heroes as well as episodes from Maranao history, and tackles the immortal themes of life, death, courtship, politics and love. Darangen contains Maranao social values, customary law, ethics and aesthetics.[21]

Singkil, on the other hand, is an elegant, stylized performance dance that usually involves performers interpreting archetype characters inspired by and interpreted from the thread of storylines found similarly in the Indian epic the Ramayana. They include those of a princess, her faithful assistant, friends and ardent suitors, who step in and out, sit or stand on two sets of crossed bamboo poles, which are thumped on the floor and clashed together in order to make percussive music. Native musical instruments such as the agung (gong) and the kulintang (made of eight small gongs set on a rack) complete the ensemble. The Maranaw people in the southern Philippines, even before the arrival of the Spaniards in the sixteenth century and the arrival of Islam in the twelfth century, observed these oral traditions by retelling similar stories from the Ramayana in

---

[18] Nagasura Madale. "The State of the Darangen Studies". *Society and Culture: The Asian Heritage* (Quezon City: University of the Philippines Asian Center, 1999), 32.

[19] Ma. Delia Coronel. *Introduction. Darangen Volume 1* (Marawi City: Mindanao State University, 1986), 6.

[20] Juan Francisco. *Maharadia Lawana* (Quezon City: University of the Philippines, 1969), 4.

[21] Roel Manipon. *Dancing Darangen: The Way to the Maranao Epic.* National Commission for Culture and the Arts. 2008. Accessed February 5, 2012. http://www.ncca.gov.ph/about-culture-and-arts/articles-on-c-n-a/article.php?i=293&subcat=13.

darangen. These retellings are the basis of the stories that are interpreted and performed whenever the singkil is danced.[22]

In particular, the swaying of body, arms and hands as well as movements in the dance are reminiscent of ancient dance forms from many countries that are based on the Hindu style. In the singkil this can be explained by the extensive influence of the Sri-Vijaya and Majapahit empires, which reached Indonesia as well as the many islands of the Philippines. In the performance, the main dancer, Princess Gandingan, interprets the movements after learning the rituals for gathering medicinal plants and herbs from the forest from her mother, the powerful village healer. These movements represent Gandingan's sojourn in the forest, either alone or with her friends and her faithful assistant, who usually bears a beautiful parasol for the princess wherever she goes.[23]

Other than the performing arts, the most extensive evidence of Indian influences in the Philippines is to be found in the Sanskrit elements of the country's languages. These have persisted since their introduction in the Philippines between the tenth and fifteenth centuries and have been fully assimilated into these speech systems. In a survey conducted by Francisco in 1988, there are 336 words in Philippine languages that are recognizably Sanskrit in origin and 50% of these have definitive provenance in Sanskrit.[24] William Henry Scott even gives a statistical count of Sanskrit words in Philippine languages, listing some 150 separate words as the origin of Philippine terms. The majority are in Tagalog and the rest in Bisaya, Ilocano and Sulu (Tausog).[25] Table 6.1 provides a glimpse of Sanskrit influences on Filipino languages.

It is interesting to note that some common words found in Philippine languages and Sanskrit have meanings that have changed semantically through the years. Words such as *pitaka* (basket in Sanskrit) becomes wallet in Philippine languages, *bana* (arrow in Sanskrit) is *pana* in Philippine languages, and interestingly means husband in the Visayan region, while *kama* (love in Sanskrit) becomes bed in Filipino.

Moreover, it may be observed that the hierarchy of gods and goddesses of the pre-Islamic Filipinos is also profoundly influenced by Hindu reli-

---

[22] Santarita. SEACOM Studies, 2.
[23] Jerome E. Baladad. *Singkil: The Maranao native dance.* Accessed last February 5, 2012. http://www.helium.com/items/2293684-singkil-the-maranao-native-dance.
[24] Francisco. 1988, 31.
[25] William Henry Scott. *A Critical Study of the Pre-Hispanic Source Materials for the Study of Philippine History* (Manila: University of Santo Tomas Press, 1968), 52–53; also cited by Francisco, 1988.

Table 6.1 Selected Sanskrit terms in Filipino languages

Filipino	Meaning	Sanskrit	Meaning
Bakti (T)	Gift, token, devotion	Bhakti	Homage, love, worship
Guro (Tag)	Teacher	Guru	Teacher
Bangsa (T)	People, race, nation	Vamsa	Lineage, race
Bichara (T, M)	Speak, talk	Vicara	Deliberation, reflection
Dukka (T) Dukha (tag)	Poverty, misery poor	Duhkha	Grief
Guna (T, I)	Usefulness, profit	Guna	Good quality, merit
Hina (Tag)	Weak, reduced	Hina	Fatigue, weak, defective
Pana (Tag)	Arrow	Bana	Arrow
Saksi (Tag, I, B)	Witness, testimony	Saksi	Witness
Suchi (T, P)	Clean, pure, neat	Suci	Pure, neat, innocent

Origins: *T* Tausug, *B* Bikolano, *M* Maranao, *Tag* Tagalog, *P* Pampango, *I* Ilokano
Source: Francisco (1988)

gious thoughts and practice.[26] For example, the word *bathala* is the pre-Islamic Filipinos' chief god, being a form of the Hindu–Indian word *bhattara* (god).

Furthermore, Indian imprints are also noticeable in the customs and culture of the Philippines. In particular, the ancient Filipino sarong, turban, bronze bells, armlets, anklets and many other ornaments are of Indian origin. The practice of bending the head and pressing hands together in salutation (pranamanjali) may still be seen. The custom of knitting together the scarves of the bride and the bridegroom on the occasion of marriage recalls the granthibandhana of India. In northern Luzon, the costumes of the Igorot women resemble those of Assam and northern India. The textiles of Iloilo are similar to the silk fabrics of Banaras, and the brocades of Mindanao are similar to those of Banaras and Bengal. The famous barong tagalog appears as the kurta of Lucknow.

In terms of tangible manifestations of Indian presence in the Philippines, Francisco identifies some artefacts that are housed either in the National Museum of the Philippines or abroad.[27] These include the Buddhist Tara of Agusan, the votive stamp of Calatagan, the Golden Garuda of Palawan and other glass beads.

The Golden Tara, an 8 in tall image of a woman in pure gold, was discovered in the early 1920s at Maasin, Esperanza, and a molten jar

[26] Sarangani, *The Islamization of Mindanao*, 26.
[27] Francisco, 1988, 31–32.

unearthed at Bahbah, Prosperidad, in the early 1960s marks the Agusan's pre-Hispanic cultural history which was greatly influenced by India. The former, a 21-carat gold figurine, is presently kept at the Gem Room of the Chicago Field Museum of National History, Chicago, USA. The said Buddhist image of the Sailendra Period (900–950 CE) is the earliest known image of Indian origin which depicted early Indian–Philippine relations. Francisco concludes that the image was a Buddhist Tara.[28]

Another significant discovery was the clay medallion or votive stamp on whose obverse face is an image of the Avolokitesvara Padmapani in bas relief. The image, found in Calatagan, Batangas, stands in the classic Indian pose known as 'tribhanga', or three bends, and appears to hold a padma, lotus, in his right hand. This item was associated with the fourteenth or fifteenth century and has recently been housed in the National Museum of the Philippines. The medallion is semi-oblong in form, measuring 2.6 in high and 1.9 in wide. Francisco postulates that the medallion is of local manufacture.

Another proof of Indian influence in the country is the Golden Garuda pendant. This ornament was found at Brookes Point in the island province of Palawan, and is now stored in the National Museum of the Philippines. It is believed to depict the vehicle of the Hindu god, Vishnu, having been made at the height of power of the Hindu-influenced Majapahit empire.[29]

Indeed, it may be certain that whether these artefacts were brought to the Philippines directly or indirectly, they have a lasting place in the historico-cultural perspective of the Filipino people.[30] In fact, Krober believes that the Indian influence, perhaps because it was older and continued longer, was more pervasive than that of Islam. It was profound, of course along the coast and the lowlands, but penetrated even to the mountainous interior of the larger islands. He further opines that there is no tribe in the Philippines, no matter how primitive and remote, in whose culture of today elements of Indian origin cannot be traced.[31]

---

[28] Juan Francisco. "Reflexions on the Migration Theory Vis-a-Vis the Coming of Indian Influences in the Philippines". *Asian Studies* 42.1–2 (2006): 84.

[29] Elizabeth Bacus. "The Archaeology of the Philippine Archipelago". *Southeast Asia: From Pre-history to history* Ian Glover and Peter Bellwood, eds. (New York: RoutledgeCurzon, 2004), 272.

[30] Juan Francisco. "A Buddhist Image from Karitunan Site, Batangas Province". *Asian Studies* 1.1 (1963): 18.

[31] Kroeber, *Peoples of the Philippines*, 11.

Conclusion

The reference made by ancient people on the Philippines to Panyupayana is a clear indication that the archipelago has been on the radar of Indians for millennia. Such a reference indicates that full interaction with Indians took place. Buddha Prakash observes that the diverse interactions occurred between different groups in various periods, and the value of such relations was recognized by the references made to different places either on the basis of location or according to the resources they produced. Some of the regions referred to were designated with picturesque and sometimes poetic names by the Indians, these either being based on important products indicating significant traits of life, evoking religious sentiments or expressing safety, comfort or distress.[32] As a matter of fact, Indian sailors and geographers looked upon the islands and countries as places of enchantment, considering them the home of idyllic pleasure, bucolic beauties and sylvan attractions as well as the source of fabulous wealth and precious products.[33]

As for the rajahnates, their presence is proofs that the Philippines or parts of Panyupayana were once Hindu-influenced polities. Casino clearly cements this argument when he says that Butuan is an example of a chiefdom that experienced Indian influences but did not evolve into an Indianized state. There are several indications of Indic influences in the Butuan trading community. The first is that the officials who went on the first Butuan tribe/trade missions to China had Hindu/Buddhist names, such as Sari Bata Shaja. Second, some gold strips found in Butuan are related to Javanese strips that date back to the twelfth and fifteenth centuries. Third, the golden Tara of Agusan is said to be 'the image of the goodness of the Buddhist pantheon, in the Mahayana group ... may be a female bodhisattva, or the counterpart of the Hindu goddess Sakti'. Fourth, a number of golden ornaments and sword handles uncovered in Butuan and Surigao have designs that are suggestive of Garuda or Naga, both deriving ultimately from Indonesia/Indian iconography.[34] There are similar finds from the Rajahnate of Cebu.

---

[32] Buddha Prakash. *India and the World: Researches in India's Policies, Contacts, and Relationships with Other Countries and Peoples of the World* (Horshiarpur: Vishveshvaranand Vedic Research Institute, 1964), 60.
[33] Ibid., 73.
[34] Eric Casino. "Chiefdoms: Mapping the Contours of Complex Societies in the Central Philippines". *SEACOM Studies* (2013): 84.

By and large, the process of Islamization gradually dissipated. The advent of massive colonialism in Southeast Asia, including the Philippines, greatly contributed to the fall of Hindu polities that once thrived in the area. It is a consolation that a few vestiges managed to survive and were integrated into mainstream Philippine society. Several aspects of these Indian encounters were preserved in the languages, practices and traditions of the country and some were immortalized in stones and beads. These vestiges have to some extent contributed to the historical legacies of Indian-influenced polities, and subsequently to the making of a Filipino identity.

CHAPTER 7

Indian–Southeast Asian Contacts and Cultural Exchanges: Evidence from Vietnam

Le Thi Lien

INTRODUCTION

The cultural histories of South Asian and Southeast Asian countries are considered to be closely correlated with cultural exchanges and trading networks (Nandana Chutiwongs 1996: 3). Long before the opening of the so called "silk route" and the construction of Buddhist and Hindu temples, which were the result of cultural absorption from Chinese and Indian civilizations, the primitive people already had contacts with each other. Having studied the Bronze Age on mainland Southeast Asia (1500–1000 BCE), Charles Higham believes that long-distance exchanges were mainly along the river systems, including goods such as metal ingots, gemstones, shell, carnelian, fine pottery and (now surely perished) organic materials. These goods were used to express social status and make offerings to the dead (Higham 2004: 57). He also notices that from about 500 BCE, following the invading route of the Qin and Han China, several

---

L. Thi Lien (✉)
Institute of Archaeology, Vietnamese Academy of Social Sciences, Hanoi, Vietnam

© The Author(s) 2018
S. Saran (ed.), *Cultural and Civilisational Links between India and Southeast Asia*, https://doi.org/10.1007/978-981-10-7317-5_7

societies in mainland Southeast Asia developed with direct influences from Chinese culture. Other areas, further to the south and in the islands, were only indirectly influenced by the expansion of the Han. The long coast and various river systems from the lower delta of the Mekong River to the Chao Phraya created the best conditions for the development of interregional and international exchanges and trading. The demand for luxury goods and local products from the Chinese and Roman empires speeded up the formation of trading mechanisms and societies in South and Southeast Asia (ibid.: 59; Borrel et al. 2014: 110–111). The seafarers, traders and migrants who gradually settled in the islands and on the mainland of Southeast Asia fostered the process of cultural interaction and exchanges. The monsoon offered great chances, firstly for the Indians and the Arabs and then the Romans to expand their trade and cultural exchanges with Asians, in particular the Southeast Asian people (Moorhead 1957: 10–11).

Trading activities thus acted as the catalyst to begin the development of Southeast Asian societies. Archaeological evidence mainly represents two phases of early contacts and exchanges with the Indian and the Roman worlds, which resulted in the formation of early Southeast Asian states:

Phase I: From the fifth century BCE to early CE, evidence indicates that the exchanges were regular but not large in scale. Elements of Indian culture can be recognized mainly in the grave good assemblages and the craft-workshop settlements in South and Southeast Asia.[1]

Phase II: The first half of the first millennium CE witnessed the strong development of trading networks and the rise of early Southeast Asian states. Changes in social life, burial customs and religious practice allowed them to be called "Indianized states" by R.C. Majumdar (1952).

The nature and connotation of cultural contacts and exchanges between Southeast Asia and the Eastern and Western civilizations have been long discussed. G. Coedés, who also considered Southeast Asian to be "Indianized states," admitted that the Indians were not facing ill-defined groups of people but well-organized societies that possessed civilizations

---

[1] Researches of Glover and Bellina (2011), Lam (2011), Dussubieux and Gratuze (2010) are among the most interesting references.

with several similar elements to their own culture (1968: 17). The first Southeast Asian civilizations had long traditions dating from prehistory, as attested by the archaeological discoveries at several sites such as Ban Don Ta Phet (Thailand), Sa Huynh (Central Vietnam), Pre-Óc Eo (Southern Vietnam), Phum Snay, Angkor Borei and Prohear (Cambodia), Beikthano, Halin, Mongmao and Srikshetra (Myanmar).[2]

Discussing the polity of the early states, Miriam T. Stark considers that the transition from prehistory to history in Southeast Asia took place from about the second century BCE to the fifth century CE (2004: 96). During this period, Southeast Asians first settled in large nucleated communities, organizing themselves into small warring polities and engaging in international trade. Although new archaeological evidence relating to the late prehistoric period, which chronicles a gradual indigenous trend toward socio-political complexity, has compelled most historians to revise their outlook on the role of indigenous Southeast Asians in the process of early state formation, Indian culture was clearly playing an important role in the enrichment of indigenous civilizations. A survey of the evidence found in Vietnam gives a better understanding of this cultural interaction.

CONTEXT OF MARITIME TRADE NETWORK ALONG THE COAST OF VIETNAM DURING THE EARLY CHRISTIAN ERA

Geographical Setting

Vietnam is located at the crossroads between South and Southeast Asia, the continent and the Pacific Ocean. The country has a coastline that is over 3000 km long. Geological development has resulted in the formation of large and small coastal bays, and scattered islands that could serve as transit points, places to escape from storms or major ports. River networks, which mainly connect to the sea on a northwest to southeast bearing, contribute to the formation of river deltas, including the largest ones—the Red River and the Mekong River deltas. This natural context

---

[2] These sites have been discussed by several authors, including Charles Higham (2004: 64), Bui Chi Hoang et al. (2012), Nguyen Thi Hau (2004: 874–893), Miriam T. Stark (2004: 96, 99), Andreas Reinecke et al. (2009), and Pamela Gutman and Bob Hudson (2004: 157–161).

provides favorable conditions for transportation and cultural exchanges between the inland and coastal areas, as well as with distant areas belonging to great civilizations (Fig. 7.1).

Prehistoric Cultures on the Coast of Vietnam and Evidence of Cultural Exchanges

Archaeological findings relating to the development of coastal cultures in the late Neolithic Age reveal evidence of cultural exchanges, most probably via the sea routes. Along the northern coastline, the Ha Long culture remnants (4000–3500 years BP) are distributed in Quang Ninh and Hai Phong provinces. They are considered to be commercial spots. The people could have possessed the knowledge to make boats for traveling and exchanging, as indicated by shouldered axes and adzes typified by Ha Long marks, and Ha Long-typed terracotta found in contemporary sites in Northern Vietnam, Thailand, the Philippines and coastal sites in the Guangdong, Fujian, Hongkong provinces of China (Ha 1998: 264–275).

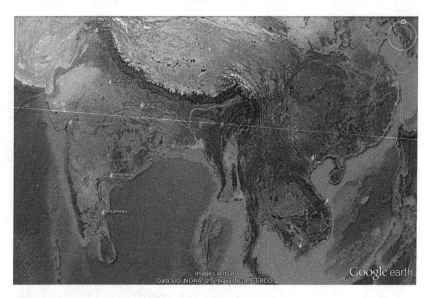

Fig. 7.1 Google map of Vietnamese and Indian early cultural centers: (a) center of the Jiao Chi realm; (b) center of the Liny–early Champa realm; (c) port-city of the Óc Eo–Funan realm. Source: Google

They could also have exchanged with inland mountainous peoples via the Gam, Lo, Da and Hong rivers, which speeded up the development of Pre-Dong Son communities in the lower delta as the basis for the formation of the Van Lang state during the Dong Son period (Trình 2012: 264–269).

On the northern central coast (including Nghe An, Ha Tinh and Quang Binh provinces), artifacts of Bau Tro culture, dated to 4000–3500 years BP, reflect the interchange with the Hoa Loc and Ha Long cultures to the north, the Xom Con culture to the south and the mountainous areas of Nghe An, Quang Binh, Upper Laos and Bien Ho in Tay Nguyen highland (Ha 1998: 275–285). Archaeological evidence includes shouldered and quadrilateral adzes, leech-shaped earrings, mollusk shell currency, ox-tooth shaped adzes and colored pottery (Phạm 2000: Bv 45.1, 2, 3; Ba21.a; Nguyễn 2009: 267). Various shapes and decorative patterns of Hoa Loc pottery are also considered to be linked with the Sa Huynh-Kalanay culture (Ha 1999: 171).

Contacts made by the coastal groups could have created favorable conditions for long-distance exchanges. As a result, the sharing of beliefs and art among these groups was fostered. During the Metal Age, especially in its late phases, the invention of bronze and iron tools dramatically increased the population and cultures significantly developed. Various sites could have been densely populated settlements with craft manufacturing spots, as indicated by the number of unearthed burials, remains of production, tools, raw material and waste. They were not only transit stops or entrepôts along the coastline, but also developed into commercial centers connecting with the inland areas via the river networks and with far regions via the sea routes.

Dong Son culture flourished during the seventh–sixth centuries BCE to the first–second centuries CE in the large river deltas of Hong River, Ma River and Ca (or Lam) River in northern Vietnam (Ha 1999: 268). This culture is characterized by a high level of bronze technology and production which were exchanged with various regions in the East and Southeast Asia. The artifacts of the Viet Khe burial (500–200 BCE) indicate that the coastal plain of the Hai Phong area probably had direct contacts with southern China via the sea route (Wei and Shiung 2014). The jar burials unearthed from various Dong Son sites, such as Lang Ca, Lang Vac, Dong Mom, Hoang Ly), a lingling-o glass earring (Lang Vac site) and an earring in the shape of a double-headed animal (Xuan An site, Ha Tinh province) indicate that the Dong Son people maintained a cultural relationship with the people of Sa Huynh culture in Central Vietnam directly via the sea route and indirectly via the river network to the inland areas (Ha 1999: 339). The occupation of the Han Chinese in Northern Vietnam from the first century BCE and the enforcement of its governing policies from the first century CE created major changes in local societies. A new style of brick tomb with a large amount of grave goods, bronze bells and pottery in Chinese style came into vogue. However, the model of terracotta thatch house and a particular lamp found from Lach Truong Tomb No. 3 (Thanh Hoa province) owe much more to local and Indian inspiration than to the Chinese (Higham 1989: Fig. 5.19).

The Lang Vac is a typical burial site of Dong Son culture on the lower reaches of the Lam River, and dates from the third–first centuries BCE. Archaeological evidence indicates a wide range of cultures that could have been in contact and exchanging with the Lang Vac people. The drums discovered at the Lang Vac site are similar to the popular type unearthed at Thach Trai Son as well as other sites in South China and those found scattered in Southeast Asia, up to Indonesia at their furthest point. Among the Dong Son type ornament assemblage, a lingling-o glass earring of Sa Huynh type and carnelian and agate beads are indicators of a trading relationship with Southeast Asia and India (Fig. 7.2).

Sa Huynh culture flourished in the first millennium BCE, with a large number of sites distributed along the central coastline. Artifacts found at these sites manifested the prosperous development of marine trade networks. Based on this maritime trading, Sa Huynh people were able to integrate outside cultural elements with their own knowledge to create diversified cultural patterns. In addition to the bronze tools and weapons which are indicators of a relationship with the Dong Son people, Sa Huynh-type double animal-headed earring and lingling-o were also unearthed from the East and Southeast Asian sites, such as those in the Philippines, Indonesia, Taiwan, Hong Kong, Thailand and Myanmar (Ha 1999: 338–39; Hung and Bellwood 2010: 234–237).

Various sites unearthed along the coast of Thua Thien Hue, Quang Nam, Quang Ngai, Binh Dinh, Khanh Hoa and Ninh Thuan provinces have been assigned to the second half of the first millennium BCE to early centuries CE. The rich and diverse assemblages of the grave goods indicate the intensively expanded trading networks that were crossing this area (Bui 2014: 266–269). In addition to the Dong Son type weapons, utensils for daily life and jewelry; Han type small bronze bells, bronze mirror, Wushu coins and various types of beads originating from India and the

Fig. 7.2 Beads from Lang Vac site, Nghe An province (Photo: Le Thi Lien). Source: Author

Mediterranean more regularly appeared than in the earlier period. The assemblages of artifacts unearthed from the sites of Con Rang (Thua Thien Hue), Go Mun, Binh Yen and Lai Nghi (Quang Nam), Hoa Diem (Khanh Hoa), Go Que, Nam Tho Son (Quang Nam) and Ly Son Islands (Quang Ngai) are the most typical representatives of this period (Lam 2011: 11–12) (Fig. 7.3).

Further to the south, hundreds of low mounds arise from the swampy land of the Dong Nai river mouth following a decrease in sea level. The inhabitants who lived in this area from the first millennium BCE to the early Christian era produced goods that probably served the need of traders, including pottery containers (the kiln sites and wastes at Cay Keo mound site, Can Gio), big jars for burials and glass ornaments (Giong Phet site, Can Gio). Meanwhile, they received rare imported goods from the traders. Typical products include the double animal-headed earrings from the Sa Huynh people, bronze mirrors and several types of Chinese pottery, intaglio and ornaments, such as agate, serpentine, amethyst, crystal round or oval beads and gold beads from the Mediterranean and Indian worlds.

Fig. 7.3 Beads from Nam Tho Son (Quang Nam province). Source: Author

These ornaments were also traded to the Binh Duong region (Phu Chanh site), Lam Dong (Phu My site) via the Dong Nai river and to the Dong Thap Muoi region (Go O Chua, Go Hang sites and early cultural evidence from Go Thap) via the Vam Co river networks (Bui et al. 2001; Le 2006a: Figs. 227, 22.10).

Archaeological evidence thus indicates that long before the early Christian era the maritime trade route made several Indian products known, and that they became favorite goods for the ancient communities in Vietnam. However, Indian civilization did not yet play a role in the social structure; Indian beliefs and religions were not yet commonly practiced among the local communities, until the appearance of the first states.

The Diffusion of Indian Civilization

Nowadays, traces of Indian influences are observed clearly in the cultural heritage of the Champa civilization in Central Vietnam, are scattered as temple ruins and sculptures in Southern Vietnam and are almost unidentifiable in Northern Vietnam. Archaeological discoveries and other sources provide valuable information that allows us to reconstruct the penetration and diffusion of Indian culture into local societies.

In Northern Vietnam, the most interesting story that should be taken into account is the origin of the four Dharma Buddhas. The legend in Dau area (present Thanh Khuong village, Thuan Thanh district, Bac Ninh province) relates to a monk named Khau-Da-la. The story is that he stepped over a local girl, Man Nuong, who served in the monastery kitchen. She then gave birth to a child and brought it back to the monk. By reciting the magic words, the monk made a dau tree (mulberry tree) opened and the child was placed inside. One day, the tree fell down to the river after a big storm. No one but Man Nuong could pull it out of the water, using her waist-sash. Images of the four Dau sisters were then sculptured from the tree and worshipped in four pagodas. The story seems to agree with the chronicle record about the presence of Indians and their religions during the reign of Si Nhiep (*Shi Xie*) in this area, which served as the headquarters of the Jiao Chi in the second century CE (*Dai Viet Su ky Toan thu, Vol. III*). The four Dharma Buddhas are also called by the local people the four Lady Buddhas: Phap Van (Cloud Lady), Phap Vu (Rain Lady), Phap Loi (Thunder Lady) and Phap Dien (Lighting Lady). They were prayed to for rain by the kings and the people. Their seventeenth- to eighteenth-century images are made of wood in a special form, with a female face and a sexless body (Fig. 7.4). The child is represented in the form of a stone named "Thach Cuong" (Lighting Stone). The tradition of worshipping the four Dharma Buddhas is witnessed in various areas of the Red River delta. This is an old tradition that could have been

Fig. 7.4 Dau Lady Buddha, Bac Ninh Province. Source: Author

influenced by the Indian Vedic cult and overlaid with Chinese elements during the Han domination in the early Christian era. The political center of Luy Lau in the Dau area was in contact with Central and Southern Vietnam, as indicated by the similarity of the roof tile-ends with kala face that were found in Tra Kieu, the Champa ancient capital, and the kendi and grinding stone which were also found at both the Champa and Óc Eo sites (Nishimura 2012: Figs. 122–127, 123–124, 5, 124–122, 4). These typical artifacts reflect the great inspiration that was taken from Indian culture.

The branches of the Red River, one of which reached the Dau area, served as convenient transport to the sea and inland areas. The mouth of the river was developed as a trading center and meeting point that received new cultural elements, as indicated by the discovery of a stone Buddha image datable to the sixth–seventh century from Ben Cui, Nam Dinh city (Lê and Tống 1994). Other areas in Northern Vietnam, such as Lach Truong in the old Ma river mouth (Thanh Hoa province) and Vinh in Lam river mouth (Nghe An province), were active centers from the early first millennium CE. The Nhan Thap Buddhist stupa (Nam Dan district, Nghe An province) is the outcome of a mixture between Viet, Chinese and Indian elements during the seventh–ninth centuries (Trần and Nguyễn 1987). It is also very interesting that the tenth-century stone pillars inscribed with Indian Buddhist sutra using an old Chinese alphabet have been found at the Hoa Lu ancient capital, Ninh Binh province (Ha 1997: 802). They indicate that, although covered by an imposed layer of Chinese culture under the Han domination, the earlier Viet culture which was strongly dominated by Indian elements still survived.

In Central Vietnam, the Cham civilization was nourished by the strong absorption of an Indian cultural element, particularly after the raising of Khu Lien in the second century CE. Archaeological evidence indicates that in the valley of Thu Bon and along several other rivers, the Champa ports were developed and citadels were built. Tra Kieu citadel (Duy Xuyen district, Quang Nam province) was the most important capital city of Champa during the first millennium CE. The Cham kings constructed their citadel and palaces applying both Chinese and Indian techniques and decoration, with Indian inspiration most strongly seen on roof tile ends and in other architectural decoration (Southworth 1995). Thu Bon River connected the great port of Champa, which included Cham Island, to the Tra Kieu capital city and the settlements surrounding what is now Hoi An city. It also connected the capital with its royal sanctuary—the Mỹ Sơn temple complex. The earliest temple there was built of wood in the fourth century CE by King Bhadravarman, who dedicated the entire valley of Mỹ Sơn to Bhadresvara—one epithet of the Siva god. The main surviving architecture is much later in date, mainly from the tenth century. The kings of various Champa dynasties continued to build Hindu temples and worshipped Siva in the form of Sivalinga in the main pantheon in Mỹ Sơn. Meanwhile, various groups of Hindu temple constructed on the coastal plains of Champa, flourishing most in the seventh–ninth century and continuing to the thirteenth–fourteenth century in the southern realm of Champa kingdom. Buddhism was also followed by the Cham people. The largest monastery was built at Dong Duong in 875 by the Cham king Indravarman II. There were a number of Buddhist followers who resided along the coast of Central Vietnam, as indicated by various small bronze Buddhas and Avalokitesvara images. Terracotta votive tablets depicting the Buddhist triad were discovered at Tra Kieu and produced in a kiln site at Nui Choi (Quang Ngai province), representing a long history of development from the seventh to about the twelfth centuries CE (Trần 1994; Ngô 2001).

In southern Vietnam, the Dong Nai and Mekong river systems played essential roles in the diffusion of Indian civilization to the inland areas of what is now southern Vietnam and southern Cambodia. Before the development of the first port city at Óc Eo, trading networks seemed already active in what are now the coastal swampy lands of Can Gio and Giong Lon in Ho Chi Minh city and Ba Ria-Vung Tau city respectively. The traders and middlemen could follow the waterways to Phu Chanh, Go O Chua, Go Dung, Go Thap and Go Hang, and then promote these sites so that they developed into manufacturing and exchange places for pottery and ornament, including Indian-style carnelian beads and metal earrings. Phallic type Sivalingas, representing the earliest Hindu beliefs, have been unearthed at the late prehistoric sites at Giong Noi (Ben Tre province) and Go Cao Su (Long An province) (Trần et al. 1999; Trần and Lại 2007). Buddhist and Hindu beliefs were popularly practiced by the Óc Eo people during the first half of the first millennium CE in the low Mekong river delta (Le 2015b: Figs. 5–7). Indian tastes in ornaments, experiences in pottery making, architectural building and sculpture carving can be witnessed by the archaeological discoveries in Southern Vietnam (Lê et al. 1995; Le 2006b, 2011a, b, 2015a, b).

FUNAN AND THE ÓC EO CULTURE: THE EARLIEST STATE IN SOUTHEAST ASIA FOLLOWING THE INDIAN MODEL

Óc Eo archaeological culture, with hundreds of sites discovered in southern Vietnam, has been identified as the tangible heritage of the Funan, the earliest state in Southeast Asia. Analysis of archaeological data has helped to reconstruct the Funan–Óc Eo society. Influences from Indian civilization are strongly imposed on daily life as well as on the social structure.

Social Organization of the Oc Eo People

According to Vickery (1998: 34, Table 1), Funan (first–sixth century CE) belongs to the pre-proto-history period in the history of Cambodia. However, based on Chinese chronicle records (the earliest one is *Han shu*), archaeological data and inscriptions on gold and stone found at the Óc Eo sites, Óc Eo society represented a full development of a state. Several researchers have realized that the appearance of ideas and their tangible expressions are the key point in identifying the development of civilizations. The construction of monuments and great works, such as dikes, roads, citadel walls and moats, as well as stone and brick monuments, was an important part of this. Archaeological evidence of these monuments can be identified in Southeast Asia from the middle of the first millennium CE (Stark 2006). In southern Vietnam, the canal network, the brick monuments found at Go Thap (Dong Thap province), Cay Gao, Go Ong Tung (Dong Nai province) and the brick-cum-stone monuments found at Óc Eo, Da Noi (An Giang province), Nen Chua and Da Noi (Kien Giang province) were built before the fifth century CE and largely during the fourth–sixth century CE (Lê et al. 1995; Le 2006b). They represent the so-called architecture of consensus. Indian culture was a strong influence on the monuments, as attested by their architectural style and decoration, and the contents of the deposits in the temple foundations. The tendency towards political unification began to happen in about the seventh century CE in Cambodia (Stark 2006: 21.15). However, it could have been much earlier in southern Vietnam, as attested by the appearance of the Harihara image (Le 2015b: Fig. 10) and the Sivalinga in various forms (Fig. 7.5). Social organization followed the model of a nuclear center and satellites, as attested by the remains of ports, cities and villages found in Southern Vietnam. These can be recognized as the Indian model, and this is further attested by the mandala idea that is represented by the

Fig. 7.5 Mukhalinga, Óc Eo site, An Giang province. Source: Nguyen Huu Thiet

images of the Dikpalakas, the Vedi and god Brahma on the gold plaques found at Cat Tien Hindu temple (Witzel and Lê 2007). Thus it is presumed that, from the first half of the first millennium CE, the political state in southern Vietnam was closely organized.

Religions

While settlement remains were studied and excavated at only a few sites, architectural remains and religious artifacts, such as statues and altars, religious symbols, incarnations of Hindu gods and goddesses, images of Buddha and Bodhisattva, and inscriptions have been found at many sites. Some of these have been systematically excavated and studied. The size and characteristics of architecture and the art at several religious sites are valuable sources for the study of the development and the role of the major Óc Eo sites. They are also valuable for the history of the propagation and development of the two main religions in the Óc Eo society—Buddhism and Hinduism.

There are very few Hindu temples where above-ground remains still exist, and they are all dated to the flourishing period of the Óc Eo culture. There are several standing monuments dating from the second half of the first millennium CE, including the Vĩnh Hưng tower (Minh Hải province), Bình Thạnh and Chót Mạt (Tây Ninh province) and several ruins of the Cát Tiên temple complex in Lam Dong province. The artifacts found in situ inside the Cat Tien temples help to determine the religious function of many architectural ruins in the lower delta of the Mekong River, such as those at Gò Tháp and Đá Nổi sites (Le 2011a).

The artifacts found inside the temples' foundations also demonstrate a rich and diverse Hindu pantheon, which developed from simple symbols to images of various gods and goddesses. The art, iconographic features and Hindu architecture reflect a long history of cultural interaction and exchanges with various Indian areas and art centers (Le 2011a: 427–428, 2015a: 119). The archaeological context of these artifacts confirms that the Óc Eo people thoroughly understood and followed the practices of the *gabhanyāsa* ("the depositing of the embryo") and the *Prathameṣṭakānyāsa* ("the placing of the first brick") ceremonies during the construction of the Hindu temples and Buddhist stupas, as described in Indian texts and followed by other Southeast Asian communities (Ślączka 2007).

Hindu sculptures from the Óc Eo culture tend to be simple anthropomorphic forms of gods and goddesses. The absence of the Siva god in human form leads to the consideration that Vishnuism played the main role in the Óc Eo culture. However, research into the number and evolution of the Sivalinga indicates that Sivaist belief was very common and played an important role in the Óc Eo sites (Le 2006a: 82–100, Table 2.3). Even the worship of the phallic-form linga or 'Ong Ta' (it could be the local word '*Rudra*'), was probably practiced earlier, as indicated by finds from proto-historical sites (Trần et al. 1999). Buddhism was commonly followed by the Óc Eo people. So far, Gò Xoài is the only site that has been clearly defined as a Buddhist stupa. The remnant of this building that survives has a square brick foundation with a central sacred hole slightly slanted to the west. Twenty-six gold artifacts were deposited in the hole, including four rings and several gold plaques cut in the form of a snake, tortoise, lotus and water lily, incised with the image of an elephant, and one with an inscription which is datable to the eighth century (Bui et al. 2001: 203–217; Le 2005). They indicate that the ceremonies of a Buddhist stupa construction were strictly followed.

Although a distribution map of Buddhist architecture has not yet been completed, Buddhist artifacts, mainly images of Buddha, have been found at many sites. Some wood and stone sculptures found at Óc Eo, Gò Tháp and Mỹ Thạnh Đông (Long An province) represent the earliest art style, which was influenced by the Mathura and Amaravati schools. Later on, influences of other Indian art styles, such as those of Gupta, can be identified (Le 2006a: 60, Map I). Like Hindu art, the Buddhist art of the Óc Eo culture in South Vietnam developed on the basis of imported prototypes which were then imitated, subsequently resulting in the creation of their own style, as witnessed by the bronze Buddha head in Gandhara style from the Óc Eo site and a stone image in Sarnath style from Nen Chua site (Le 2014: Fig. 87, 2015a: Fig. 24). Buddha images in wood are among the most typical art products that make up the so-called Funan style of art (Le 2006a: 42–47). Go Thap site was an important carving center for the Buddha image in wood and Hindu images in stone.

The Beliefs and Practices of Religious Ceremonies of the Óc Eo People

The meanings of the images on gold plaques unearthed from the central part of the temple foundations vividly represent ceremonial practices and beliefs at different levels of society. Gold plaques found in the temple ruins at the Gò Tháp, Đá Nổi and Cát Tiên sites suggest that many people, including royalty and high-ranking officers, joined in the ceremonies of temple construction. This is based on the repeated appearance of some motifs in the same collection or prayers with personal names.

It is possible that before the appearance of the Hindu temples the Óc Eo people, probably including immigrants, practiced religious ceremonies in several ways. From the settlement layers and graves at Gò Tháp have been unearthed a tortoise shell cut into the Linga shape with an incised trident, a terracotta triangle and small colorful gravel which looks like beans or have a triangular shape after cutting the end (Lê and Nguyễn 2003). Evidence of Buddhist practices is not very clear. However, the frequent appearance of lotus motifs (although they are used in both religions) on pottery, swastika images and terracotta stupa-shaped covers found at Óc Eo sites are probably indications of Buddhist followers. Both Buddhism and Hinduism were followed simultaneously at the major sites of the Óc Eo culture, such as Óc Eo, Nền Chùa and Gò Tháp. This could be the outcome of the internationalization and diversification of the Óc Eo culture during its participation in the international network of trading and cultural exchanges.

Funeral Rites and Grave Goods

Traditional rites and funeral customs of different ethnic groups might have interacted with each other, as can be seen from the different remains found in the same area. The cremated tradition seems to be closely related to contact with Indian people. The first cremation jar burial was unearthed on the slope of Ba Thê Mount (Manguin and Vo 2000: Figs. 4, 6). At the Gò Tháp site, both inhumations and cremations were unearthed. The ash of the cremated bodies was not only contained in a jar, but also put on bricks and covered with half-cut jars or scattered in a rectangular earthen pit. The customs of scattering potsherds at the bottom of a burial or covering the top, marking the burial with stone and using clay or sand around the burial pit indicate elements of earlier burial traditions. Compared with the burial traditions of the Metal Age, the grave goods show a great change in burial customs, resembling several Indian elements (Dubois and Beauchamp 1936: 490). Pottery was broken before laying it around the burial pit. However, in some cases the burial jar was excluded. The simple sets of grave goods found in burials at the foot of Minh Sư mound consist mainly of daily ceramics and ceremonial pottery, such as kendi or kundika. This may indicate funerals of common people. Some of these burials might have been of craftsmen, as indicated by the presence of glass fragments and grinding stones (Le 2006b: 237–239, 2015a: Fig. 7).

Other Indian elements that strongly influenced the Óc Eo culture can be realized from the writing (*Brahmi* was used for inscriptions on stone and gold plaques), entertainment (Indian type music instrument, dice) and daily life (pottery, ornaments) (Le 2011b, 2013, 2015a: Fig. 11, 2015b: Figs. 11. 16–11.18, 11.21).

Conclusion

From various sources, archaeological data in particular, it is impossible to deny the profound influences of Indian civilization on the art, religion, writing and other aspects of daily life of the groups of ancient people in Vietnam. The setting up of a number of Indian seaports along the coast, spanning the west to the east of the Indian subcontinent, which initiated trading relations between Southeast Asia and the West, the Greco-Roman world and the Middle East, provided great chances for Southeast Asians, including Vietnamese people, to develop their contact with the outside world.

Archaeological evidence clearly proves that cultural influences were adopted from various areas of India at different times. In addition, traces of cultural exchanges with other civilizations and cultures are attested. Evidence also proves that the development of the maritime trade network particularly flourished during the first millennium CE. As a result, several states in Southeast Asia made their way into the wider world. Funan—the first maritime state, which left profuse tangible remains in Óc Eo archaeological sites in Southern Vietnam—was deeply influenced by the Indian civilization.

Acknowledgement The author would like to express special thanks to RIS, India for publication of this chapter. It is the outcome of various research projects conducted over more than twenty years, supported by the Institute of Archaeology (2001–2003), Toyota Foundation (1998–2000), Harvard-Yenching Institute (1999–2000, 2006–2007) and the NAFOSTED (National Foundation for Science and Technology Development, the Ministry of Science and Technology, Vietnam) (2011–2015).

REFERENCES

Borrel, B., Bellina, B., Chaisuwan, B. 2014. Contact between the Upper Thai-Malay peninsular and the Mediterranian World, in Nicolas Revire & Stephen A. Murphy (eds.), *Before Siam – Essays in Art and Archaeology*, pp. 98–117, Bangkok: River Books & The Siam Society.
Bui C. H., Pham, C. T., Nguyen K. T. K. 2012. *Khao co hoc Ba Ria-Vung Tau – Tu tien su den so su* [Archaeology in Ba Ria-Vung Tau province – from Prehistory to history], Ho Chi Minh City: Social Sciences Publishing House.
Bui, P. D., Dao, L. C., Vuong, T. H. 2001. *Khao co hoc Long An – Nhung the ky dau Cong nguyen* [Archaeology in Long An Province – Centuries in early Christian Era], Long An: Long An Department of Culture and Information.
Bui, V. L. 2014. *Cac di tich so su Mien Trung-Tay Nguyen* (Prehistorical sites in Central and Highland of Vietnam), unpublished document of the Institute of Archaeology.
Coedés, G. 1968. *The Indianized States of Southeast Asia*. Trans. By S. B. Cowing. Honolulu.
Dubois, ABBe J.A. and Beauchamp, H.K. 1936. *Hindumaners, customs and ceremonies*, Oxford: University Press.
Glover, I. C. and Bellina, B. 2011. Ban Don Ta Phet and Khao Sam Kaeo: The earliest Indian contacts Re-assessed, in Manguin, P. Y., Mani, A. and Wade, G. (Eds.), *Early Indian influences in Southeast Asia: Reflection on Cross-cultural Movements*, pp. 17–46. Singapore, Manohar Publishers and distributors.

Ha, Van Tan 1997. *Theo dau cac van hoa co* (Following the Remains of the Ancient Cultures, Hanoi: Social Sciences Publishing House.
Ha, Van Tan (ed.) 1998. *Khảo cổ học Việt Nam*, Tập I, Thời đại Đá Việt Nam (Vietnamese Archaeology, Vol. I, The Stone Age in Vietnam), Hanoi: Social Sciences Publishing House.
Ha, Van Tan (ed.) 1999. *Khảo cổ học Việt Nam*, Tập II, Thời đại Kim khí Việt Nam (Vietnamese Archaeology, Vol. II, The Metal Age in Vietnam), Hanoi: Social Sciences Publishing House.
Higham, C 1989. *The Archaeology of Mainland Southeast Asia: From 10,000BC to the Fall of Angkor*, Cambridge University Press.
Higham, C. 2004. Mainland Southeast Asia from Neolithic to the Iron Age, in Glover, I. C. and Bellwood, P. (eds.), *Southeast Asia from Prehistory to History*, pp. 41–67, New York: Routledge Curzon.
Hung, H. C. & Bellwood, P. 2010. Movement of raw materials and manufactured goods across the South China Sea after 500 BCE: From Taiwan to Thailand and back, in Bellina, B., Elisabeth A. Bacus, Thomas Oliver Pryce and Jan Wisseman Christie (eds.), *50 years of Archaeology in Southeast Asia – Essay in Honour of Ian Glover*, pp. 235–246, Bangkok: River Books.
Dussubieux, Laure & Gratuze, Bernard 2010. Glass in Southeast Asia, in Bérénice Bellina, Elisabeth A. Bacus, Thomas Oliver Pryce& JanWisseman Christie (eds.), *50 Years of Archaeology in Southeast Asia –Essays in Honour of Ian Glover*, pp. 247–259, Bangkok: River Books.
Lam, Thi My Dzung. 2011. Central Vietnam during the period from 500 BCE to CE 500, in Manguin, P. Y., Mani, A., Wade, G., *Early Interactions between South and Southeast Asia: Reflection on Cross-Cultural Exchange*, pp. 3–16, Singapore: ISEAS.
Le, Thi Lien. 2005. Gold plaques and their archaeological context in the Oc Eo Culture, *Bulletin of the Indo-Pacific Prehistory Association* 25: 145–154, The Taipei papers (Vol. 3).
Le, Thi Lien. 2006a. *Buddhist & Hindu Art in the Cuu Long River Delta Prior to 10th Century AD*, Hanoi: The Gioi Publishing House.
Le, Thi Lien 2006b. Excavations at Minh Su Mound, Go Thap site, Dong Thap Province, South Vietnam, in *Uncovering Southeast Asia's past* – Selected papers from the 10th International Conference of the European Association of Southeast Asian Archaeologists, pp. 232–244. Singapore: NUS Press.
Le, Thi Lien 2011a. Hindu Deities in Southern Vietnam – Images Seen on the Tiny Archaeological Artefacts. In Manguin, P. Y., A. Mani & Wade, G. (eds.), *Early Indian influences in Southeast Asia: Reflection on Cross-cultural Movements*, pp. 407–431. Singapore: Institute of Southeast Asian Studies.
Le, Thi Lien. 2011b. Metal ornaments and traces of their manufacturing in Oc Eo culture (Southern Vietnam), in Stephen Chia & Barbara Watson Andya (eds.),

Bujang Valley and Early Civilization in Southeast Asia, Chapter 15, pp. 299–309, Malaysia: Department of National Heritage.

Le, Thi Lien. 2013. *Brahmi inscription from archaeological sites in Southern Vietnam during the 1st millennium CE*, paper presented at The First SEMEO SPAFA International Conference on Southeast Asian Archaeology, Burapha University, Chonburi, Thailand, 7–10 May 2013.

Le, Thi Lien 2014. Hindu-Buddhist Sculpture in Southern Vietnam: Evolution of icon and style to the Eighth Century, in John Guy (ed), *Lost Kingdoms – Hindu-Buddhist Sculpture of Early Southeast Asia*, pp. 118–121, New York: The Metropolitant of Art.

Le, Thi Lien 2015a. History of Maritime Contacts between Vietnam and India: Archaeological Evidence from Oc Eo culture in Southern Vietnam, in Sila Tripati (ed.), *Maritime Contacts of the Past: Deciphering Connections amongst communities*, 95–123, New Delhi: Delta Book World.

Le, Thi Lien 2015b. Hindu Belief and Maritime Network in Southern Vietnam during the Early Common Era, *Journal of Indo-Pacific Archaeology* 39: 1–17.

Lê, Thị Liên and Nguyễn, Đăng Cường 2003. Về những viên sỏi nhỏ và mảnh gốm ghè tròn ở di chỉ cư trú Chân gò Minh Sư (Gò Tháp, Đồng Tháp) [On the small gravels and chipped potsherds from the settlement site of Minh Su mound (Go Thap site, Dong Thap province)], *NPHMVKCH nam 2002*, 864–865, Hanoi: Social Sciences Publishing House.

Lê, Xuân Diệm, Đào, Linh Côn, and Võ Sĩ Khải. 1995. *Oc Eo Culture –Recent Discoveries*. Hanoi: Social Sciences Publishing House.

Lê, Thị Liên and Tống, Trung Tín 1994. Ve mot pho tuong Phat dang duoc luu tru trong Bao tang Nam Ha [On a Buddha Image Housed in the Nam Ha Museum), *NPHMVKCH nam 1993*: 193.

Majumdar R. C. 1952. *Greater India*, Motila Banarasidas.

Manguin, P. Y. & Vo, S. K. 2000. Excavation at the Ba The/Oc Eo Complex (Vietnam), A Preliminary Report on the 1998 Campaign, *Southeast Asian Archaeology 1998*, Center for Southeast Asian Studies, University of Hull, Great Britain, 107–112.

Moorhead, F. J. 1957. *A History of Malaya and her neighbours*, Vol. I. London: Longmans.

Nandana Chutiwongs. 1996. Trade route and the diffusions in South and Southeast Asia, in *Ancient trades and Cultural Contacts in Southeast Asia*, pp. 3–42, Bangkok: The Office of the National Commission.

Ngô, Văn Doanh 2001. Ve nhung tieu pham Phat giao bang dat nung cua Champa o nui Choi (Quang Ngai) [On the small terracotta artworks of Champa from Nui Choi site (Quang Ngai province)], *NPHMVKCH nam 2000*: 724–724.

Nguyễn, Khắc Sử 2009. *Di chỉ tiền sử Cái Bèo, đảo Cát Bà* (Cai Beo Prehistorical site, Cat Ba Islands), Hanoi: Social Sciences Publishing House.

Nguyễn, Thị Hậu 2004. Hệ thống di tích khảo cổ học vùng sinh thái ngập mặn ở Cần Giờ, Thành phố Hồ Chí Minh (The archaeological site complex in the salt-marsh ecological area of Can Gio, Ho Chi Minh City), in *Một thế kỉ Khảo cổ học Việt Nam (One Century of Vietnamese Archaeology)*, Vol. I, 874–893. Hanoi: Social Sciences Publishing House.

Nishimura, Masanari 2012. *Archaeology and Ancient History of Vietnam*, Tokyo: Doseisha (in Japanese).

Pamela Gutman and Bob Hudson. 2004. The Archaeology of Burma (Myanma) from the Neolithic to Pagan), in Ian Glover and Peter Bellwood (eds.), *Southeast Asia from Prehistory to History*, pp. 149–176. London and New York: Routlegde Curzon.

Phạm, Thị Ninh 2000. *Văn hóa Bàu Tró* [The Bau Tro culture]. Hanoi: Social Sciences Publishing House.

Reinecke, Andreas, Vin Laychour, and Seng Sonetra 2009. *The First Golden Age of Cambodia: Excavation at Prohear*, Bonn: Thomas Muntzer.

Ślączka, Anna A. 2007. *Temple Conseration Rituals in ancient India – Text and Archaeology*. Leiden, Boston: Brill.

Southworth, William A. 1995. Ngoi mat he o di chi Tra Kieu (Quang Nam – Da Nang) [The tile-ends with human-mask design from Tra Kieu site (Quang Nam-Danang)], *NPHMVKCH nam 1994:* 455–457.

Stark, Miriam T. 2004. Pre Angkorien and Angkorien Cambodia, in Glover, I. and Bellwood, P. (eds), *Southeast Asia from Prehistory to History*, pp. 89–119. London and New York: Routlegde Curzon.

Stark, Miriam T. 2006. Early Mainland Southeast Asian Landscapes in the First Millennium A.D. ANRV287-AN35-21 ARI 16 June 2006 21:48, online Review in Advance on June 27, 2006.

Trần, Anh Dũng and Nguyễn, Mạnh Cường. 1987. *Thap Nhan o Nghe Tinh qua hai lan khai quat* (Thap Nhan site in Nghe Tinh province after the two excavations), doccument of Vietnam Institute of Archaeology.

Trần, Kì Phương 1994. Ghi chu ve nhung tieu pham Phat giao moi phat hien tai Tra Kieu (Quang Nam – Da Nang) [Notes on the small Buddhist artifacts newly found from Tra Kieu site (Quang Nam-Da Nang province)], *NPHMVKCH nam 1993*: 301–303.

Trần, Anh Dũng, Bùi Văn Liêm, and Nguyễn Đăng Cường. 1999. *Bao cao khai quat di chi Go Cao Su (Long An)* [Report on the excavation in Cao Su Mound site (Long An province)], document of Vietnam Institute of Archaeology.

Trần, Anh Dũng and Lại, Văn Tới 2007. Di chi Giong Noi (Ben Tre) qua ba lan khai quat (The three excavations at Giong Noi site (Ben Tre province). *Khao co học* 2 (146): 13–35.

Trình, Năng Chung 2012. *Cao Bang thoi Tien su va So su* (Cao Bang during the prehistory and Protohistory). Hanoi: Social Sciences Publishing House.

Vickery, Michael 1998. *Society, Economic, and Politics in Pre-Angkorian Cambodia: The 7th – 8th centuries*, Tokyo: Center for East Asian Cultural Studies for UNESCO, Tokyo Bunko.

Wei, Weiyan and Shiung, Chung-Ching. 2014. Viet Khe Burial 2: Identifying the Exotic Bronze Wares and Assessing Cultural Contact between Dong Son and Yue Cultures, paper presented in the 20th Congree of the IPPA, Siem Riep, 13-17/1/2014.

Witzel, Michael and Lê, Thị Liên 2007. Gop them thong tin tu cac manh vang cua Go 6B (Cat Tien, Lam Dong) [More information from the gold plaques of Go 6B (Cat Tien site, Lam Dong province)], *NPHMVKCH nam 2007*: 685–687.

PART III

Representations of Religions and Rituals

CHAPTER 8

From Śivaśāsana to Agama Hindu Bali: Tracing the Indic Roots of Modern Balinese Hinduism

Andrea Acri

INTRODUCTION: RECEIVED IDEAS AND NEW PARADIGMS IN THE STUDY OF BALINESE HINDUISM

A significant number of anthropological studies on Balinese religion has been published since the 1970s. Those studies—primarily tackling sociological issues connected with ritual, politics, and hierarchy—have paid particular attention to the reformed version of Hinduism (*Agama Hindu Bali*) that came to the fore from the early twentieth century onwards. According to the most influential theories, Balinese religion emphasized orthopraxy rather than orthodoxy, lacking a proper theological and philosophical tradition as well as a set of shared beliefs expressed in a body of canonized sacred scriptures. It was only after contact with the ideologies carried by representatives of Christian, Islamic, and Indian Hindu faiths that the Balinese reformers sought to promote a shift from a kind of embedded orthopraxy to a universalistic and abstract dogmatic religion, the allegiance to a single deity, and the 'scripturalization' of traditional beliefs.

A. Acri (✉)
EPHE, PSL, Paris, France
e-mail: andrea.acri@ephe.sorbonne.fr

Such views may be traced back to the influential essay '"Internal Conversion" in Contemporary Bali' by North American anthropologist Clifford Geertz (1973). Geertz posited that Balinese religion, in contrast to the 'rationalized' world religion that is Indian Hinduism, is thoroughly 'traditional', being characterized by 'metaphysical nonchalance', its ritual and religious specialists being 'more professional magicians than true priests' (pp. 176–179). Traditional Balinese palm-leaf manuscripts are 'more magical esoterica than canonical scriptures', in other words religious paraphernalia traditionally used as sacred heirlooms and bearing no relevance to our understanding of current Balinese religious discourse and ritual practice (p. 185).

Following Geertz, James Boon (1990: 158–164) argued that Balinese religious texts constitute 'dispersed fragments of Tantric influence [...] not doctrinal, seldam corporate, not coherent or even necessarily cultic, and orthodoxies' (p. xiii). In a similar fashion, Fredrik Barth (1993: 216–217) pointed out that Balinese texts 'fail to function in a way that enhances a unity of doctrine and dogma' and, rather than constituting a 'literary heritage allowing reference, comparison, and a critical scholarship of establishing a shared authentic knowledge', they must be regarded as 'separate, independent sources of authority to their priestly possessors, at best read for their unique and place-and-person-specific knowledge'. Jean-François Guermonprez (2001: 277) maintained that there is no demonstrable relation between Sanskrit Śaiva scriptures from South Asia and Balinese texts, for the latter would be 'aides-mémoires' concerned with mystical and yogic practices rather than proper manuals of religion. In a recent contribution, Annette Hornbacher (2014: 316) argues that the texts called Tuturs do not contain any religious beliefs and therefore are not canonical scriptures, but rather 'sacral texts' (*sakralen Texten*) whose 'often dark' (*oft dunklen*) speculations describe cosmogony and deliverance, micro-macrocosmic analogies, and powerful and ambivalent knowledge of life and death. To her, unlike the canonical texts of the reformed version of Balinese Hinduism, Tuturs convey neither a doctrine nor even a tutorial or explanation of Balinese ritual practice, requiring not a primary theoretical understanding of the text but rather an existential and transformative implementation of what is written in the life of the practitioner (ibid.: p. 317). Further, Hornbacher casts doubt on the validity to interpret the Tutur genre as an expression of an Indic Śaiva system.[1]

---

[1] See, for instance, Hornbacher (2014: 332, fn. 25), referring to Acri 2011a and 2013 (the latter article does not, however, appear in her bibliography); she claims that all the names,

Writing from the disciplinary perspective of philology, in 1971—hence before the publication of Geertz's study—Haryati Soebadio argued that

> In Bali, the more speculative parts of the religious texts are no longer evident in present day religious life. [...] The Tutur are not so much used as treasured as *pusaka*, a sacred heirloom, and venerated as such. [...] Balinese religious life as we witness it at present seems thus to show that since the day Tutur were composed, theological speculation has receded into the background to the point of near oblivion. (Soebadio 1971: 61–62)

Building on these premises, and on the theories of Geertz and his epigones, Sanskritist Frits Staal (1995: 31) bluntly stated that 'Balinese ritual is a classic case of ritual without religion'.[2]

Such views (subliminally) imply a higher position of the 'intellectual West' over the 'ritual East'. To sum up: the majority of Western scholars of Balinese religion have denied Balinese agency by ignoring its sophisticated religious discourse stemming from a pre-modern tradition of Śaiva theology and philosophy. Not recognizing a scriptural basis for Balinese religion, they have perceived ethnographic data as more significant than data mined from texts; those texts have been generally regarded as belonging to a dimension removed from daily life, to the point of becoming totally irrelevant to the study of Balinese religion and its living manifestations.

Even the anthropologists who have (marginally) engaged with the Balinese scriptural corpus, such as Barth, Guermonprez, Picard, and Hornbacher, have characterized it as a heterogeneous mass of mystical, esoteric, and obscure texts that can be understood uniquely in their own terms. Not surprisingly, those scholars have refrained from embarking on a comparison of features of Balinese religion(s) and ancient South Asian religions and philosophies, which since the first millennium AD have con-

---

designations and personifications of the highest form of Śiva as the Absolute (such as Saṅ Hyaṅ Tuṅgal, Saṅ Hyaṅ Nora, etc.) that are found in Tuturs 'get completely out of sight if one accepts the fact of monism and his sporadic connection with Śiva as a sufficient reason to interpret Tuturs overall as expression of an Indian Śivaite system' (*Sie geraten vollkommen aus dem Blick, wenn man die Tatsache des Monismus und seine sporadische Verbindung mit Shiva als hinreichenden Grund dafür nimmt, die tutur insgesamt als Ausdruck eines indischen Shivaitischen Systems zu deuten*). This statement over-simplifies the matter; elsewhere (Acri 2011b: 7, 2011e: 549) I have pointed out that the proliferation of names of God in His various aspects that are rarely found, or altogether unattested, in the Śiva Sanskrit literature from South Asia is a distinctive feature of apparently late, more 'localised' Tuturs, but not of Tattvas, which follow Sanskrit prototypes more closely.

[2] See also Howell (1978: 265), Picard (1997: 188, 1999: 42), Howe (2001: 148).

tributed to shaping the religious discourse on Bali. The opinion that these materials must be understood exclusively in their own (i.e. Balinese) terms and that any comparison with South Asia and other areas of the Sanskritic world is bound to be, or ill advised, has hampered a full understanding of Balinese religion and its foundational scriptural body. This perspective has favoured a 'parochialization' of Balinese culture, denying as it does its trans-local, Indic cosmopolitan dimension.

The corollary ensuing from this perspective is that any trans-local, intellectual, and 'universalizing' elements of the religious discourse are to be regarded as having been triggered by external influences that occurred during the colonial and post-Independence period. Indeed, the synchronic approach championed by anthropology has paid little attention to the historical dimension of Balinese religion, thereby failing to distinguish between features that are the result of reformist influence from those that have been inherited from the pre-colonial period. Finally, one notes a lack of ethnographic documentation and study of the discourses and practices current among the Brahmanical Śaiva religious/ritual specialists (*pedanda śiva*), who constitute the elite in charge of the preservation of the specialised (and esoteric) knowledge upon which the edifice of Balinese ritual rests.

In a series of articles (Acri 2011a, 2013, 2014a, b), I have offered a critique of the current scholarly opinions on Balinese Hinduism. My critique has revolved around the fact that most Western scholars have largely, and surprisingly, ignored an important source of data on the latter aspects of Balinese religion, namely the extensive corpus of Old Javanese-cum-Sanskrit Śaiva texts known as Tuturs and Tattvas—a body of literature reconfiguring materials of South Asian provenance within a Javano-Balinese doctrinal framework. Balinese society in the pre-colonial period had a relatively high degree of literacy (Rubinstein 2000), as well as a high number of manuscripts per capita; it is, therefore, deeply ironical that it has been treated virtually as an oral, pre-literate one. Indeed, Balinese religion involves a 'specialization' and 'compartmentalization' of knowledge, which reflects different levels of knowledge accessible to, and dominated by, different social groups. Thus, one needs to acknowledge that different persons have different schemes of knowledge, depending on their status, education, needs, personal abilities, and interests. Since texts written on palm-leaf manuscripts (*lontar*) are agreed on by most Balinese to be the ultimate source of authority, even by those who cannot read them or understand them, they have to be regarded as providing insight—either directly or indirectly—for Balinese culture as a whole (Stephen 2002: 63). However, scholars have tended to treat Balinese Hinduism as a virtually pre-literate religion consisting in village-rituals and ancestor-cults with an uppercrust of universalizing beliefs and ritual practices introduced in the colonial and post-colonial period, after the contact with Semitic religions and Indian (Neo-)Hinduism, thereby imparting a monochrome and ahistorical characterization of it.

Making use of textual and historical data that have so far been neglected by both anthropologists and scholars of Old Javanese, I have made a case for the existence of a trans-local, and text-based, shared tradition of theology and philosophy in the (Javano-)Balinese world. This tradition constitutes the link connecting modern Balinese Hinduism with its pre-modern Śaiva formative phase in Java. Building on the compelling arguments advanced by text-savvy anthropologist Michele Stephen in her groundbreaking monograph Desire, Divine and Demonic (2005), I have presented textual evidence supporting the claim that the cultural exchanges with South Asia that started at the beginning of the Common Era led to the existence on Bali of a sophisticated theological tradition predating twentieth-century reformism. The existence of a dialectic relationship between the modern and contemporary religious discourse and the past tradition is suggested by the great number of translations into modern Indonesian of Sanskrit religious texts published on Bali since the advent of printing, and by the even greater number of publications on Hinduism written in modern Balinese and Malay-Indonesian. The same dialectic is documented in the cultural events during which Old Javanese sources are either (re)interpreted, (re)enacted and commented upon in Balinese, or 'performed' in a variety of manners.

My starting point is the assumption that the use of data drawn from pre-modern Śaiva sources from both the Indonesian Archipelago and South Asia is indispensable for a better understanding of the more recent religious discourse on Bali, where reformist groups have attempted to adopt (and adapt) the canon of neo-Hinduism as a constitutive part of modern Balinese Hinduism. I argue that the Javano-Balinese religious discourse is characterized by a remarkable continuity with the earlier tradition, especially when it comes to its exegetical and text-building practices, but also by important elements of change. To appraise the nature of such changes, single them out, and explain them in the light of their context-specific historical, literary, and theologico-philosophical background remain scholarly desiderata. If we are to understand the (trans)formation of the religious discourse on Bali, it is imperative to use data drawn from pre-modern textual sources, and contrast them with the newly imported beliefs from various neo-Hindu trends; to determine the textual strata within the available corpus through text-historical research; and to investigate how the Balinese have (re)interpreted and reconfigured their own textual tradition at different historical junctures to the present.

In what follows, my analysis mainly focuses on the treatment of doctrine and yoga featuring in selected texts belonging to the pre-modern body of Javano-Balinese Tattva literature (*Dharma Pātañjala*, *Tattvajñāna* and *Vṛhaspatitattva*) and in textbooks of Balinese Hinduism published in the twentieth century (*Aji Sangkya* by Ida Ketut Jelantik and *Rsi Yadnya Sankya dan Yoga* by Shri Rsi Anandakusuma). My comparison shows that independent, yet related, Javano-Balinese cultural products were shaped by analogous historical conditions and epistemic paradigms.

Pre-modern Tattvas: Dharma Pātañjala, Vṛhaspatitattva, Tattvajñāna

On the basis of intertexual and comparative analysis, I have argued (Acri 2011a: 152, 2011b: 8–11, 2013: 71–72) that within the wider corpus collectively referred to as Tutur a distinct subclass (or subgenre) of speculative and systematic scriptures can be distinguished, namely Tattvas. The three pre-modern Old Javanese sources discussed here belong to the corpus of Śaiva Tattvas. It is difficult to ascertain the date of composition of both Tuturs and Tattvas, which may have spanned from the eighth to the fifteenth century AD. Be this as it may, Tattvas, on account of their intrinsic textual and doctrinal features, are likely to form a relatively early stratum of the corpus, based on/compiled after sources (in either Old Javanese and/or Sanskrit) pre-dating the tenth/eleventh century. While an 'early core' of Tuturs may have been composed in the same period, the majority of them are clearly late compilations post-dating the fifteenth century, and continuing well into the modern period on Bali.

Tattvas can be distinguished from Tuturs on account of their peculiarities of style, textual features, and contents. Tuturs are usually (and explicitly) esoteric, often unsystematic, oriented towards mantric and yogic practice, and mystically minded; further, they display a higher degree of localization. On the other hand, Tattvas reveal Śaiva doctrines and philosophical, epistemological, and ontological matters in a systematic and coherent manner, and share a core of fundamental tenets through the corpus. Like the early Tuturs, but to a much greater extent, Tattvas show a lesser degree of localization, and indeed appear to have inherited their main doctrinal elements directly from the pan-South Asian early Śaiva Saiddhāntika literature in Sanskrit (circa sixth–tenth century AD), which may be regarded as the scriptural canon through which Śaivism was transmitted to the Indonesian Archipelago in the pre-modern period (see Acri 2006).

The most representative text of the Tattva genre is the *Dharma Pātañjala*, written in Old Javanese prose interspersed with a handful of Sanskrit verses. It has come down to us in a single fifteenth-century *gebang* palm-leaf manuscript of West Javanese provenance, but allegedly found in the Central Javanese Merapi-Merbabu collection and now kept in the Berlin Staatsbibliothek.[3] It has not been handed down in Bali.

The *Dharma Pātañjala*, arranged in the form of a dialogue between the Lord and his son Kumāra, is remarkable in that it provides what is as yet the most complete, coherent and detailed exposition of Śaiva doctrine to be found in an Old Javanese text. It also constitutes the unique testimony for the existence of (theoretical knowledge of) the yoga of Patañjali in Java. Nearly a third of it is based on parts of the Sanskrit *Yogasūtra* and a commentary that is closely related, albeit by no means identical, to the one, popularly referred to as *Bhāṣya*, embedding the *Yogasūtra*. The *Dharma Pātañjala* appears to be the work of a single author or mastermind, who carried out a conscious operation of doctrinal innovation insofar that he tried to intelligently incorporate Pātañjala yoga into a predominantly Śaiva theological framework.

The *Vṛhaspatitattva* consists of seventy-three Sanskrit verses provided with an Old Javanese exegesis. It opens with a rather long prose introduction. Judging from the significant number of extant palm-leaf manuscripts containing copies of the text, the *Vṛhaspatitattva* held a prominent and authoritative position in Bali, where it has remained popular until today. Come down to us in single the primary prototypical source of many twentieth-century Balinese textbooks of Hinduism, the *Vṛhaspatitattva* has been translated into English by Sudarshana Devi (1957, along with a critical edition) and into modern Indonesian by Mirsha (1995).

The *Vṛhaspatitattva* is a composite and complex text integrating materials belonging to various Sanskritic doctrinal traditions, such as Pāśupata Śaivism and Sāṅkhya, within a Śaiva Saiddhāntika framework.[4] The Sanskrit–Old Javanese translation dyads 53–59 features a detailed descrip-

---

[3] Gunawan (2015) has convincingly argued that the manuscripts that have been hitherto described as Nipahs (*Nypa fructicans*) were called by the pre-modern indigenous sources *gebang*, which corresponds to a different writing support (*corypa gebanga* or *corypa utan*).

[4] See Nihom 1995 (on the Sāṅkhya and Pāśupata parallels) and Acri 2006, 2011d (on the early Śaiva Saiddhāntika parallels).

tion of the variety of (non-Pātañjala) Śaiva yoga that became paradigmatic in Javano-Balinese Tuturs.

The *Tattvajñāna* is composed entirely in Old Javanese prose; unlike the other two Tattvas discussed here, it is not arranged in the form of a dialogue but expounds its arguments in the form of a lesson given by an anonymous teacher. This scripture is remarkable in the Tattva and Tutur genres insofar that it has been preserved not only in Balinese manuscripts, but also in two complete palm-leaf manuscripts (*lontar*) from the Central Javanese collection of Merapi-Merbabu (now at the National Library of Indonesia in Jakarta) and the (East Javanese?) Mackenzie collection (now at the British Library in London), as well as in a short fragment of palm-leaf manuscript (*gebang*) from the West Javanese collection of Ciburuy (Acri 2000b). The text was edited on the basis of the Balinese manuscripts, and translated into Hindi, by Sudarshana Devi (-Singhal) at the International Academy of Indian Culture (1962). Besides being characterized by a less sophisticated argumentative style, the *Tattvajñāna* features a more localised approach to religious experience, as it mixes the speculative themes found in the *Dharma Pātañjala* and *Vṛhaspatitattva* with the kind of esoteric and mystical themes thriving in Tuturs, thereby constituting a 'link' between the two genres.

Textbooks and Pamphlets of Hinduism: Aji Sangkya and Rsi Yadnya Sankya Dan Yoga

Numerous mimeographed pamphlets and printed booklets, written in either Balinese or Malay-Indonesian, sprang up on Bali soon after the introduction of modern stencilling and printing techniques in the early twentieth century. These publications, aiming at those Balinese—the majority—who could not read the scriptures in their original languages and scripts, quickly superseded, yet never entirely replaced, *lontar* as the favourite medium of dissemination of the religious lore on the island (Hooykaas 1963). The main reason to study such literature is that it documents a crucial phase in the (re)formation of what is now called Agama Hindu Bali, during which the Balinese intellectuals and religious leaders were intent upon (re)creating a textual canon that, through the incorporation of elements of Indian Hinduism, would have sanctioned recognition of Balinese religion as a fully fledged, and pan-Indonesian, world religion.

The *Aji Sangkya* ('Textbook of the Sāṅkhya Philosophy', Jelantik 1947) is a short theologico-philosophical treatise (fifty-seven pages), composed in Balinese by the intellectual Ida Ketut Jelantik (d. 1961) of Banjar, Singaraja. First published, as a mimeographed pamphlet, in 1947, the work circulated in Bali through a number of printed editions, the last dating from 1979, as well as in *lontar* manuscripts. Not long after the publication of the original work, a Dutch translation by Hooykaas (1951) appeared as 'Çāngkhya-leer van Bali' in the *Tijdschrift voor Indische Taal-, Land- en Volkenkunde*. The *Aji Sangkya* was subsequently rediscovered among the *lontar* of the late Jelantik's library in 1972 by Gede Sandhi, who translated it into modern Indonesian and republished it. As far as I know, the only subsequent reprint of the work appeared in 2012, published by Paramita Press (Surabaya and Denpasar).

In the foreword to his work, Jelantik explains that he wished to produce a small booklet describing the Śaiva religion (*Igama Siwa*) in low-level Balinese (*bahasa Bali kapara*) and not in the Old Javanese and Sanskrit used in the available body of sacred texts, in order that his work be read and understood by a larger public. The author declares that he has taken as his basis a body of foundational sacred texts preserved in *lontar* manuscripts, which he chose according to their contents, and which he thought to be more important for the edification of his readers. The listed sources are the following (spelling standardized): *Bhuvanakośa*, *Vṛhaspatitattva*, *Tattvajñāna*, *Brahmāṇḍapurāṇa*, *Pañcaviṁśatitattva*, *Buku Yogasūtra*, *Nirmalajñāna* (otherwise known as *Navaruci*), *Saṅ Hyaṅ Daśa Ātmā*, *Sārasamuccaya*, lontar *Samādhi*, *Catur Yuga Vidhi Śāstra*, *Sapta Bhuvana*.

While the *Aji Sangkya* constitutes a synthesis and restyling of materials drawn from Sanskrit–Old Javanese sources, it displays unmistakable traces of originality. Jelantik, himself a proficient theologian and eclectic intellectual, should not be regarded as a mere synthesizer and systematizer but rather as an author in his own right, aiming at implementing a well-defined doctrinal and moralistic agenda. To study his treatise is therefore interesting in order to establish where the boundaries between originality and adherence to a canon lie in the Javano-Balinese tradition.

Jelantik's main intention is to describe the characteristics of Ida Sang Hyang Widhi, who created the world and everything living there, especially human beings; and to characterize the basic dichotomy described in Tattvas, namely between the metaphysical principles of Sentience (*cetana*) and Insentience (*acetana*), which accounts for the entire creation. This dichotomy reflects the one espoused by the Sāṅkhya school of Indian philosophy, which names the two principles Spirit (*puruṣa*) and Nature (*prakṛti*). The treatise unfolds through ten chapters, each dedicated to a particular (set of) constitutive principle(s) of the universe (*tattva*), beginning from the uppermost, that is the Lord in His various aspects (*paramaśivatattva, sadāśivatattva, śivatattva*), the Soul, the lower twenty-five *tattva* of Sāṅkhya from Spirit down to the five gross elements, and Man. Besides dealing with ontology, Jelantik provides his readers with directions to the worship of God and the practice of yoga.

The *Aji Sangkya* has been appraised by various Balinese authors as a document of great importance for the study of Balinese religion (Dharma Palguna 2009). Hooykaas (1951: 434–435) regarded it as groundbreaking since it benefited from the advantages of printing technology, which enabled the work to have a far-reaching impact among the common Balinese. Hooykaas further remarked that, unlike contemporary manuscripts, the *Aji Sangkya* was reproduced free of copying mistakes, therefore any mistakes in the exposition could be attributed to the author himself rather than to sloppy anonymous copyists. More importantly, Jelantik may be regarded to be among the first Balinese reformers to have looked at India as the cradle of Hinduism (see Bakker 1993: 302).

Another theologico-philosophical treatise is the *Rsi Yadnya Sankya dan Yoga* (sixty-eight pages), written in Bahasa Indonesia and published in Klungkung in the early 1970s (Anandakusuma 1973). The author, Shri Rsi Anandakusuma (for the record Gusti Ngoerah Sidemen, 1912–1992), was a polymath with ninety books to his name (Bakker 1993: 335–339). He was a respected religious personality of the reform movement. Bearing the prestigious title of Rsi ('seer'), he served as the head of the Satya Hindu Dharma Pusat from 1959 to his death. In an interview he gave in 1989, Anandakusuma stated that through his work he wished to spread 'true Hinduism' among the Balinese so that they would gain 'greater knowledge of the philosophical background and more emphasis on the mystical side of the religion'. He was influenced by Hindu philosophers and religious leaders such as Swami Vivekānanda (1863–1902), Swami Śivānanda (1887–1963) and Sarvepalli Radhakrishnan (1888–1975).

Like his predecessor Jelantik, Anandakusuma composed his textbook by making use of existing sources, which he listed in a bibliography; these are, following the original order, *Rsi Shasana*, *Wrehaspati Tattwa*, *Swatika Sutra* (*sic*, read *Swastika Sutra*) by Anandakusuma himself and *Kundalini Yoga* by Swami Śivānanda. His treatise is divided into three parts, entitled respectively *Rsi Yadnya*, *Sankya* and *Yoga*. Part I, *Rsi Yadnya*, forms an extended introduction in which the author explains the background and aims of his literary and edifying endeavour. He embarks on a semantic analysis of the words *guru* and *sattwam*; declares that in the Veda the Lord (*tuhan yang maha esa*) is Sat-Chit-Ananda; explains the prerogatives of a

Rsi or Bhagawan; narrates the story of the Rsi Wyasa; lists the moral duties of human beings; defines the supreme principle of Brahman as Atman Aikyam ('one with the Self'); and describes the characteristics of an Acharya or Wiku.

Part II, *Sankya*, starts with introductory remarks about the meaning of Sāṅkya philosophy and its sharing the same aim (*mempunyai satu tujuan*) with yoga. Anandakusuma's declared aim is to improve spirituality (*kerokhanian, kejiwaan*), which is a part of philosophy (*tattwa*), by clarifying or disentangling (*menguraikan*) the teaching of the Lord (*Ishwara*), so that that after death one may become one with Him. He then very briefly introduces the frame story of Ishwara teaching the gods on the peak of the Kelasa, who are joined by Wrehaspati. From this point onwards, the text closely follows the *Vrhaspatitattva*, except for a few additions as well as doctrinal divergences, most notably the description of Pātañjala yoga in part III (*Yoga*). Although Anandakusuma is likely to have been familiar with Jelantik's *Aji Sangkya*, his *Rsi Yadnya Sankya dan Yoga* does not bear any specific influence traceable to the latter work and must therefore be regarded as a largely independent endeavour in the panorama of Balinese reformism.

The Javano-Balinese Tutur/Tattva Corpus as the Scriptural Basis of Pre-modern Śaivism and Modern Hinduism on Bali

In my comparative investigation of the sources summarized above, I suggested (Acri 2011a, 2013) that modern Balinese Hindu writers appropriated and restated the main doctrinal items found in the pre-existing scriptural corpus of Old Javanese Śaiva texts, which therefore ought to be regarded as constituting the basis of an Indic-inspired, (Javano-)Balinese Śaiva theology. Their pamphlets and manuals of Hinduism were considered normative, and indeed their doctrines found their way to the curricular textbooks used in Balinese schools.

Annette Hornbacher (2014: 321), discussing the fascinating subject of 'orthographic mysticism' as a medium of esoteric speculation and ritual efficacy on Bali, admits the usefulness of philological research on Tuturs, yet at the same time advances a critique of my view that Old Javano-Balinese Śaiva texts have the same character, and thus have to be treated in the same way, as canonical scriptures—that is, as the basis of religious orthodoxy. She claims that my thesis not only ignores the specifically

Balinese orthographic practices, but also the internal relationship between esoteric orthographic theory and related ritual practices, as well as the local understandings of ritually effective orthography. Hornbacher (ibid.: 334) contends that Tuturs convey a mystical theory of written characters that is not the expression of canonical doctrine, but which unfolds—as a mystical manifestation of God in the world, embodying the presence of divine power—ritual significance and efficacy. Further, she regards as anachronistic and 'politically questionable' my thesis that the Indonesian religious policy, with its pressure to reach the status of a canonical monotheistic 'Religion of the Book', is linked to a much older and genuine Balinese scriptural religion.

Frankly speaking, I fail to see how my thesis could be anachronistic and politically questionable. In fact, the contrary can be said to be true: my thesis actually rehabilitates the Balinese tradition, showing that it is not derived uniquely from the encounter with Abrahamic religions and the pressures of the newly constituted Indonesian state, but represents an orthogenetic development stemming from a pre-existing Śaiva religious discourse and its normative textual canon. Furthermore, I should like to point out that at the basis of Hornbacher's critique there seems to lay a fundamental misunderstanding of my thesis; that is, a failure on her part to distinguish the Tutur from the Tattva genres. For my part, I have argued that within the vast and heterogeneous Tutur corpus there lies an 'inner core' of (early) normative texts—the Tattvas—whose nature is mainly speculative and systematic.[5] It is these texts that inform the basic doctrinal framework of many (later) Tuturs, as well as of modern pamphlets of Hinduism, and therefore may be considered canonical (for a lack of a better term). Furthermore, Hornbacher uses the general term 'Tutur' as if it only referred to the subclass of texts dealing with the theory and practice of the phenomenon of orthographic mysticism, which however forms just a fraction of a much larger and variegated corpus. In my opinion, this phenomenon has little if any relevance to the issues of canonicity and religious orthodoxy. Unlike those Tuturs that treat the topics of orthographic mysticism and ritual (such as the *Aji Saraswati*, the *Tutur Svara Vyañjana*, etc.),[6] which are indeed practice-oriented and may still be employed in certain Balinese ritual contexts, Tattvas do not directly play a significant role in the ritual

---

[5] See Acri 2011a: 152, 2013: 71–72.
[6] On which see Rubinstein 2000 and, for an overview of this phenomenon and a description of its South Asian prototypes, Acri forthcoming.

contexts mentioned by Hornbacher. The onus remains on ethnographers to describe the contemporary Balinese practices in which texts, in both their intellectual/intangible and material dimensions, are used as constitutive elements.

Hornbacher claims that, in spite of substantial parallels with Sanskrit original texts, Tuturs (Tattvas?) have to be understood on the basis of their culturally specific integration into a ritual practice that is realized only performatively and orally in the teacher–student relationship and their foregrounding in a local form of knowledge. Although there is certainly a lot truth in her claim, Hornbacher does not produce much concrete evidence besides references to the well-known Balinese beliefs in, and representations around, the supernatural power of these texts: their use in a context of initiation or magical practice (including sorcery), the warnings against their purely intellectual use, and what may be defined as a 'cult of the book-manuscript'. In fact, my personal experience is that Tattvas on Bali are also *read* and *discussed*, in both restricted/religious and public/secular contexts, as *books*, that is, as media of philosophical and doctrinal truths ('*tattva*'), which inform many aspects of the Balinese complex ritual edifice insofar that they constitute its ultimate theological and ontological foundations. It is from the Tattvas that the pamphlets and textbooks of modern Balinese Hinduism draw upon. This context hardly constitutes a form of performative/oral teacher-student relationship, and should rather be studied in the framework of modern institutionalized religious education. In spite of this attempt to 'democratize' the religious knowledge through the school curriculum, the doctrinal foundations contained in Tattvas are traditionally considered to be the preserve of the highest ritual and religious authorities—the Śaiva Pedandas—and not of the many other categories of lower-status ritual agents and practitioners mentioned by Hornbacher—like Pemangkus, Balian, Leyak, and so on. Those categories are indeed associated with different texts: certain Tuturs, Warigas and ritual manuals dealing with, for example, magic, astrology, medicine and yoga. I basically agree with Hornbacher that the main purpose of many of those texts is—at least nowadays—not to convey theory that can be understood, believed or criticized purely intellectually, but to manifest knowledge as a transformative power to be realized performatively (ibid.: 317). Those texts, however, are a far cry—both linguistically, stylistically and in terms of content—from the 'śāstric' register and theoretical contents of Tattvas, where we find few if any references to ritual practices.

Clearly, Hornbacher's research is extremely valuable since as it explores the intriguing, chronically understudied and no doubt crucial relationship between texts and ritual practices on Bali. I think, however, that a more careful reading of the sources,[7] detailed ethnographic descriptions of the actual rituals and 'body-techniques' linked to Tuturs,[8] and a comparative investigation, from a synchronic and diachronic perspective, of the relationship between these Balinese texts and practices and prototypical texts and practices in the Indian subcontinent are in order before any claims can be made about the nature of these phenomena, let alone about their cultural specificity.

Contrarily to the received view that Balinese religion lacks a proper theological and speculative tradition, let alone a body of sacred canonical scriptures carrying the foundation of its 'orthodoxy', I reiterate the points that (1) the reformed 'rationalized theology' and (allegedly) ensuing 'scripturalization' of Balinese religion is no new (and derivative) phenomenon, but has its root in the sophisticated Old Javano-Balinese corpus of speculative Śaiva scriptures; (2) the 'Tattva' corpus was not an uniquely local, embedded and place- and person-specific Balinese product, but partook of a complex trans-local cultural phenomenon that flourished along the networks of intra-Asian contacts within the geographical and cultural entity called by Pollock (1996, 2006) 'Sanskrit Cosmopolis'; (3) Tattvas present a shared 'minimum common denominator' of Śaiva (monotheistic) theology, which constituted the basis for what we may call an 'orthodoxy' of religion; and, (4) Tattvas share a similar agenda of 'translation' of Sanskrit doctrinal elements into a local linguistic and intellectual framework, displaying a similar degree of faithfulness to the common and prototypical Sanskrit canon—the corpus of South Asian Siddhāntatantras.[9]

---

[7] Hornbacher (2014: 332, fn. 25), referring to Acri 2011a and 2013 (the latter article does not, however, appear in her bibliography), claims that all the names, designations and personifications of the highest form of Śiva as the Absolute (such as Saṅ Hyaṅ Tuṅigal, Saṅ Hyaṅ Nora, etc.) that are found in Tuturs get completely out of sight if one accepts the fact of monism and his sporadic connection with Śiva as a sufficient reason to interpret Tuturs overall as expression of an Indian Śivaite system. This statement over-simplifies the matter; elsewhere (Acri 2011d: 549). I have pointed out that the proliferation of names of God in His various aspects that are rarely found, or altogether unattested, in the Śiva Sanskrit literature from South Asia is a distinctive feature of apparently late, more 'localised' Tuturs, but not of Tattva, which follow Sanskrit prototypes more closely.

[8] Detailed accounts of the death-ritual and the internalized yoga-praxis informed by orthographic mysticism have been published by Stephen (2010, 2014, respectively).

[9] On this corpus of texts, mainly formed by mildly Tantric, dualist scriptures, see Goodall (2004: xii–lvii).

It is important to stress that the Balinese reformers themselves, including Jelantik and Anandakusuma, never claimed to add anything new to their religion but only to find its 'true' meaning, which was 'hidden' in the body of Old Javanese scriptures. In fact, both Tattvas and Tuturs constituted, to a great extent, the very object of debate among the various factions of the Balinese intelligentsia who sought to reform their religion: the *Vṛhaspatitattva* and *Tattvajñāna* are listed among the sources used by Jelantik in his *Aji Sangkya*; the *Vṛhaspatitattva*, which is in all respects the most systematic and speculation-oriented treatise to have survived on Bali, constituted the main prototypical source for both Jelantik and Anandakusuma,[10] among other authors. It is those texts that, supplemented with Indonesian translation, have been published again and again on the island since the early twentieth century; it is those texts that find a widespread diffusion in the form of palm-leaf manuscripts in several Brahmanical *griya*s on Bali. It seems thus hardly deniable that those texts formed a sort of canon, to which those in search of Balinese 'Śaiva orthodoxy' must turn.

Indeed the idea of orthodoxy, referred to in Old Javanese as 'true knowledge' (*samyagjñāna*), as opposed to heterodoxy, 'false knowledge' (*mithyājñāna*), is apparently featured in pre-modern Tattvas, such as the *Vṛhaspatitattva* and the *Dharma Pātañjala*. Their exposition is carried out in the form of a debate between the Lord, his divine interlocutor and an adversary (*saṅ para*). The latter, usually a follower of materialist doctrines, is a bearer of a 'false view', as he negates the existence of (1) God; (2) *karma* and its fruits (*karmaphala*); (3) heaven and hell; (4) *mokṣa*; and (5) the *ātman*.[11] These five points can be compared to the so-called *pañcaśraddhā* of orthodox Hinduism, generally acknowledged by scholars to be a recent addition to Balinese Hinduism, where they were supposedly unknown.[12]

---

[10] Anandakusuma in his *Pergolakan Hindu Dharma* (1966) too resorted to the *Vṛhaspatitattva* whenever he sought to explain philosophical and theological concepts. The author's reliance on that Old Javanese text also results from his interview published by Bakker (1993: 62–64).

[11] Cf., e.g., *Vṛhaspatitattva* 2 and 52; similar passages are found throughout the *Dharma Pātañjala*.

[12] Cf. Ramstedt 2004: 14; with regard to *karma* and *mokṣa*, see Bakker 1993: 72–73, and Guermonprez 2001: 278. Howe (2001: 72), by contrast, maintains that 'though ideas about karma can be found in indigenous Balinese texts, the doctrine has not had much influence among ordinary Balinese until relatively recently'. In agreeing with Howe that these ele-

Balinese intellectuals perceived a close relationship between ideas and rituals, and claimed that 'their particular form of Hinduism comprises three closely related components, namely philosophy, ritual, and ethics' (Bakker 1993: 22). Such threefold compartmentalization, which must be considered an indigenous categorization, appears to have already existed in the past, for we find scriptures dealing with different aspects of 'religion' such as theology and philosophy (*tattva*), 'applied' theology and yoga (*tutur*), conduct for religious people (*śāsana*) and ritual (*kalpa*, etc.). This categorization roughly corresponds to the ideal division into four parts: doctrine (*vidyā*), *yoga*, behaviour (*caryā*) and ritual (*kriyā*) that a scripture within the South Asian Sanskrit Śaiva Saiddhāntika tradition must possess in order to be considered complete and authoritative. Although one rarely notes the presence of ritual elements within speculative texts, it is also true that the two aspects, as the Balinese maintain, are closely related.

Conclusion

This chapter has advocated the idea that if we are to do full justice to the intellectual and historical dynamics that have shaped Balinese Hinduism up to the present day we have to study the pre-colonial body of Śaiva literature as well as the modern textbooks of Hinduism, which constitute their natural continuation. In doing so, we need to move beyond a scholarly paradigm focusing uniquely on the context-specific Balinese cultural instances, and realize that Balinese Hinduism was the product of a complex, trans-regional Javano-Balinese discourse having its roots in the South Asian Śaiva tradition (i.e., the wider 'Sanskrit Cosmopolis' and ensuing 'Vernacular Millennium' theorized by Sheldon Pollock). Anthropologists need to engage with these scriptures and their use in Balinese literate high-culture, thereby ceasing to regard the methods appropriate for pre-literate cultures as sufficient to deal with the former (the ongoing research by Michel Picard and Annette Hornbacher on Balinese written sources goes in the right direction). Conversely, philologists need to pay closer attention to Old Javanese and Sanskrit Śaiva scriptures preserved in Balinese lontars, and at the same time explore the way in which texts are received,

ments already existed in the Tattva and Tutur literature, I should like to point out that local proverbs widespread among the Balinese of all social classes and ages seem to refer to the law of *karma pala* in prosaic terms, illustrating situations and images understandable to anybody (cf. Departemen Pendidikan dan Kebudayaan 1984: 6–10, 18–20; etc.).

reproduced and performed in contexts that are not the preserve only of the elites. This will pave the way for an investigation of the multifarious dimensions of 'specialized' knowledge and its entanglement in 'non-specialized', or lay, milieux. Indeed, in Bali it is often difficult to neatly separate the prescriptive and theoretical dimension of texts from the everyday practice as lay actors in the domains of ritual, belief, folklore, performance, and visual arts all have interiorized elements from the textual tradition of the elites. Such levels of entanglement inevitably call for a wider, multidisciplinary approach.

With an understanding of the basic—yet deep—concepts that structure and give meaning to Balinese ritual, and which may be found in Balinese texts, the mistaken impression of 'meaninglessness' of Balinese ritual is revealed. Similarly, with knowledge of Tantric Śaiva literature in Sanskrit, Balinese texts cease to appear 'disperse tantric fragments' and 'place-and-person-specific knowledge', becoming localized manifestations of a wider Sanskritic cosmopolitan phenomenon.

References

Acri, A. 2006. 'The Sanskrit-Old Javanese Tutur Literature from Bali. The Textual Basis of Śaivism in Ancient Indonesia'. *Rivista di Studi Sudasiatici* 1: 105–135.

Acri, A. 2011a. 'A new perspective for "Balinese Hinduism" in the light of the pre-modern religious discourse; A textual-historical approach'. In: M. Picard and R. Madinier (eds). *The Politics of Religion in Java and Bali; Syncretism, Orthodoxy, and Religious Contention*, pp. 143–167. London/New York: Routledge.

Acri, A. 2011b. *Dharma Pātañjala; A Śaiva Scripture from Ancient Java Studied in the Light of Related Old Javanese and Sanskrit Texts*. Groningen: Egbert Forsten Publishing.

Acri, A. 2011c. 'Javanese manuscripts of the *Tattvajñāna*', in M. Gupta (ed) *From Beyond the Eastern Horizon; Essays in honour of Professor Lokesh Chandra*, pp. 119–129. New Delhi: Aditya Prakashan.

Acri, A. 2011d. 'Glimpses of early Śaiva Siddhānta; Echoes of doctrines ascribed to Bṛhaspati in the Sanskrit-Old Javanese *Vṛhaspatitattva*', *Indo-Iranian Journal* 54: 209–229.

Acri, A. 2011e. 'Re-configuration of Divinity in Old Javanese Śaiva texts from the Indonesian Archipelago (with special reference to *Jñānasiddhānta*, chapter 19)', *Travaux de Symposium International: Le Livre. La Roumanie. L'Europe. Troisième édition, Tome III*, pp. 546–565. Bucarest: Éd. Bibliothèque de Bucarest.

Acri, A. 2013. 'Modern Hindu Intellectuals and Ancient Texts: Reforming Śaiva Yoga in Bali', *Bijdragen tot de Taal-, land- en Volkenkunde* 169/1: 1–36.
Acri, A. 2014a. 'Text and Reality in the Study of Balinese Hinduism', *Journal of Hindu Studies* 7/2: 137–145.
Acri, A. 2014b. 'Pañcakuśika and Kanda Mpat. From a Pāśupata Śaiva Myth to Balinese Folklore', *Journal of Hindu Studies* 7/2: 146–178.
Acri, A. 2016. 'Imposition of the Syllabary (*mātṛkā/svaravyañjana-nyāsa*) in the Javano-Balinese Tradition in the light of South Asian Tantric Sources', in A. Hornbacher and R. Fox (eds), *Balinese letters: Materiality, Efficacy and Scriptural Practices*, pp. 123–165. Leiden/Boston: Brill.
Anandakusuma, Sri Reshi. 1966. *Pergolakan Hindu Dharma*. Denpasar: Balimas [two volumes.]
Anandakusuma, Sri Reshi. 1973. *Rsi yadnya Sankya dan Yoga*. Singaraja: Toko Buku Indra Jaya.
Bakker, F. 1993. *The Struggle of the Hindu Balinese Intellectuals; Developments in Modern Hindu Thinking in Independent Indonesia*. Amsterdam: VU University Press.
Barth, F. 1993. *Balinese Worlds*. Chicago: University of Chicago Press.
Boon, J. 1990. *Affinities and Extremes; Crisscrossing the Bittersweet Ethnology of East Indies History, Hindu-Balinese Culture, and Indo-European Allure*. Chicago and London: University of Chicago Press.
Departemen Pendidikan dan Kebudayaan. 1984. *Ungkapan tradisional sebagai sumber informasi kebudayaan daerah Bali*. Jakarta: Departemen Pendidikan dan Kebudayaan, Proyek inventarisasi dan dokumentasi kebudayaan daerah.
Dharma Palguna, I.B.M. 2009. 'Aji Sangkhya dan Ida Ketut Jelantik; Sumber Ilham dan Masalah Intertekstualitas', *Bali Post, Apresiasi* (Sunday 28 Juni 2009).
Geertz, C. 1973. 'Internal conversion" in Contemporary Bali', in *The Interpretation of Cultures*, pp. 170–189. New York: Basic Books inc. Publishers.
Goodall, D. 2004. *The Parākhyatantra; A Scripture of the Śaiva Siddhānta; A Critical Edition and Annotated Translation*. Pondichéry: IFP/EFEO.
Guermonprez, J.F. 2001. 'La religion balinaise dans le miroir de l'hindouisme'. *Bulletin de l'École Française d'Extrême Orient* 88: 271–293.
Gunawan, Aditya. 2015. 'Nipah or Gebang? A Philological and Codicological Study based on Sources from West Java', *Bijdragen tot de Taal-, Land- en Volkenkunde* 171: 249–280.
Hooykaas, C. 1951. 'Sangkhya-leer van Bali (1947)', *Tijdschrift voor Indische Taal-, land- en Volkenkunde* 84: 434–484.
Hooykaas, C. 1963. 'Books made in Bali', *Bijdragen tot de Taal-, Land- en Volkenkunde* 119: 371–386.
Hornbacher, A. 2014. 'Machtvolle Zeichen: Schrift als Medium esoterischer Spekulation, rituellen Wirkung und religiöser Kanonisierung in Bali', in Joachim

Friedrich Quack and Daniela Christina Luft (eds), *Erscheinungsformen und Handhabungen Heiliger Schriften*, pp. 311–336. Berlin: De Gruyter.

Howe, L. 2001. *Hinduism and Hierarchy in Bali*. Oxford: James Currey/Santa Fe, School of American Research Press.

Howell, J.D. 1978. 'Modernizing Religious Reform and the Far Eastern Religions in Twentieth Century Indonesia', in S. Udin (ed) *Spectrum; Essays Presented to Sutan Takdir Alisjahbana on his Seventieth Birthday*, pp. 260–276. Jakarta: Dian Rakyat.

Jelantik, Ida Ketoet. 1947. *Adji Sangkya*. Banjar.

Mirsha, I Gusti Ngurah Rai. 1995. *Wrhaspati tattwa; Kajian teks dan terjemahannya*. Denpasar: Upada Sastra.

Nihom, M. 1995. 'Sāṅkhya and Pāśupata Reflexes in the Indo-Javanese Vṛhaspatitattva', *Wiener Zeitschri für die Kunde Südasiens* 39: 203–220.

Picard, M. 1997. 'Cultural Tourism, nation-Building, and Regional Culture; The Making of a Balinese Identity', in M. Picard and E. Wood (eds), *Tourism, ethnicity, and the state in Asian and Pacific societies*, pp. 181–214. Honolulu: University of Hawai'i Press.

Picard, M. 1999. 'The Discourse of Kebalian; Transcultural Constructions of Balinese Identity', in R. Rubinstein and L.H. Connor (eds) *Staying local in the global village: Bali in the twentieth century*, pp. 15–49. Honolulu: University of Hawai'i Press.

Pollock, S. 1996. 'The Sanskrit Cosmopolis, 300–1300 CE: Transculturation, Vernacularization, and the Question of Ideology', in J.E.M. Houben (ed) *Ideology and Status of Sanskrit; Contributions to the History of the Sanskrit Language*, pp. 197–247. Leiden, New York and Köln: Brill.

Pollock, S. 2006. *The Language of the Gods in the World of Men: Sanskrit, Culture and Power in Premodern India*. Chicago: University of Chicago press.

Ramstedt, M. 2004. 'Introduction. Negotiating identities—Indonesian "Hindus" between local, national, and global interests', in M. Ramstedt (ed.), *Hinduism in modern Indonesia: a minority religion between local, national, and global interests*, pp. 1–34. London and New York: RoutledgeCurzon.

Rubinstein, R. 2000. *Beyond the realm of the senses; The Balinese ritual of kekawin composition*. Leiden: KITLV Press.

Soebadio, H. 1971. *Jñānasiddhānta. Secret Lore of the Balinese Śaiva Priest*. The Hague: M. Nijhoff.

Staal, F. 1995. *Mantras between fire and water; Reflections on a Balinese rite*. Amsterdam: North-Holland Publishing.

Stephen, M. 2002. 'Returning to original form; A central dynamic in Balinese ritual', *Bijdragen tot de Taal-, Land- en Volkenkunde* 158: 61–94.

Stephen, M. 2005. *Desire, Divine and Demonic; Balinese mysticism in the paintings of I Ketut Budiana and I Gusti Mirdiana*. Honolulu: University of Hawai'i Press.

Stephen, M. 2010. 'The yogic art of dying: Kuṇḍalinī Yoga and the Balinese *pitra yadnya*', *Bijdragen tot de Taal-, Land- en Volkenkunde* 166: 426–474.
Stephen, M. 2014. 'The Dasaksara and Yoga in Bali', *Journal of Hindu Studies* 7/2: 179–216.
Sudarshana, Devi (-Singhal). 1957. *Wṛhaspati-tattwa; An Old Javanese philosophical text*. Nagpur: International Academy of Indian Culture.
Sudarshana, Devi. 1962. *Tattvajñāna and Mahājñāna*. New Delhi: International Academy of Indian Culture.

CHAPTER 9

Power, Prestige and Possession: Interwoven Legacies of Ida Pedanda Istris 'Priestesses' in Balinese Hinduism

Madhu Khanna

INTRODUCTION

This chapter is a spin-off from my constructive engagement with an ongoing research project on life and religious roles of Ida Pedanda Istris, 'Priestesses' in Balinese Hinduism. It is based partly on historical continuities of Hindu culture in Bali, complemented by ethnographic and field explorations that I conducted on the living culture of Ida Pedanda Istris, their power and prestige, and the interwoven legacies in a variety of ritualistic religious practices that are traceable to the Hindu tradition in India.

Bali is an island that has embraced a cosmopolitan modernity in every possible way. At the same time; it has staunchly guarded its ancient religious faith rooted in Vedic tradition and several aspects of Hindu culture. The transmission of Hinduism to Indonesia, though difficult to trace in the early period, was facilitated by maritime trade. Hinduism was imposed

M. Khanna (✉)
National Museum, New Delhi, India

Centre for the Study of Comparative Religion & Civilisations, Jamia Millia Islamia, New Delhi, India

© The Author(s) 2018
S. Saran (ed.), *Cultural and Civilisational Links between India and Southeast Asia*, https://doi.org/10.1007/978-981-10-7317-5_9

151

as a layer over the pre-existing animistic and indigenous religions prevalent at that time. Over the centuries, through a long process of adoption, assimilation and adaptation, Bali evolved a distinct type of worship, cultural patterns, unique modes of religious transactions, all shaped by the living indigenous faiths and the green ecology of the island.

In the early nineteenth century many scholars from the West—among them Geertz, Pritchard, Gonda, Goodriaan, Hooykaas and Pott, to name a few, in their numerous scholarly studies and anthropological discourses were compelled to study and research Javano-Balinese culture. These authors engaged a growing body of core cultural themes and values around Balinese religion, visual and performative arts, ancient history, societal patterns, origin stories of local clans, rituals and belief systems. These authors undoubtedly made an important contribution to the current post-colonial scholarship. In their studies one gains an insight into the many-layered and dense Balinese religion and culture, but surprisingly the subject of Istri Pedanda is conspicuous by its absence, even where the roles of religious specialists assigned to male Brahmins are discussed.[1] What is astounding, in retrospect, is that there is not even a passing mention of the resilient legacy of women Pedandas in Bali, even where priestly functions are outlined. This smacks of a kind of orientalism that assumes the invisibility of women lock stock and barrel, rooted in the assumption that status and power will always rest in a male, hierarchalized order, with no reference to the possibility of the 'dual-sexed' model of a shared powerbase in society. Even a prominent Indologist such as Jan Gonda overlooked the monumental role Ida Pedanda Istris have played in Balinese society. What is attempted in this chapter is to redress this imbalance and to offer a revisioning of perception towards women in the religious processes of Hindu Bali, yet unrecognized but contributing substantially to the archipelago's spiritual and religious life.

Research and exploration into historic cultural narratives and alternative philosophies of life in non-Western cultures is a widely neglected subject and an under-researched area in feminist scholarship.[2] This is so because there has been an outright dismissal of spiritual issues by academic Western philosophy,[3] mainly because the adherents of postmodernism

---

[1] Hooykaas, C. (1974). *Cosmogony and Creation in Balinese Tradition*, pp. 129–161.
[2] Falk, Nancy and Rita M. Gross. (1980). *Unspoken Worlds: Women's Religious Lives in Non-Western Cultures*, pp. VII–XII.
[3] Ahmed, Durre S. (1997). *Women and Religion*, Vol. II, p. VII ff.

mistrust the authenticity of spiritual experience and its theological foundations.[4]

The grand narrative of feminist studies in religion begins from the way in which the single-sexed model of dominance in governance and institutions has subordinated women in all areas of life. In all parts of the world womanhood is generally linked to silences and absences in history. In no other area is sexism in religion more prominently displayed than in the area of the ordination of women. In the early stages of development, women enjoyed an equal status. With the death of the founders, misogynist interpretations of commentators changed the original import of scriptures. All the major scriptures of mainstream religions, whether Hinduism, Islam or Buddhism, have a sexist core that advocates the marginalization and subordination of women. Religious canonical scriptures are often used to justify discrimination against women. In Semitic cultures such as Islam and Christianity, there were strict laws prohibiting women from playing powerful religious roles. Christianity and its conservative denominations opposed the admission of women as priests and bishops. Similarly, in the conventional sects of Islam women cannot lead mixed gender congregations or become imams.

In the case of Hinduism, the storyline is somewhat different. In the Vedic age (2500–1500 BCE), women enjoyed a high status, girls had the right to be educated and also went through ceremonial initiation (*upanayan*) into Vedic studies, common to both boys and girls. Female students were divided into two classes. The *Brahmavādinīs* pursued the study of theology and philosophy, and mastered the art of chanting Vedic hymns, prescribed for daily worship, and were entitled to perform sacrificial rites. The others, known as *Sadyodvāhās*, studied until the age of puberty and then opted out and were given to a suitable groom in marriage.[5] This is borne out by the fact that there were as many as thirty Rishikās, women seeresses, who wrote notable hymns of the Rig Veda. This was an age of unsurpassed opportunity for women: we learn about Viśvavarā (Rig Veda 5.28.1), the priestess of the Ātri family and seeress Apālā, and later Gārgī,[6] who won dialectical arguments in a philosophical tournament. During the age of the Dharmaśāstras (400–700 CE) that cod-

---

[4] For discussion see: Ahmed, Durre S., *Women and Religion Vol. II*, Introduction and *Gendering the Spirit*, Introduction, pp. 1–32.
[5] Altekar, A.S. (1995). *The Position of Women in Hindu Civilization*, pp. 7–16.
[6] Findly, Ellison Banks, "Gargi at the King's Court: Women and Philosophic Innovation in Ancient India", in *Women, Religion and Social Change*, pp. 37–58.

ified the norms, actions and privileges of orthodox Hinduism, the *pativrata* ideal was introduced, stripping a women of her previous choices and freedom to play powerful roles in the religious and theological spheres, in that women were ineligible for Vedic studies. The ceremonial initiation that facilitated her role as a priestess was replaced by the ideal of *vivāha* (marriage). After nearly a thousand years of dominance, counter cultures such as the tradition of Śākta Tantra, a radical sect within Hinduism that flourished in the post-medieval period, in which women could play powerful religious roles, become gurus, initiate disciples and run ashrams.[7]

In India we find that a period of women's liberation was followed by a period of depression. It is not so in Bali, which has enjoyed an unbroken tradition of Istri Pedandas from an early period without any major breaks, a situation that is indeed unique.

The tradition of Istri Pedanda, developed through a process of integration with Hinduism, is represented in the archipelago in purely Balinese terms and has no parallel anywhere else where Hinduism has survived outside India. In the context of this historical reality, I propose to outline some case histories that I recorded during my conversations with many dynamic religious practitioners. The chapter also seeks to explore reasons for the continuity and survival of the tradition: why is it that while the ordination of women is prohibited in other cultures such as in orthodox Hinduism, it has survived in Bali?

Types of Pedanda Istris

The tradition of Ida Pedanda Istri, a class of women priestesses, is ancient and has survived with relatively little interference. In Bali, several grades of priestesses can be distinguished. The most common are the Istri Ida Pedandas who are wives of ritual specialists and priests. My first encounter with one such priestess was with Pedanda Istri Mayun at Dempasar, who lived in a palatial traditional Balinese home with a large compound with four pavilions, each with a shrine. There was a shrine for the presiding deity of the guardian of the compound/land; an ancestor's shrine; a Padma-asana shrine, reserved for the supreme god, Sadā Śiwa; and an open pavilion where ceremonial offerings are placed and the pūjās are performed. She was a wife of a well-known priest and was initiated at the

---

[7]For a discussion see: Khanna, Madhu. (2002). "Goddess Women Equation in Śākta Tantra", in Ahmed, *Gendering the Spirit*, pp. 35–59.

age of fifty-four. After a series of purification rites and ceremonial offerings, she was given a simple mantra of Śiwa. After three years, she underwent another initiation by her husband so that she could pray for people, gods and *bhūtas*. She was asked why she opted out to be a priestess. Born of Brahmin parents, she felt that it was an obligation she owed to society. As a Brahmin lady she needed to fulfil her hereditary obligations. She recalled that 'my life became better, more peaceful, more beautiful, after that'. Ida Pedanda Istri Mayun represents the most general category of priestesses, whose main obligation is to be a helper to a ritual specialist, in this case her husband. Their main work is to act as an assistant to the priests to facilitate rituals (Fig. 9.1).

Pedanda Tāpinī is considered as one of the royal or professional religious leaders or 'offering makers', someone who organizes the endless number of items in an offering, and is aware of the ritual practice and its symbolism and inner meanings. They are supra-managers of rituals in large public temples such as the Pura Besakih temple, Batur. Pedanda Istri Mas was one of the most celebrated Istri Pedanda Tāpinī, who died at the ripe old age of 121. She was a well-respected figure at the Besakih temple, and

Fig. 9.1 Pedanda Istri Mayun with her husband, Denpasar. Source: Author

has now been replaced by Pedanda Istri Karang from Grihya, Gibetan, Karangasen, from eastern Bali. They are highly respected among the spiritual practitioners (Fig. 9.2).

The third kind are known as Ida Pedanda Istri Kania, young women who are identified as possessing a special spiritual power to become fully fledged priestesses. The fourth, a special type, is when a Śūdra, a low caste woman who marries a Brahmin priest, acquires the right to make special offerings (*bantan*) inside the temple. They are called Jero Istri Pedanda. The next, of a higher status, is *Sūtri*, or a female priest (*Pumangko*) of a temple. Then there are the *Balian*, an exclusive group of diviners or those who acquire their power through divine inspiration. The *Balian* is a healer who has mastered the art of trance and spirit-possession. Before 1960 only those from the Brahmin caste could aspire to become a high-level priest or priestesses, but since this time there has been a sea change in attitudes. Owing to the rise of the tourist industry, new opportunities have raised the economic condition of the service sector which has been the preserve of lower castes, resulting in caste mobility that has raised their status in

Fig. 9.2 Ida Pedanda Istri Kania Mas Kajeng in her shrine, Badung. Source: Author

society. A person from a lower caste may now assume the role of a priest or priestess. There is, however, no formal institution or organization for religious teachers. There have been families of Brahmin priests to which Bali–Hindu families of other castes are normally linked as disciples (*sisia*). These families have preserved the oral heritage of spiritual transmissions.

This categorization is not frozen but fluid, as I discovered when I met Ida Ayu Agung Mas. She is a remarkable example of one who shifts her identity between multiple alternate roles. Born into a well-known family of Padandas, her Brahmin origins demand that she should be a priestess, but she opted out to play a public role (Figs. 9.3, 9.4, and 9.5). In 2004, she decided to be a senator and a public figure, a member of the 'representative of provinces' from Sua Bali. She is a politician and activist, and has been fighting for nature rights and local rights for farmers and people in her province. Development tourism has entered the pristine landscapes of Sua Bali and destroyed the environment. She spearheads an alternative tourism movement. She said, 'my political statement was that modern Western tourism will break us apart. We need a different indigenous policy to reduce our tourism. We need to put a current

Fig. 9.3 Senator, Ida Ayu Agung Mas, Sua Bali. Source: Author

Fig. 9.4 Ida Ayu Agung Mas in the ceremonial attire of Pedanda Istri. Source: Author

Fig. 9.5 Pedanda Istri Ida Ayu Agung Mas honouring a young priest with a crown. Source: Author

zoning between alternative indigenous and modern tourism.' Despite her strong convictions about her public involvement in social causes, she has not renounced her role as a priestess.

As a modern Brahmin woman, she offers her personal interpretation and redefinition of Āgama dharma.

I do not know words from Sanskrit, nor do I chant the Gāyatrī mantra. I believe in nature as a creator ... I believe there is a power ... I do not make huge offerings. I offer myself ... Religion plays a major role in Bali but many women may not understand the Gāyatrī Mantra. If they value themselves and have enough self-worth, wherever they may be, they would be [the goddess] Gāyatrī themselves!

Although it is difficult to get an accurate census of the number of Pedandas in Bali, I was informed that the Bandung Regency and surrounding areas alone have as many as 500 Istri Pedandas and five Kanias. The oldest Pedanda is Istri Mas who is 125 years old in Budakalug village, while Istri Sasih is 100 years old and the youngest is in her twenties. On 13 March 2007, a legend was born in Bali. Ida Pedanda Istri, Resi Alit, is the youngest priestess, barely twenty-eight years old. At the age of twenty she suffered depression and was advised to study yoga, whereupon she began to have out-of-body experiences and spontaneous trances. She was ordained by the Hindu Dharma Parishad as the youngest priestess of the Hindu Dharma.

In order to frame the discourse on Balinese priestesses it is necessary to give an overview of the religious ideas and concepts that underlie their lives. The Balinese believe that the religion they practise, Āgama Hindu Dharma (traditionally referred to as Trita, Trimūrti, Āgama Tirta, Śiwa, Buda) is a blend of seven different religious currents: Tantra (Bhairava Tantras found in the old Javanese manuscript tradition); Buddhism; Śaivism; Vaiṣṇavism; the cults of Durgā Śakti and Gaṇapati; and the tribal or the pre-modern indigenous forms of animistic beliefs. Between the ninth and tenth centuries the king of Udayan, Varma Dewa, whose wife Śrī Guṇa Priyā Dharma Patni was the daughter of Dharma Vaṃśa guru from East Java, had three sons. Rishi Kutaran was a prime minister in the court of Varma Dewa. It is believed that Sage Mpu Kuturan laid the foundation for Hinduism in Bali (in the eleventh century) and also introduced the concept of *Trimūrti* (worship of the Hindu Trinity Brahmā, the creator god, Wiṣnu the preserver and Śiwa the transformer (or destroyer). He was an expert in administrative law, religious philosophy and *Vāstuvidyā*. He is said to have laid out the design of the famous Besakih Temple, 'Mother Temple' and Goa Lawah Temple, built around a 'bat cave' in Pesinggahan, Dawan district, in the eleventh century).

Legend holds that during his time the eclecticism that characterized the existent religions was synthesized through interpretative exegesis and mainstreamed into two major traditions, namely Śaiwism and Buddhism. It is quite obvious from the extant ancient texts of Śiwa-Siddhānta in Javanese such as *Bhuvanasaṃkṣepa, Bhūvanakośa* that there was a strong undercurrent of Tantric Sādhanās employing seed syllables (*bījamantras*), mystical diagrams (*yantras*), the ritual of *nyāsas*, infusing the power of the deity on specific parts of the body, and *tantric-yogic kriyās*. While Javanese Śaiwism is greatly indebted to Āgamic forms of Śaiwa and Śākta practices that flourished in India,[8] the Hindu elements in their ritual praxis are integrated and woven in such a skilful way that they acquire a well-defined Balinese imprint.

FIERCELY BALINESE BUT PASSIONATELY HINDU

The transmission of the Hindu faith to Indonesia, though difficult to trace in the early period, was greatly facilitated through the maritime trade that stretched from China to India between the first and the fifth centuries. On the evidence of early archaeological sources; it appears that Tarumanagara was one of the earliest known kingdoms, whose fifth-century ruler Purnawarman was associated with the Hindu god Wisnu (Viṣṇu) and Brahmin priests.[9] Local chiefs were greatly influenced by the Indic style of kingship rooted in the Hindu social system, and regarded the new religion as an asset. This was mainly because the Hindu model of kingship (*rājadharma*) mirrored a divinely sanctioned role for a form of kingship that united fragmented social groups and was more conducive to the continuity of groups. The ruler was often compared to the sun, a solar luminary whose overlordship extended beyond fragmentary social groups. This symbology was in sync with the development of power relations in Indonesia. What gave unity to Bali was its deeply rooted cultural identity based on the Hindu faith. It is noteworthy that behind the war and hardship, and the shifting of the centres of power from the Central Javanese kingdom (732–928 CE) to the east Javanese kingdoms of the Hindu emperor (929–928 CE), of the Majapahits (1293–1500), dominating so much of the history of Indonesia, there thrived a rich and vital cultural

---

[8] Headley, Stephen C. (2000). *Mary Somers, Southeast Asia: A Concise History*, pp. 270–274; Pott, pp. 102–142.

[9] For early history see: Heidhues. (2000). *Mary Somers, Southeast Asia: A Concise History*, p. 45 and 63; Coedes, George and Walter F. Vella (editors). (1968). *The Indianized States of Southeast Asia*. Trans. Susan Brown Cowing.

tradition that was well grounded in its Hindu roots. Hinduism had been virtually wiped out and dethroned when Islam made inroads into Java during the fifteenth–sixteenth centuries through powerful trade networks. Hinduism lost ground, the only exception to this being in Bali. When the ruler of the Majapahit was conquered, he sought refuge in Bali from the conquest of Islamic forces. This set the stage for Indonesia's emergence as the world's largest Muslim nation. The Balinese, on the other hand, resisted Islam, and kept alive their literary and religious heritage. The modern period, extending from the nineteenth to the twentieth century, only strengthened the religious continuities but with some differences. By the 1970s a new Hindu revival, as a 'utopian' movement, began to sweep across the archipelago.[10] The Hindu Religious Council of Indonesia was set up to reform, centralize and redefine Hindu Navya Shastra.

In Bali, Hinduism is a recognized religion in the Indonesian constitution's 'pancashila clause'. Balinese are Hindus who describe their religious lineage as coming down from Hindu Śaivism, but they fiercely defend their Hindu identity by tracing it to the Balinese Śaiwite sect of Hinduism! The form of Hinduism they follow, though rooted in Hindu theology and ritualism, bears their own individualistic signature. The cross-fertilization of pre-existing animistic beliefs and Hindu faith with well-defined archaic folk features, indigenous to their soil, has created a Hinduism on their own terms. There are no monastic or ascetic orders, nor is their religion grounded in forms of yogic meditation. The Balinese form of Hinduism is centred on ritual praxis, dominated by *Caryā* and *Kriyā*,[11] deriving its sanctity from the notions of *Karma* and *Bhakti*. The religious practices are highly ritualistic, ornate and abundant in offerings. While the ideology of Balinese Hinduism is rooted in Hindu theological concepts and the Indian legacy of priesthood, a large number of rituals that form the backbone of their cultural expressions are based in pre-existing indigenous folk beliefs. On even a casual visit to Bali's lush environment, with its beautiful vistas of clouds, palm trees, bamboo groves and terraced rice paddies, one cannot fail to notice that at every home, every shop, supermarket, hotel and even government department there will be a sacred offering made from

---

[10] Acri, Andrea. (2013). "Modern Hindu Intellectuals and Ancient Texts: Reforming Saiwa Yoga in Bali", pp. 68–103, cf. Reuter, Thomas Anton. (2002). *Custodians of the Sacred Mountains: Culture and Society in the Highlands of Bali*, pp. 1–14.

[11] For a collection of a substantial number of hymns and mantras that are used for exoteric worship of deities, see: Goodriaan (1971) and Hooykaas (1974) *Stuti and Stava*.

agricultural products (*bantan*) placed on the threshold, with coconut leaves shaped as a tray holding flowers, incense, coconut, betel nuts, herbs and so on. People pray at least three times a day, morning, noon and night, and on average each family makes as many as fifty daily offerings. In temples Ida Pedandas play a major role in the preparation of ritual and ceremonial offerings. The Hindu religion in Bali is a blend of pre-existing Balinese local indigenous Austronesian culture called *adat*, over-layered with a complex theocentric ritual system of Hindu *saṃsakāras*, daily and seasonal ceremonies framed in the perennial principles of the doctrine of imminence and transcendence and the Advaitic notion of *dharma, mokṣa, saṃsāra, karmaphala* and *punarjanma*.

The five principal Hindu–Dharma beliefs that structure their religious lives are the existence of a supreme divine being called Sang Hyang Widi Wasa; the existence of the eternal soul (*ātman*); retribution (*karma-phala*) and that every deed has a reward; the cycle of reincarnation (*punarbawa*) or rebirth; and the final aim of unity with the Supreme Reality/god (*mokṣa*). Besides these beliefs, the primal substratum of ancestor worship, with traits of pre-modern tribal customs in its treatment of ritual and large-scale social organization that existed before the arrival of Islam, have survived. New-born babies are often taken to the spiritualist to identify which ancestor's soul is in the child.

These beliefs are lived through religious ceremonies day after day and they define the religious roles of a large number of Istri Pedandas. Ritualism and elaborate ceremonies are intrinsic to the Balinese lifestyle and have remained unchanged despite the inroads of modernity. The most important are the five forms of *yadnyas* (Sanskrit yajñas):

1. *Deva Yadnya*: dedicated to the Supreme Being, Sanghyang Widhi Wasa who is also referred to as Acintya.
2. *Reshi Yadnya*: in favour of the Maharṣis, such as Agastya-muni, Markaṇḍeya, Mpu Kutaran, who is regarded as one who simplified rituals in Bali.
3. *Pitṛ Yadnya*: ancestor sacrificial rituals.
4. *Manuṣa Yadnya*: the Hindu sacraments from birth to death along with the indigenous form of the rite of the filing of teeth (*Matata*),

which symbolically empowers individuals to distinguish between what is good and bad.[12]

Pratiṣṭhā-rituals are presided over by the god Viswakarma, the deity who presides over domestic buildings. One of his indigenous manifestations is Rave Angon, who takes care of animals. The deity Tumpek Uduh represents the spirit of nature as manifested in trees, rivers and mountains. He is invoked for showering abundance.

The Balinese observe two diametrically opposed calendars: the Balinese Pawuk of 210 days and the luni-solar Saka calendar. The cyclic order of time dictates the two major festivals: the Galungan every 210 days lasts for ten days, and is about the victory of *Dharma* over *adharma*, with Kuningan performed at the end when the deities are dismissed. In the six-month period a variety of blessings are invoked: there are five Tumpak, thanksgiving ceremonies for expressing gratitude to all material things (*tumpek landep*), plants (*tumpek andang*), for puppets (*tumpek wayang*) and for well-being and flourishing of the world. Apart from this, every six months, they perform Saraswatī-Pūjā, Śiwalatri (*Śiwarātri*), a thanksgiving to Śiwa for amelioration of sins; Paperwasi, to drive away malevolent forces; Sabuh Emas a day for purchasing gold. Besides these there is the customary full moon (*purṇimā*) and 'dark moon' night rituals and Nyepi, the day of complete silence, which announces the commencing of the new year.

It may be noted that the Pedanda Istris are well versed in conducting these rituals. When I questioned why the Balinese perform so many different kinds of rituals, one of them stated that the fractured ego-bound consciousness of each individual needs to be established in the doctrine of Tri Hita Karaṇa, the 'three causes of happiness'. These consist of three forms of harmony between human and god, between humans and fellow beings, and between humans and the entire flora and fauna and biological web of the natural world. The enduring principle of interconnectedness of all creation inspires respect for all life and fosters togetherness. Wherever one is, at home or in the marketplace, these three must be kept in equilibrium and harmony, 'We give back to the gods what we receive from them', she said. This approach to the unending cycle of rituals is based on the belief that one must pay spiritual debts throughout one's life to the pantheon of gods, to one's ancestors and to the entire creation.

---

[12] A ritual digest on *Manuṣa Yadnya* used by female priests was given to me by Istri Kania Mas Kajeng. See bibliography Tapini (2009).

IDA PEDANDA ISTRI KANIA MAS KAJENG

Badung Regency located in the centre of Bali island is divided into 117 traditional villages (*desa adat*) and 522 administrative subvillages (Banjar), with a population density of 794 persons per square kilometre. Most people who live here are Hindus and follow the religious ceremonies and unique traditions that have survived through generations. Ida Istri Kania Mas Kajeng, whom I met, is a leader of over 500 Ida Pedandas Istris who live in Bandung Regency and the surrounding area, and is the head of the society of Pedandas. As a leader, her main task is periodically to hold interactive meetings of all the Istri Pedandas, to perfect the ceremonies, decode the symbolism and complex ritual procedures, collect donations and to advise, guide and inspire the young to follow a religious life. She has in her possession as many as twenty family books, mostly ritual manuals and digests listing the *upcāras* of worship, and manuscripts (*argha patra*) of Śiwa Āgamas. Explaining the need for conducting outer rituals and ceremonies, she observed that the Hindu Dharma cannot change but people change:

> It is Kaliyuga, the dark age. People are becoming more and more evil every day. The ceremonies are made to protect the people from the influence of materialism and to stabilize the universe. There must be a balance between good and evil and amity among diverse people.

In order to be a Istri Pedanda, one has to undergo initiation (*dīkṣā*), which marks entrance into the religious group. The true Brahmin Pedanda Istri status is conferred by a symbolic second birth in the form of an initiation rite. Initiation rituals for becoming a Pedanda are the same for men and women. In the ritual of initiation, the officiates symbolically become *dvi-jāti* and acquire second birth into priesthood. They go through the ritual of Matiraga, to be reborn into priesthood. The ritual consists of a symbolic death and rebirth. First they undergo Majayajaya, which prepares the Pedandas mentally to become priests. They are given a mantra of Śiwa. The second stage consists of giving up the old garments and sleeping in white clothes. After Matiraga, there is a ritual of purification, and the Nabi (guru) prepares them for the role of a priest by giving them a new name, a new garb and by touching the crown of the head with the foot. While Guru Nabi gives the initiation, Guru Vaktra gives the divine mantra. The priestesses have to wear white clothes and tie their hair into a top-knot, which marks and defines their status and identity as a religious specialist. Goodriaan went on to describe her initiation into the order of priestesses:

In order to be a priest one has to leave the life of saṃsāra. My mother (Ida Pedanda Istri Made) and father (Ida Pedanda Ide Rai) were both priest and priestess. It is obligatory that the family has a priest. We are fifty-two persons in all from eight families. My initiation began from a *tritha-yātrā*, pilgrimage to seventy temples which lasted six months. In the formal initiation one must die and be re-born to a new life. After several purifications, I slept in a temple and was reborn (*dvījāti*). The next day I formally acquired the new name Istri Kania, and a mantra. Three days later I was given a Weda book in Pali, belonging to the [Śaiwa] lineage. To read or touch the book and to perform ceremonies, I was given a white attire ... when we do big ceremonies as I will this year, I will wear a crown which will complete the attire (Fig. 9.6).

The Pedanda Istri sports a special hairstyle reminiscent of the tuft of an orthodox Brahmin (*Śikhā*). A knot of hair is tied as a top-knot and adorned with flowers. She has to follow a strict spiritual discipline. The day of the priestess begins from the ritual of Sūrya-sevana,[13] worship of the sun, chanting of mantras, performing prāṇāyama, conducting offerings and

Fig. 9.6 Ida Pedanda Istri Kania Mas Kajeng adorned with a crown. Source: Author

[13] For *Sūrya-sevana stavas* see: Goodrian and Hooykaas, *Stuti and Stava* ..., p. 854, 4, 7, 16, 19, 22, 226, 679, 588, 715, 851.

making special prayers to the deities, conducting ceremonies along with other priests in temples, performing lifecycle rituals for families and offering blessings, gratitude prayers on auspicious full moon days for individuals, families and village communities. The custom of *dakṣiṇā*, offering a fee for religious ceremonies, has survived. When priestesses became very proficient in their religious duties, they adorn themselves with a sacred crown which symbolizes their unity with god Śiwa.

Is there any gender discrimination, I enquired.

Ida Istri Kania Mas Kajeng said:

> On account of patrilineal culture in Bali men tend to be superior but I do not think so. I have complete right to lead the ceremonies I perform. I also initiate men and women when I lead and conduct ceremonies with other male priests, everybody, men and women have the same rights ... studying dharma and meditation in front of the shrine, conducting ceremonies for others give us our spiritual power.

Women priestesses are the main performers of ritual and have mastered the manual skills of producing diverse offerings that form a very significant part of the ritualcentric religion of Bali. The highly refined craft of making aesthetically placed offerings is an orally transmitted tradition within the household and family, and may be transmitted in the community congregation of Istri Pedandas.

The entire ritual is managed by women, who are responsible for the preparation and placement of offerings. Young girls are socialized by their mothers in the art of the placement of offerings. What appears to be a basket of greens to the untutored eye veils a deep symbolic message. The elements used in the offering remind believers about the ephemeral nature of existence: fire symbolizes birth, holy water the flow of life, wind, represented by the smoke of incense, symbolizes death. The ritual of offerings conducted by women and the Pedanda Istri is a sacred art in an endless cycle of spiritual transaction between human beings and the divine reality, traceable to the Vedic ritual philosophy 'give me, I give you' (*dehi me dadāmi te*, Taittirīya Saṃhitā 1.8.4.1).[14]

Ida Pedanda Gede Made Gunung, one of the most respected Śaiwa masters in Bali, explained to me that the basket of offerings (*Canong*) is a

---

[14] Witzel, Michael, "Vedas and Upaniṣads", in Flood, Gavin, (2003) (editor), *The Blackwell Companion to Hinduism*, p. 79.

representation of a complete system of cosmic complexes and correspondences that can be interpreted symbolically. The *Upcāra* is a symbol of god or the highest reality. The *Canong Sari* basket of offerings placed on thresholds is a mirror of the Balinese world view. The basket offering has a square created by strips of palm leaves, which symbolizes the ground of creation of Brahmā and the deities presiding over eight directions of the square. The flowers of various colours decorated in the squares are symbolic of Śiwa's presence in His wholeness and His manifested parts. The centre (*Prosan*) is for the Trimūrti, or three gods; Viṣṇu is represented with Kempangrampe herbs, white edible lime for Śiwa/Īśvara and Brahmā by a small fragment of Catchu. Sacred symbols function, as Clifford Geetz pointed out in his several works, to synthesize a world view and ethos of the Balinese people—the character and quality of life, its moral and ethical basis, its aesthetic representations, their ideas of order, and states of interconnectedness and transcendence that embody their total cosmology. The symbols are evocative of a deeply felt aesthetic sentiment about their connectedness with a higher reality. The system of ritual complexes has survived primarily owing to the contribution of women who are the principal offering makers.

The women in the family or the Ida Pedanda Istri are the sole decision-makers as to whether certain rituals should be conducted or not. In recent years a manual book of offerings (*Pengelutuk*), a ritual digest, has been followed by women. The rules and ethical and moral dimensions of the ritual are derived from *Tutur*, the book of guidance for life and the variegated rules of lineage which connect the *Tattwa* and *Upacāra*, the theory and practice of ritual. Rituals, they believe, teach them the value of humility and respect for every aspect of creation:

> Our ego is effaced when we meet trees through our offerings, without them, there would be no air to breathe. Better to put *saiban* [rice offering] in front of the house, store in a marketplace, gods in the shrine, rather than to meditate and perform yogas without a feeling of gratitude and thankfulness for the wonders of creation.[15]

---

[15] As explained by Cok Sawitri (2015).

BALIAN METWUN: A TRADITIONAL HEALER OR A MASTER OF NON-INVASIVE THERAPY?

Several forms of pre-Islamic practices of tribal origin have entered the tradition of Istri Pedandas. One category of traditional healers is known as *Balian*, or healers, who are chief practitioners of trance and trance possession and are understood to have psychic abilities. They are supposed to be adepts in attaining trance-possession states, the physical, psychological and psychic processes that are involved in the treatment of the problems and illnesses of people who come to them. They treat both mental and physical problems that the Balinese believe to have arisen from negative karmas in previous lives. It is estimated that there are 2500 *Balians* in Bali. Each uses a distinct mode of diagnosis and techniques for treatment. They have been classified in accordance with the methods of cure they employ. For instance, those who derive their power from reading Lantor or ancient Balinese sacred manuscripts and books are called *Balian-usad*; those who use mantras, ritual offerings and massages on the body with invocations of mystical powers are known as *Balian-apun*. They are also skilled in healing bone fractures and sprains, and correcting dislocations. The third kind is the *Balian-taksu*, who are trance-mediums who have access to occult powers. They are believed to be able to channel the powers of gods and spirits through the subjective possession of divinities who act, speak and heal through them, using their bodies as a conduit. They treat illnesses, sometimes considered to be incurable through other means, caused by bereavement and family problems associated with kārmic debts of deceased relatives. They want to be referred to as *pengadeg dasaran*, which means 'gods uses the body', or *taksu* (Sanskrit Cakṣu, Cosmic Eye), those who have a special gift of the divine eye. Some others, known as *Balian-kebal*, offer protection against evil spirits by giving clients amulets, talismans and rings infused with spiritual power[16] (Fig. 9.7). What is extraordinary about the *balian* tradition is that practitioners are able to diagnose the problem without any prior information from the clients and can reveal the exact reason for their visit. The Balinese prefer to go to a faith-healer than a general physician, and prefer a person-to-person interaction with their respective *Balian*.

---

[16] Suryani, Luh ketut and Gordon D. Jeusen. (1993). *Trance and Possession in Bali*, pp. 49–51.

Fig. 9.7 Balian Metwun, Denpasar. Source: Author

In the year 2009, I had the chance to meet one such trance-medium healer. Her name is Balian Metwun. I visited her house at Denpasar, and was awed by the arrangement of symbolic magical spaces where she met her clients. There was a raised veranda, a square (approximately 15 ft) covered with a pagoda roof. To the northwest was a raised platform where the *Balian* sat and conducted her rituals. In front there was another large raised platform, which acted as a table to place offerings. On the northeast axis there were three open air shrines in the pavilion. The first had an image of Sūrya, the second a platform of ancestors (*Rongtiya*) while the third was for the guardian deities.

When questioned about how she became a *Balian-taksu* and acquired the techniques of divine healing, she described her transformation thus:

> When I was young, I was given a white shirt. I had a dream that a patient was being cured by a guru. The guru looked at me and spoke to me and said 'since you are dressed in white, I am asking you to treat the patient.' Since that dream I got my authorization from the guru. I learn the techniques of healing from my teacher, Dewa Khamaredi. My instructions did not take long since I was born with signs to heal. I have a [sign] of cakra on my palm. The technique consists of a test. I pray seven times. I feel the vibration, which is like an electrifying white ray, as if my forefinger functions like an antenna. Sometime there is a sensation of heat or cold, which I have to capture. I stroke or pat three times on the shoulders of the patient to open the illness. My touch opens out the block and uproots the disease [by means of vibration]. I also use mantras in Indonesian language, and Sanskrit mantras. I received these mantras directly from my ancestors. The mantras work when we pray every day to retain their powers. To cure certain illnesses, I have to make a vow/pledge that I will eat only white rice.

What type of illness did she treat? She said, 'I treat illnesses like *Bebai*, caused by black magic (*ilmu-pengiwa*). *Babinan* is believed to be caused by the possession of the soul by a malignant spirit (evil spirit of an old Balinese).' She went on to explain, 'I make white water and wait for a cure and ask for the origin of the illness. Because water is a symbol of *sañjīvinī*, I give water to the patient to drink, I close the crown-cakra. After the patient has drunk the water, I ask the power to heal the patient. By then the patient is in a trance ... then, the patient may begin to talk to himself about his own illness ... slowly the evil influences melt away.'

She also practises a specialized form of trance-possession for the treatment of grief and bereavement. While I was interviewing her, a group of seven people came to her asking for help regarding their relative who had died and to learn whether any kārmic debt was to be paid to the deceased. She prayed, and the souls of the deceased appeared to her and communicated to her about the problem. She advised the family that 'when the body was cremated the *pañchmahābhūtas* [the five elements, earth, water, fire, air and space of which the body is composed] were not cleansed'. Hence, a ritual with fifty offerings was prescribed for their liberation. Most *Balians* claim that they are unaware of what they do under the spell of trance-possession. For me, *Balian* Mutwan is a master healer practising non-invasive therapies, orally inherited from generation to generation.

It is quite obvious that the tradition of *balian* healers is intimately tied up with cultural and religious beliefs in their pre-modern world view that has survived the onslaught of time and is both unique in its historical and cultural contexts. Although the *Balians* are a class by themselves, their popularity, affective power and acceptance has given them a unique status in Balinese society. It is plausible that the universal acceptance of this class of healers has given a stronger place to the Istri Pedandas in Bali.

BALINESE GENDER PHILOSOPHY

There are several reasons for the continuity and survival of the Istri Pedanda tradition. Three reasons need to be elaborated: philosophical, social and religious/cultural. In many cultures of the world the ordination of women has been a contentious issue. It is not so in Bali. The answer to this question lies in the Balinese version of Hindu Saṃkhyā philosophy that they have adopted to suit their value-based culture. It is primarily based on Balinese gender philosophy according to which Puruṣa, the masculine principle, essentially passive, is in contrast to the active Pradāna energy, which is feminine. In the popular marriage rituals, the Balinese man assumes the Puruṣa role while the women assumes the Pradāna role. But in some forms of marriage (i.e. Raja Santena marriage), the roles are reversed. What is unique in the context of Bali is that gender roles are not determined by sex, but by the obligations, social and religious duties that a person is meant to play. Given that this philosophy is the basis, it is quite natural that Balinese society has created a space where women can play powerful religious roles. As Cok Sawitri, a famous writer, states:

Only in Balinese Hinduism can a woman become a high priest with equal authority and position as a male priest. Moreover, when a Balinese man wants to be a high priest with equal authority and position he must marry first, because without a women companion, he will be considered imperfect for priest hood, and they are inducted as high priests together, on the other hand, a women can become a high priest without having to marry. It is a spiritual acknowledgement that a women is perfect in herself. A senior Ida Pedanda Istri is treated first among equals in all Balinese Hindu ceremonies.[17]

Pedanda Istri Kania Mas Kajeng (ante) has no need to symbolically transform into Puruṣa, because in her body and consciousness both Puruṣa and Pradāna are said to be ever present, as she integrates the dormant male power and active essence of the feminine. As a Kania, her unity of male and female potential is intact, but in other Pedanda Istris the unity of male and female is split apart and is not complete any more. The male Pedandas have to marry in order to become a priest, based on the belief that the Puruṣa principle in Balinese philosophy and culture is considered to be passive. He cannot create or regenerate without a Pradāna, who is considered to be active, dynamic and creative. According to the esoteric Śaiwa school, women's spiritual powers are attributed to their innate possession of the powers of five sacred syllables that lie dormant in five parts of their bodies: Sa, ba, ta, am and Ing representing the five forms of Brahmās or Pañca Tirta (the five syllables that comprise the Śiwa mantra, *na-ma-śi-vā-ya*).[18] Men also possess this power but it is inactive in them: the potential power of the mantra can only be activated by women. As Cok Sawitri explained: 'Spiritually, the male and female Pedandas are equal, but the women is the potential Śakti and the Balinese value her potential and her inherently spiritual nature.'[19]

Balinese society is dominated by a patriarchal family structure where the male member is the centre of power. This is attested by the patrilineal Mapadik system of marriage, which is highly respected over other forms of marriage. The matrilineal form of marriage, though rare, deriving its philosophy from the supremacy of Pradāna, has survived in Bali in some isolated pockets. Gadung, Tabanan Regency, accepts the reversal of a Hindu system of marriage based on the matrilineal system. In this system,

---

[17] Ibid.
[18] As related by Cok Sawitri during my last meeting on 10 August 2015.
[19] Ibid.

the groom has to symbolically transform into a Pradāna and assume a womanly status and roles, whereas the bride has the upper hand and assumes the role of a Puruṣa. The role of a Puruṣa is assigned when there is an absence of sons. The daughters have the authority to become head of the family and are called Putrikā (female-sons!). Husbands then become their followers, who assist and accompany their wives and may have a subordinate position (Fig. 9.8).

The second reason for the survival and continuity of the women Pedandas, Cok Sawitri went on to explain, stems from the social status and the ritualistic base of Balinese Hinduism, which is grounded in certain ethical codes and moral principles unique to Bali. The obligation and duties assigned to each family in Bali, for example, extend beyond the immediate members of the family. Each family in Bali has an obligation to its ancestors. This is reflected in the continuity of the traditional community organization rituals by maintaining the family's temple and compound. The next is the duties towards its respective clan, thirdly to its traditional neighbourhood association (*Banjar*) and lastly, to its customary village.

Fig. 9.8 Author with two Ida Pedanda Istri, Denpasar, 2009. Source: Author

By participating in the elaborate ritual ceremonies an unbroken continuity is maintained with one's family (*griha*) community, ancestors and indeed with the whole of creation. The Balinese believe that the world is in a state of flux and turmoil between binary opposites, of good and evil; creation will fall apart into a state of disorder if balance and harmony are not restored by the correct performance of ritual enactments and following the set principles of moral behaviour and customary rules which are part of the divine order. The highly ritualistic lifestyle of Bali demands the total involvement of both genders. The family takes precedence over the individual. Decision in a traditional community organization is first made through consensus and the guidance of elders in critical matters, with approval from high priests and royalty. Cok Sawitri further stated that 'one family is entitled to one vote. Unlike other imperfect democratic systems, that follows one man/women one vote system.' If we raise the question about how modernity has been embraced by the Balinese, we would say that it is not by secularization alone, but it is by resisting change and by celebrating the cosmopolitan character of a shared hierarchy of values.

What the tradition of Istri Pedandas has proved to me is that masculine and feminine are products of culture and not products of biology as has been misconstrued by patriarchy. While men have held power over women through patriarchal structures, and several forms of hierarchical relationships, in societies such as Bali there has been a conscious breakdown of boundaries between sexual identity and social roles, where the time-honoured andocentric models of humanity have been challenged by the persistence of traditions such as those of Istri Pedandas. The greatest boon has been that such women are no longer the profane objects of the male gaze but their position, social status and spiritual power give them an opportunity to critique and reconstruct their religion from the woman's point of view, inspired by values they hold dear to their hearts. Tragically, the flame of high ranking seeresses that originated in India as early as 2500 BCE was extinguished, but it was rekindled and kept alive in Bali, but with a difference.

One of the critical responses to the Ida Pedanda Istri tradition is that it reflects an isolated case study from insular Southeast Asia.[20] Bali has been able to retain the ancient pattern of female empowerment in the religious sphere because of its relative isolation. In other areas of social life patriarchy reigns supreme and women are not acknowledged as equal partners. Indonesian men prefer not to marry highly individualistic professional

[20] I am indebted to Prof. Tom Hunter for this input and discussion.

women who occupy a position of power in society. Women in Bali are responding to the fast pace of change. Ancient patterns of female empowerment are being replaced by newer roles for women, owing to modernization, Western education and the inroads made by radical women's groups, such as the Indonesian women's movement. Their agenda is somewhat different from the recovery of women's share in religious history. These feminist groups aim for greater equality, labour rights and reform regarding marriage, work and polygamy. When we juxtapose these two parallel approaches to women's empowerment, some significant differences come to light. Whereas Ida Pedanda Istris have thrived under the patronage of patriarchy, they have survived within strict patriarchial norms. They are highly respected by male Pedandas and the laity at large and do not form an alienated group in society; whereas modern women's issues are a site for tension and violence, where the position for equality has to be fought and negotiated at every step.

What is interesting about the modern Balinese women whom I met is that they are not looking for stereotype role models of emancipation from the West. The Balinese understanding of Āgama Dharma and Weda, as Cok Sawitri explained, is that the 'Balinese form of Hinduism, far from condoling gender inequality, asserts equality. It is the misinterpretation of Weda that has led to the inequality witnessed in daily life.'[21] The tradition of Pedanda Istris, as it appears to me, is here to stay because it forms the cement that glues together the ritualcentric religion of Bali. As long as the faithscape of Bali survives, the Ida Pedanda Istris will continue to illuminate the religious and cultural landscape of Bali.

Acknowledgements The author is grateful to several people, especially scholars and Pedanda Istris in Bali, who were willing to share their knowledge and experiences during my research tours in 2009 and 2015. I am obliged to Luh Ketut Suryani for her useful advice. Ida Pedanda Istri Kania, Kajeng, at Badung; Ida Ayu Agung Mas at Sua Bali; and Mutwan at Denpasar shared their knowledge and experience with me with the utmost intimacy. I am also indebted to Cok Sawitri, the eminent writer and theatre personality, for her insightful comments. Ida Pedanda Gede Made Gunung, the Śaiwa master, ritual specialist, shared his rich understanding of the tradition. Ms Malini Saran in Delhi inspired me to take up the challenge of this study. I am grateful to Prof. Tom Hunter, who raised critical questions and clarified many complex issues. I am also grateful to Prof. Andrea Acri for providing influential contacts in Bali and Windhu Sancaya for his timely support during my last visit.

[21] Cok Sawitri's individualistic statement on gender dharma of Balinese Weda.

References

Acri, Andrea. 2013. "Modern Hindu Intellectuals and Ancient Texts: Reforming Śaiwa Yoga in Bali" Bijdragen tot de Taal-, Land- en Volkenkunde 169, 68–103.
Ahmed, Durre S. 1997. *Women and Religion* Vol. II *The Hidden Woman* Lahore: Heinrich Boll Foundation.
Altekar, A.S. 1995. *The Position of Women in Hindu Civilization*, Delhi. Motilal Banarasidass.
Coedes, George and Walter F. Vella (editors). 1968. *The Indianized States of Southeast Asia*. Trans. Susan Brown Cowing. Honolulu: University of Hawaii Press.
Eisman, Fred, Bali Sekala and Niskala, (1989) Vol. 1 *Essays on Religion, Ritual and Art.*, Singapore: Periplus Editions.
Haddad, Yvonne Yazbeck and Ellison Banks Findly. 1985. *Women, Religion and Social Change*, Albany: SUNY Press, p. 37–58.
Fox, James. 1998. "Indonesian Heritage: Religion and Ritual", Vol. 9 of *Indonesian Heritage*, (Editor) Timothy Anger, Singapore: Archipelago Press.
Falk, Nancy A. and Rita M. Gross. 1980. Unspoken Worlds: *Women's Religious Lives in Non-Western Cultures*, London: Harper & Row Publishers.
Gonda, Jan. 1975. "The Indian Religions in Pre-Islamic Indonesia and Their Survival in Bali," in *Handbook of Oriental Studies*. Section 3, Southeast Asia, Religions, Google Books pp. 1–54.
Geertz, Clifford. 1966. *Person, Time and Conduct in Bali: An Essay in Cultural Analysis*, New Haven, Yale, Southeast Asia Studies.
Geertz, Clifford. *The Religion of Java*. New York: Free Press of Glencoe, 1960
Geertz Clifford (1975). *Kinship in Bali* Chicago: University of Chicago Press.
Goodriaan, T. and C. Hooykaas. 1971. *Stuti and Stava (Baudha, Śaiwa and Vaiṣṇava) of the Balinese Brahmin priests*. Verhande lingen der Konin Klijke Nederlandse Akademie van wetenschappen, ofdeeling Letter kunde, Nederlandse Akademic van watten schappen, a f deeling Letter kunde, nieuwe reeks, No. 76.
Headley, Stephen C. 1991. "The Javanese Exorcisms of Evil: Betwixt India and Java". In *The Art and Culture of South-East Asia* edited by Lokesh Chandra, pp. 73–110. Delhi: Aditya Prakashan.
Hedihues. 2000. Mary Somers, *Southeast Asia: A Concise History*, London: Thames and Hudson.
Hooykaas, C. 1974. *"Cosmogony and Creation in Balinese Tradition*. KITLV, Bibliotheca Indonesica, 9. The Hague: M. Nig ho66.
Headley, Stephen C. 1980. *Drawings of Balinese Sorcery* Leiden: E. J. Brill.
Headley, Stephen C. 2004. *Durga's Mosque: Cosmology, Conversion and Community in Central Javanese Islam*, ISEAS, Singapore: Institute of Southeast Asian Studies.
Howe, Leo. 2001. *Hinduism and Hierarchy* in Bali. Oxford: James Curry; and Santa Fe School of American Research in Bali.

Khanna, Madhu. 2002. "The Goddess-Woman Equation in Śāktā Tantras", in Durre S. Ahmed (Editor) *Gendering the Spirit-Women, Religion and the Post-Colonial Response*. London: Zed Books, pp. 35–54.
Pott, P.H. 1946. "Pantheons in Java and Bali" in, *Yoga and Yantra, Their Interrelation and Their significance for Indian Archaeology*, Leiden: E. J. Brill.
Ram Seejer, U. 1986. *The Art and Culture of Bali*. Singapore: Oxford University Press.
Ramstedt, Martin (Editor). 2003. *Hinduism in Modern Indonesia – A Minority Religion between Local, National and Global Interests*. London: Routledge.
Reuter, Thomas Anton, *Custodians of the Sacred Mountains: Culture and Society in the Highlands of Bali*, Hawaii: University of Hawaii Press, 2002.
Stuart-Fox, David J. 2002. *Pura Besakih: A Study of Balinese Religion in Bali*. KITLV Verhandelenpen No. 193. Leiden: KITLV Press.
Sudarshana Dewi. 1957. *Ganpati-tattwa* Satapitaka Series No. 4, New Delhi. International Academy of Indian Culture.
Suryani, Luh ketut and Gordon D. Jeusen. 1993. *Trance and Possession in Bali*, Oxford: Oxford University Press.
Tantrajnana and Mahajnana Satpitaka. 1962. Series No. 23, New Delhi: International Academy of Indian Culture.
Wrhaspati-Tattva, An Old Javanese Philosophical Text, critically edited and annotated. New Delhi: International Academy of Indian Culture, 1958.
Witzel, Michael, "Vedas and Upaniṣads", in Flood, Gavin, (2003) (editor), *The Blackwell Companion to Hinduism*, Oxford: Blackwell Publishing, pp. 68–98, especially p. 79.
Wulandari, N. Putu Desi, Ni Nyoman Padmadewi, IGede Badasi. 2013. "Communication Strategies in Tabanan Nyentana Couples Related to Gender Difference and Matrilineal Marriage System", in *e-Journal Program Pascasarajana Universitas Pendidikan Ganesha Program Studi Pendidikan Bahasa Inggris* (Volume 1 Tahun).

WIKIPEDIA

"Bali Cultural Ceremony and Rituals". Balispirit.com retrieved April 7, 2009.
"Balinese Hindu Dharma", www.shastra.org/shastras-balinese-01.htm retrieved February 5, 2009.
Sawitri, Cok, "Feminism is Not a Problem for Balinese Women" BaliDaily.com retrieved June 12, 2015.
"Other Ways of Looking at Balinese Feminism" www.thejakartapost.com retrieved June 11, 2015.
"Hinduism in Indonesia" – www.wikipedia, retrieved July 1, 2015.
Reuter, Thomas, *Great Expectations: Hindu Revival Movements in Java, Indonesia*. www.swaveda.com, Retrieved June 8, 2009.

PRACTICAL RITUAL HANDBOOKS IN BALINESE

Tapini, Wiku and Kabupaten Buleleng, *Manusa Yadnya (Iepacara Tiga Bulanan Dan Otonan)*, Singaraja, 2009.

Mekarya Tetangunan Sumber Sastran Ipin Ring Bama Kertih Ian Panugrahan Bhagawan Wiswakarma Raryangon Widhi Sastra.

PART IV

Textual Traditions and Transmissions

CHAPTER 10

Transmission of Textual Traditions in South and Southeast Asia: A View from India

Sudha Gopalakrishnan

INTRODUCTION

This chapter looks at some of the common features and differences in the context, form and dispersal of textual knowledge across South and Southeast Asia. With a focus on the multiple cultural flows pertaining to knowledge transmission in the pre-modern era, it looks at patterns of adaptation and recreation of knowledge across the region. While there has been assimilation, adaptation and integration of a predominantly classical Sanskrit textual idiom across the region from early times, there have also been other parallel processes of knowledge dispersal with manifold evolutions across time and space.

According to the Oxford English Dictionary, a text is 'a book or other written or printed work, regarded in terms of its content rather than its physical form'. Textuality has a broader significance than the physical text, and in this chapter it is an inclusive term to suggest knowledge beyond the written, which includes the oral, ritualized and performative expressions that embody, interpret and extend the scripted form. The processes of

S. Gopalakrishnan (✉)
Sahapedia, New Delhi, India
e-mail: sudha.gopalakrishnan@sahapedia.org.in

such interaction include the transmission of textual knowledge through a vibrant oral tradition, the transition from an oral to a written form of expression, the adaptation of textual knowledge into ritual and performance domains, and lastly the development of common practices for the perpetuation and preservation of this knowledge.

Oral Transmission of Texts

All cultures of the world have from ancient times found ways to pass on their knowledge through formal and informal ways of communication and preservation. While looking at the broad sweep of such transmission of knowledge, we find that there are some recurrent patterns that may have directly or indirectly influenced the development of the literatures of many countries.

In India, the oral transmission of knowledge continues to be one of the most important methods for conveying messages, transmitting stories, educating children in their lessons, learning scriptures and nurturing knowledge about life and art. Much of India's sacred literature, myths and epics such as the Mahabharata and the Ramayana, tales, legends, songs and a multitude of knowledge and skills in every field were passed on through a largely flexible mode of oral communication and transmission. There were professional storytellers attached to temples who narrated stories from the Ramayana and the Mahabharata. Wandering storytellers told and retold the epics and legends not merely in temples but in other public spaces across the country. In this manner, different texts and narrative traditions emerged, with local variations including stories and substories, which began to be integrated into the main plot. These stories were gradually expanded through local interpolations and by embedding subnarratives. With the interpretive skills of the storytellers, even complex ideas in the stories of the Ramayana and the Mahabharata became accessible to a wider audience. The emphasis on orality was so strong that it was believed that 'the knowledge from books and the money lent to another person are not useful, because they cannot come to one's aid when needed'.[1]

In India, a complex, highly codified method of oral transmission was in place from early times to preserve large portions of Vedic texts. This method of recitation was so elaborate, highly sophisticated and foolproof that it eliminated or decreased the danger of losing words, syllables or

---

[1] The Sanskrit saying goes, *pustakeshu cha yaa vidyaa/parahastagatam dhanam/samaye tu paripraapte/na saa vidyaa na taddhanam.*

accent. The basic mnemonic method which was used to instruct and memorize these compositions was *padapatha*, the straightforward recitation of the Vedas, by splitting them word by word and combining with hand gestures (*mudra*s) to signify appropriate sound patterns. A student slowly graduated to the next level of recitational complexity called *krama*, where the first word of the mantra is added to the second, the second to the third and so on, until the whole verse is completed. This method enabled the student to know the individual words, and also combine words and integrate the changes in recitation that occur in the sound and the word as a result of the combination. While pada and krama are a direct mode of recitation, there are also indirect methods called *vikrti* which follow eight memorization patterns of increasing complexity such as *jata*, *mala, sikha, rekha, dhvaja, danda, ratha* and *ghana*. This elaborate system was developed with the purpose of preserving the purity of sound, word, pronunciation, intonation as well as the pitch-and-sound combinations of the verses of the Veda and to facilitate the absorption of massive amounts of data as oral memory. Accounts from early times including those of visiting travellers such as I-tsing and Buhler in the late nineteenth century give evidence of the system of the oral memorization of texts in ancient India.

In the Buddhist world, it is believed that the Tipitaka textual corpus was handed down orally through a strong monastic tradition in countries such as Korea, Thailand and Laos. The need to safeguard a vast magnitude of verses led monks to devise incredibly fail-safe methods to commit these texts to memory. The training and education of monks included different recitational devices and mnemonic features such as repetition, formulae, metre and numbered lists. The oral tradition was entrusted to specially trained monks called *bhanaka*s (reciters). The bhanakas were divided into several groups, each of whom was responsible for memorizing a different part of the canon, and the oral tradition continued to be the prevalent mode of transmission of texts even much after the texts started to be preserved in the form of manuscripts. Monks well versed in the Tipitaka were referred to as 'Tipitakadhara', a title that signified the three different kinds of texts, including the Vinaya, Sutta and Abhidhamma, as well as the memorization of a significant part of the Tipitaka.[2]

---

[2] Daniel M. Veidlinger. 2007, *Spreading the Dhamma: Writing, Orality and Textual Transmission in Buddhist Northern Thailand*. Honolulu: University of Hawai'i Press, p. 31.

Oral to the Written: Manuscripts and Textual Knowledge

The first instance of written forms of expression in India and other South and Southeast Asian countries is in the form of inscriptional records from the beginning of the first millennium, composed initially in the Prakrit language, later replaced by Sanskrit and the regional languages. What the introduction of writing meant for the codification and the fixing of textual knowledge, and its relations with the oral and performative, is a complex field to which this chapter can only provide some signposts.

The spread of Sanskrit across India and Southeast Asia, according to Sheldon Pollock, resulted in its transformation from a solely liturgical language to a medium of literary use, for example in *kavya*s and *nataka*s:

> As the turn to Sanskrit is taking place in the Indian subcontinent for the creation of inscriptions at once political, literary, and publicly displayed, precisely the same phenomenon makes its appearance in what are now the countries of Burma, Thailand, Cambodia, Laos, Vietnam, Malaysia, and Indonesia, and with a simultaneity that is again striking. The first Sanskrit public poems appear in Khmer country Champa, Java and Kalimantan all at roughly the same time, the early fifth century at the latest, or not much more than a couple or three generations after their widespread appearance in India itself. And they will continue to be produced in some places for centuries.[3]

Perhaps roughly around the same time, the knowledge that was transmitted from generation to generation entirely through an unbroken oral tradition gradually came to be written down in the form of manuscripts on different materials such as stones, copper plates, birch bark, palm leaves, parchment and paper. Composed in different languages and scripts, these manuscripts are spread all over the Asian region in *mutt*s, monasteries, temples, libraries and private collections. While a large number of manuscripts deal with knowledge relating to sacred literature from multiple religious traditions, including philosophy, scripture, hymnal literature, liturgy and texts on rituals and worship, there is a larger corpus that deals with different facets of worldly knowledge such as history, sciences and the arts, relating to such varied branches of knowledge as astronomy, metallurgy,

---

[3] Sheldon Pollock, "The Cosmopolitan Vernacular", *The Journal of Asian Studies*, Vol. 57, No. 1 (February, 1998), pp. 6–37.

medicine, agriculture, architecture, music and drama among others. The range of languages and scripts in which manuscripts are found reflects vibrant linguistic and literary diversity spread over hundreds of years. Much of this immense corpus of manuscripts comprises copies of the same texts written by scribes down the centuries. A large portion of these texts lies on the verge of destruction owing to the ravages of time and the lack of proper management or conservation in the collections where they are housed. This may be true of manuscript collections both in India and the Southeast Asian countries.

On an investigation into the corpus of manuscripts found in collections across South and Southeast Asia, we find several connecting links that may vouch for common historical and cultural roots. There are shared patterns of movement discernible in the transmission of texts and cross-fertilization across countries as widespread as India, Bhutan and Afghanistan to Malaysia, Thailand, Indonesia and Japan. The oldest Pali manuscript discovered is from the sixth century and has twenty gold leaves containing sixty lines; it is now in the Archaeological Museum in Sri Kshetra in Myanmar.[4] In Sri Lanka, texts such as *Dipavamsha* started recording information in chronicles. Hartman records that 'these chronicles mention that the monks *(bhikkhus)* wrote down the Tipitaka in Sri Lanka for the first time in the first century BCE, but the very short passage, consisting of only two verses, does not provide details of that Tipitaka or of the commentary *(atthakatha)*'.[5]

Apart from the inscriptional records mentioned earlier, the oldest surviving manuscript collection found in India is known as the Gilgit manuscripts. Discovered by a group of shepherds in 1931, this corpus of manuscripts may have been written between the fifth and sixth centuries CE. A collection of Buddhist writings covering a wide range of subjects such as religion, ritual, philosophy, iconometry, folk tales and medicine, the Gilgit collection contains *sutras* from the Buddhist canon, including the *Saddharmapundarikasutra* (popularly known as *Lotus Sutra*). It also has the complete manuscript of the *Samadhirajasutra*, one of the important Mahayana canonical texts well known throughout

---

[4] Richard Gombrich, 2006, *How Buddhism Began: The Conditioned Genesis of the Early Teachings*. London and New York: Routledge, p. 9.

[5] Jens-Uwe Hartman, 2009, "From Words to Books: Indian Buddhist Manuscripts in the First Millennium CE", in *Buddhist Manuscripts: Knowledge, Culture and Art*, Eds. Stephen C. Berkwitz, Juliane Schober & Claudia Brown, London: Routledge, pp. 95–105.

the ancient Buddhist world, particularly where Mahayana Buddhism was practised.[6] The National Archives of India recently compiled the Gilgit manuscripts in collaboration with the Institute of Oriental Philosophy and the Soka Gakkai Institute in Japan.

ADAPTATION OF THE TEXT INTO LANGUAGE

The supremacy of Sanskrit as a written and literary language in the first millennium and its gradual shrinking to give way to local languages is a phenomenon by and large common to regions across India and Southeast Asia. However, the first language to be used in the early inscriptions in India was Prakrit, followed by Sanskrit not merely in inscriptions but as a language of literary, liturgical and courtly use and transaction. Gradually, Sanskrit came to wield great influence in India and Southeast Asia between 300 and 1300 CE, and became localized, as signified by the term 'Sanskrit cosmopolis' to refer to the 'trans-regional power-culture sphere of Sanskrit'.[7] Pollock maintains that Sanskrit was not the language of common parlance but the main language for political expression in the region for a long time.

The existence of Pali or an admixture of Pali and Sanskrit in inscriptional records from early times points out to a flourishing language context, as evidenced by its Buddhist literature. By the seventh century, the regions slowly started adapting the Sanskrit phonetic system to write in their own vernacular languages, though in the field of vocabulary adaptation into the vernacular was not considerable. In his crucial study of the role of language and early state formation in Southeast Asia, Hunter speaks about the spread of scriptoria associated with Buddhist and Hindu institutions over a large geographical area, and how this is linked to exchange not

---

[6] Lokesh Chandra, who took the initiative to forge the collaboration between the National Archives and the Japanese institution, refers to Gilgit manuscripts as 'the glory of India—the Lotus Sutra has deep pan-Asian significance for a more meaningful study of all, Sanskrit, Chinese, Korean and Japanese languages and literature. Mantras in this even form a part of Gandhiji's Bhajanavali—even the three monkeys associated with Gandhi are from the Lotus Sutra. The publishing and easy access that scholars will get has unimaginable potential for scholarly research.' Seema Chishti, 'Countries oldest Manuscripts out in Brand New Prints', *Indian Express*, April 27, 2012. Online at http://archive.indianexpress.com/news/country-s-oldest-manuscript-out-in-brand-new-prints/942090/ Accessed on 15 July 2015.

[7] Sheldon Pollock, 2006, *Language of the Gods in the World of Men: Sanskrit, Culture and Power in Premodern India*, Berkeley, University of California Press, p. 12.

merely in language, but in beliefs, practices as well as artisanal skills.[8] Discussing the linguistic processes of bilingualism and diglossia, he quotes Jan Houben's definition of 'diglossia' as a stable language situation in which another written and codified language is superimposed on it, leading to considerable enrichment in all spheres of life.[9] He also discusses the development of vernacular languages in Java, Sumatra and the Malaysian region, as well as the spread of Sanskrit and Pali, and how the original languages were adapted to suit the local context.

In a similar vein, citing Chinese influence in Vietnamese literature and Sanskrit influence in Cambodian inscriptions and literary culture, Wolters establishes how these foreign elements acted as textual embellishments in the original language with particular significance in the local context.[10] He says, 'The question was ... how the historian should approach the study of cultural diversity. One approach was to enquire what happened to Indian materials circulating in different sub-regions, and I suggested that they were "localized" to become part of the local cultures just as Sanskrit loan words were localized.' The use of Sanskrit metric patterns in Old Javanese literature and the use of *manipravala*, a mixture of Sanskrit and the local language such as Tamil or Malayalam in the southern part of India, are two examples of such adaptation.

Adaptation into Ritual and Performance

The adaptation of textual sources for use in sacred rituals has a long history across Asia. In India, textual material forms the basis of a whole ritual complex recorded in the *grhyasutras*, standing for domestic or personal sacramental rites. Textual knowledge through the mediation of ritual accompanies every phase of a person's life. Apart from these prescriptive texts, there is a whole corpus of material belonging to the *srautasastras*, apart from commentaries according to the different *sakha*s (branches) of Vedic knowledge. These practices were adapted into local contexts and cultures subsequently, as is evident in the Nambutiri tradition in Kerala, the southwestern part of India, or the temple consecration rituals in Tamil Nadu.

---

[8] Thomas Hunter, 2011, "Exploring the Role of Language in Early State Formation of Southeast Asia", Nalanda-Sriwijaya Centre Working Paper No. 7 (October), http://nsc.iseas.edu.sg/documents/working_papers/nscwps007.pdf, p. 13.

[9] Ibid., p. 5.

[10] O. W. Wolters, 1999; rpt. 2004, *History, Culture, and Region in Southeast Asian Perspectives*, Ithaca, Cornell University Press, p. 63.

A text that is heard, performed or interpreted is a different experience from one that is simply read. The ritualistic monastic tradition of Paritta in Sri Lanka, *ye dharma hetu prabhava* of the Tibetan tradition or the Koan ritual relating to Zen Buddhism have adapted texts to suit the context of ritual performances from these regions. On the study of the Zen Koan ritual performance,[11] Barry Stephenson writes that:

> The dominant concerns of the discipline of religious studies since its inception—the category of experience and the hermeneutics of texts—have dominated the scholarly study of the koan tradition. A performative approach can knock these two meta-texts around, loosening their somewhat tyrannical hold on the conception, reception and study of the koan. Interest in performative culture has generated a wealth of theory, across disciplines, on performance, and ritual action; this work could be fruitfully brought to bear on the study of the performative basis of the Zen koan.

The process of adaptation and integration of knowledge relating to the Ramayana and the Mahabharata into South and Southeast Asia is perhaps best visible in their rich and varied theatric/dance performances and visual art traditions, where one may see how epic characters and roles are reinterpreted and terms reassessed. While the system of handing down knowledge in the region became dependent on an organized system of learning through the *guru-shishya parampara* and was later codified through manuscripts, the narrative-performative tradition of recitation carried on the dissemination of indigenous textual knowledge. In performative adaptations, the largely flexible mode of communication carried the text forward by extending the original narrative through interpolations, conscious extensions and embedding of subnarratives. The performative powers associated with the appropriate uttering through words, enacting through ritual and embodying in performance offer another way of understanding or interpreting the text itself, opening up possibilities of multiple versions and perspectives. The many valuable studies in this area are also being integrated with the material contexts of textual transmission, to deepen our understanding of how the dispersal of manuscripts such as the *Natya Sastra* and the *Gitagovinda* have, over the centuries, enhanced knowledge exchange through continuous reinterpretation and innovation among the countries of South and Southeast Asia. In a compelling article, Kapila

[11] Stephenson Barry, "The Koan as Ritual Performance", in *Journal of the American Academy of Religion*, Vol. 73, No. 2 (Jun., 2005), pp. 475–496.

Vatsyayan identifies the sixty-two dance sculptures of the Lara Djonggrang temple (Prambanan) as illustrating in stone the verses of the fourth chapter of the *Natya Sastra*, titled 'Tandava Lakshanam'. In comparison with the dance sculptures in Brhadishvara, Chidambaram, Elura and Pattadakkal, she finds that while there are similarities with the Prambanan group, the preoccupation of the sculptors is with dance poses: 'The survivals of the dance styles in these countries, particularly in Indonesia (both Java and Bali), Thailand and Khmer, and aspects of Burma, further reinforce our impression that although there is a consanguinity of fundamental vision and execution in form and technique, there is regional distinctiveness'.[12]

When a text is adapted into a ritual or musical/theatrical performance, it takes on a life of its own, becoming less fixed and more open-ended. The complex relationship between the written and performed versions of texts, each with their own identity and integrity, is explored in a significant study of the epic performances in South and Southeast Asia,[13] raising such questions as 'What do performers and audiences mean when they identify something as 'Ramayana' or 'Mahabharata'? How do they conceive of texts? What are the boundaries of the texts?'[14] In India as well as Southeast Asia, the Mahabharata and the Ramayana have countless adaptations, versions and recreations that existed as floating stories in localized contexts. In many performance styles, these stories have considerable freedom of interpretation depending on the skill and creative imagination of the narrator, and are open-ended and collaborative rather than fixed and inflexible. Even when the basic story remains the same, the interpretation changes according to *who* says it, *where* it is said and *how* it is said. This is true of the narrations of Tulsi's *Ramcharitmanas*, Malay *Hikayat Seri Rama* or Kerala's Chakyarkoothu tradition.

Performative elements such as chanting, singing and dancing are popular devices to reach out to audiences, and folk/regional performances such as Ramlila, Pandvani and a host of other performances across India popularized the Ramayana and Mahabharata stories in their multiple variations. Ramlila, the performance of the divine play of Rama based on the text of Tulsidas's

---

[12] Kapila Vatsyayan, 1977, 'The Dance Sculptures of Lara-Djonggrang (Prambanan)', *National Centre for Performing Arts Quarterly*, Vol V, No. 1, pp. 1–14.

[13] Joyce Burkhalter Flueckiger and Lauri J. Sears (ed.), 1991, *Boundaries of the Text: Epic Performances in South and Southeast Asia* (*Michigan Papers on South and Southeast Asia*, No. 35) Michigan, Centre for South and Southeast Asian Studies, p. 1.

[14] Ibid.

Ramcharitmanas, has diverse expressions across India, especially in north India. In the celebrated Ramlila of Ramnagar, the whole village is transformed into a performance arena and becomes the venue where the divine *lila* is played out year after year during the festive season of Dussehra. There are also several other versions of Ramlila from Chitrakoot, Agra and Delhi, which have carved their own niche in narrating the Rama story, as well as hundreds of neighbourhood Ramlilas that happen in villages across north India. The fact that there is a Ramlila ground in almost every village, town and city in India testifies to the popularity of the performance of Ramlila in the country.

VENERATION OF THE TEXT

Many textual traditions across South and Southeast Asia have shared practices relating to the caring for and protection of manuscripts, which has helped not only the long-term preservation of the physical text, but perpetuated its use down the centuries to the present day. Many customs and conventions arose, which pertained to all aspects of manuscript writing and preservation such as the use of material for writing (i.e. palm leaf and later paper), copying practices, scribal practices such as colophons, as well as traditions of manuscript painting reflecting different artistic styles.

One of the common features found across many regions in South and Southeast Asia pertaining to diverse faiths such as Hinduism, Buddhism, Jainism, Sikhism and Islam is the reverence accorded to texts that are considered sacred. Beyond being considered a mere object meant as reading material, and perhaps also as a significant way of protecting the faith, some texts are ascribed with powers beyond the ordinary. Accordingly, there are also notions of purity and the right decorum in handling and storing them. In the Buddhist world, the manuscript of *Prajnaparamita* is invested with such sacred power that it is considered as the Buddha's persona and is ritually consecrated.

> The public recitation and sanctification of texts, as well as the display of the manuscript itself—the physical vessel of the teaching—still form an important part of Buddhist worship. The emergence of a book-cult was certainly modeled after the stupa-cult (the stupa serving as a protective container of Buddha relics and often adorned with flags), and in a parallel way

acknowledges the physicality of the book as a physical container of the teaching that is equated with a dharma relic.[15]

Just as Buddhist relics and texts were venerated, many cultures including the Hindu, Jain and Sikh treat the text as God or as a representative of God. The Guru Granth Sahib placed in the Golden Temple in Amritsar has elaborate daily rituals of worship and singing as it is taken on a ceremonial procession across the premises; the monastic Vaishnava community of *sattra* in Majuli in Assam reveres the Bhagavata text, called *puthi*, placed inside the *namghar* (the house of the sacred name).[16] The manuscripts containing Jain scriptures, with splendid painted illustrations, are deemed to contain the wisdom of Jain religion. The Svetambara Jains recite and worship the Kalpasutra manuscripts, and take them out in ritual processions as an important event of the annual eight-day Paryushana festival during the monsoon season.

The conception of the holiness ascribed to texts also accounts for the rituals employed to dispose of the manuscript when it becomes damaged; after all, the texts held in reverence while they were intact need to be treated with the same respect even when they are out of use. In her book dedicated to the 'death' of sacred books, Myrvoid describes at length the diverse practices for the ritual annihilation of manuscripts that have served their purpose and are damaged beyond restoration.[17] Apart from the destruction of such texts, in many parts of Southeast Asia and India there was the parallel tradition of ritual concealment of important texts for use in a faraway future, including stacking away important scriptural texts along with statues and other relics for a possible discovery after several generations. Many Buddhist texts discovered in China, Japan and other places are accounted for by this fact. On the safeguarding of manuscripts, Moerman discusses the ways in which core Buddhist sutras were guarded for long-term preservation.[18] Specifically about the 'burial' motivation of the *Lotus Sutra*, he observes:

---

[15] Yana Van dyke, 2009, "Sacred Leaves: The Conservation and Exhibition of Early Buddhist Manuscripts on Palm Leaves", *The Book and Paper Group Annual* 28, pp. 83–97.

[16] Sacred rituals surrounding the text in India are described by B. N. Goswamy, 2007, in the Introduction to the exhibition catalogue *The Word is Sacred, Sacred is the Word: The Indian Manuscript Tradition*, New Delhi, National Mission for Manuscripts, pp. 11–47.

[17] Kristina Myrvold, 2010, Introduction to *The Death of Sacred Texts: Ritual Disposal and Renovation of Texts in World*. Surrey: Ashgate, pp. 1–9.

[18] D. Max Moerman, "The Materiality of the Lotus Sutra: Scripture, Relic, and Buried Treasure", *Dharma World* July–September 2010. Internet Resource. http://www.koseishuppan.co.jp/english/text/mag/2010/10_789_4.html

In the age of the Final Dharma, history and salvation provided a set of interrelated problems. To many monks and aristocrats of the period, the practice of sutra burial provided a solution of sorts. Ceremonial transcription, enshrinement, and burial of the Lotus Sutra was among the repertoire of Lotus Sutra–related practices that offered the ritual strategies and material means whereby the end-time could be prepared for and paradise secured. For historians of Japanese Buddhism, however, the evidence of sutra burials can address another set of problems and provide another kind of buried treasure. Sutra burials, like so many time capsules, offer materials for a geography of religious aspiration. They identify the desires, the individuals, the cults, and the sites central to Japanese Buddhist practice. As such they may offer a map to a new sort of history, a spatial history that might begin to explore the vast and less charted landscape of the Japanese religious imagination.

For scholars of religion beyond Japan, the history of text burial offers other lessons as well. For example, the death of Hindu texts in Vrindavan, known as *grantha samadhi*, is a ritual disposal of damaged manuscripts of *Ramcharitmanas* or *Bhagavata* into the river Yamuna. The long-term preservation of texts by hiding them between walls and vaults has become redundant with the technological changes brought on by methods such as printing the text, microfilming and digitization. It remains to be seen how far the digital archive may ensure the perpetuity of the written tradition, once protected by the veneration of texts and affected by scribal errors or interpolations. What we do know is the enormously enlarged scope that the digital archive offers for online collaboration across regions, the empirical study of linguistic flows in relation to other historical processes,[19] and the application of new tools for the critical and interpretive understanding of texts as they are configured in different knowledge traditions.

---

[19] Thomas W. Hunter, "Exploring the Role of Language in Early State Formation of Southeast Asia", p. 13.

CHAPTER 11

The Bhagavad-Gītā Sections of the Old Javanese Bhīṣmaparwa, Text-Building and the Formation of the State in Pre-modern Indonesia

Thomas M. Hunter

INTRODUCTION

This chapter, on cultural connections between the Association of Southeast Asian Nations (ASEAN) and India is based on a close comparison of the Bhagavad-gītā sections of the Sanskrit Bhīṣma-parvan and the Old Javanese Bhīṣma-parwa. This comparison will show us that the Old Javanese Bhīṣmaparwa is not so much an abridgement by a single author of the Sanskrit original as one of many works that belie the multiple voices of a pedagogical tradition that had a profound influence on the shaping of the courtly and political culture of Java in the tenth century CE.

An earlier comparison of these passages was contributed in 1973 by Barend van Nooten, an eminent scholar of Vedic and Sanskrit, in a little-known article published in Baroda that has made its way into few Western

---

T. M. Hunter (✉)
Department of Asian Studies, University of British Columbia,
Vancouver, BC, Canada

© The Author(s) 2018
S. Saran (ed.), *Cultural and Civilisational Links between India and Southeast Asia*, https://doi.org/10.1007/978-981-10-7317-5_11

193

libraries. In the present work the relationship of the two texts has been based on the Sanskrit–English edition of Cherniak (2008), the Romanized text of the Bhagavad-gītā with the commentaries of Śrīdhara, Mādhusūdana, Viśvanatha and Baladeva available on Gretil and the Old Javanese edition of Gonda (1936).[1]

As we know from the preamble to the Bhīṣmaparwa, this work was composed during the reign of Dharmawangśa Tĕguh, who reigned in East Java around 990–1006 CE. This places it alongside the Wirāṭa-parwa, which we know from internal evidence was read at the court of Dharmawangśa from October 14 through November 12 in the year 996 CE. We can surmise, too, that the Bhīṣmaparwa was composed following the same request that Dharmawangśa makes in the Wirāṭaparwa—that the work should "shun the diversion of the play of poetic invention,"[2] and present the tale in a straightforward manner that will prove useful in times of "seeking victory over insolent enemies."[3]

The religious orientation of the framers of the Parwa literature comes out clearly in the two introductory verses to the Bhīṣmaparwa that are included in order to provide a contemporary setting for the work. In the commentary on the first verse, the sage Vyāsa is characterized as a Shaiva mendicant, who is as resplendent in appearance as the god himself.[4] In the second verse Dharmawangśa is characterized as the cakravartin of the island of Java and praised as Lord Vishnu.[5] In both cases we see a configuration of religious and political streams in ancient Javanese society that is reflected, for example, in the relief sculptures of the Brahma and Shiva shrines at the Loro Jonggrang (Prambanan) complex of central Java.[6] In this configuration priest-ascetics of the Shaiva orders played a foundational

---

[1] For the Gretil text see Göttingen Register of Electronic Texts in Indian Languages (accessed 27 May 2015).
[2] yathābhūta tattwa kathānâtah [...] tan bhūṣan.āna buddhiracana.
[3] yadyapin hana jaya-prasangga-dūṣaṇa.
[4] nīlakaṇṭha kiris śarīra nira kangkĕn megha, bhinūṣaṇan de ni kalipajaṭā kangkĕn kila ta, inadyutan ing bhasma putih.
[5] sira ratu cakrawarti siniwi ring Yadadwīpamaṇḍal [...] wyaktinya n singangguh hari Wiṣṇu sira, ri de nira Śrīdhara.
[6] See further in Hunter, Thomas M. (2013) for a discussion of the reliefs at the Candi Prambanan complex illustrating sages in terms of the importance of Shaiva priest-ascetics as royal preceptors in the Early Mataram period (c. 732–928 CE). The role of these priest-ascetics continued to be decisive in the formation of East Javanese religious and political culture (c. 929–1478), when similar priest-ascetics of the Buddhist denominations shared pride of place in their relationship with the noble houses of Kediri-Daha and Kahuripan-Janggala.

role in the shaping of court life, providing instruction to the nobility and fostering the courtly cult of Vishnu and Śrī as the progenitors of the royal line.

Preliminaries

The major claim of this chapter is that the Parwa literature shares with the didactic traditions a form of text-building that grows out of long-standing pedagogical processes that stretch back to the monastic and courtly institutions of the Sumatran state of Śrīwijaya.[7] This claim assumes a number of theoretical and historical points that are detailed below.

There is no time to expand fully on the history of these institutions in the context of the present work, but a few points stand out that are worthy of note:

Theoretical preliminaries:

- This work and related works by the author represent a methodology based on applying the principles of philology, linguistics, anthropological linguistics and socio-linguistics to the study of literary and cultural history.
- It is assumed in this approach that textual artifacts represent sedimentations of generations of the experience of readers and writers. They are not in that sense unitary, but are open to investigation that can unpack information relevant to history, anthropology and other social sciences by focusing on understanding the social contexts in which textual artifacts were produced.
- From this perspective, processes of text-building that are often encountered among the cosmopolitan vernacular languages of the Sanskrit cosmopolis can be understood as textual practices parallel to processes of the production of the state that are also mirrored in the visual and performing arts.

Historical preliminaries:

- We know from the chronicle of the Chinese Buddhist pilgrim and translator I Ching that the court center of the Śrīwajayan empire was

[7] For an earlier and still authoritative survey of the Parwa literature see: Zoetmulder, P. J. (1974).

renowned for its scholarship in Sanskrit and Mahāyāna Buddhism, so that I Ching himself spent several months of study there before continuing on to India during his long journey of 671–695 CE.[8] From this we surmise that there was a strong tradition in pedagogy in Sanskrit at the Śrīwajayan court center of Palembang.

- Early Śrīwijayan inscriptions such as the Śrīkṣetra inscription of 684 CE reveal a process of incorporation of Sanskrit loan words into the morphological structure of Old Malay that was taken over by the Buddhist and Shaiva framers of the inscriptions of ancient Java and Bali. These processes produced literary languages that in time came to be understood as representing Prākrit reflections of Sanskrit, and in this sense can be understood as higher status languages of the type Pollock (1998) has termed "cosmopolitan vernaculars."
- There appears to have been a strong historical tie between the court of Śrīwijaya and the "Shailendra guru-s" who are characterized in the Kalasan inscription of 778 CE as the preceptors of the Javanese monarch Panangkāran. This suggests to me that the pedagogical institutions that were fostered in Palembang with Śrīwijaya patronage made their way to Java when the learned preceptors of these institutions began to be patronized by Javanese kings of the lineage of Sañjaya as well as by their original Śrīwijayan patrons.[9]
- We can assume from these connections between Śrīwijaya and the Javanese lineage of Sañjaya that the practices of pedagogy that we find reflected in the didactic traditions of Javanese Shaivism and Buddhism have a long "prehistory" before they appear in Buddhist works such as the Sang Hyang Kamahāyānikan and Shaiva works such as the Old Javanese Wṛhaspatitattwa.
- A close examination of the didactic literature of ancient Java will show us that this literature represents a unique form of text-building based on applying the principles of the Sanskrit tradition of commentaries in vyākhyā form to the problem of translation. In this tradition entire Sanskrit verses or sections of verses are paired with expositions in Old Javanese that initially translate the Sanskrit verses, but in time become much more expansive, in this way mirroring the expository style of the Sanskrit tradition of commentary.

---

[8] For a record of the travels of I Ching see Takakusu, J. (2006).
[9] For a study that suggests that there was only one dynasty in the Early Mataram era (*c.* 732–928 CE) see van der Meulen, W. J. (1979).

- This style of "translation" can be understood as representing the "commentarial" style of text-building characteristic of the didactic tradition that gained such prominence in the composition of prose works that it was taken over by the framers of the Parwa literature and also served as the model for creative efforts in early prose composition, such as the fourteenth-century work Tantri Kāmandaka.[10]
- We can thus expect that the Parwa literature will follow the model of textual organization that Hunter (2013) has somewhat clumsily described as "translation dyads."[11] At the same time we find in the Parwa literature many instances of shorter "quotations" from Sanskrit originals of the Mahābhārata being used to "launch" passages in Old Javanese that further develop the story line or doctrinal teaching being conveyed in the work. We can use the term pratīka for these shorter passages, thus indicating their role in linking the Old Javanese text with an authoritative original.[12]

Found in Translation: The Old Javanese Parwa Literature as a Guide to Courtly Etiquette and the Training of Political Actors

With these points in mind let us now turn to a closer look at how the Old Javanese narrative of the Bhagavad-gītā (BG) section of the Bhīṣmaparwa is developed around Sanskrit verses and pratīka that provide a crucial link

---

[10] For a discussion of the "commentarial" form of translation from Sanskrit to Old Javanese see Hunter (2011).

[11] See Hunter (2013) for a study that links the sages portrayed in relief sculptures of the Candi Prambanan complex with Shaiva priest-ascetics who are understood to represent the pinnacle of spiritual power in the religion of the Early Mataram, and served as important advisers and preceptors to the nobility of ancient Java.

[12] The primary meanings of pratīka are "turned towards, directed towards," but the term has an extensive usage in several technical meanings. In the Aṣṭadhyāyī of Pāṇini it is used in the sense of a "symbol" or "focus" and is used to refer to the particular subject matter of a commentary. A major commentary (bhāṣya), for example, should focus on the explanatory rules (vārttika) that accompany the rigorous presentation of a subject in sūtra form, while a vṛtti, the first-level glossing of a treatise, will have the sūtra itself as its pratīka. In such works as the Pratīka Index of the Mahābhārata (Poona, 1967–1972) it refers to the indexing of the quarter verses of the Mahābharata by citing their initial phrases. This is the sense intended when the term is used for the citations from the Mahābhārata found throughout the Old Javanese Parwa literature that serve both to link the OJ text to authoritative Sanskrit originals, and as a text-building device in its own right.

with the authoritative original of the Sanskrit text. The type of textual analysis that has been developed within socio-linguistics and translation studies is taken here as a model. This mode of analyses holds that a work such as the Old Javanese Bhīṣmaparwa represents the "sedimentation" of social and textual practices that are reflected in both the form and content of textual artifacts. In the particular case of the Parwa literature it appears that what we are seeing in the text-building practices of this genre reflects the work of the institutions of Buddhist and Shaiva pedagogy that played a major part in the formation of the "Indianized states" of Southeast Asia, or in Pollock's terms the formulation of an "aestheticization of politics" that meant that literature and the performing arts played a major role in shaping political life in the states he includes under the terms "Sanskrit cosmopolis" and "Sanskrit Ecumene."

We will be looking here at particular passages from the BG section of the Bhīṣma Parwa, which can give us a nuanced view of the role played by prose composition in Old Javanese in what might be called "education for governance."

Excerpt 1: Indexing and Defining Social Hierarchies

Contemporary socio-linguists who see the work of Michael Silverstein (1976, 1998) as fundamental to our understanding of the role of language in society often look to the work of Charles Sanders Peirce, whose tripartite division of linguistic signs into "icons, indexes and symbols" has allowed linguists to explore the role of social constraints in the formulation of linguistic meaning.[13] The notion of "index" has been particularly influential in that it provides a model for understanding languages such as Japanese, Javanese or Balinese that have highly developed systems of alternative vocabulary used to mark status differences in language. While it is well known that modern Javanese and Balinese have developed parallel vocabulary for at least two "speech levels" that are used to code differential status in communicative acts, it has been assumed by earlier scholars that this was a unique development that began in Java only during the period of the Later Mataram, the period following Sultan Agung's ascension to the throne in 1613. While the Old Javanese material does not

---

[13] Important works by this author include: Silverstein (1976) and Silverstein (1998).

reveal a separate vocabulary for "refined" and "informal" levels of speech, there is a complex system of pronominal usage that illustrates clearly the indexing of hierarchical social relations through language use and in this sense is entirely continuous with the later development of Javanese and Balinese, where socio-linguistic contrasts play a role in naturalizing hierarchy comparable with South Asian rules on commensality and selective endogamy.

Let us look now at an example of socio-linguistic indexing from the Bhīṣma Parwa:

BG 25.28–29; Gh 41.4–5[14]
dṛṣṭvêmān svajanān Kṛṣṇa yuyutsūn samavasthitān
sīdanti mama gātrāṇi mukham pariśuṣyati

Krishna, at the sight of my own kin standing here ready to fight, my limbs feel tired and my mouth has grown dry.

Gh 41.6–14
rahadyan sanghulun mahārāja Kṛṣṇa tan wwang waneh ta karih sang rowanga ning apranga katon ta sira kabeh kapwa kulawarga bapa kaki paman pangajyan guru wwang sanak kaka anak putu parnahnya waneh bheda sangke rama tuha mitra kula bhartiti. amogha lumay iki sarira ni-nghulun an ton sira kabeh kasatan angĕlih ike mukha ning pinakanghulun tatan pasangkan kĕtĕr nikeng sarwasandhi, nda-nda tumibakĕn śarīranya ikang gaṇḍewadhanuḥ sangke tangan ing pinaka-nghulun apayapan tan pahati kahilangan citta patik haji.

Respected sir, mahārāja Kṛṣṇa, those who are to be companions in the battle to come can be seen here to be kinsmen all—fathers, grandfathers, uncles who are our preceptors and guru-s, as well as older brothers, grandsons and other kinsmen, not to mention fathers-in-law, family friends and followers. Suddenly my body fells limp as I look upon them all. My mouth feels dry and weak and all the joints of my body are unexpectedly trembling. See here how (my trembling) has thrown down the Gaṇḍiva bow from my hand, for this the spirit of your faithful servant (is devoid of strength).

---

[14] In this article the abbreviation BG is used for verses drawn from the Bhagavad-gītā section of the Sanskrit Bhīṣmaparvan and Gh (= Ghonda 1936) for passages from the Old Javanese Bhīṣma Parwa.

The crucial term in the pronominal contrasts here is hulun, which appears to derive from hulun, "servant." When this word is used as the equivalent of a first person it is found as ng-hulun, "the servant," and pinaka-nghulun, "the one who is used/taken as the servant." While several very estimable philologists have denied that this pronoun can have "humble" reference, this seems rather to be exactly what is intended. This possibility is reinforced in Bhīṣmaparwa 41.14 by possessive use of another first person pronominal phrase patik haji, "servant of your majesty," which even in translation connotes a hierarchical relationship and the humility of the first person speaker.

A crucial point in support of this claim comes out when we look at the second person pronominal phrase rahadyan sanghulun, which can be roughly translated as "my respected royal master." Here the marker ng, which normally marks the definiteness and prominence of nominal and pronominal arguments in a clause has been replaced with sang, a title-marker used to refer to persons of higher rank. Here the respect due to a person of higher status is coded in the shift from more neutral ng-hulun to sang-hulun. Note that the higher status of the interlocutor is signaled by a corresponding shift from a more neutral first person pronominal phrase to one containing the honorific element sang that is contextually appropriate when addressing a royal patron, a ra hadyan, or "respected royal master."[15]

An argument for a crucial contrast in Old Javanese between humble first person reference and polite second person reference may not be accepted in all quarters, yet it seems appropriate to make the following claim around the pronominal usage illustrated in Bhīṣmaparwa 41-6-14:

---

[15] In 1983 the late A.L. Becker suggested that several first and second person pronouns of Old Javanese depend on a metonymy, where hulu-n represents a development from hulu, "head." Becker (p.c. 1983) held that pinaka-nghulun is a metonymous extension of the act of placing one's head (hulun) at the feet of someone of higher status and respect, so that this pronominal forms nghulun and pinakanghulun can be read "I, who am to be taken as the head in a gesture of respect where my head is placed lower than your feet."

The derivation of hulun from hulu may be problematical; however, it could be explained as developing from hulu + the "passive irrealis marker"-ĕn. This possibility opens up a rich field of lexical exploration around hulu, "head" and hulun, "servant" that should not be foreclosed by arguments that dismiss the possibility of a reading informed by post-structural approaches to the problem of the sign, and the more recent innovations in cognitive linguistics. Here the formula "head > bondsperson" might appear as a normal phonological consequence of a metonymous source of meaning.

the contrastive use of complex pronominal phrases in this passage sets up a hierarchy of persons that was to become an enduring part of the sociolinguistic landscape of Java and Bali and runs throughout the entire history of Old Javanese. This contrast was crucial to the naturalization of hierarchy that was an essential ingredient in the "education for governance" of the pedagogical institutions of ancient Java, and so was reflected at a deeply functional level of language use. In Bhīṣmaparwa 41-6-14 this contrast puts Arjuna in the humble position appropriate to even a great warrior-prince when in the presence of Krishna, an interlocutor of the highest possible status.[16]

Excerpt 2: Instructions in Social Duty (Dharma)

In a second excerpt the Old Javanese narrator expands on a well-known Sanskrit verse with a discussion that brings out several key terms and understandings in the social order of ancient Java.

BG 25.31c-d, 25.32a-b; Gh 41.15–16
na ca śreyo 'nupaśyāmi hatvā svajanam āhave
na kāṅkṣe vijayam Kṛṣṇa na ca rājyam sukhāni ca

I see no good in killing my own family in war. I don't desire victory, Krishna nor kingdom, nor pleasures.

Gh 41.17–27
ring kapanêkang inak ambĕk kabhuktya dening pinakanghulun yan tĕlas mĕjahana ng kulawandhu ngke ring palagan? matangnyan pwa, mahārāja Kṛṣṇa, tan ahyun nghulun i kawijayan tan kapengin ing rājyawibhawa. apa kārya ning bhoga lawan jīwita yan prāṇaghātakânghilangakĕn kaṭumba. <i> ng asih tṛṣṇa mangāweśê hati ning pinakanghulun.ndya ng sukha, ndya ng manah tuṣṭa? byakta ng kapāpan juga ng kapanggiha. ndya tang widhi, ndya tang prāyaścitta, tumulaka doṣa ning madamĕl kṣaya kula? yeki sākṣāt adharma-karaṇa ngaran ika, apan niyatânghilangakĕn piṇḍodaka-kriyā.

When could it be that I could enjoy a tranquil heart when I had killed my family and kinsmen there on the field of battle? And that is the reason, mahārāja Krishna, that I have no desire for victory or the majesty of ruling a

---

[16] Another striking example of the indexing of social hierarchies by way of the Old Javanese pronominal system see Bhīṣmaparwa 59.9–17, which paraphrases BG 35.1–4.

kingdom. What is the purpose of pleasure or life itself if one becomes a prāṇaghata, one who annihilates their kith and kin. Feelings of affection and attachment have overpowered my heart. Where then can there be happiness? Where satisfaction? Clearly, we will meet only with wretchedness and evil. Whither thence divine order? Whither thence the expiation that would ward off the evil of bringing about the destruction of one's lineage? That clearly is what is known as adharma-karaṇa, "action that goes against the dharma," for one thus eliminates forever piṇḍodaka-kriyā, the rituals to the sacred ancestors.

While much of this can be read as "translating" a South Asian understanding of social order, it is also quite clear that we see reflected here the ritual and social order of Javanese society during the era of the Sanskrit ecumene. This comes out most clearly in the rarely used phrase piṇḍodaka-kriyā, which refers to the annual offering of balls of rice and water to the ancestors that is an important part of South Asian śraddha rites, but was, if anything, more crucial to the social order of societies of Southeast Asia, where a great deal of attention is paid to the continuing rituals that ensure the health and prosperity of human society through the reiteration of the connection of human society with the world of sacred ancestors.

Excerpt 3: The Training of Warriors

In another excerpt the Old Javanese narrator expands on the theme of the Sanskrit original to bring home a lesson about the performance of one's social duty (swadharma) that had a special role to play in the alliance of priestly and warrior castes that was as central to the "Sanskritized" societies of Southeast Asia as it was to India itself.

BG 26.31; Gh 44.4–6
svadharmam eva cāvekṣya na vikalpitum arhati
dharmyādd hi yudhhāc chreyo 'nyat kṣatriyasya na vidyate

You should attend to your own duty and stand firm, for there is nothing better for a warrior than a legitimate battle.

Gh 44.7–14
swadharma ning kadi kita tah wawarĕngön. haywa sumandeha ng halahayu, apayapan tan hana wih dharma yukti gawayĕn de ning kadi kita kṣatriya yan lena sangkeng dharma-yuddha-karma. ya ta n gawaya ng

dharmayuddhakārya biṣama ng kīrti katinggala kapangguh pāpa magöng niyata ginuyu-guyu de sang mahāwīra upětěn de ning singhapuruṣa. ikang ulah tininda de ning śūrajana yeka duḥkha mahābāra ngaranya ring rat.

It is the swadharma of those like you that you should heed with full attention. Don't have doubts about [the teachings on] evil and righteousness, for there is no dharma more fitting to be undertaken by those who are warriors (kṣatriya) than that of a just war. It is the work of a just battle that you should carry out, lest (in failing to do so) honor and fame will desert you and you will meet with great evil, constantly mocked by great heroes and spoken ill of by lions among men. Your conduct will be censured by men of heroic nature: that is what is known as the greatest suffering in this world.

EXCERPT 4: INSTRUCTIONS ON "CARE FOR THE BODY"

Mark Hobart (1983) has noted in an article provocatively titled "How My Balinese Neighbor Became a Duck" that his Balinese interlocutors could not envision a self (ātmā) that has a separate existence from the body. A similar set of beliefs seems to be at work in the Old Javanese expansion on BG 30.1, where the narrator emphasizes the importance of "care for the body" in the pursuit of spiritual attainment, thus introducing what seems a very Southeast Asian cultural theme into the original discourse on ātmā.

<u>BG 30.5; Gh 51.30–31</u>
uddhared ātmanâtmānaṃ nâtmānam avasādayet
ātmâiva hy ātmano bandhur ātmâiva ripur ātmanaḥ

A man should elevate himself by himself, and shouldn't degrade himself, for the self is the self's only friend, and the self is the self's only foe.

<u>Gh 51.29</u>
kunang pinakajāti sang paṇḍita nihan:
<u>Gh 52.1–10</u>
awak nira juga sādhana nirânghanakěn śarīra nira, tatan dadi mirsakit ing swaśarīra, apan tan hana kadang ny awak nira lena sangke swaśarīra nira. musuh ny awak nira ya ta swaśarīra nira. seng (?) nikang ujar mangkana: ngke śarīra ta pwa sangkan ing mitra mwang śatru, udāsina. ring awak mūla ning hala lawan hayu. yan apa n hayu? yan hayu kawangun de ning śarīra. yan kakawaśa ng indriya de nikang wang pisih yatikâmangun hayu. yapwan ta n kakawaśa pwa ng wang dening indriya irika ta ya n hala kawangun de nikang awak.

"Going on, the true condition of a wise man is as follows: His (physical) body (awak) is his spiritual means for brining into existence his (true) body" (śarīra). It isn't proper to bring pain to his own body (swaśarīra), for there is no other friend of his (physical) body than his own body. And the enemy of his (physical) body is indeed his own body. The teaching is thus: the body itself is the source of friends, enemies and those who are indifferent. And the source of evil and auspiciousness (hala hayu) is the body. If there is goodness and auspiciousness (hayu) it is raised up by the body. If the sense-organs (indriya) of an attentive man are brought under control that brings goodness and auspiciousness (hayu,) but if a man is controlled by the sense-organs that is the source of the evil and pain (hala) that is brought into being by the body.

A very similar caution about extreme practices of asceticism can be found in an important early work of the Buddhist didactic tradition in Old Javanese. These lines that expand on Verse 31 in the Sang Hyang Kamahāyānan Mantranaya carry a very similar message to those of Bhīṣmaparwa 52.1–10. Constructed around a Sanskrit śloka that is explicated through a combination of Old Javanese and Sanskrit glosses, this example from the didactic tradition rounds out the argumentation of this chapter by revealing the close links between the literary practice of the court of Dharmawangśa Těguh and the didactic practices of the Buddhist and Shaiva monastic and pedagogical institutions. These were the institutions that were responsible for the training of young royals and the wider nobility, both those destined for the court and defense of the nation and those destined to play a role in the religious institutions that provided models for governance such as those embodied in the Parwa literature.

Sang Hyang Kamahāyānan Mantranaya (SHM), verse 31
svam ātmānaṃ parityajya tapobhir natipīḍayet/
yathāsukhaṃ sukhaṃ dhāryaṃ sambuddho 'yam anāgataḥ//31//[17]

---

[17] In 1974 de Jong summarized the findings of the Japanese scholars Wogihara Unrai (1915) and Sakai Shiro (1950), who had shown that the Sanskrit portions of the Sang Hyang Kamahāyānan Mantranaya (SHM) can be traced to the Chinese version of the Mahāvairocanasūtra and to Chinese and Tibetan versions of the Adhyardha-śatikā-prajñapāramitā-sūtra. Two versions of the Mahāvairocanasūtra were brought to China by Wu-hsing and Śubhakara and translated into Chinese between 724 and 725 CE by Śubhakara and I-hsing (cf. de Jong 1974: 633–635). These considerations suggest that the doctrinal basis of the later Mahāyāna and Mantrayāna was well known in Java by at least the ninth century, and that the composition of the SHM could easily have taken place not long afterward.

Having given up the things of this world, you should not oppress your Self with severe acts of penance, Your way of bearing yourself should be one of ease, according to your ability; (in this way) you will attain Buddhahood in the future.

kalinganya/patiwar ikâwakta/
svakāyanirapekṣataḥ kita haywa tṛṣṇa ring awak/
tapobhir natipīḍayet haywa pinisakitan ring tapa/
haywa wineh gumawayakĕn kawĕnangnya /
yathāsukhaṃ sukhaṃ
dhāryaṃ yathāsukha lwiranta t' gawayakĕn ng boddhimārgga/
sambuddho 'yam anāgataḥ haywa gyā hyang buddha kita dlāha

The meaning is: you should abandon your body to its fate;
    svakāyanirapekṣataḥ: you should have no attachment to your body;
    tapobhir nâtipīḍayet: don't torture it with austerities; don't allow them to take power over you;
    yathāsukhaṃ sukhaṃ dhāryaṃ: as you carry forward the way to enlightenment the path you take should be one of ease, according to your ability;
    sambuddho'yam anāgataḥ: don't rush; you will become the Lord Buddha one day in the future.

Conclusions

I have endeavored to show in this chapter that even a cursory glance at the relationship of Sanskrit verses to their Old Javanese "translations" in the Parwa literature shows us that we are not dealing with translation as it is conventionally understood, but rather with text-building practices that derive ultimately from the didactic traditions of the religious institutions central to the formation of the state in the lands of the Sanskrit cosmopolis. It seems clear that these traditions go back to pedagogical practices in institutions where "cosmopolitan vernacular" languages such as Old Malay, Old Javanese and Old Balinese were consciously developed as instruments of statecraft and vehicles for literary practice in a world where literature was central to the interests of the state. If the choice of examples and comments on the verses cited from the Bhagavad-gītā and Old Javanese Bhīṣmaparwa has been successful, this chapter has perhaps revealed some small part of the story of cultural interchanges that marked an era when Indian cultural practices and ideas spread far from their original home in the Indus Valley and Gangetic plain. That these ideas spread along ancient trading networks that were active well before the era of the cosmopolis (*c*. 300–1500) attests to the importance of taking into account the local concerns of South Indian and Southeast Asian partners in a trans-cultural world where each local development bears the double stamp of indigenous ideas and practices and the impact of the linguistic ideology of Sanskrit, and all that implied for the formation of the languages and rituals of the state.

REFERENCES

Cherniak, Alex (2008) Mahābhārata, Book Six, Bhīṣma, Volume One, Including the "Bhagavad Gītā" in context. New York: New York University Press & JJC Foundation.
Gonda, Jan. 1936. Het Oudjavaansche Bhismaparwa. [Bibliotheca Javanica 7] Batavia (Jakarta): Koninklijk Bataviaasch Genootschap van Kunsten en Wetenschappen. Bandoeng: A.C. Nix.
Hobart, Mark (1983) "Through Western Eyes, or How My Balinese Neighbor Became a Duck." Indonesia Circle Newsletter 11:30, pp. 33–47. [Anniversary Lecture, University of London: School of Oriental and African Studies]
Hunter, Thomas M. 2011. 'Translation in a World of Diglossia,' in Jan van der Putten and Ronit Ricci (eds.) Translation in Asia: Theories, Practices, Histories. Manchester, pp. 9–26. Great Britain: St. Jerome Publishing.
Hunter, Thomas M. 2013. 'Religion', in Véronique Degroot (ed.) Magical Prambanan, pp. 32–41. Jakarta: BAB Publishers.
de Jong, J.W. 1974. 'Notes on the Sources and the text of the Sang Hyang Kamahāyanan Mantranaya.' Bijdragen tot de Taal- Land-en Volkenkunde, 136 (4): 619–636.
van der Meulen, W.J. 1979. 'Sañjaya and His Successor', Indonesia, 28: 17–54.
Pollock, Sheldon (1998) "The Cosmopolitan Vernacular:" The Journal of Asian Studies 57 (1): 6–37.
Takakusu, J. 2006 [1896]. A Record of the Buddhist Religion: As Practised in India and the Malay Archipelago (A.D. 671–695). Delhi: Cosmo Publishers.
Silverstein, Michael. 1976. 'Shifters, linguistic categories, and cultural description,' in K. Basso, and H. Selby (eds.) Meaning in anthropology, pp. 11–56. Albuquerque: University of New Mexico Press.

Silverstein, Michael. 1998. 'The Uses and Utility of Ideology: a Commentary," in Bambi B., Kathryn A. Woolard, and Paul V. Kroskrity (eds.) Language Ideologies, Practice and Theory, pp. 68-100. [Oxford Studies in Anthropological Linguistics, No. 16] New York, Oxford: Oxford University Press.

Zoetmulder, P.J. 1974. Kalangwan: a Survey of Old Javanese Literature, pp. 68-100. [KITLV, Translation Series 16] The Hague: Martinus Nijhoff.

CHAPTER 12

The Reworking of Indian Epics in the Hands of Javanese and Malay Authors

Ding Choo Ming

INTRODUCTION

As a natural junction of sea routes between India and China, the so-called Malay World—comprising the present Republic of Indonesia, Malaysia, Singapore, Brunei, southern Thailand and southern Philippines—has for centuries been the meeting point of Chinese, Indian, Arab and European influences, which in turn played a decisive role in the development of early Malay World literature, both in manuscript and oral forms. The arrival of Hinduism, before the coming of Islam, provided a great surge of artistic expression in the Malay World's traditional literature.

The earliest stream of Indian language, culture and literature is believed to have come to the Malay World with Brahmin and Ksatriya adventurers, traders and others. Their arrival strengthened trade and cultural ties between India and the Malay World. This cultural contact and literary migration of the Indian epics along the trading route to Langkasuka,

---

This paper is an expansion of The Reworking of Indian Epics in the Other Side of the Indian Ocean, published in Dialogue vol. 13 no. 1 (2011).

D. Choo Ming (✉)
Former Principal Research Fellow, Institute of Malay World & Civilization, National University of Malaysia, Selangor, Malaysia

© The Author(s) 2018
S. Saran (ed.), *Cultural and Civilisational Links between India and Southeast Asia*, https://doi.org/10.1007/978-981-10-7317-5_12

Kadaram and others, some of the earliest 'Indian-influenced' states in the region then known to the Indians as Suvamabhumi and Suvamadvipa, found a permanent home not only in the local texts and temples, but also in the heart of the local folk who cherished the universal values enshrined in the stories, such as love, truth, solidarity and the ultimate triumph of righteousness over evil. To these must be added the fantasies of demons which enthral the local audience, who carry them from place to place so that they remain ever popular, without linguistic barriers, among the Javanese and Malays (Sarkar 1983: 206–208; Ratnam 1983: 231).

Following the arrival of Hinduism, we also witness the development of complex socio-cultural rituals that encompassed practically all areas of life, ranging from politics and government to family law and interpersonal relationships (Farish A. Noor 2005: 38). In the process, new social, political and religious systems transformed the mental, moral, aesthetic and cultural universe of the local people. In the end, there emerged a rigid and highly ordered religio-political social system with *raja* and *istana* occupying a pivotal position in society (Milner 1982, 1986). In this way, Indian influences were established in Java, Sumatra and the Malay Peninsula before the emergence of the Islamic sultanates on both sides of the Straits of Malacca in the early thirteenth century.

As ties with India grew in strength, 'Indian-influenced' kingdoms in the region began to emerge around 100 CE. Chronologically, the ensuing development of 'Indian-influenced' kingdoms from 100 CE onwards in the region provided increasing evidence of the long history of interaction between 'foreign' and local cultures in early Malay civilizations, with kings, rulers, sultans and *raja* in the region contributing a great deal to the process of 'Indianization' of Southeast Asia. Among them was Srivijaya, a maritime empire in the island of Sumatra, from the seventh to the thirteenth centuries. It controlled the Malay Peninsula and parts of Java through the Hindu–Buddhist Sailenda dynasty, and flourished in central Java from the eighth to the thirteenth century, when Islam was accepted in Demak, Pasai and Malacca.

It is in the Hindu period, when Hinduism was reaching the peak of its development and importance in the Sailendra and Srivijaya dynasties, that Javanese rulers and Malay rajas took some of the Hindu concepts of caste and the caste system and further modified them to fit their local needs. Noticing that the pre-Islamic Javanese and Malay *kerajaan* was firmly focused upon the near-omnipotent *raja*, Farish A. Noor (2005: 39) adds that the term *kerajaan* ensures that the rulers or *raja* constitute the primary object of loyalty from the people under their rule. In this context, the concept of *derhaka* is also taken from Hinduism to be contextualized in the pre-existing power structure. Following this, the hierarchy and structure of Malay *kerajaan* is referred to in Milner's works (1982, 1986). In the same way, the Hindu concept of *sakti* was grafted on to give the local ruling elites a sacral-supernatural power and authority (Farish A. Noor 2005: 38–40), dubbed as *daulat*, an important component in the traditional concept of Malay kingship.

Indian Influences Enriched Malay World Literature

As important monuments in early Javanese and Malay literature, the early and mostly anonymous and undated works from the various Javanese and Malay courts all over the Malay World not only reflect the ingenuity and wisdom of the Malay World authors, but also their unique synthesis of early Malay culture and tradition. Winstedt (1969) argues that much of the early Malay literature is not only full of allusions to Hindu, Arabic and Persian mythologies, but is also mostly translations, reworkings and localizations of Sanskrit, Arabic and Persian literatures. He cites *Hikayat Seri Rama* as a free translation of Ramayana and *Hikayat Bayan Budiman* as an adaptation of *Sukasaptati*. In recent years, scholars have tried to explain many of the problems raised by different versions of the Indian epics in the composition of *Hikayat Seri Rama and Hikayat Pandawa Lima*, for example, which are based on the reworking of some stories from the epics. Solutions to many of these complex problems will continue to challenge them for many years to come.

From the extant literary work, including the *kakawin* and *hikayat*, it is obvious that authors in the Malay World in the early days did not adopt a confrontational approach to Hindu-Buddhism, nor did they accept them totally. This means the acceptance of stories from the Indian epics was also very selective. This resulted in the region's literature tradition becoming a rich tapestry of many and varied multicoloured designs, interwoven and layered upon each other within the framework of native tradition (Roxas-Lim 2005: 16). This not only demonstrates a process of intellectual engagement, adaptation, interaction and transformation, but also the fact that new stories that were accommodated were used to widen the scope and range of local literature. It was this interaction that formed the heritage that shapes and enriches the early Javanese and Malay literatures.

The extant resources indicate that Malay 'traditional' literature was not written until about 1400, though Javanese literature is believed to date from 900 CE. The problems of dating Malay World literature from the Hindu period are insurmountable not only because of the natural destruction of *lontar* leaves and other easily perishable fragile organic materials in a harsh tropical climate, but also the rapid evolution of local languages and scripts, namely the Pallava, Kawi and Renchung, and the destruction of many other Hindu literary works following the ascendancy of Islam.

Interestingly, though, the extant literature can be used to give us a glimpse of the history of 'Indianization' in bygone days. An important point to bear in mind is that 'Indianization' did not break the early Javanese and Malay literary traditions, but reinforced them in the sense that stories, values, motives and characterization from the Indian epics were accommodated in one way or another into the existing Javanese and Malay literatures to widen their scope and range. The outcome was something old and new, in the sense that we find different Indian, Islamic and Javanese influences coexisting, indicating a tolerance, flexibility and adaptability in the traditional Javanese and Malay literatures.

One obvious example can be cited here of the coexistence of Hinduism and Islam. It is none other than the *Hikayat Merong Mahawangsa*. Therein, we come across the marvellous and fantastic tales that tell not only of the adoption and adaptation of Hinduism in the region, but also a paradigm shift in the local people's understanding of themselves: who they were and where they were located in the universal scheme of things. This comingling between the past and the present, between Hinduism and Islam, is also evident in many of the extant Malay *hikayat* in Jawi, including the *Hikayat Indera Jaya* and *Hikayat Shah Mardan*, in addition to the already mentioned *Hikayat Merong Mahawangsa*, which was written after Islam had taken root in the Malay World. Various linguistic, cultural and religious currents flow through them. They are also pregnant with Hindu, Islamic, animistic and indigenous tales.

From the literary point of view, the multifarious beliefs, ideas and symbols in the Mahabharata and Ramayana gave the Javanese and Malay court artisans plenty of tales, ideas, myths and legends to work on, thus keeping them occupied for hundreds of years. Works included *Nagarakertagama* by the Javanese court poet Mpu Prapancha (1365–), from the Majapahit kingdom (1293–1500), valorizes the ruler Rajasanagara or Hayam Wuruk (1334–1389) as the Dewaraja, placing him at the narrative centre of the Java-centred universe. The extant *kakawin* and *hikayat* that 'originated' in the Hindu period bear all the elements of the Javanese and Malay people's lives: their land, beliefs, values, wisdom, customs, feelings, romanticism and fantasy, among many other aspects, interact with those from the two Indian epics.

Contents of Encompassing Nature

The Indian epics, the Ramayana and Mahabharata, were also used to pass on a wide-ranging philosophy and moral teachings, *darmasastra* (moral lessons), *arthasastra* (lessons on politics and war craft) and *nitisastra* (lessons on how to lead a noble life), but also provided examples of the ideal way of life. The core of these moral teachings was manifested in the main characters in the epics. For example, in the Ramayana Rama is the epitome of virtues; Sita, the beloved wife of Rama, is symbol of female purity and virtue; Hanuman, who plays an important role in locating Sita in the ensuing battles, is believed to live until our modern world; Laksamana, the younger brother of Rama, chooses to go into exile with the former to protect Sita and Rama; Ravana, a *raksasa*, the king of Lanka, is epitome of a powerful demon king; and Jatayu is a demi-god who has the form of an eagle and tries to rescue Sita from Ravana. These powerful themes of universal values have had a very deep influence on the people of the Malay World.

The immense popularity of these stories is not only because they illustrate the spiritual struggle of man—an eternal struggle between good and evil—but also because of their affirmation of life and the knowledge of a life which negates the concept of death as final. Here, Javanese and Malays see the continuity of life in the grand panorama of the epics as an everrejuvenating process, a principle that is eternally alive. This can be seen clearly in *Hikayat Hang Tuah* too, especially with the expression of immortality in the message bestowed on *Hikayat Hang Tuah* that 'tak Melayu hilang di dunia' (Never shall Malays vanish from the earth) and the fact that Hang Tuah becomes a hermit and does not die (Kassim Ahmad 2008). Another interesting point is the convention of choosing the young and brave to portray the character of Hang Tuah in the *Hikayat Hang Tuah*, in the way that Rama in the Ramayana and the five warriors of Lord Krishna in the Mahabharata are portrayed to symbolize life and its struggle, which is ageless and transcends time (Ratnam 1983: 249–250). Besides that, many historians and literature critics point out that warrior Hang Tuah and his four warrior friends—Hang Jebat, Hang Kasturi, Hang Lekir and Hang Lekiu—are a Malay version of the five warriors of Lord Krishna in the Mahabharata.

Another interesting point here is that the unknown author of *Hikayat Hang Tuah* knows how to construct a story or 'romance' to keep the audience enthralled from the beginning to the end, with tales of an idealized feudal Javanese and Malay hero whose life follows in a familiar and intricate pattern of jealousy, conflict, fate and divine intervention as in so many other Malay *hikayat*, including those were remodelled on the Panji tales and the Ramayana and Mahabharata, which respectively also demonstrate the ideals of right and wrong, good and bad. We must not forget the importance of literary imagination in the heroic stories in providing entertainment and enjoyment, in generating emotions, thoughts and feelings, and more importantly in inspiring the audience to greater heights of imagination (Muhamamad Haji Salleh 1992). The audience of these early Javanese and Malay literary works certainly enjoyed the tales because of the clever interplay of absorbing romances, tragedies, duels and the adventures of heroes and heroines who dare to venture into a fantastic world in which humans jostle with supernatural beings. The heroes, their characterizations and their stories in the Indian epics provided role models for how to deal with the perplexities of life.

MORE INFLUENCES OF THE INDIAN EPICS

On the other influences of the Indian epics on early Javanese literature, it is stated that during the rule of King Dharmawangsa (990–1006) a prose summary of the eighteen books of the Mahabharata in the Javanese language became a great source of inspiration for Javanese poets. This has continued to be the case over the centuries, as some of the stories from this work have continued to be adapted at the order of Javanese rulers. Its influence has been so strong that the Javanese consider the forefathers of their monarch to be incarnations of the Indian warriors in the epic. It has been regarded as having a certain magical power that its translation and reworking has not diminished: not only does it honour the Javanese forefathers, but it also confers special power on their rulers (Liaw 2013: 80). Its tremendous influence can also be seen in a great variety of other literary works from the region, including the *Hikayat Pandawa*, another very popular work in Malay traditional literature.

Related to Pandawa's brothers in the *Hikayat Pandawa*, we have other stories such as the *Hikayat Pandawa Lebur*, the *Hikayat Darmawangsa* and the *Hikayat Angkawijaya*, which are either translations, adaptations or reworkings from the Javanese *kakawin*: the *Hikayat Sang Boma* is a translation from the *Kakawin Bhomakawya*, the *Hikayat Perang Pandawa Jaya* is an adaptation from the *Kakawin Bharata Yudha*, while the *Kakawin Ghatotkacasraya* and *Kakawin Arjuna Wiwaha* can be traced back to the *Hikayat Pandawa Lima* or *Hikayat Panca Kelima* (Zoetmulder 1974).

In the meantime, in the Malay literature there are also such works as *Hikayat Pandawa*, *Hikayat Pandawa Lima*, *Hikayat Pandawa Jaya*, *Hikayat Perang Pandawa Lima* and *Pandawa Panca Kelima* (Knappert 1999: 73; Liaw 2013: 81). But Winstedt (1969: 52) argues that many of these romances were composed after Islam had been firmly established, with the relics of Hinduism being adapted to a changed world. All of these examples, and also the *Hikayat Inderaputera*, *Hikayat Maharaja Puspa Wiraja*, *Hikayat Sang Boma*, *Hikayat Seri Rama* and *Hikayat Hang Tuah*, clearly bear the traces of Indian epics and Javanese shadow-play tales.

But we have a problem with the authorship in Malay manuscript culture. It is messy and is made worse by the indifferent copying that has taken place (Ding 1999, 2003, 2008), not to mention the inherent problems in writing on the *lontar* leaves with their rough fibres: these do not allow the easy flow of ink or let the scribes put the necessary dots in appropriate places. Some of the confusion can be due to another important factor: that the writers, artists and storytellers have adapted the tales to suit the already changed conditions of contemporary life.

Although local people in the Malay World do not reject the cultural and literary heritage from India, their knowledge of the Indian sacred texts has dwindled so much over time that they have to secularize, modify and even localize some of the popular stories for contemporary public entertainment. This can be seen in the change of names in the *Hikayat Seri Rama* by Mir Hassan from Kampar, Perak, Malaysia, published by Maxwell (1886), To summarize the changes, Sri Rama is called the king of Tanjung Bunga, Sita the Princess Sekuntum Bunga Setangkai, Hanuman is called Kera Kecil Imam Tengganga, Laksamana is a shaman (*pawang*) and the names of the different kingdoms are given as Syah Noman, Gunung Inggil Beringgil and Gunung Inggil Beringgil (Liaw 2013: 64–65).

Products of Literary Synthesis Over a Period of Time

Many would agree that many of the early Javanese and Malay literary works were not composed all at once, but gradually from many sources over a period of time, an example being the *Hikayat Hang Tuah* (Braginsky (2004: 471–473). This argument is based on the fact they not only have wide breadth and scope, but also include the conventional background of fantastic adventure romances, spiced with Malay interpretations of Panji tales, the Ramayana, Mahabharata and others. This means they are the outcomes of literary synthesis in the early Malay literature. This may lead us to other puzzling questions regarding authorship, as mentioned earlier, and creativity around the reworking of the Indian epics in the Malay World.

Though early or traditional Malay literature is seen to be receptive to external influences, it is far from being a passive recipient. This being the case, it is indeed an extraordinary alchemy and interaction of diversity, localization and assimilation of external influences, whatever their sources, and the achievement of Malay World authors' very open- minds. There has been a slow, gentle, selective, stylistic and subtle adaptation and absorption over a period of decades, if not centuries, to give enough time for new ideas and other changes to percolate through and be synthesized. This long process involves copying, which is followed by accommodation, socialization, toleration, localization, hybridization, elaboration and other stages, in response to stimuli depending on circumstances. As a result, there are different versions of the *Hikayat Seri Rama* (Ikram 1980), the *Hikayat Pandawa Lima* and others, with stories which may and may not be the same as in Ramayana and Mahabharata after they have been reworked with new stories and characters added to reflect the contemporary Javanese and Malay authors' interpretations of the stories in the two epics, so that they could be accepted in the region. This is important because in addition to entertainment, the *kakawin* and *hikayat* tradition served also to strengthen communal ties and help to restore peace and harmony in the Javanese and Malay societies as they underwent changes (Muhammad Haji Salleh 1992).

All the above could be better understood as part of a big synthesis process that went on for centuries regarding early Javanese and Malay literary authorship. In this synthesis, the chronology of history is ignored to allow the authors to elevate the status of their principal characters, examples being Hang Tuah in the *Hikayat Hang Tuah*; Yudistira, Arjuna, Bima and Nakula dan Sadewa in the *Hikayat Pendawa*; Raja Ahmad and Raja Muhammad in the *Hikayat Raja-Raja Pasai* and Raja Bikrama Puspa in the *Hikayat Inderaputera*. Another plausible explanation for this synthesis is the convention among Javanese and Malay authors that allows them to assimilate stories to bring them within the compass of the common man's knowledge and taste.

In this process, we see the obvious features of 'similarity in variety' and vice versa in some of the episodes, motifs and values of Hang Tuah as identifiable in the main characters in the Panji tales, the Ramayana and Mahabharata, for example. Though we do not know when the first Javanese *kakawin* and Malay *hikayat* in the Hindu period were composed, as indicated earlier, we now have some ideas of the circumstances of their creation, and some of the various stages through which many of the *kakawin* and *hikayats* evolve until they reach the form familiar to us now. This means that we are not only interested in what has been created, but also what has been accepted into local tradition. This approach can hopefully shed new light on the creative process and the kind of stimuli given to authors in bygone days.

THE INDIAN EPICS ARE ROOTS OF EARLY LITERARY WORKS

Based on the extant literary works, we can say for certain that the Indian epics, the Ramayana and Mahabharata, are the roots of some of the earliest Javanese and Malay literary works. The former has also been recounted in Malay in *Hikayat Seri Rama*, and the latter in *Hikayat Pandawa Lima*, for instance. Retrospectively, the Sanskrit original of the latter was abridged in an Old Javanese prose of about 1000 CE, in which the kernel story of *Bharatayudha* was turned into a lovely poem in 1157 by Sedah and his brother Panuluh. This was in turn adapted in modern Javanese as *Baratayuda* (Zoetmulder 1974).

Over the centuries, the Indian myths have also seeped into Malay folktales, following the immense popularity of the Indian epics. Thus, we find lots of them not only in *cerita penglipor lara*, for example the *Hikayat Anggun Cik Tunggal* and *Hikayat Malim Deman*, but also in many court literary works, such as the *Hikayat Hang Tuah* and *Hikayat Raja-Raja Pasai*. Equally interestingly, many of the Hindu spirits and gods have also been modified to suit the Javanese and Malay cultural, social and religious needs as they were believed to be able to yield the power expected from the spirit of the Wind (Mambang Angin), the spirit of the Waters (Hantu Ayer) and the spirit of the Sun (Mambang Kuning). Therefore, in Malay folklore we find versions of Vishnu, the preserver, Brahma the creator and Batara Guru (Kala), among others (Haron Daud 2004).

Related to the above, Batara Guru is unquestionably the greatest of all the Indian deities. It appears in *Hikayat Sang Sembah* that it is the Batara Guru who has the elixir of life that can restore life to the dead. Another notable character in Malay folklore is the *gergasi*, the half-human forest spirit represented as a tusked ogre who feeds on human flesh in the Kedah annals, *Hikayat Merong Mahawangsa*. He leads a group of giants and establishes Langasuka, the present state of Pattani. Here, we must be aware that in the past the forests surrounding the Javanese and Malays were an unknown mystery. Demons and ghosts lurked there looking for wandering human beings. People did not dare upset the natural equilibrium that maintained the balance and harmony between the world of men and nature, and in addition the Malay World abounded with legends and folktales about heroes who underwent trials along every step of their journey through the foreboding forests (Sharifah 1993). We find such mythical birds as the *geruda*, *jentayu* and *cenderawasi*, beastly creatures including the *naga*, *raksasa*, *mambang*, *polong* and *pontianak*, lycanthropic humans such as the *harimau jadian* in *Hikayat Inderaputera*, *Hikayat Inderjaya*, *Hikayat Malim Deman*, *Hikayat Panca Tanderan*, *Hikayat Cekel Waneng Pati* and *Hikayat Bayan Budiman*.

As it is, in literary works from the Hindu period, human beings seem to be in contact with spirits and, interestingly, can speak with animals and spirits in the forest. It is not surprising, therefore, to find in the *Hikayat Shah Mardan* that Raja Indera Jaya is portrayed as transforming into a bird and later a monkey. In addition to many strange and wonderful things that happen one after the other, he meets Ulama Tuan Shekih al-Din and Tuan Sheikh Lukman al-Hakim (Farish A. Noor 2005: 24).

An Insatiable Hunger for Fantastic Tales

This hunger for fantastic tales continues in *Hikayat Hang Tuah*, believed to have been composed in 1700. After picking up the arts of self-defence and meditation from Adi Putera, Hang Tuah can change his form at will. In a duel with Sang Winara, a Majapahit warrior, he changes himself into a log, a dog, a man again, an insect, a cat, a tiger and back to his usual self. Likewise, in an attempt to defeat Hang Tuah, Petala Bumi, another Javanese warrior, changes himself into a cat, a log, a dog, a tiger and a monster. In response, Hang Tuah changes himself into a tiger and then back to his ordinary self. This is just one of the many examples of the 'similarity in variety' between Hang Tuah in the *Hikayat Hang Tuah* and Rama and his friends in the Ramayana.

Here we must also be aware that much Malay court literature on the adventures and daring exploits of members of the elite shows them in association with deities and spirits. In these stories, human and supernatural worlds interconnect with one another as part of one united cosmos. It is obvious here that many different local myths and needs have been interwoven in *Hikayat Hang Tuah*, *Hikayat Raja-Raja Pasai*, *Hikayat Seri Rama* and *Kakawin Bhāratayuddha*, for instance. This also suggests that some Rama stories in the Ramayana have been localized in these literary works through a long process of reworking and rebalancing. It is from this process that new versions of the *Hikayat Hang Tuah*, *Hikayat Raja-Raja Pasai*, *Hikayat Seri Rama* and also the *Kakawin Bhāratayuddha* appear from time to time in the early Javanese and Malay literatures.

The above literary works can be cited as examples that include rather than exclude, or accommodate rather than differentiate, Hinduism and Islam. In these literary works, the encounter between Islam and the pre-Islamic past is negotiated with care in the same way that Hindu temples and Muslim mosques have been built next to one another in the region over the centuries. This indicates the tolerance and readiness of local people to absorb different faiths from elsewhere, as well as continuing their local religious practices and revering ancestral spirits, as in the Hindu-inspired *Hikayat Sri Rama*. It is the encompassing contents of these literary works that brings out the richness of the Malay literature and culture, and the creativity of hundreds of Malay authors, anonymous and known.

All in all, we not only find that both indigenous animistic beliefs and nature worship have been incorporated into Buddhist, Hindu and Islamic belief systems in one way or another, but also that the spirits invoked are appeased to ensure health, prosperity, fertility, to ward off evil or *bala* and to obtain general well-being, *pahala*, for oneself, the family and the community. Here, literary works in their myriad forms have served to ratify social relations and deal with the risks and uncertainties of life (Roxas-Lim 2005: 50–53). Over the centuries, generation after generation of Javanese and Malay authors had been composing literary works that tell their story, their people and how they view the universe.

But we do not know when or where most of these literary works were originally composed, as mentioned earlier. To divine an answer to this, we have to turn to history.

In central Java, there are the Sailendra (eighth century) and Sanjaya (732–760) kingdoms, among many others. It is believed that Sanskrit texts were actively translated into Javanese and other local languages in the region, including in the Mataram kingdom that rose to power in the early tenth century. One of the most significant rulers from the Mataram kingdom was Airlangga (1019–1042). He extended his power and rule to Bali and other areas. Historically, the *Panji* tales, a cycle of romances about Prince Panji and Princess Kirana, and Panji's search for his long-lost bride, are believed to have been created in the kingdom, while a famous Javanese court poet, Arjuna Vivaha, wrote poems in honour of Airlangga. In religious life, the tantric teachings from India gained influence, thus adding yet another element to the syncretism of Javanese religion.

THE RECREATION OR REWORKING OF 'NEW' LITERARY WORKS

Until now, we have generally accepted that early Javanese and Malay traditional literary works are mostly anonymous. We have also generally accepted that a well-known *hikayat*, whether from the Ramayana, Mahabharata or the others, becomes familiar generation after generation as the tales grow in popularity. This means that many of the tales that have been inherited today are those that were popular yesterday. As it is, the last 'edition' is perhaps the creative act of a single author, unlike the earlier ones which are the cumulative work of many unknown authors and have undergone a long process of recreation. The stories produced in this way can have their roots in those that are floating around n oral form, being recreated according to these authors' individual creativity in response to certain stimuli. Describing the author as a creator is a bit ambiguous, but in the strict sense of the word any creation is a creative act as long as it brings into being something new and special. The primary concern of these authors is to make these tales as appealing and beneficial as possible, and this is a cardinal concept of authorship in Javanese and Malay traditional literature.

From the extant literary works, whether derived from the Mahabharata, Ramayana or other sources, we can see that literary works in the Malay World were specifically oral for centuries (Sweeney 1994). The thousands of manuscripts that we have inherited were written in old Javanese script in Java and in Jawi script after the arrival of Islam in the thirteenth century. The transition from oral to written literature, from the Hindu to the Islamic period, entails the use of preexisting structural and decorative forms, as shown in the *Hikayat Seri Rama*, *Hikayat Pandawa Lima*, *Bhraratayuddha* and others. In this way, oral tales are transposed into manuscripts by recomposing them. Since the Hindu period, Javanese and

Malay authors are believed to have been 'producing' literary works using familiar schematic compositions from oral discourse that was known to them.

Transforming and adapting oral tales into written form is certainly another aspect of the creative process in Malay authorship. Authors charged with transforming these works had the creative freedom to reinterpret and recreate. Here, Sweeney (1994: 4–5) explains that as long as the mode of consumption is aural, the written tradition continues to employ schematic modes of composition. The reliance on schemata is to ensure relative stability in the content of what is produced and transmitted.

However repetitive the tales may appear, every author has contributed something valuable and special, because within the system there is enormous scope for creativity, though not necessarily originality in the strictest sense of the word. The authors know that scope and space, and more importantly their own capabilities and creativity. Once we comprehend the workings of the system in which they operate, it becomes apparent that their genius can be appreciated in their terms and ours (Sweeney (1994: xiii). It is in this way that we can assume that different authors have worked on and reworked different stories from the Ramayana and Mahabharata for a very long time. In this process, we can understand not only their burden as preservers of oral and written literature, but also the increasing weight of collective memory that grows with each passing generation. As a result, we have the *Hikayat Perang Pandawa Lima*, *Hikayat Song Boma*, *Hikayat Seri Rama*, *Hikayat Maharaja Ravana*, *Bhagavatapurana*, *Bhaumakavya*, *Serat Kanda*, *Hikayat Pandawa Jaya*, *Hikayat Perang Puting*, *Hikayat Inderaputera*, *Hikayat Langlang Buana*, *Hikayat Marakarma* and others cited in the history of Javanese and Malay literature.

Studying them, we know very well that Javanese and Malay authors, scribes and editors over the centuries have changed words, altered names of characters, reinterpreted meanings, added tales or even changed titles in the process of writing and rewriting. These changes are made consciously to make them better in one way or the other. In this way, many 'new' literary works are created, however much they may resemble others. Thus we find repetition of tales, characters, messages and plots not only in one particular work, but also across many works (Ding 2003; Maier 1985). What is involved here is adding something new to make the stories appear different.

Conclusion: The Influence of the Indian Epics Continues

As it stands, the Mahabharata and Ramayana have been immense sources of inspiration for Malay and Javanese authors, artists, storytellers, writers and others. For centuries, they have continuously rewritten and reworked their own versions of stories with similar but different motifs, including hunting, tough life in the jungle, attractive princesses, strong and handsome princes, curse, liberation, abandonment, divine favour, rejection, revenge, incarnation, magical power and duels (of wits and strength), all involving the main characters in the Indian epics. On this, Farish A. Noor (2005: 23) notes that much of what passes today as culture of the Malay World is the consequence of 'Indianization' in the region. Nevertheless, we cannot overlook another important historical legacy: there are numerous accounts of the interplay between the local indigenous culture and Hindu and Islamic religions in the *Hikayat Pandawa Lima*, *Hikayat Panji Semirang* and *Hikayat Merong Mahawangsa*, written after the sixteenth century.

In these works, the genius and creativity of Javanese and Malay authors and scribes are obvious in their bringing together of diverse cultural traditions. This has not only opened up a dialogue between civilizations, but it has also helped to bolster the pluralist culture now inherent in the Malay World. Hence, it does not come as a surprise if local people and Javanese and Malay authors from the past were able to deal with these early encounters between Hinduism, Islam and indigenous cultures creatively in their daily lives and in the above-mentioned *hikayat*. This is just one example of the golden age of pluralism and diversity in the Malay World, which is one of the most globalized regions in the world.

The above observation must be seen against the background that Javanese and Malay peoples have received the Indian epics in many waves over the centuries. Having an insatiable hunger for mystery and fantasy tales, they have also been translating and adapting many Islamic legends, no less fantastic than those in the two Indian epics. Even in the Javanese and Malay court chronicles, that narrate the history of Javanese and Malay rulers, there are tales of heroes from Javanese and Malay literary works, comprising mainly the princes and princesses. Given the interest, variety and the quality of the myths and legends, they are chosen and presented in a new light, such as the idealized heroism in Hang Tuah in the *Hikayat Hang Tuah*, which also contains instructions and advice that distinguish between good and evil (Knappert 1999: 192).

To do it justice, the Javanese and Malay literary tradition since the Hindu period needs to be seen as a creative expression that has emerged from a specific socio-cultural milieu, deeply shaped by many authors' open minds in creatively managing and blending local beliefs, philosophical outlooks and traditional values with those from Hinduism and Islam. It is partly through these writings that hundreds of authors and scribes, anonymous and otherwise, have preserved for posterity their and their peoples' spirit, humour, pain and longing. In is in these works that we read the evolution history of the local peoples, who have coexisted peacefully with immigrants from near and far. It is also in these compositions that we catch a glimpse of an ordered universe, a cosmos that is balanced between alternatives, and more importantly the generation of a new hybrid of culture. To understand all this, we need new ways of looking not only at the reworking of the Indian epics, but also the Malay social cultural experiences that have grown out of actual historical circumstances over the centuries.

References

Braginsky, Vladimir. *The Heritage of Malay Literature: a Historical survey of genres, writings and literary views*. Singapore: Institute of Southeast Asian Studies, 2004.

Ding Choo Ming. *Raja Aisyah Sulaiman: Pengarang Ulung Wanita Melayu*. Bangi: Penerbit Universiti Kebangsaan Malaysia, 1999.

———. *Kajian Manuskrip Melayu: Masalah, Kritikan dan Cadangan*. Kuala Lumpur: Utusan Publications and Distribution, 2003.

———. *Manuskrip Melayu: Sumber Maklumat Peribumi Melayu*. Penerbit: Universiti Kebangsaan Malaysia, 2008.

Farish A. Noor. *From Majapahit to Putrajya: Searching for Another Malaysia*. Kuala Lumpur: SilverfishBooks, 2005.

Haron Daud. *Ulit Mayang: Kumpulan Mantera Melayu*. Kuala Lumpur: Dewan Bahasa dan Pustaka, 2004.

Ikram, Achadiati (ed). *Hikayat Sri Rama: Suntingan Naskah Disertasi Talaah Amanat dan Struktur*. Jakarta: Penerbit Universitas Indonesia, 1980.

Kassim Ahmad (ed). *Hikayat Hang Tuah*. Kuala Lumpur: Dewan Bahasa dan Pustaka, 2008.

Knappert, Jan. *Mythology and Folklore in South-East Asia*. Kuala Lumpur: Oxford University Press, 1999.

Liaw Yock Fang. *A History of Classical Malay Literature*. Translated by Razif Bahari and Harry Aveling. Singapore: Institute of Southeast Asian Studies, 2013.

Maier, Hendrik Meno Van. *Fragments of Reading: the Malay Hikayat Merong Mahawangsa*. Alblasserdam: Offsetdrukkerij Kanters, BV, 1985.

Maxwell, W. E. *Hikayat Sri Rama* by Mir Hassan from Kampar, Perak. *JSBRAS* 17 (June 1886): 87–115.

Milner, A. C. *Kerajaan: Malay political culture on the eve of colonial rule*. Tucson: University of Arizona Press, 1982.

———. Malay local history: an Introduction. *Journal of Southeast Asian Studies* 17 (1) 1986: 1–4.

Muhammad Haji Salleh. *Puitika Sastera Melayu: Suatu Pertimbangan*. Bangi: Penerbit Universiti Kebangsaan Malaysia, 1992.

Ratnam, Kamala. Socio-cultural and Anthropological Background of the Ramayana in Laos: 230–251. In Iyengar, K. R. Srinivasa (ed). Asian Variations of Ramayana: papers presented at the International Seminar on *Asian Variations of Ramayana in Asia: their cultural, social and anthropological significance*. New Delhi, January 1981. New Delhi: Sahitya Akademi, 1983.

Roxas-Lim, Aurora. *Southeast Asian Art and Culture: Ideas, Forms and Societies*. Jakarta: Asean Committee on Culture, 2005.

Sarkar, H. B. The Ramayana in Southeast Asia: a General Survey: 206–220. In Iyengar, K. R. Srinivasa (ed). Asian Variations of Ramayana: papers presented at the International Seminar on *Asian Variations of Ramayana in Asia: their cultural, social and anthropological significance*. New Delhi, January 1981. New Delhi: Sahitya Akademi, 1983.

Sharifah Maznah Syed Omar. *Myths and the Malay Ruling Class*. Singapore: Times, 1993.

Sweeney, Amin. *Malay Word Music: a Celebration of Oral Creativity*. Kuala Lumpur: Dewan Bahasa & Pustaka, 1994.

Winstedt, R.O. *A History of Classical Malay Literature*. Kuala Lumpur: Oxford University Press, 1969. (Oxford in Asia Historical Reprints).

Zoetmulder, P. J. Kalangwan. *A Survey of Old Javanese Literature*. The Hague: Martinus Nijhoff, 1974.

CHAPTER 13

Camille Bulcke's *Ramakatha-Utpatti aur Vikas*: An Important Reference Work for Scholars in the Field of Ramayana Studies

Malini Saran and Vinod C. Khanna

INTRODUCTION

The Ramayana and Mahabharata epics are among the most enduring and pervasive of many historical and cultural threads that bind India to the Association of Southeast Asian Nations (ASEAN). Large regions of Asia that today comprise modern nation states which are members of ASEAN were for more than 1500 years part of an expansive cultural zone that shared a fascination for India's encyclopaedic narrative traditions,[1] particularly the stories of Rama and Sita. The fact that some of these regions embraced Buddhism and some Islam did not diminish the Ramayana's influence on the political, social and ethical aspects of daily life. The epic

[1] Sheldon Pollock described it as the Sanskrit Cosmopolis (1996).

M. Saran (✉)
Independent Researcher, New Delhi, India

V. C. Khanna
Former Ambassador of India to Indonesia, New Delhi, India

© The Author(s) 2018
S. Saran (ed.), *Cultural and Civilisational Links between India and Southeast Asia*, https://doi.org/10.1007/978-981-10-7317-5_13

melded so seamlessly with local traditions that people in Southeast Asia rightly regard the Ramayana as part of their own cultural heritage, with no obvious connections to India.

While the Ramakatha tradition flowered in Southeast Asia, its roots were deeply embedded in India, its birthplace. The Rama story's inherent ability to adapt to any environment was already evident in India, where it was first immortalized in Valmiki's Ramayana and from where its geographical spread began.

An enormous body of scholarship in several languages has explored the range, depth and complexity of the Ramayana's unparalleled legacy. However, many gaps remain in our understanding of the proliferation of this civilizational phenomenon. This chapter discusses the important contribution to the field of Ramayana studies made by Camille Bulcke's seminal work entitled *Ramakatha-Utpattiaur Vikas* [The Story of Rama, its Genesis and Evolution].[2] We will abbreviate this to *Ramakatha* when referring to Bulcke's work, but use the generic term Ramakatha to indicate the story of Rama. This comprehensive scholarly study, first published in 1950, was his PhD dissertation in Hindi from Allahabad University. It discusses in one volume the literature of all the Ramayanas known at that time, Indian and foreign, including those written in Southeast Asia. Bulcke was an outstanding Sanskritist, and his additional fluency in Hindi, English, German, French, Dutch and Latin enabled him to garner research materials in those languages as well. In the second and third editions, respectively produced in Bulcke (1962) and Bulcke (1971), Bulcke incorporated and acknowledged new research material from other scholars, particularly on Southeast Asia.[3]

Professor Stuart Robson draws our attention to the four approaches to literary history as classified in 1986 by Prof. A Teeuw: looking at a work as part and parcel of cultural history; adopting a periodization according to the major periods of national history; merely enumerating chronologically the main works; or studying the origins of the literary motifs and themes.[4] Bulcke does not consciously follow any one of these categories, and yet his *Ramakatha* appears to reflect something of all four.

---

[2] Camille Bulcke, a Jesuit priest by vocation, was born in Belgium in 1909. From his arrival in India in 1935 to his death there in 1982, he steeped himself in India's literary culture. In 1974, he was awarded the Padma Bhushan by the President of India for his contributions to Indian education and literature.

[3] Published by the Hindi Parishad Prakashan, Allahabad University, Allahabad.

[4] Raghavan and Robson (2014).

The subject matter of *Ramakatha* is organized into four parts. The survey and analysis of ancient and modern Ramakatha literature is found in the first and third part respectively. The second relates to the origins and genesis of Ramakatha. The fourth is devoted to a detailed study of the evolution of Ramakatha through an examination of the individual parts of the story, following the sequence of episodes in Valmiki Ramayana.

RAMAKATHA IN ANCIENT LITERATURE

Bulcke begins his magnum opus with a survey of Vedic literature, to see if the origins of Ramakatha lie there. He concludes that, despite references in various Vedic compositions to individuals bearing the same name as leading characters in Ramayana, nothing suggests that the epic can be traced to Vedic literature. Names such as Janaka, Rama and Sita appear, but occur in contexts totally unrelated to Ramayana epic. Bulcke argues further that, though there may have been earlier legends relating to Ramakatha, these are no longer available. Valmiki's Ramayana, he concludes, is the most ancient extant telling of the Ramakatha.

Scholars have long been aware that a divergence existed between the two main recensions of the available Valmiki Ramayana, the Northern and Southern. The Northern recension is often split into the Northwestern and the Eastern. Although Bulcke wrote his work before the monumental Critical Edition was completed by the Baroda Oriental Institute,[5] his summary of the differences between the three recensions provides the reader with a useful guide to how Valmiki's composition was transmitted down the centuries in different parts of India.

Bulcke devotes a chapter to the relationship between Valmiki Ramayana and the other great Indian epic, Mahabharata. Borrowing from the work of many scholars, he notes that while there is no mention of Mahabharata in the Ramayana, there are four major references to Ramakatha in the Mahabharata, as well as another fifty or so occasions where the Mahabharata uses Ramakatha and its characters in similes. He gives a detailed comparison of *Ramopkhyana*, the most extensive Ramakatha in the Mahabharata, and Valmiki's Ramayana, and concludes that *Ramopkhyana* is based on Valmiki's epic and not the other way around.

---

[5] *The Valmiki Ramayana: Critical Edition*, 7 vols. General Editors: G. H. Bhatt and U. P. Shah Baroda Oriental Institute (1960–1975).

Bulcke then examines the Ramakathas in the literature of the two great non-Brahmanic movements of ancient India, Buddhist and Jaina. He gives a synopsis of Rama-related stories in the *Dasharatha Jataka, Anamakam Jatakam* and *Dasharatha kathanam*. He also summarizes the relevant Jaina works: Vimalasuri's *Paumachariyam* and Gunabhadra's *Uttarapurana*. In the latter, Sita is portrayed as Ravana's daughter, a motif which appears in an earlier Jaina work, Sanghadasa's *Vasudevahindi*, and was to reappear in Southeast Asia.

THE ORIGINS OF RAMAKATHA

The second part of Bulcke's work surveys the birth and source of the Ramayana. As he himself states, even though this investigation reaches no new conclusions, it clarifies and classifies all the published material relating to debatable subjects.

On the subject of the genesis of the Valmiki Ramayana, Bulcke examines and refutes the theories of scholars such as A. Weber, H. Jacobi and Dineshchandra Sen. He demonstrates, for instance, how Weber wrongly traced the Sanskrit epic to *Dasharatha Jataka*, consequently misleading several other scholars.

He does not hesitate to give his views on other controversial issues, such as the dating of Valmiki, Rama's divinity, the issue of interpolations and so forth. Other equally good scholars have persuasively expressed different views of the same subjects. This is particularly true for the vexed issue of interpolations in the Valmiki Ramayana as it has come down to us. Thus, for instance, many scholars believe that Bulcke was wrong in judging that the entire Balakanda was not part of the original epic.[6] Similarly, Sanskritist Sheldon Pollock agrees with Indian traditionalists on the complex problem of Rama's divinity, arguing that it is an integral and authentic feature of Valmiki's epic, while Bulcke regards it as a later development.[7] The latter subject becomes a point of divergence in Southeast Asian Ramayanas, in which Rama is seen as the symbol of a just and perfect ruler, rather than as a god to be worshipped.

Bulcke's remarks on the dating and historicity of the Valmiki Ramayana, and on whether or not *Vanaras* and *Rakshasas* were respectively meant to be monkeys and demons, are more controversial: he states that Valmiki

[6] Goldman (1984).
[7] Pollock (1991).

composed his work around the third century BCE, and argues that *vanaras* and *rakshasas* were actually aboriginal tribes, so named because of their totems. However, his lucid presentation of these views ensures that entrants into the field of Ramayana studies are aware of important themes requiring further study.

Ramakatha in Later Literature

Bulcke turns here to the Ramakatha literature that appears in subsequent centuries. He divides this survey into four chapters:

- Ramakatha in Sanskrit religious literature
- Ramakatha in the Sanskrit *belles lettres*
- Ramakatha in modern Indian languages, and
- Ramakatha in foreign lands.

In Religious Literature

Bulcke documents the Rama story's appearance in a very large number of ancient Hindu religious texts known as the Puranas. As with almost all ancient Sanskrit literature, it is difficult to date the Puranas precisely; they may stretch over a thousand years from the early centuries of the Christian era. They often contain certain episodes that are not part of Valmiki Ramayana, and appear in later Indian and Southeast Asian Ramayanas. Thus, for instance, Bulcke refers to the *Shivamahapurana* narrative in a later part of his work when describing the various birth stories of Hanuman that are not found in Valmiki. In this case Shiva, aroused by the beauty of Vishnu in his Mohini form, fathers Hanuman on Anjana. The story bears a striking resemblance to the one found in the Malay *Hikayat Seri Rama*. Although such similarities might be of interest to scholars looking for connections between these works, the precise route by which such non-Valmikian Puranic tales travelled to Southeast Asia remains unknown.

Other religious works entirely devoted to narrating the Rama tale are devotional in nature, and linked to one or another Hindu belief system. Bulcke's research reveals that Rama worship started much after Rama was recognized as an *avatara* or incarnation of Vishnu. He believes that as religious devotion to Rama became more widespread, the Ramakatha was deliberately cast in a similar mould, leading to the composition of such well-known sectarian Ramayanas as *Adhyatmaramayana*, *Anandaramayana* and *Adbhutaramayana*. Of these, the *Adhyatmaramayana* is the most important. Bulcke believes it was written in the fourteenth or fifteenth century, and, enjoying much prestige in the Ramananda sect, it went on to inspire the famous *Ramacharitamanas* of Tulasidasa and the Marathi Ramayana of Eknath. Sita outperforms Rama in many of the religious Ramayanas: in *Adbhutaramayna*, written perhaps shortly after the *Adhyatmaramayana*, she slays a 1000-shouldered Ravana; and in the *Tattvasangraha* Ramayana she kills the 100-faced Ravana.

In Sanskrit belles lettres

The Valmiki Ramayana has inspired several Sanskrit poets and playwrights, and Bulcke briefly summarizes all their well-known creations. Subsequent research has proved that Sanskrit *kavya* literature in particular profoundly influenced the formation of the poetics and prosody of *kakawin* literature in the classical language of Old Javanese.

Perhaps the most celebrated of the Ramayana-based poems is *Raghuvamsa*, authored by Kalidasa, the greatest of Sanskrit poets, who probably lived and wrote in around the fourth or fifth century CE. Bulcke also introduces us to many other Ramayana-based poems including *Bhattikavya* (sixth or seventh century), whose influence on the Old Javanese Ramayana (ninth to tenth century) has been established. In the *Udararaghava* (fourteenth century), Sita best expresses the plurality of the Ramayana tradition, telling Rama, who is reluctant to expose her to the dangers of a forest exile: 'Many are the Ramayanas which one has heard, but none in which Rama goes to the forest without Sita.'[8]

Equally useful are the brief glimpses that Bulcke gives us of Sanskrit plays devoted to the Rama story: *Pratimanataka* and *Abhishekanataka*, whose authorship by Bhasa has been contested, as well as *Uttararamacharita* and *Mahaviracharita* of Bhavabhuti, and many others. Here, as elsewhere, he draws on the work of many other scholars, such as V. Raghavan.[9] The *Uttarakanda* of Valmiki Ramayana provides plentiful source material for dramatic literature in India. Similarly, in Southeast Asia, the *Uttarakanda*, translated into Old Javanese prose in the tenth century, provided a reservoir of themes for the performing arts of Java and Bali.

Besides poems and plays, Bulcke documents the rich repertoire of Sanskrit story literature in which Ramakatha was incorporated. One of the

[8] Bulcke, section 219 (Revised 6th edition 1999).
[9] Raghavan (1961).

most celebrated such works is *Kathasaritsagara* [Ocean of the Stream of Stories], written in the eleventh century by Somadeva. Ramakatha is narrated twice here. Found in one of them is the story of Valmiki creating Kusha as the second son for Sita when he fears Lava is missing, a theme that is reflected in Southeast Asian literature and sculpture.

In Modern Indian Languages

Bulcke summarizes the well-known Ramayanas of every major modern Indian language, starting with Kamban's *Iramavataram* in Tamil, written in the twelfth century.[10] Though a basic continuity with the Sanskrit Ramayanasis evident, Bulcke identifies many new twists of plot and character. A characteristic feature of many of them is deep devotion to Rama.

Several motifs in the Rama stories in regional languages are missing from the Valmiki Ramayana, but appear in Southeast Asian Ramayanas. These Indian works themselves may or may not have travelled across the Bay of Bengal, but the specific episode may indeed have been carried across in some oral narrative by Indian travellers. To cite some examples:

- Unlike the Valmiki Ramayana, Trijata is Vibhishana's daughter in the Tamil Ramayana of Kamban, a theme which takes much more impressive form in the Old Javanese Ramayana *kakawin*.
- Rama recognizes Hanuman on the basis of ornaments the latter has had since birth. Variants of this appear both in the Telegu Ramayana of Ranganatha and in several Southeast Asian Ramayanas.
- The story of Rama abandoning Sita because she draws Ravana's picture is in the Bengali Ramayana of Krittivasa and in Southeast Asian Ramayanas, but not in the Valmiki Ramayana.

Borrowing once again from the work of other specialists, Bulcke also gives us some idea of Ramayana legends prevalent in an oral form among certain Indian tribes such as the Santhals and the Mundas.

This chapter concludes with a mention of the Persian Ramayanas, written during the reigns of Akbar and Jahangir. Some Muslim kings, both in India and Southeast Asia, took a deep interest in Hindu literary compositions.

---

[10] Bulcke starts with the Ramayanas of south India in Tamil, Telegu, Kannada and Malayalam; then proceeds to those written in Assamese, Bengali, Oriya, Marathi, Gujerati, Hindi and Kashmiri; and includes the Ramayanas in Nepalese and Sinhalese.

Ramayana in Foreign Countries

Having demonstrated how Ramakatha pervaded Indian literary forms, Bulcke proceeds to map its spread in neighbouring countries and discuss the forms it acquired there. Surveying the literature of Tibet, Khotan and Southeast Asia, he attempts to trace the route and chronology of the Rama stories. While subsequent investigations into individual works have yielded much more information, Bulcke's comparative approach offers food for thought.[11]

Bulcke speaks of Ramakatha emanating from ancient India in two streams, one northwards and the other eastwards, in the third and fifth centuries respectively. He first looks at the one that went northwards, as manifested in the Buddhist Ramayanas, *Anamakam Jatakam* and *Dasharathakathanam*, which survived thanks to Chinese translations. This northward-spreading stream includes the Ramayanas of Tibet and Khotan, in ancient Tibetan-language manuscripts dated to the eighth or ninth century. The entire story, from the character of Ravana to the renunciation of Sita and the Rama–Sita reunion, appears here. In both the Tibetan and Khotanese Ramayanas, Sita is regarded as Ravana's daughter, as she is in Gunabhadra's *Uttarapurana*. At the same time, Bulcke points out enough differences between the two to suggest that the geographical proximity of the regions should not lead one to presume that the Ramayana of Khotan derives from that of Tibet. In the Khotanese Ramayana, Rama is an incarnation of the Buddha and Lakshmana of Maitreya.

The second stream travelled quite early to Indonesia as is evident from the Old Javanese Ramayana and the Ramayana reliefs in the Prambanan temples (ninth century) and to Cambodia, Thailand, Laos and Burma. Bulcke provides a bird's-eye view of this region's Rama-related literature, starting from the Old Javanese *Ramayana Kakawin*, based on the *Bhattikavyam* that adheres closely to Valmiki and proceeding to the later Ramakathas in modern Javanese and Malay which vary considerably from the Sanskrit epic. In the course of this journey through Southeast Asia, he provides a relatively detailed introduction to such major works as the Malay *Hikayat Seri Rama*, the Khmer *Ramaker*, the Thai *Ramakien*, the Lao *Rama Jataka* and the much later plays written in Burma.

The following extract from what Bulcke has to say on the *Hikayat Seri Rama* demonstrates that this section is not merely an inventory of various

---

[11] See the works of Josselyn de Jong (1983) and Michael Kapstein (2003) et al.

tellings of the Rama story. It is a study replete with cross-references to Ramakatha material in other parts of his book which are indicated in brackets:

> There is no scope for doubting the basis of Indonesia's ancient Ramakatha (see section 314) but to determine the main source of *Seri Rama* is impossible. Even so what is clear is that of the many different episodes in *Seri Rama* which differ from Valmiki, the basis is Indian. The influence of the Jaina (sections 446, 585, 605, 632, 655 and 723) and Bengali (sections 343, 388, 552, 576, 598, 613, 614 and 723) Ramakathas is indisputable. The influence on *Seri Rama* of the Rama literature of Orissa, the *Ranganathan* Ramayana and the Kamba Ramayana, that is, the works from the eastern coast of India is evident (see sections 454, 474, 512, 514, 519, 552, 578, 583, 585, 591, and 675). Several episodes of *Seri Rama* are present in *Ananda Ramayana* (sections 350, 428, 517, 539 and 552), *Kathasaritsagar* (sections 745, 756) *Mairavanacharita* (section 614) or *Torave Ramayana* (section 513). The impact on *Seri Rama* of *Ramayana Kakawin* (sections 466, 574 and 583) and the Islamic religion (sections 336 and 749) was unavoidable.[12]

In Bulcke's survey, three traits of Ramayana spring to our attention from the range of Ramakatha stories that take root in these lands. The first trait is the regions' continuous familiarity with Rama stories, told and retold in multiple languages until modern times. The second trait is that these varied stories, both Valmikian and non-Valmikian, were adapted to the religion of the land, be it the Buddhism of Burma, Thailand, Cambodia and Laos, or the Islam of Indonesia. The third is that while the stories continued to be told, they were firmly localized in the process, so that names of characters and places changed and new characters were invented. Each Ramayana bore a distinctly local character.

The same chapter also documents Ramakatha works by various Western travellers and missionaries who came to India from the fifteenth century onwards.

---

[12] Bulcke *Ramakatha* 1999 (sixth revised edition), section 320, p. 215. Translation by Khanna and Saran in unpublished work.

The Evolution of Ramakatha

The last and most original part of the book is extremely valuable to researchers. Comprising more than half of Bulcke's work, it is devoted to a detailed study of the evolution of Ramakatha. He examines the individual components of the Rama story, following the sequence of episodes in Valmiki Ramayana, and laying out an impressive comparative study of important characters and themes in various Ramayanas in diverse cultural settings, often with very different objectives. To this end he makes detailed references to the ancient and modern Ramakatha literature described in his book's first and third parts.

Bulcke starts with the Balakanda, selecting important themes, episodes and characters to survey how each is dealt with in various Ramakathas. He examines each of the following six kandas similarly.

One example of this, on the theme of Sita's birth, will serve to illustrate Bulcke's method.[13] Scholars have long been aware of how differently various Ramayanas depict the birth of Sita. Bulcke outlines her birth story in more than twenty Indian and Southeast Asian Ramayanas. His analysis of these diverse accounts indicates that there is perhaps no other figure in the history of literature whose birth has been so creatively imagined. Indian orthodoxy, largely familiar with Valmiki's Sita—miraculously born and adopted by Janaka—might still accept those Ramayanas that suggest she was actually Janaka's biological daughter, with variant versions in which he succumbs to the irresistible charms of some divine damsel who magically conceives Sita. But they tend to be shocked to learn that many Ramayanas describe her as the daughter of Ravana, some even as the daughter of Dasharatha, making her not only the wife of Rama but also his sibling. In the first chapter Bulcke speaks of references in Vedic literature to Sita as a presiding deity of agriculture, and later suggests its possible link with the story of her miraculous emergence from the earth.[14] Similarly, he reminds us that stories which in some way connect her birth to Ravana and Lanka may perhaps be traced back to an episode in Valmiki's Uttarakanda. There, according to the story recounted by Sage Agastya to Rama, Ravana attempts to molest Vedavati, a beautiful young woman who curses him before immolating herself, foretelling her own return in a future birth to become the

---

[13] Ibid. Sita's Birth Story (Chap. 14, section 405–428).
[14] Ibid. Chap. 1, section 11 and 19.

cause of his death. These very ideas are developed in the Javanese *Serat Kanda* and in other Southeast Asian Ramayanas.

As Bulcke demonstrates how the Ramakatha evolved through the centuries, his thorough research technique is evident in the way he traces the diverse appearances of even a comparatively minor character such as Trijata in more than a dozen Ramayanas, including in Southeast Asia.[15] He begins by summarizing her relatively marginal role in the Valmiki Ramayana as an aged *rakshisi* placed by Ravana to intimidate the captive Sita. She turns out, instead, to be sympathetic to Sita. Bulcke then takes us through numerous retellings of the Rama story in which Trijata acquires greater salience. He shows how, in this process, the poets tended to conflate into the single character of Trijata several other *rakshasis* of Lanka who figure briefly in the Sanskrit epic as well-wishers of Sita. His brief summary of her role in the Old Javanese *Ramayana Kakawin* hints at her greater presence there. A close study of the *Kakawin* published in 1993, several decades after Bulcke's work after Bulcke's work brought into sharper focus the fact that the Javanese Trijata surpasses all her Indian forebears with her pluck and formidable courage, particularly in the episode where she not only testifies to Sita's chastity during her incarceration in Lanka, but goes further in denouncing Rama for doubting his wife.[16]

In his concluding chapter Bulcke emphasizes that his work shows that the number and diversity of Ramakatha renderings, its sheer spread over time and space, is unparalleled in the history of literature. According to him the main conclusion of his study is that no matter how great the variations in these hundreds of Ramayanas, their basic unity stems from a common ancestry, ultimately traceable to Valmiki's great epic.

CONCLUSION

Bulcke's comprehensive study ably captures the enduring phenomenon of diverse Ramakathas in multiple languages, adopted by different religions, both in India and Southeast Asia. His study of the evolution of characters, motifs and themes in the literature illustrates the capacious nature of this story, as malleable in the hands of its Indian redactors as in those of the poets, dramatists and performance artists of Southeast Asia.

---

[15] Ibid. Chap. 18, section 545–547.
[16] See Khanna and Saran (1993) and Saran and Khanna (2004).

Of great value to any research scholar would be Bulcke's comprehensive bibliography covering seventeen pages. Three of these are in Hindi and devoted to Indian works from ancient to modern times; and the remaining fourteen pages in English refer to works in English and other foreign languages. Naturally his list does not extend beyond 1971. In another useful annexure, Bulcke draws a timeline indicating the dating of works related to Ramakatha from ancient times down to the seventeenth century. Given the perennial interest in various facets of Ramayana, many scholars in India and worldwide have made important new contributions since Bulcke's work. These have been extensively collated in the Sahitya Akademi's critical inventory,[17] and the *Rama Sahitya Kosh* of the Ayodhya Shodh Sansthan has a useful compendium in Hindi.[18] However, the comprehensive scope and meticulous comparative analyses of Bulcke's *Ramakatha* render it invaluable to a scholar entering the field of Ramayana studies.

Bulcke's masterly work is not designed to cover any single Ramayana text so comprehensively as to make it the sole source for a detailed research study. Rather, it is of great use to any scholar attempting to decode the relationship between various literary texts and a particular narrative sculpture; or in the study of acculturation, how different themes and characters are handled in the important Ramayanas of diverse regions.

It must be pointed out that Bulcke's study is written in Hindi, limiting its use to those familiar with that language. In order to make this work of encyclopaedic scope deservedly accessible to non-Hindi speaking scholars, the present authors have undertaken the task of translating it into English. The Ramayana universe is increasingly viewed as a cultural zone of which Southeast Asia is an integral part. If available in the widely used language of English, Bulcke's study could be a valuable aid in situating individual works in a larger context to explore regional interconnections through the stories circulating there at different times. In this form it could also be of use to those in ASEAN countries working in the fields of literature, ballet and drama, who continue to draw their inspiration from the stories of Rama and Sita.

Bulcke's *Ramakatha* vividly demonstrates how the Ramayana epic tradition has endured, transcending barriers of politics, language and religion. The multiplicity of Ramayanas in India and many other lands is history's tribute not only to the genius of the original composer but also a monument to the talents of the countless known and anonymous participants in this unique transnational phenomenon.

---

[17] Krishnamoorthy, K. (ed.) 1991, 1993.
[18] Singh, Y. P. (ed.) 2014.

References

Bulcke, Camille (1962) *Ramakatha: Utpatti aur Vikas* (second edition), Allahabad University, Allahabad. Hindi Parishad Prakashan.
────── (1971) third edition Allahabad University, Allahabad. Hindi Parishad Prakashan.
────── (1999) Revised Sixth Edition. Allahabad University, Allahabad. Hindi Parishad Prakashan.
De Jong J.W (1983) "The Story of Rama in Tibet" in K.R Srinivas Iyengar (ed.) *Asian Variations in Ramayana*. Delhi: Sahitya Akademi.
Goldman, Robert P. (1984). 'Introduction' in *The Ramayana of Valmiki: An Epic of Ancient India* Volume I *Balakanda*. Princeton: Princeton University Press.
Kapstein, Matthew (2003) "Indian Literary Identity in Tibet" in Sheldon Pollock (ed.), *Literary Cultures in history; Reconstructions from South Asia*. New Delhi: Oxford University Press, pp 747–802.
Khanna V.C and Malini Saran (1993) "The Ramayana Kakawin: A Product of Sanskrit Scholarship and Independent Literary Genius" in *Bijdragen tot de Taal- en Volkenkunde*, 149 2e.pp 226–249.
Krishnamoorthy, K. (ed.) (1991 and 1993) *A Critical Inventory of Ramayana Studies in the World* Vol I (1991) and II (1993) New Delhi. Sahitya Akademi in collaboration with Union Academique Internationale. Bruxelles.
Pollock, Sheldon (1991) "The Divine King of the Ramayana" in *The Ramayana of Valmiki: An Epic of Ancient India*, Vol. 111. Princeton University Press.
────── (1996) "The Sanskrit Cosmopolis, 300–1300: transculturation, vernacularization and the question of ideology' in J.E.M Houben (ed.) *Ideology and Status in Sanskrit, Contributions to the History of the Sanskrit language*. Leiden.
Raghavan, V (1961) *Some Old Lost Rama Plays*, Annamalai.
Raghavan, V and Robson, Stuart O. (2014) 'The Ramayana in Java and Bali: Chapters from its literary History' presented at an international Workshop at ISEAS in Singapore in April 24–25, 2014 on *Traces of the Two Great Epics Ramayana and Mahabharata in Javanese and Malay Literature*.
────── (2015) *The Old Javanese Ramayana: A New English Translation with an Introduction and Notes*. Research Institute for Languages and Cultures of Asia and Africa. Tokyo University of Foreign Studies.
Saran, Malini and Vinod C. Khanna (2004) *The Ramayana in Indonesia*, Delhi. Ravi Dayal Publishers.
Singh Y.P (2014) (ed.) *Rama Sahitya Kosh*, Delhi. Rajkamal Prakashan.
Srinivas, K.R (1983) (ed.) *Asian Variations in Ramayana*, New Delhi. SahityaAkademi.

PART V

Sacred Geographies and Localisations of Beliefs

CHAPTER 14

Archaeology as Soft Power in ASEAN–India Cultural Contexts

Sachchidanand Sahai

INTRODUCTION

In the first decade of the twenty-first century, 'soft power' has emerged as a much-touted concept. The term, arguably used to gain lost ground for the USA, was first enshrined in the writings of Joseph Nye (1990, 2004, 2011), and began to be used against the backdrop of the Vietnam War, the dwindling military might of the USA and the American withdrawal from Vietnam.

Soft power is more than influence; it is also the ability to attract. Soft power is more difficult for governments to wield than hard power. Culture is one of the three categories of soft power, the other two being political values and policies. Governments can generate soft power only partially. Non-state actors have a major role to play in this respect, and in modern parlance soft power is used as a universal term. Yoga is widely thought to be an instance of India's soft power.

S. Sahai (✉)
Preah Vihear National Autimhority, Royal Government of Cambodia,
Preah Vihear, Cambodia

UNESCO Expert for the Archaeological Complex of Sambor Prei Kuk,
Phnom Penh, Cambodia

© The Author(s) 2018
S. Saran (ed.), *Cultural and Civilisational Links between India and Southeast Asia*, https://doi.org/10.1007/978-981-10-7317-5_14

However, it should be stressed that soft power does not capture all the nuances of Asian relations. From prehistoric times India and the Association of Southeast Asian Nations (ASEAN) have been an integral part of monsoon Asia, which offers a community of culture and sharing of living traditions based on the idea of intimate relations between nature and living beings. Animistic beliefs, ancestor worship, cosmic perspectives and a pluralistic world view are the main pillars of monsoon Asia, which carry the cultural edifice of India and ASEAN nations. Cultural relations have been geared through dynamic routes that involve public participation rather than state-sponsored projects. Dissemination of knowledge and the mutual appreciation of cultural streams have been the responsibilities of non-state actors. It is true that Devapala, the Pala king of Magadha, created residences for Indonesian students at Nalanda in northern India and in the far south in the ninth century AD, but the basic infrastructures of cultural relationships and mutual understanding took shape through a network of trading skills and technical expertise. The exchange of goods followed the exchange of ideas. This symbiosis was responsible for material growth and cultural ramifications. New experiments in art, architecture, medicine, astrology and astronomy, language and literature were possible in spite of pirates in the Indian Ocean, travelling was safer 1500 years ago, when the texts in Sanskrit were engraved in West Java and in East Kalimantan.

From this traditional Asian perspective, the celebration of common, shared culture is the ultimate expression of soft power. There has been no role for hard power in 2000 years of cultural dialogue between India and Southeast Asia. It was a mutual appreciation of a common culture, except for the so-called Chola expedition—which I personally treat as the fancy of a Chola king rather than a serious military enterprise: no conquest of territories resulted from the establishment of Chola rule.

Language

The Sanskrit, Malay, Mon-Khmer, Vietnamese and Chinese languages are the storehouses of data that outline the development of various languages and literature as a result of close cultural and economic contacts. Sanskrit was instrumental in the growth of the regional languages of India, enriching their technical vocabularies and content base. It was also instrumental in enriching the languages of Southeast Asia. In the fourth–fifth centuries CE, Sanskrit was not sponsored in Southeast Asia by any of the Indian states, nor was the script taught by the teachers who were sent by Gupta,

Pallava or Pala kings of India. To learn about the latest advances in medicine, architecture, engineering and so many other branches of knowledge, the rest of Asia read and researched from the Sanskrit sources.

In the fifth century CE, Sanskrit inscriptions were inscribed on the sacrificial posts (*yupa*) in Kutei (Borneo), present-day East Kalimantan in Indonesia, by Mulavarman, an Indonesian ruler of that epoch. Mulavarman admired Sanskrit and Sanskrit-based culture, so he took a Sanskrit name— although his father Kundung bore a purely local language name. I read the seven Sanskrit *yupa* inscriptions of Kalimantan in my student days, and have taught them to my students for the last forty years. But before writing this chapter, I did not realize that modern Indonesians have already commemorated and celebrated Mulavarman by establishing Mulavarman University in East Kalimantan.

In India, however, nobody knows about Mulavarman, except a few specialists, professors and students. Since Mulavarman University's establishment in 1962, no Indian university has established contact with it. Another icon of India–Indonesia, India–ASEAN cultural relations is the fifth-century king Purnavarman of Tarumanagara in West Java. Sanskrit inscriptions are inscribed on the boulders in the riverbed of Chi Trauma. Indonesians have celebrated Purnavarman by establishing a university that commemorates his name.

In Southeast Asia Sanskrit retains its charm and potential. In mainland Southeast Asia, no political leader would deliver a satisfactory speech without using some words of Sanskrit origin. Even in the twenty-first century, in the Thai, Lao and Khmer languages technical words are formed with the help of Sanskrit. We in India use the English word telephone in our languages, but Thai, Lao and Khmer are happy with *durasabda*. Hun Sen, the Prime Minister of Cambodia, and his colleagues, tell people how they are taking into consideration the factors of *desa* (place) and *kala* (time) in the formulation of their policy. In the modern love songs of Cambodia, there are two catchwords—*neary* (*nari*) and *sneha*. After hearing the first word for a few times I realized myself without the help of any teacher or interpreter that the Cambodians write *naarii* (women) and pronounce it as *neary*; the other word *sneha* (love) is pronounced as it is pronounced today in Sanskrit.

In their daily conversation, the common people in Southeast Asian cities and villages use a number of words of Sanskrit origin. Once the driver of my car in the streets of Siem Reap (Angkor) was worried about a policeman who might impose upon him *pinai*. When I asked him what that meant, he replied that it was the imposition of a fine. The original Sanskrit word is *vinaya*, which has the dictionary meaning of fine. The same word has been used from the early Angkor period in 802 AD to the present day.

Heritage Sites

The vast and variegated landmass and coastal areas of South and Southeast Asia are studded with archaeological sites and monuments. They are an unlimited testimony to cultural interaction, and are sites that illustrate the social, economic and cultural empowerment of rural neighbourhoods. Borobudur, Prambanan, Panataran in Indonesia, Pagan in Myanmar, Mi-s'on in Vietnam and Angkor Wat in Cambodia are some of the major sites in Southeast Asia, and these wonderful sites amaze us—but perhaps the general public in India and Southeast Asia has yet to realize the density of archaeological monuments. There are over 4000 temples of Pagan (Myanmar), over 2000 Khmer archaeological sites in mainland Southeast Asia, some 200 brick temples still standing on the sea coast of Vietnam, working as lighthouses for ships navigating the Indian ocean—such is the panorama of the ASEAN–India cultural interface. As I have shown elsewhere, these temples were as much spiritual centres as agencies of rural development, urbanization and state formation (Sahai 2012).

In mainland Southeast Asia, besides monumental temples, there used to be a small brick temple every 50 km, preserving a Sanskrit and/or Khmer text that is engraved on its door frame. Most of these temples are dying monuments; many of them have disappeared. Those that remain will disappear during the course of the twenty-first century, and with them will disappear the records of our past relationships.

It is urgent to use the traditional storehouse of our soft power to protect and preserve these small but crucial archaeological ruins.

For the last twenty-five years, several nation states, including India and China, have been vying to mark their presence at Angkor. I have asked some of them. 'Why are you all flocking here?' The answer is simple: to acquire visibility on behalf of their country at this internationally famous site.

India and ASEAN nations have to join hands to give life to all the small brick and stone temples that are spread over mainland and island Southeast Asia which will otherwise soon breath their last, taking with them important testimony related past regional cooperation.

In the application of archaeology as 'soft power', the danger of politicization looms large, leading Luke and Kersel (2012) to plead for bottom-up initiatives with long-term effects, whereby archaeologists act as unofficial ambassadors. Archaeology is today an integral part of cultural diplomacy in the widest sense of the term. It has to be applied to improve the lives of the general public in foreign lands, and not simply as an effort to establish closer official relations with foreign countries. Archaeology is for 'small d diplomacy' involving the grassroots segments of the society. It should not be used as 'big D diplomacy', leading to government encouraged and enabled actions. Only in this way can archaeology be a useful instrument of soft power.

Independent, non-governmental institutions, with a genuine apolitical profile, can successfully represent the soft power of a nation in a host country, though mediation of governments may be required for facilitating their task. The Ambassador's Fund should be provided for cultural and archaeological preservation for smaller, more open-ended, local projects. The real villages, which shelter archaeological sites, are ideal partners in conserving the site and in pioneering rural development through the promotion of cultural assets.

A Seventh-Century Heritage Site

The seventh-century archaeological site of Sambor Prei Kuk (Ishanapura) in central Cambodia offers an interesting example of collaborative efforts on a non-governmental basis between India and Cambodia.

A total of 291 structures and vestiges of structures have been recorded to date at Sambor Prei Kuk. Out of 291 temples, seventy-one survive with visible ground plan, sixteen survive up to the roof-top, sixteen halfway up to the roof, three up to the bottom of the roof, twelve up to the top of the walls, sixteen halfway up the walls and eight up to the lower portion of the wall. Of the remainder that are ruinous, forty-five retain part of their walls, sixty-two retain no wall, but there are sandstone architectural elements in their vicinity. Nearby, 100 mounds survive with brick and laterite elements. The existence of eleven sanctuaries can be deduced from small mounds that are situated symmetrically in relation to the sanctuaries that lie within the enclosures.

The O Kru Kae River divides the whole archaeological complex into two distinct parts. The ancient city of Ishanapura is on one side of the river. To the other side of the river, there are three distinct temple complexes: north, south and central groups.

Until recently the ancient city of Ishanapura was barely known. Parmentier (1927) mentioned only one temple in the area—Prasat Rousei Roliek. Shimoda reports a total of fifty-six sites consisting of eighty-two sanctuaries. Mostly these are independent single structures; on thirteen sites multiple structures appear to form a temple complex.

On the other side of the river, the North Group of Temples or the Gambhireshvara Complex is locally called Prasat Sambor, after the neighbouring village of Sambor. This group consists of temples within two enclosure walls and a number of temples outside these enclosure walls. It covers less space than two other campuses: central and south. However, a number of peripheral temples were attached to the north group, which were brought to notice in the course of later studies. The presiding deity of this complex is Gambhireshvara, a form of Shiva, variously interpreted as the god of depth, profundity and seriousness.

The South Group of Temples, dedicated to the Smiling Lord, Prahasiteshvara (Shiva), constitutes a central rectangular temple, open to the east, surrounded by a number of secondary temples which give an idea of a quincunx plan. Two enclosure walls define the space occupied by these temples. The enclosures are not concentric; they are decentred in a way that provides more space to the east. Quite homogeneous, this group is supposed to have been built in a very short period during the reign of Ishanavarman I in the first half of the seventh century (AKP, 52).

In fact, Prahasiteshvara (Shiva) or the Smiling Lord figures in three inscriptions belonging to the reign of Ishanavarman I: K 440, K 442 and K 90. K 440 (IC: 4, 5–11) is a Sanskrit text inscribed on each of the two uprights of the eastern gate of the outer enclosure wall of the south group of temples at Sambor Prei Kuk. The location of this inscription at the outer gate clearly suggests that the principal god of this southern complex of temples was Prahasiteshvara, and the inscription begins with a stanza in praise of this god, no other god being invoked. This also indicates the primacy of Prahasiteshvara here.

Prahasiteshvara figures in the additional list of the linga in the *Skandapurana*, as a temple of Shiva in Pataliputra (Patna) in the state of Bihar (India): 'Another sanctuary (ayatana) of Pinakin in Magadha is Prahasiteshvara, in the town of Pataliputra. One who has visited that Lord obtains [the result of] a vajimedha' (Bisschop 2006, 218). There also exists a linga named Prahasiteshvara in Varanasi (Aiyangar 1942, 89, I.17). It may be noted here that today no such temple survives physically in

Pataliputra (Patna), nor in the memory of today's mainstream Hindu population of India.

The Central (C) complex of the temples of Sambor Prei Kuk, the Lion Temple (Prasat Tao) is the biggest of the three main groups. Its composition is comparable to that of the Prasat Yeai Poan (South Group). The second enclosure of both the complexes, south and central, is bigger in size than the northern complex (Bruguier and Lacroix 2011, 185). Both have a sacred pond to the northeast. The central complex is less densely constructed and its central tower is isolated.

It may be noted that not only the principal god of the South Complex of temples was a smiling divinity (Shiva), but the figures portrayed on the walls of a large number of temples of this site are portrayed as beaming with an otherworldly smile. Such is the case of the figures portrayed in the kudu of the early seventh-century N 17 temple of Sambor Prei Kuk/Ishanapura (Fig. 14.1).

Fig. 14.1 Temple N 17, Smiling Face in the Kudu, Ishanapura, Cambodia. One of the salient features of the temple is the kudu or semi-circular arches in which divine and semi-divine figures are placed. This feature also known as chaitya window, is popular both in South and North Indian temples. In this Cambodian example from Ishanapura, one of the several faces smiles in the kudu placed around temple N 17. Source: Author

The Octagonal Temples

Sambor Prei Kuk assumes special importance in the global history of architecture for its surviving ten octagonal temples: S 7, S 8, S 9, S 10, S 11, N 7, Z 2, Z 6, Prasat Y, and Khnach Tol. Objects referenced by the number eight and octagons are somewhat rare in the natural world. Spiders, sponges and octopuses aside, octagonal structures are mainly a human construct, and the logical result of the geometric relationships that exist and develop between the square and the circle and related forms. The octagon represents a variety of meanings in many cultures and religions.

The ten known examples of octagonal temples at Sambor Prei Kuk are the only specimens of this type in Southeast Asia, in addition to the two examples from Champa (South Vietnam). The five octagonal temples are in the south group of Sambor Prei Kuk: S 7, S 8, S 9, S 10, and S 11. The N 7 is the only octagonal temple in the north group of Sambor Prei Kuk (Fig. 14.2). No octagonal temple has been reported from the central group. The two temples of Z group, the temple Y and Khnach Tol are the four octagonal temples outside the three main groups of the Sambor Prei Kuk temples. No example of an Indian temple, octagonal in shape from the base to pinnacle, survives from the seventh century.

If we follow South Indian texts of architecture (*shilpashastra*), the octagonal temples of Sambor Prei Kuk should be considered as a product of the Dravida or South Indian School of architecture. This may appear as most convincing in the light of the epigraphic evidence available at Sambor Prei Kuk (Ishanapura). Durgasvamin, the son-in law of Ishanavarman who was quite active in Ishanapura, claims to have been originally a resident of Dakshinapatha.

In fact, the Mayamata 19/36 considers the octagon to be a defining element of the Dravida-style temple. The Ajitagama (Kriyapada12/67), the Suprabhedagama (Kriyapada 30/42) and the Svāyambhu Āgama unanimously say: 'The prāsada that is octagonal from the kantha (neck) onward up is Dravida.'

Flying Palaces

The site of Sambor Prei Kuk is famous for its reductions of flying palaces, attaining the highest aesthetic perfection in their realization. To understand the deeper meaning of Sambor Prei Kuk art it is essential to understand various nuances of the term *vimana*, a word of Sanskrit origin,

Fig. 14.2 Title: The N 7 Temple in Ishanapura (Cambodia). There are ten octagonal temples in Ishanapura. In the north group of temples only N 7 is octagonal. These temples are octagonal from the base to pinnacle. Top to bottom octagonal brick temples in India are not known. These temples are called flying palaces since on the outer side walls of the temple, palaces are shown being carried by sculpted winged animals. Source: Author

integrated both in the ancient and modern Khmer language. At the base of the octagonal temples are depicted winged mythical animals carrying the temple on their upturned palms. From the Vedic period the gods travelled on their flying chariots (*ratha*). In later literature *ratha* is replaced by Vimana, the flying devices of the gods (Fig. 14.3).

One of the monuments of Angkor is popularly known as Phimeanakas (*vimana* + *akasha*) or the celestial *vimana* in the modern Khmer language. The expression carries several meanings, ranging from temple or

Fig. 14.3 Winged animals, horse, garuda and lion shown carrying the octagonal temple as flying palace, Ishanapura, Cambodia. The octagonal temples have been documented from different parts of India, but the motif of winged animals carrying the temple/palace is absent in Indian examples. Source: Author

palace to mythological flying machines described in Sanskrit epics. References to these flying machines are commonplace in ancient Indian texts, which even describe their use in warfare. Indra's *vimana* is called Trivishtapa; it is octagonal in shape.

BHARAVAHAKAS

The *bharavahaka* or the weight-bearers are the precursors of the winged animals at Sambor Prei Kuk that carry celestial structures on their outstretched palms. The Silpa Prakasha uses it as a general term to describe various types of *yaksha*-like figures that seem to uphold sections of a temple. These pot-bellied, dwarf-like figures usually have their hands above their shoulders as if bearing a weight. *Bharavahakas* are seen only occasionally in the earlier temples, and seem to gather popularity later at the Chaurashi, Baudh, Tirtheshvar and Mukteshvar temples. The Shilpa Prakasha (I, 343–353) tells that these figures should be seated in *kukkutasana*, like a cock, or in other words in a squatting position. The text suggests that they should be depicted preferably in pairs (Boner and Sarma 1966). In the later temples of our groups, single *bharavahakas* appear at the top of the pilasters of the temple walls. A unique occurrence of the motif is in the Gauri temple where the entire base of the temple is supported by rows of *bharavahakas* (Dehejia 1979, 60–61).

Ishanapura is distinguished by the presence of the Saka Durgasvami, who was a native of peninsular India—*dakshinapatha janmā*. After political dislocation in the western Deccan, migration of Saka people to other parts of Dakshinapatha and beyond India was a natural process. Durgasvami must have been born somewhere in the present-day region of Maharashtra, Telangana or Andhra, which together constitute the ancient Dakshinapatha. He might have migrated to Ishanapura (Sambor Prei Kuk) in around 610 when Ishanavarman was the ruling king. With his scholarship and mastery over the esoteric Brahmanical practices of India, he was quick enough to attract the attention of King Ishanavarman, take the hand of his daughter and lead the Ishanapura community to new heights.

In fact, an inscription from the archaeological site N 16-1 expressly mentions Durgasvami, the Saka Brahmin, as the son-in-law of King Ishanavarman, responsible for carrying out a number of projects in Ishanapura. He was an Indian who came to Ishanapura from Dakshinapatha, the region south of Vindhya in India.

The worship of Hindu gods, Shiva in the form of Smiling Lord and the Serious Lord, and the cult of Harihara, a combined form of Vishnu and Shiva, was popular in Ishanapura. The Sanskrit language was highly cultivated as evidenced from a number of inscriptions found at the site. The local Khmer language was growing as a result of contacts with the Sanskrit-speaking population in the city. This is evident from the Khmer language inscriptions found at the site.

The combined testimony of inscriptions, monuments and pottery suggests that Ishanapura flourished as a capital city during the rule of Ishanavarman, and became famous as an international city for Asia during his regime. However, as an important settlement, the site pre-dates Ishanavarman. A Robang Romeas inscription offers the dateline of 598. Four hundred years later, when the site was no longer the capital city, a high official of the tenth-century king Rajendravarman came to carry out restoration work at the north group of temples, trying to revive the cult of Gambhireshvara. The site shows its political importance in the eleventh century with the inscription of Suryavarman I at Robang Romeas, in the neighbourhood of Ishanapura.

Various types of pottery unearthed from the site confirm that the site flourished as a living settlement for many centuries after Ishanavarman. Khmer stoneware is predominant in the ceramic assemblage of the site, dating from the Angkorean period. Most of this work, ash-glazed, was produced locally in the eleventh century. The Chinese ceramics found from the site range from the eighth to fourteenth centuries. The parallel evolution of both Khmer and Chinese ceramics, with a peak in the eleventh century, points to an innovative time at Sambor Prei Kuk (Shimoda 2010, 45).

Concluding Remarks

It would be useful to establish a consortium of archaeologists, social scientists and engineers from India and ASEAN countries to carry out holistic projects in which archaeological conservation, rural development, cultural awareness and economic empowerment are integral and complementary components. Conservation for conservation's sake, inspired by the nostalgia of the past, does not respond to the ground realities of the economic stress apparent in Third World countries. Some pilot projects will pave the way for better understanding of the aspirations of the rural communities that are the real custodians of archaeological sites.

References

Aiyangar, K.V. Rangaswami (ed.), 1942. Lakshmidhara. Krityakalpataru. Ashtamo bhagah. Tirthavivecanakandam, Gaekwad's Oriental Series XCVIII. Baroda.
Boner, Alice and Sarma, Sadasiva Rath, 1966. Silpa Prakasha of Ramachandra Kaulacara (translated and annotated), Leiden.
Bisschop, Peter C., 2006. Early Saivism and the Skandapurana. Sects and Centres. Groningen: Egbert Forsten.
Bruguier, Bruno and Juliette Lacroix, 2011. Sambor Prei Kuk et le basin du Tonlé Sap. Guide archéologique du Cambodge. Phnom Penh: Les editions du Patrimoine.
Dehejia, Vidya, 1979. Early Stone Temples of Orissa. New Delhi: Vikas Publishing House Pvt Ltd.
Luke, Christina and Morag M. Kersel, 2012. US Cultural Diplomacy and Archaeology: Soft Power, Hard Heritage. New York: Routledge.
Nye, Joseph S., 2011. The Future of Power. New York: Public Affairs.
———., 2004. Soft Power: The Means to Success in World Politics. New York: Public Affairs.
———., 1990. Bound to Lead: The Changing Nature of American Power. New York: Basic Books.
Parmentier, Henri, 1927. L'Art Khmer Primitif. Van Oest: Paris.
Sahai, Sachchidanand, 2012. The Hindu Temples in Southeast Asia. Their Role in Social, Economic and Political Formations. New Delhi: Aryan Publishers.
Shimoda, Ichita. 2010. Study on the Ancient Khmer City Isanapura. Tokyo: Waseda University. Ph.D. Thesis (in Japanese language).

CHAPTER 15

Shiva's Land: Understanding the Religious Landscape of Early Southeast Asia

John Guy

INTRODUCTION

This chapter explores the earliest evidence for the practice of aspects of Brahmanical culture in mainland and insular Southeast Asia. Archaeological traces of commercial links between the Indian subcontinent and Southeast Asia recovered in the past two decades have been revealed to date from at least the second century BCE.[1] Southern Indian black and red polished rouletted ware ceramics, such a feature of the southern Coromandel coast, have also been reported at Red Sea sites (some with Southern Brahmi, so-called 'Grantha', inscriptions), and, extending the reach eastward, from north coast Java and Bali.[2] Thin-bodied bronze bowls previously known from northwestern India, distinguished by a high tin content and engraved figurative designs, have been recovered from the river bed at Khao Sam Keo in peninsular Thailand, and are assumed to have been deposited there as a

[1] Chaisuwan, Boonyarit 2011; Bellina, Berenice, in Guy, John 2014.
[2] Wayan Ardika 2008.

J. Guy (✉)
Florence and Herbert Irving Curator of South and Southeast Asian Art, The Metropolitan Museum of Art, New York, NY, USA

© The Author(s) 2018
S. Saran (ed.), *Cultural and Civilisational Links between India and Southeast Asia*, https://doi.org/10.1007/978-981-10-7317-5_15

253

result of slippage from early habitation sites immediately uphill.[3] This same source recently produced a post-Mauryan ring-stone of the classic type previously only known from northern Indian sites stretching across the width of Gangetic plains, recorded from Kausambi to Pataliputra.[4] The site of Khao Sam Keo has previously revealed quantities of intaglio seals and a carnelian lion miniature of a type also known from central Thailand and central Vietnam,[5] and previously only known in northern Indian Buddhist stupa reliquary deposit contexts. Likewise, an ivory comb excavated at Chansen, central Thailand, is a first–second-century luxury import from the Deccan, likely Andhra Pradesh. The famous ivory mirror handle in the form of a standing female figure, excavated at Pompeii (terminal date 76 CE), inappropriately often described as representing Lakshmi, was likely produced at one of the great urban centres of the northern Deccan; Ujjain is a strong contender, though Ter is conventionally suggested because of much inferior examples excavated there.[6] Finds of Roman glass are reported from southern India with increasing frequency, as the recently published finds at Pattanam in Kerala affirm.[7] These include the ribbed coloured glass bowl types previously known from Chinese dated tomb contexts of the Western Han period; identical glassware has been reported from the Thai peninsula, affirming the pan-regional nature of this long distance trade. As these finds make increasingly clear, the West Asian and late Roman trade with the Indian peninsular was part of a wider network of exchange that encompassed not only Sri Lanka but also peninsular and insular Southeast Asia.

Early Trade and Inscriptional Record

Centres of early trade exchange in mainland Southeast Asia, all on river systems that linked to the sea, have yielded a rich array of terracotta imagery, both imported and local artefacts of the Brahmanical derivation. Amulets depicting Gaja-Lakshmi and Kubera, both propitious Indic deities associated with success and prosperity—highly appropriate deities of personal veneration in merchant communities—are found in abundance at such first millennium sites as U Thong, Chansen and Lopburi in Central

---

[3] Glover, Ian, paper presented to The 15th European Association of Southeast Asian Archaeologists Conference, Paris, June 2015.
[4] Gupta, S. P. 1980.
[5] Glover, Ian C., and Bérénice Bellina 2011.
[6] Prince of Wales Museum 1975, no. 27.
[7] Cherian, P. J. and V. Venu. 2014.

Fig. 15.1 Comb decorated with auspicious emblems (*astamangala*) and *hamsa*. Ivory, Deccan or Andhra Pradesh, *c*, second century CE, excavated Chansen, central Thailand. Source: National Museum, Bangkok

Thailand, a region of great importance for interregional trade, both overland to Myanmar and to the coast connecting to the Gulf of Thailand. Such Indic deities may best be understood in these early urban contexts as the 'patron saints' of merchants, cults shared no doubt by local as well as Indian merchants. An ivory comb undoubtedly imported from the Deccan, likely Andhra Pradesh, decorated with the eight auspicious emblems (*astamangala*), was similarly excavated in the Chansen area (Fig. 15.1).[8] A remarkable Shaiva seal with boxed-Brahmi script from

---
[8] Bronson, Bennet (1973).

Fig. 15.2 Seal impression from an Indian matrix, probably Bihar; clay impression found U Thong, central Thailand, early to mid-sixth century. Source: U Thong National Museum, Suphanburi

U Thong, and near identical sealings from Chansen, carry a moulded inscription best read as the property of a merchant of Saiva allegiance, pointing to close mercantile connections (Fig. 15.2).[9]

While such finds confirm the early nature of Indian trade and exchange with mainland and insular Southeast Asia, it is only around the fifth and sixth century that a secure epigraphic record begins to appear, engraved on natural boulders as well as stele. Amongst the earliest are those of two western Indonesian rulers, one a local Borneo chief who titled himself Mulavarman, and in Sunda—western Java—the ruler of the Tamanagara kingdom, Purnavarman. These inscriptions are the earliest records in insular Southeast Asia of the enactment of Brahmancial ritual for the spiritual protection and material welfare of local rulers. The familiarity of those responsible for these inscriptions with propitious Brahmanical rites suggests that Indian priests, or their immediate descendants, were the agents of these rituals. Southeast Asian clan leaders are witnessed here assuming, for the first time, Indic kingly titles expressed in Sanskrit, and sponsoring efficacious rites based directly on Indian practice. The devotional allegiances expressed in the inscriptions suggest that these rulers were espousing a personal iden-

---

[9] The iconography and inscription of the clay seal are discussed in Guy 2014.

tification with the Brahmanical gods, especially Vishnu, and that they were actively enacting Brahmanical rituals through the agency of Brahmin priests.

This is demonstrated most vividly in one of the oldest suite of inscribed Sanskrit steles known in Southeast Asia, the seven *yupa* stones of king Mulavarman, of Kutei, in eastern Kalimantan (Borneo).[10] These roughly shaped stone stele are referred to in the inscription as *yupa*, a Sanskrit term for a consecrated sacrificial post associated with Vedic ritual. They were here erected to record a local ruler's declaration of allegiance to the religious authority of a new religion, Brahmanism, and the gifts bestowed on those who performed the worship. This ruler is the earliest recorded kingly *bhakta* in Southeast Asia. He provided a three-generation lineage, with Mulavaraman and his father Asavarman assuming Indic reign names, while his grandfather, Kundunga, appears to be have a local name.[11] This stele may thus be read as the earliest record of the process of cultural appropriation of Indic models of kingship and religion, witnessed over three generations. This linage likely extends back to the fourth century CE.

The Vedic fire sacrifice enacted on Mulavarman's behalf must have been performed by Brahmin priests. We may assume that it followed Vedic prescription, enacted on a temporary platform of geometrically arranged bricks; no structural shrine would have been required. Seven inscribed memorial stones record the ritual sacrifice and the abundant gifts bestowed on the priests; of these, one records the sacrifice, and the remainder are devoted to an inventory of the gifts. The priests were rewarded with a feast and gifts of cattle, land, lamps, oil, sesame seeds and ghee, the latter a required ingredient in the performance of Vedic *homa* rituals. These accord with the Puranic list of *mahadanas* ('great gifts'), indicating that ritual procedure was correctly observed. It is clear then that this was a wholly Indian ritual enacted for the benefit of a local Southeast Asian ruler.

Located on the eastern coast of Borneo, the kingdom of Kutei may have been less remote in the fourth–fifth century than perhaps it is today, linked already to the early gold trading networks of the Indian Ocean. The presence of a court strongly influenced by Indic models, as witnessed here, makes it clear that Indian traders, and Brahmins, must already have been well established in the region. Brahmins appear early in the recorded history of Southeast Asia as the first witnesses and agents of an imported religious system.

---

[10] Chhabra, Bahadura Chanda 1947, 1965.
[11] Bahadura Chanda Chhabra 1965, pp. 107–108.

This process is witnessed again, likely in the sixth century, in west Java, with a series of four rock boulder inscriptions from sites which span an area from the village of Ciampea in the hills near modern Bogor to the coast at modern-day Jakarta. We may understand these as marking the extent of the earliest known kingdom in the region, Tarumanagara. In these records, King Purnavarman pronounced his allegiance to Vishnu and to Indra, the first explicit Indic religious affiliations declared in Southeast Asia. The choice of natural rocks, rather than shaped pillars as seen at Kutei perhaps a century earlier, or in the famous Vo Canh stele from Nat Trang, central Vietnam,[12] points to a conscious act of empowering the living landscape with Indic scripts and sacred syllables, metaphors of divinity, the latter in so-called Shell script associated with Gupta-period sites in India, including Udayagiri, near Vidisha in Madhya Pradesh.

Three of the inscriptions are located at the site of a fortified citadel situated on a riverine island between two branches of the Ciaruteun River, near Bogor. One of the Ciampea inscriptions, the *Prasati Ciaruteun*, depicts a pair of feet (*pada*), denoting a divine presence. The massive boulder, carved in situ in the bed of the river, identifies the footprints as being those of Vishnu by the appearance of the name Trivikrama. This alludes to Vishnu's *avatar* as the dwarf Vamana, who assumed gigantic proportions in order to encircle the earth in three strides—whereby he is named Trivikrama ('He of Three Strides')—so both asserting Vishnu's authority as divine ruler and evoking the earth's passage around the sun, alluding to Vishnu's origins as a solar deity (Fig. 15.3). A small radiating circle appears as part of the composition, perhaps to be understood as a sun symbol. The inscription describes king Purnavarman as 'the great king, ruler of the world, whose footprints are the same as those of Lord Vishnu', identifying him with Trivikrama. Vishnu is widely understood as the divine universal monarch, a concept shared with the Buddhist *Cakravartin*. The close identification of earthly rulers with Vishnu's divine kingship was clearly a familiar concept to early Southeast rulers. The second inscription at Ciampea, the *Telapak Gadjah*, depicts a large pair of elephant feet (*gajapada*), again with which Purnavarman is identified, the inscription likening him to the mighty elephant Airavata (Indo: Airwata), the vehicle of Indra, the Vedic weather god and harbinger of the monsoons.[13]

The choice of location of the *Prasati Ciaruteun* inscription, on a boulder in the river bed, was repeated on a further inscription on a boulder at

[12] Illustrated Guy 2014, fig. 58, p. 69.
[13] For *Prasati Ciaruteun* and *Prasati Kebon Kopi* I, De Casparis 1975.

Fig. 15.3 Rock-cut inscription of Purnavarman, ruler of the kingdom of Tarumanagara, Sunda, west Java, Indonesia, early sixth century (photographed in situ, Ciaruteun River, Ciampea, *c.* 1920). Source: Author

a nearby river junction. This is engraved in a highly cursive script which has defied a secure reading and likely represents *mantras*, sacred syllables serving as protective charms and spells, again in shell scrip. Taken together, these three inscribed river boulders can be seen as providing magical protection to Purnavarman's river island citadel.

The fourth Purnavarman inscription, found at Tegu, near the modern harbour of Tanjuk Priak, Jakarta, records his construction of a canal system at a location near the coast named *Sundapurna*. This is the earliest confirmation of the antiquity of the name Sunda for the region of west Java. The presence of this inscription on the coast would indicate that Purnavarman's territory extended over a considerable distance, from the hills of modern day Bogor to the shores of the Java Sea. Access to the sea ensured that the Tarumanagara kingdom could engage in regional and international trade. King Purnavarman's inscriptions tell us that he was the third ruler of Tarumanagara, so we may date the beginnings of this development to the sixth century.

These four inscriptions mark the geographic reach of the Tarumanagara kingdom, whose regional importance may be gauged from the seventh-century Kota Kapur inscription found on Bangka Island, which records the victory of Srivijaya's fleet in conquering a kingdom in Sunda in 684.[14] That victory was very likely over Purnavarman's descendants. Eighth-century Chinese sources speak of a kingdom of 'Duo-lou-ma', likely Taruma, suggesting it prospered for around three centuries before coming under the suzerainty of Srivijaya, as indicated by the Kota Kapur hexagonal pillar inscription.

Tarumanagara is the earliest kingdom for which we have extensive inscriptional sources demonstrating the existence of upland–lowland exchange systems in all of Southeast Asia, a model which provides a key to wealth generation and early state formation in later periods. It is likely that Mulavarman's Kutei kingdom functioned on the same model, given that the presence of Indians Brahmins presupposes Indian traders, undoubtedly attracted by the island's rich supplies of alluvial gold, harvested upstream in the Borneo interior. This region is encompassed in the Sanskrit nomenclature for early Southeast Asia, Suvarnadvipa.

In mainland Southeast, the inscription of paramount importance is that of King Devanika. Sometime in the later fifth century a local chief, who titled himself by the Indic name Devanika, journeyed on pilgrimage from an unknown place to the early Khmer city at Champasak, now in southern Laos, famous for its holy mountain, Sri Lingaparvata. This mountain, whose summit resembles a natural *linga*, was known already at this time as an abode of Shiva and hence a *tirtha*, a sacred site for pilgrimage on the early Hindu landscape of Southeast Asia.

In the presence of this holy mountain, this ruler engaged Brahmin priests to perform a consecration ceremony to affirm his authority in the presence of Lord Shiva. The rite performed was an *abhisheka*, a lustration ceremony whereby this king was, so says the inscription, 'installed in supreme royal power by the auspicious Sri Lingaparvata, honoured since antiquity'. Devanika assumed a new title in the inscription, that of *maharajadhiraja*, 'king of kings', one who is blessed to be Shiva-like. The dedicatory inscription he installed to record his pious devotion (*bhakti*) to

[14] Trigangga 2009.

Shiva, inscribed on the four sides of a tripartite *linga*, has proved to be the oldest Sanskrit inscription known from Khmer-speaking territory.

To honour this *tirtha*, Devanika constructed a bathing tank for the cleansing of pilgrims' sins, which he titled Kurukshetra, after the famous location in northern India where the climatic battle of the *Mahabharata* took place. As the contemporary Indian *Vishnudharmamottara Purana* states, no temple is complete without a bathing tank, so we may assume that an image-house, probably an open *linga* shrine, already existed locally. Structural shrines are unknown from this period, but stone-built platforms are, presumably originally enhanced with timber and thatch superstructures.

The reality beyond these functional inscriptions is captured in a series of contemporary sources. Chinese dynastic histories of the second half of the first millennium preserve rare descriptions of Southeast Asian court life as witnessed by Chinese envoys. These have recently been studied to great benefit by Geoff Wade.[15] The early sixth-century *Nan shi* describes the king of a Buddhist kingdom, Po li (Panei), likely located at Padang Lawas in north Sumatra, a region rich in forest products such as camphor, benzoin and alluvial gold much in demand in China. It tells us that the king wore variegated silks and cords or chains of rank across his chest, a high gold crown decorated with seven varieties of gems, a gold-adorned sword, that he sat on a golden throne and when he went out he rode in an elephant sedan chair of fragrant woods, accompanied by attendants blowing conches and beating drums.[16] This description captures an image of mid-first millennium kingship which seems to be a blend of locally conceived display of wealth with Indian trappings.

Another evocative image is from Kedah, on the Malay Peninsula, in the early seventh century. The *Sui Shu* tells us of the capital, likely located near the estuary to the Bujang river valley, that 'at each gate there are painted flying spirits, fairies and Bodhisattva images ... the king's throne is a golden crouching bull, and above it bejeweled parasol and bejeweled fans left and right ... Hundreds of Brahmins seated in rows facing each other on left and right.'[17]

Such descriptions, presumably based on envoy or merchant first-hand observations, were intended to reflect the trade wealth of these small polities engaged in tribute trade with China. A remarkable Chinese hand-scroll from the sixth century, preserved in an eleventh-century copy,

---

[15] Wade 2014.
[16] The full source in cited in Wade 2014.
[17] *Sui Shu*, cited in Wade 2014.

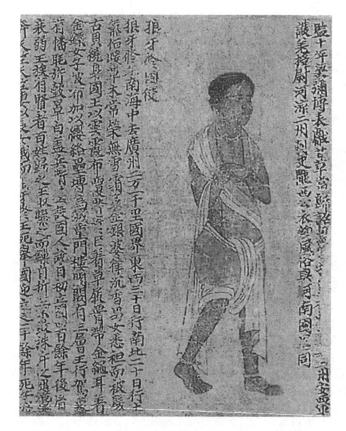

Fig. 15.4 Envoy from Langkasuka; detail of *Liang zhgong tu* (Illustrated History of the Liang). Handscroll. Eleventh-century copy of sixth-century original. Source: National Museum of China, Beijing

records portraits of foreign envoys received at the Liang Dynasty court. Most are from Central Asia but one, depicted bare chested and wearing a waist-skirt, is named as being from Langkasuka, a known polity on the Gulf of Thailand, likely located in the region of modern Nakhon Sri Thammarat (Fig. 15.4). This is a unique depiction of a high-ranking Southeast Asian of the sixth century.

From the sixth century onwards, we witness in Southeast Asia, as in India, a rapid emergence of a built-temple tradition. Integral to the earliest brick sanctuary towers that characterize the first phase of Brahmanical temple construction in Cambodia was the use of sandstone lintels, many of them unique in their innovative interpretation of Brahmanical imagery and myths. Among the rarest is the lintel from Wat Eng Khna, central Cambodia, belonging to the cultural sphere of the seventh-century royal city of Isanapura, today's Sambor Prei Kuk. It uniquely combines two narratives, both central to the enactment of Khmer kingship. The upper register of the lintel depicts the creation myth of the *linga*, the *Lingodbhavamurti*, which recounts a dispute between Brahma and Vishnu, each challenging the other's claim to be the creator of the universe. A great flaming pillar, seemingly without limit, appears before them both, with Shiva's face within the shaft of the *linga*, asserting his supremacy over them both. Depictions of this myth are extremely rare in Southeast Asia and in India being predominantly confined to Pallava-era Tamil Nadu. The myth features prominently in Indian textual sources known in Cambodia, especially the *Skandapurana*, a favoured text by the Shaiva Pasupata sect who rose to prominence in seventh-century Cambodia.[18]

In the second register of the Wat Eng Khna lintel appears a scene unique in Khmer art. It depicts a royal consecration, such as that implied in Devanika's inscription of two centuries earlier (Fig. 15.5, detail). Here we see the enthroned king, installed in an open pavilion (*mandapa*), flanked by dignitaries and Brahmins, the latter identified by their piled-up dreadlocks, beards and sacred cords. Two priests immediately adjacent to the ruler pour holy waters over the enthroned figure, performing an *abhisheka*. This act of lustration in the context of kingship is associated with consecration and legitimization of divine status (*rajasuya*), as made explicit in Devanika's inscription, whereby he not only becomes a king of kings but in his person 'Shiva-like'.

From Vishnu's to Shiva's Land

The sculptural record suggests that in the earliest associations of Southeast Asian kingship with Indic ideas, in the fifth and sixth centuries, it was the worship of Vishnu, not Shiva, that predominated. The inscriptions of Purnavarman make the personal identification of that ruler with Vishnu explicit, as do the numerous Vishnu images surviving from western Indonesia, the Thai peninsula, and Mekong delta. The Indic mode of conceptualizing kingship—with Vishnu as the divine role model—clearly

[18] Guy (2000).

Fig. 15.5 Detail of lintel depicting the *Lingodbhavamurti* myth and a king's consecration, mid-seventh century. Found at Wat Eng Khna, Kampong Thom province, Cambodia. Sandstone. Source: National Museum of Cambodia, Phnom Penh

offered local rulers a new means of setting themselves apart, as the embodiments of divinities on earth.

By the seventh century, however, the linkage with Shaivism was increasingly accepted as a universal principle of Southeast Asian kingship. Several aspects of Shaivism developed a uniquely Southeast Asian character in this period. A prevailing feature was the emphasis on asceticism; Shiva is proclaimed supreme yogi, the first of the ascetics. This emphasis in Cambodian Shaivism may be largely attributable to the predominance of the Pasupatas Brahmins, a sect of early medieval Indian Saiva ascetics. An extreme sect of Shaivism, they placed great emphasis on Shiva as the supreme yogic master (*Mahesvara-yoga*) and on the principles of ascetic renunciation and austerities (*tapas*): the *Skandapurana* speaks of them having a white radiance from the smearing of their bodies with cremation ash.[19] They were a powerful force in the Indian Deccan in the mid-first millennium and are known from inscriptions to be a major presence in early Cambodia, being the recipients of royal favours, grants and appointments in the early seventh century. Isanavarman I appointed a Pasupata to oversee one of his royal temples at Isanapura; others served as spiritual and temporal advisors to kings, one is even recorded as a court poet. It is likely then that it is Pasupata who are depicted performing the king's *abhiseka* in the Wat Eng Khna lintel.

Inscriptions indicate that Pasupata were themselves active in the commissioning of *lingas* and sculptures in honour of Shiva. A unique sculpture in the seventh-century Khmer repertoire celebrating Shiva as an ascetic may have been associated with Pasupata patronage or produced under their guidance. A life-size male deity, moustached and with a forehead third eye, dressed only in a short loincloth and with piled up dreadlocks, was discovered in a ruined sanctuary in Stung Treng province, northeast Cambodia, in 1920 (Fig. 15.6). The only attribute is an ascetic's water bottle (*kundika*), a rare but recognized feature of anthropomorphic representations of Shiva from the early Gupta period in northern India. The appearance is that of a Shaiva ascetic, and given its scale and obvious role as a cult image was undoubtedly intended to represent Shiva himself. The singular nature of this sculpture defies comparison with other pre-Angkorian sculpture and we must look to contemporary Champa for the closest iconographic analogy, the ascetic Shiva recovered at sanctuary A4, My Son (Fig. 15.7). This site served as the principal Cham religious sanctuary in central Vietnam, located in the mountains southwest of Tra Kieu, the citadel capital of the dominant Cham lineage in Quang Nam province. The My Son ascetic Shiva shares the same features, with the addition of a crescent moon in his dreadlocks, as seen routinely in Indian depictions.

Shaiva asceticism appears in another guise at My Son in the seventh–eighth century, in a cult icon of Shiva's son, Ganesha (Fig. 15.8). The survival of a number of large-scale images of Ganesha from sites in central Vietnam, Cambodia and eastern Thailand demonstrate that this deity enjoyed a special status in early Southeast Asia and was the subject of an important cult. This icon was recovered from chapel E5 in the southwest corner of temple complex E at My Son. Ganesha is here represented as the embodiment of the asceticism exemplified by Shiva, displaying the third eye and a *yajnopavita* cord represented as a snake, bracelets that adorn

---

[19] Bisschop 2006.

Fig. 15.6 Shiva as an Ascetic, seventh century. Found in Stung Treng province, northeastern Cambodia. Sandstone, h. 164 cm. Source: National Museum of Cambodia, Phnom Penh

each wrist and the tiger-skin hip-cloth of a *rishi*. Two hands are now lost, but a 1903 site photograph allows identification of the missing attributes, one a horseradish (*mulakakanda*), an elephant's favoured treat and a reminder of Ganesha's early Indian origins as an agricultural deity. The flayed tiger skin and snake garlands point to India Gupta and Vakataka-era prototypes of the fifth and sixth centuries.

Also recovered at the My Son temple complex, and preserved there today, is a tympanum relief depicting Shiva Natesha with his assembled family and celebrants, including a royal devotee, to the right (Fig. 15.9). This is the earliest known representation of this subject from Southeast Asia, and likely dates to the eighth century. In this work we can find a strong Indian prototype in the rock-cut depiction of a sixteen-armed Shiva Natesha at the early seventh-century Chalukyan site of Badami, in the Deccan (Fig. 15.10). Not only is the ensemble and configuration strik-

Fig. 15.7 Shiva installed on a lustration pedestal, eighth century. Recovered from temple A4, My Son, Quang Nam province, central Vietnam. Photographed in situ in 1903. Source: Author

ingly similar, but the precise dance position assumed by Shiva, one foot down, one with heel raised only, is identical, pointing to artistic direction by priests or *stapathis* from a shared tradition.

Siva assumed other startlingly original forms in early Cambodia. A shrine platform depicting a pair of footprints (*pada*) was discovered in 1911, identified by inscription as *Civapadadvayambhoja*, 'the pair of lotus feet of Shiva' (Fig. 15.11). Fragrant flower imagery is closely associated with Shiva, routinely celebrated as the 'lord of flowers'. While *Vishnupada*, and *Buddhapada* are frequently found in India, those linked

Fig. 15.8 Ganesha, late seventh–eighth century. Recovered from temple E5, My Son, Quang Nam province, central Vietnam, Sandstone, h. 96 cm. The Museum of Cham Sculpture, Da Nang, Vietnam. Source: Author

Fig. 15.9 Tympanum depicting Shiva dancing before his assembled family and royal devotee. My Son, Champa, central Vietnam. Sandstone, h. 143 cm, w. 170 cm. Source: My Son Site Museum, Quang Nam

Fig. 15.10 Shiva Natesha, rock cut, Badami, Karanataka, India. Chalukya dynasty, early seventh century. Source: Author

to Shiva are extremely rare. *Shivapada* are for the focus of *bhakti*, intense personal worship which has as its goal complete identification with Shiva himself. One of the few recorded *Shivapada* in India is rock cut at Sultanganj, overlooking the River Ganges, in Bihar, eastern India, inscribed in a Gupta-era script as *rudra mahalaya*, 'Shiva, the supreme lord'. Sixth-century texts such as the *Skandapurana*, favoured by the Pasupata sect, speak of places where Lord Shiva left his footprint, from the Himalayas to Andhra Pradesh, and it is likely that the appearance of a *Shivapada* in pre-Angkorian Cambodia is thanks to their influence. Several Cambodian Sanskrit inscriptions refer to the worship of *Shivapada*, one in Kampong Cham dated to around 680. The *Shivapada*

Fig. 15.11 Shiva's footprints (*Shivapada*), second half of seventh–eighth century. Found in Stung Treng province, northeastern Cambodia, in 1911. Sandstone, 17 × 32 × 32 cm. Source: National Museum of Cambodia, Phnom Penh

from Stung Treng province is a unique survivor of its type, but fits into a broader setting of early Khmer Shaiva worship, in which the *trisula* emblem, the sacred bull and the footprint are used to invoke Shiva's presence, along with the ever-present *linga*.

Shiva has been accompanied by a bull and has displayed a trident (*trisula*) since his earliest representations in northwestern Indian coinage of the Kushan era, in the early centuries CE. A stele recovered from a ruined temple site in Kampong Cham in 1919 witnesses the *trisula* celebrated as Shiva's attribute par excellence, depicted rising from a vase of plenty (*purnaghata*) and with the blade of Shiva's axe projecting sideways from the vase (Fig. 15.12). The association of the woodsman's axe with Shiva as forest hunter is a distinctly South Indian feature, and points to the likely regional origins of this imagery in Cambodia. The distinctive profile of the *trisula*'s three blades appears across seventh-century Southeast Asia, from Champasak (the Wat Phu stele of Jayavarman, *c.* 657–681) in northern Khmer territory to the Mekong delta in the south and to My Son in central Vietnam.[20] An inscription on the central shaft of this depiction links the personal dedication to a named *rishi*, and from

---

[20] Coedes (1956).

Fig. 15.12 Stele with Shaiva Trident, Axe and Vase of Plenty, second half seventh century. Found at Vihar Thom, Kampong Cham province, southeastern Cambodia. Sandstone, h. 102 cm. Source: National Museum of Cambodia, Phnom Penh

the tone of the dedication likely also to be a Pasupata, who offered this stele, along with a *linga*, in honour of Shiva in his eightieth year.[21]

Conclusions

These expressions of Shaiva devotionalism establish a strong sense of seventh-century Khmer rulers being imbued with the spiritual values of their mentors, the Brahmins who taught that success in kingship could flow from immersion in the grace of the Indic gods. The power of Shaiva devotionalism rapidly expanded across mainland and insular Southeast Asia in the course of the seventh century, challenging the ascendant position of Vaishnavism which had first captured the attention of local rulers seeking new conceptual and religious models upon which to construct their expanding notions of kingship. The evolution from clan leader to kingly sovereign, with the moral and religious authority that concept implied in the early Indic world, is known to us only through the medium of Sanskrit inscriptions. No 'alternative histories' exist, or at least have survived.

The only independent sources for first millennium Southeast Asia are the contemporary Chinese descriptions of courtly life in some of the Southeast

---

[21] Louis Finot 1920, cited in Guy 2014, pp. 160–62.

Asian polities known to Chinese commentators from accounts provided by visiting envoys. Indeed, the earliest polities are known to us only by Chinese renderings of lost local names, or names the Chinese assigned. The earliest extant Chinese historical reference to political entities in Southeast Asia are found in a Chinese text entitled *Han shu* (History of the Han Dynasty) written in about 100 CE. It describes a voyage to the Nanhai (Southern Sea) and the places visited en route. These place names are the earliest known in Southeast Asia, though their locations remain uncertain and contentious. This and later second-century sources make clear that the region was already engaged in facilitating long distance trade that supplied the riches of the Indian subcontinent, notably precious stones and pearls, in exchange for Chinese silk and gold. Chinese knowledge of Southeast in the first millennium seems largely confined to the mainland, the Thai/Malay peninsula and the Sumatra/Java region. By the mid-millennium these sources speak of rulers with Indic names and courts, with rulers parading on elephants seated on silver howdahs, accompanied by conch-blowing brahmins and fairy-like bodhisattvas attending the gates. The *Nan shi* expressly states that a Funanese ruler who conquered the Panpan kingdom on the Thai isthmus 'changed the systems and employed the Indian laws'.[22] By the early seventh century the *Sui shu* speaks of Zhen-la (roughly equivalent to modern day Cambodia) as having thirty large cities, a remarkable level of urbanization. Likely referring to the northern Khmer urban centre at Champasak (Wat Phu, now in southern Laos), the *Sui shu* records that at the capital near the Lingaparavata mountain 'they greatly revere the law of the Buddha and also greatly trust in Brahmanic practitioners'.[23] It was here, as noted above, that a King Devanika performed an *abhisheka* in the late fifth century, and recorded this auspicious event in the oldest Sanskrit inscription extant in Khmer territory.

This otherwise unknown mainland ruler who titled himself Devanika was enacting a personal cult in a Hindu environment, enlivened and given meaning by identified holy places (*tirthas*) in the local landscape. These were not understood as surrogates of Indian holy sites, but bona fide sacred places of worship whose efficacy was equal to that of those in India. Seventh-century Cambodia was, in the mind of those Southeast Asian rulers immersed in Hindu *bhakti*, a world permeated, and defined, by Shiva's presence.

---

[22] *Nan shi*, a fifth-century Chinese source, Wade: 26.
[23] *Sui shu*, Wade translation, in Wade 2014: 26.

References

Bisschop, Peter, *Early Saivism and the Skandapurana*, Groningen Oriental Series 21, Groningen, Egbert Forsten, 2006.
Bronson, Bennet 1973. 'Excavations at Chansen, Thailand: An interim report', in *Asian Perspectives*, No. 91: 315–36.
Chaisuwan, Boonyarit 2011. "Early Contacts between India and Andaman Coast in Thailand from the second century BCE to eleventh century CE". In *Early Interactions between South and Southeast Asia: Reflections on Cross-Cultural Exchange*, edited by Pierre-Yves Manguin, A. Mani, and Geoff Wade, Singapore: Institute of Southeast Asian Studies, Nalanda-Sriwijaya Series 2, New Delhi, Manohar: 83–112.
Cherian, P.J. and V. Venu 2014. *Pattanam*. New Delhi, National Museum of India
Chhabra, Bahadura Chanda 1947. "Yūpa Inscriptions," in *India antiqua a volume of oriental studies; presented by his friends and pupils to Jean Philippe Vogel on the occasion of his fiftieth anniversary of his doctorate*, Leiden Brill: 77–82.
Chhabra, Bahadura Chanda 1965. *Expansion of Indo–Aryan Culture during Pallava rule as evidenced by inscriptions*. Delhi: Munshi Ram Manohar Lal.
Coedes, George 1956. 'Nouvelles donnees sur les origines du royaume khmer: La Stele de Văt Luong Kău pres de Văt P'hu, *Bulletin de l'Ecole Française d'Extrême-Orient* 48: 209–220.
De Casparis, 1975. *Indonesian Palaeography: A history of writing in Indonesia from the beginnings to C. A.D. 1500*, Leiden/Köln: E.J. Brill.
Glover, Ian C., and Bérénice Bellina 2011. "Ban Don Ta Phet and Khao Sam Kaeo: The Earliest Indian Contacts Re–assessed." In *Early Interactions between South and Southeast Asia: Reflections on Cross-Cultural Exchange*, edited by Pierre-Yves Manguin, A. Mani, and Geoff Wade, Singapore: Institute of Southeast Asian Studies, Nalanda-Sriwijaya Series 2, New Delhi, Manohar: 17–45.
Gupta, S.P. 1980. *The Roots of Indian Art*, Delhi, B.R. Publishing.
Guy, John 2000. "The Kosa Masks of Champa: New Evidence," in *Southeast Asian Archaeology 1998: Proceedings of the 7th International Conference of the European Association of Southeast Asian Archaeologists, Berlin, 31 August–4 September 1998*, edited by Wibke Lobo and Stephanie Reimann, Hull: Centre for South-East Asian Studies: 51–60.
Guy, John 2014. *Lost Kingdoms: Hindu Buddhist Sculpture of Early Southeast Asia*, New York, The Metropolitan Museum of Art/Yale University Press; Southeast Asia edition River Books, Bangkok.
Prince of Wales Museum of Western India, *Dawn of Civilization in Maharasthra*, Bombay, Prince of Wales Museum of Western India, 1975.

Trigangga 2009. "History of Indic Writing and Scripts in Sumatra." In *Sumatra: Crossroads of Cultures*, edited by F. Brinkgreve and R. Sulistianingsih. Leiden: Royal Netherlands Institute of Southeast Asian and Caribbean Studies: 84–95.

Wade, Geoff 2014. "Beyond the Southern Borders: Southeast Asia in Chinese Texts to the Ninth Century", in John Guy, *Lost Kingdoms: Hindu Buddhist Sculpture of Early Southeast Asia*, New York, The Metropolitan Museum of Art/Yale University Press: 25–31.

Wayan Ardika 2008. "Archaeological Traces of the Early Harbour Town," in *Burials, Texts and Rituals: Ethnoarchaeological Investigations in North Bali, Indonesia*, edited by B. Hauser-Schäublin and I. Wayan Ardika. Göttinger Beiträge zur Ethnologie 1. Göttingen: Universitätsverlag Göttingen.

CHAPTER 16

Ancient Architectural Influence Between Bali and Majapahit: Drawing Upon the Affinities with Ancient Indian Architecture and the Way It Is Developed in Bali

Ir Nyoman Popo Priyatna Danes

INTRODUCTION

Indonesia has around 2000 ethnic groups. There is religious pluralism in the country, even though the majority of the inhabitants are Muslims. The country not only strongly promotes Universalism, but demonstrates in its culture a rich history that is deeply influenced by all the major religions.

The culture of Indonesia has also been shaped by long interaction between original indigenous customs and multiple foreign influences. Indonesia is centrally located along ancient trading routes between the Far East, South Asia and the Middle East, resulting in many cultural practices being strongly influenced by a multitude of religions, including Hinduism, Buddhism, Confucianism, Islam and Christianity, all strong in the major trading cities. The result is a complex cultural mixture that is very different from the original indigenous cultures.

I. N. P. P. Danes (✉)
Scholar and Architect, Bali, Indonesia

© The Author(s) 2018
S. Saran (ed.), *Cultural and Civilisational Links between India and Southeast Asia*, https://doi.org/10.1007/978-981-10-7317-5_16

The architecture of Indonesia reflects the diversity of cultural, historical and geographic influences that have shaped Indonesia as a whole. Invaders, colonizers, missionaries, merchants and traders have brought cultural changes that have had a profound effect on building styles and techniques. Much cultural diffusion occurred before, during and after the time of the Majapahits.

Many of the cultures of the Majapahits descend from Indian culture, for the kingdom itself was 'Indianized', with aspects such as architecture and religion being greatly influenced by Indian ideas. Another factor that helped the Majapahits to flourish was trade. Merchants from China, India and many parts of Southeast Asia entered and left almost every day. This brought many new ideas from different parts of the world, many of which influenced Majapahit culture.

EXPANSION OF HINDUISM IN INDONESIA

Arrival of Hinduism

Hinduism evolved from early Indian philosophy, incorporating an immensely complex body of literature, oral traditions, visual arts, sciences, rituals, metaphysics and social systems. The holy Mount Meru, a cosmological abode of gods and goddesses, is the focus of the Hindu religion (Fig. 16.1).

Hindu influences reached the Indonesian archipelago as early as the first century. At this time, India started to strongly influence Southeast Asian countries. Trade routes linked India with southern Burma, central and southern Siam, lower Cambodia and southern Vietnam, and numerous urbanized coastal settlements were established in this area.

For more than 1000 years, Indian Hindu/Buddhist influences were therefore the major factor that brought a certain level of cultural unity to the various countries of the region.

Prior to the arrival of Hinduism and Buddhism, the indigenous population of the archipelago practised forms of animism. But when Hinduism arrived in the western part of the archipelago through a trade network stretching from China to India in the first century of the Common Era, local rulers regarded this new religion as an asset to their power as they could start to represent themselves as Hindu deities, thereby increasing their status. The pre-existing animistic beliefs are thought to have become blended with Hinduism, resulting in the formation of new hybrid types of Hinduism which contained specific features of its own, thus making it

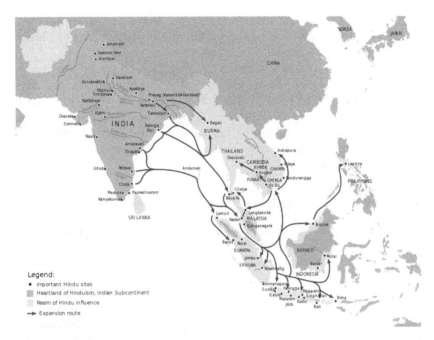

Fig. 16.1   Expansion of Hinduism in Southeast Asia. Source: www.wikipedia.org

rather different from Indian Hinduism. The caste system, for example, was never rigidly applied throughout the history of the archipelago.

Hinduism spread to Indonesia from India around 100 CE. As mentioned, when local rulers adopted new religions, these were diffused to surrounding populations. On the islands of Java and Sumatra, large empires developed, with Indian philosophies adapted to and mixed with local beliefs. Hinduism also took hold in Bali through long, close links with Java, including intermarriage between royal families.

A number of important Hindu empires were established in Kalimantan, Sumatera and Java between the fifth and the thirteenth century; some of which had also absorbed Buddhist influences.

The Sriwijaya empire to the south and the Khmer empire to the north competed for influence. From the fifth to the fifteenth centuries the Sriwijaya empire, a maritime empire centred on the island of Sumatra in Indonesia, had adopted Mahayana and Vajrayana Buddhism under a line of rulers named the Sailendras. The empire of Sriwijaya declined owing to conflicts with the Chola rulers of India.

The archipelago's last major empire, the Majapahit (±1293–1500), showed an interesting blend between Hinduism, Buddhism and animist beliefs.

The Majapahit empire succeeded the Singhasari empire; it was one of the last and greatest Hindu empires in maritime Southeast Asia. But after Islam had established itself in the archipelago as a socio-political force starting from the thirteenth century, Hinduism gradually lost ground to this quickly expanding religion. The only exception was Bali, where the ruler of Majapahit (originating from East Java) sought refuge from the conquest of Islamic forces.

Hinduism in the Colonial Era

Indonesian people continued their old beliefs and adopted a syncretic version of Islam. In other cases, Hindus and Buddhists left and became concentrated as communities in islands that they could defend. Hindus of western Java, for example, moved to Bali and neighbouring small islands. While this era of religious conflict and intersultanate warfare was unfolding, and new power centres were attempting to consolidate regions under their control, European colonialism arrived. The Indonesian archipelago was soon dominated by the Dutch colonial empire. The new rulers helped to prevent inter-religious conflict, and slowly began the process of excavating, understanding and preserving Indonesia's ancient Hindu–Buddhist cultural foundations, particularly in Java and the western islands of Indonesia

Hinduism in the Contemporary Era

After Indonesia gained independence from Dutch colonial rule, it officially recognized only monotheistic religions under pressure from political Islam. Further, Indonesia required an individual to have a religion to gain full Indonesian citizenship rights, and officially Indonesia did not recognize Hindus.

In 1952, the Indonesian Ministry of Religion declared Bali and other islands with Hindus as needing a systematic campaign of proselytization so that they accepted Islam. The local government of Bali, shocked by this official national policy, declared itself an autonomous religious area in 1953. The Balinese government also reached out to India and former Dutch colonial officials for diplomatic and human rights support. To gain official acceptance and their rights in a Muslim-dominated country,

Hindus in Indonesia were politically forced to adapt. Currently Hindu Dharma is one of the five officially recognized monotheistic religions in Indonesia.

Varieties of Indonesia Hinduism

The large Indonesian Hindu communities are located on the islands of Bali, Kalimantan, Sulawesi and Sumatra (and smaller pockets of Hindu villages can be found in East Java). Hinduism was placed as a layer on top of the pre-existing variational animist traditions, and therefore the resulting version of Hinduism differs in the various regions. In fact, on the small island of Bali one can discern an interesting level of variety across different regions. In some cases, particularly in East and Central Java, Hinduism became blended with Islamic traditions.

Javanese Hinduism

Both Java and Sumatra were subject to considerable cultural influence from the Indian subcontinent. The earliest evidence of Hindu influence in Java can be found in fourth-century Tarumanagara inscriptions scattered around modern Jakarta and Bogor.

In the sixth and seventh centuries many maritime kingdoms arose in Sumatra and Java. These controlled the Straits of Malacca and flourished with the increasing sea trade between China and India and beyond. During this time, scholars from India and China visited these kingdoms to translate literary and religious texts. From the fourth to the fifteenth century, Java had many Hindu kingdoms, such as Tarumanagara, Kalingga, Medang, Kediri, Sunda, Singhasari and Majapahit. This era is popularly known as the Javanese Classical Era, during which Hindu–Buddhist literature, art and architecture flourished and were incorporated into local culture under royal patronage.

During this time, many Hindu temples were built, including the ninth-century Prambanan Temple near Yogyakarta, which has been designated a World Heritage Site. Among these Hindu kingdoms, the Majapahit kingdom was the largest and the last significant one in Indonesian history. Majapahit was based in East Java, from where it ruled a large part of what is now Indonesia. The remnants of the Majapahit kingdom shifted to Bali during the sixteenth century after a prolonged war with and territorial losses to Islamic sultanates.

Balinese Hinduism

Balinese Hinduism is an amalgamation of Indian religions and indigenous animist customs that existed in the Indonesian archipelago before the arrival of Islam and later Dutch colonialism. It integrates many of the core beliefs of Hinduism with the arts and rituals of the Balinese people. As in India, Hinduism in Bali grew in flexibility, featuring a diverse way of life. It includes many Indian spiritual ideas, cherishes legends and myths of Indian Puranas and Hindu Epics, and expresses its traditions through a unique set of festivals and customs associated with a myriad of hyangs—the local and ancestral spirits, as well as forms of animal sacrifice that are not common in India.

The Majapahit Empire

By the thirteenth century descendants of the mighty Kediri–Singosari lineage had established a new settlement at Trowulan, Mojokerto, which they named Keraton Majapahit. Majapahit was one of the last major empires of the region and is considered to be one of the greatest and most powerful empires in the history of Indonesia and Southeast Asia, one that is sometimes seen as the precursor of Indonesia's modern boundaries (Figs. 16.2 and 16.3).

The Majapahit empire (Javanese: Keraton Mojopahit; Indonesian: Kerajaan Majapahit) was a vast archipelagic empire based on the island of Java (modern-day Indonesia) from 1293 to around 1500.

The nature of this empire and its extent are subject to debate. It may have had a limited or entirely notional influence over some of its tributary states, including Sumatera, the Malay Peninsula, Kalimantan (Borneo) and Eastern Indonesia—over which authority was claimed in the Negarakertagama. Geographical and economic constraints suggest that rather than a regular centralized authority, the outer states were most likely to have been connected mainly by trade, which was probably a royal monopoly.

The empire also claimed relationships with Champa, Cambodia, Siam, Southern Burma and Vietnam, and even sent missions to China. Although the Majapahit rulers extended their power over other islands and destroyed neighbouring kingdoms, their focus seems to have been on controlling and gaining a larger share of the commercial trade that passed through the archipelago.

ANCIENT ARCHITECTURAL INFLUENCE BETWEEN BALI AND MAJAPAHIT... 281

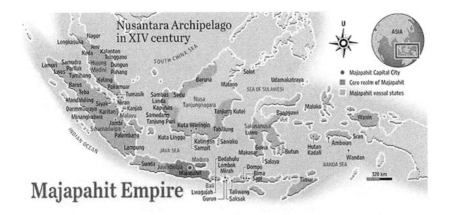

Fig. 16.2 Majapahit Empire. Source: www.wikipedia.com

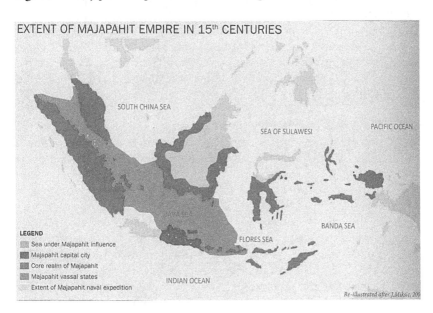

Fig. 16.3 Extent of Majapahit Empire in fifteenth centuries. Note: Majapahit was a thalassocracy, extending its territory through maritime trade and dominance. At its height the realm and its diplomatic relations extended as far as Japan and South India. Source: Wijaya (2014)

About the time the Majapahit empire was founded, Muslim traders and proselytizers began entering the area. After Gajah Mada, the prime minister of Raja Hayam Wuruk, conquered Bali, East Javanese influences spread from purely political and religious spheres into the arts and architecture. Bali became an outpost in a mighty empire—Indonesia's greatest—which encompassed nearly the entire archipelago.

Indianization During the Majapahit Era

By the late sixth century, many of the kingdoms of Southeast Asia had been Indianized, adopting the Hindu or Buddhist religion as well as Indian systems of governance. These systems were most probably introduced by priests travelling with Indian traders. They influenced local rulers, who were keen to adopt a more sophisticated system that fitted, fairly snugly, over existing hierarchies and the tribal belief system (Wijaya 2014: 72). What this shows is that the vast growth in knowledge was passed from one generation to the next, becoming a precedent. During the process, it is safe to presume that interpretations developed as well, with familiar translations being based on these precedents. There are seven points that show how Indianization occurred during the Majapahit era, according to Wijaya (2014):

1. The oldest evidence of a *pendopo agung* pavilion is found in the forecourt of the Arjuna Temple complex. An essential part of South Indian temple architecture, the temple pavilion, called *mandapa* (Sanskrit), was possibly first introduced into the local architectural vernacular at Dieng. In Java, mandapa became *pandapa* or *pendopo*—a formal Indianized meeting hall.
2. In the tenth century, the Indianized kingdoms of Central Java adopted the South Indian system of geomancy (*vastu sastra*), a science of construction based on directional alignments, known in Bali today as *Hasta Bumi* and *Hasta Kosala-Kosali*.
3. During this era, Javanese and Sumatran kings started to build manmade tanks—large rectangular water containers—sometimes with temples or pavilions as islands in the centre.

These pavilions were called *bale kambang*. In Bali we can find this type of architecture in Taman Ayun Temple (Badung) and Kerthagosa (Klungkung).

4. *Patirtaan* water temples dating from the ninth century have been found in East Java—the most famous being Jalatunda and nearby Belahan—and probably abounded in Bali during the early Hindu era. The worship of holy water most probably pre-dates this era, but it was during this era that these holy springs and wells—recalling the splendour of the stepped wells of India—such as Candi Tikus in Trowulan were popular in Java.

One may also find familiar architectural elements in Pura Taman in Bali today and at Chand Baori Step Well in Rajasthan, India.

5. One of Majapahit's greatest architectural legacies is the *candi bentar*, or split gate. Carved panels featuring images of *candi bentar* can be found on temples as far back as the ninth century (Borobudur) but, realized in red brick, they became emblematic of Majapahit era temple and palace architecture. 'Exported' to Bali, they became the symbol of Bali during the Dutch colonial era, and eventually appeared on Bali's first 'coat of arms', with a *candi bentar* featured in North Bali in 1910.
6. The use of red bricks and terracotta tiles was widespread around Trowulan, the centre of the Majapahit kingdom, throughout the era. Many gates and temples remain but only suggestions survive—on temple bas-reliefs—of what the timber buildings and pavilions may have looked like.

The use of terracotta bricks in construction is a defining feature of Majapahit, as were its towering architectural structures—split gates, prasada shrines and temple gates. The solid stylobate or raised plinth—of pavilions, gates and shrines—was another. Although some of the temples dating from the Majapahit period used andesit or sandstone, red bricks are also a popular construction material.

7. The shape of Majapahit temples tends to be slender and tall, with a roof constructed from multiple stepped sections that form a combined roof structure curving upwards smoothly, creating the illusion that the temple is taller than its actual height.

The pinnacle of the temple is usually a cube (mostly Hindu temples), sometimes a dagoba cylindrical structure (Buddhist temples).

Bali in the Majapahit Empire Era

Bali, one of Indonesia's major tourist attractions, is not only famous for its beautiful beaches, landscapes and rice fields but also for its unique cultural tradition: a Balinese Hindu tradition that mainly consists of art and ritual. This religion is rather different from Hinduism as practised in India because before Hinduism arrived in Bali it underwent some radical changes on the island of Java. One important feature of this change was the union between Hinduism (or more specifically Shivaism) and Buddhism.

Traditional Balinese architecture is more intricate, balanced and has different colours than Indonesian architecture. Balinese architecture is part of the legacy of an architectural tradition that dates back to the last great empire of Indonesia's Hindu Buddhist past, namely the East Javanese kingdom of Majapahit, which at the height of its influence between the fourteenth and fifteenth centuries held sway over most of the Indonesian archipelago.

Construction techniques employed by the ancient Javanese are still used today in Bali and many architectural elements, most notably the distinctive split gateway, or *candi bentar*, can be traced back to the golden Majapahit era. Much of Indonesia is shrouded in Majapahit mystique but nowhere as much as Bali, where it lies over the culture like a richly embroidered cloak. From this period many of the classic works of ancient Indonesian literature, the Indian poems known as *kekawin*, began to be written and circulated more widely.

By the middle of the Majapahit era, the courts in many areas of Bali were under Majapahit empire control. The Balinese were slowly educated in the ways of Majapahit; this was achieved by subduing the Bali Mula and Bali Aga villages and colonizing them through the influence of a series of vassal princes and Brahman priests who were sent to Bali by the Majapahit king Hayam Wuruk.

We know from manuscripts that some Balinese rajas even invited architects (*undagi*) from Majapahit to design their temples—the fourteenth-century Pura Maospahit in Denpasar is one such example—and that Majapahit architectural traditions had already been layered over existing archaic Balinese and early Hindu-Bali era models. Ceremonies were likewise embellished, one imagines, with Majapahit refinements (Wijaya 2014: 139) (Fig. 16.4).

The very idea of state temples (*pura agung*) and their link to royal palaces (*puri agung*) was most probably introduced to Bali at this time; as was

Fig. 16.4 Maospahit temple in Denpasar. Source: Author

the principle, so central to Majapahit statecraft, of having important temples dotted over the realm, covering, symbolically, the 'cardinal points' on the eight-leafed *nawa sanga* (the eight principal deities plus the centre, Shiva), the very symbol of Majapahit (Wijaya 2014: 140).

One imagines that during the fifteenth century various far-flung communities in the mountains of both Bali and Java were being 'Majapahitized', and that their reverence towards the mountain deities was absorbed by the belief systems of the coastal communities whose populations were, culturally, more Majapahit. Many of the ancient terraced sanctuaries of both Mount Penanggungan in Java and Mount Agung in Bali were given 'Majapahit makeovers' and reconsecrated as pedarman or ancestor temples (Wijaya 2014: 140).

The golden era of Majapahit in Java, under Raja Hayam Wuruk and his prime minister Gajah Mada, ushered in an equally golden era of palace and temple building in Bali. Many of the eight *arya* generals sent over to subjugate Bali in 1343 stayed on to build homes which were eventually turned into palaces or even temples (Wijaya 2014: 141).

Another important orientation may have been introduced to Bali at this time. The fourteenth-century East Javanese temple Candi Jawi was a funerary monument to Kertanegara, the father of the founder of Majapahit. In shape, it is very similar to the eleventh-century funerary monuments at Gunung Kawi, Tampak Siring, Bali, long rumoured to be the funerary monument of Anak Wungsu, Airlangga's brother, who ruled Bali in the latest era of the Warmadewa dynasty. Candi Jawi was the first East Javanese candi to be oriented towards both the holy mountain and the east (Shiva) (Wijaya 2014: 141).

This tradition of allocating shrines for Gods and deified ancestors to the northeast corner in compounds and pavilions is possibly a Majapahit era construct, which continues in Bali today.

By the late sixteenth century, the Dutch expedition of Cornelis de Houtman recorded a quite different scene: one of impressive majesty in the Gelgel court and of impressive ceremonies. It is quite possible that the variation in reports is because Pries stopped in Kuta and Cornelis de Houtman in Gelgel. It is also possible that the sixteenth century was a period of enormous change in Bali, with cultural refinements introduced by the Majapahit influence (Wijaya 2014: 143).

Balinese Architecture Concepts Influenced by Majapahit Style During the Post-Majapahit Era

Hilltops and mountain gods are both prominent in Balinese legend. The landscape of the islands has deeply influenced their cultural, political and economic life for thousands of years. Old traditions have persisted remarkably, despite the successive impacts of colonialism, political strife and the travel industry.

The Balinese are thought to be descendants of migrants from southern China who arrived in about 2000 BCE. Their legacy is believed to include the growing of rice as a staple crop, the craft of metal-working and the prevalence of mountain cults. These cultural traits, still clearly observable in traditional Balinese life today, suggest broad affinities with other peoples of Southeast Asia and the Pacific Ocean.

The essence of Bali style in architecture is not the performance, the materials or body, but the feeling inside. The space and how to live in balance with the world around them is the essence of this. The Tri Hita Karana is the most essential philosophy, which explains how we live in harmony; people with people, people with nature, and people with God. Tri Hita Karana has become the basis of every concept in Balinese traditional architecture.

There are a macro- and a micro-system (Bhuana Agung and Bhuana Alit). For example, the crossroads in a small village, called Catus Patha, governs where the palace, the market and the temple should be located, this idea coming from Java in the Majapahit era. The Hindu Brahmans developed it first and Empu Kuturan came to Bali with it in the eleventh century, when they were bringing Hinduism to the island. Empu Kuturan introduced the concepts of Hinduism, such as Tri Murti, that became the guidelines for temple-building and religious processions. He also made the scripts that contained all of the rules of traditional Bali architecture—known as Hasta Kosala Kosali for buildings and Hasta Bumi for the layout. Materials, proportions and position are all controlled by these laws.

There are three concepts related to directional placement: Tri Loka (Bhur, Bwah, Swah), the natural axis which is called Nyegara-Gunung, and the ritual axis which is according to the sun's movement (east–west or kangin-kauh). All houses and buildings should face towards the mountain and temple, according to Hasta Bumi.

This system has been in place for almost a thousand years, governing aspects of construction, materials and orientation in Balinese architecture. With the arrival of foreigners, and the opportunity for the Balinese to travel, outside influences have crept into the Balinese domain and especially its architecture.

The original Balinese, the Bali Aga and the Bali Mula, initially resisted Majapahit colonization, having preferred less feudal ways for centuries. But even they, over time, adopted Majapahit era-style touches into their temple architecture and courtyard shrines.

During the century of Java's conversion to Islam, it is quite possible that many architects stayed on in Java during the Islamic era of the Majapahit empire. The others, who wanted to remain Hindu, moved to Bali to continue the Hindu Majapahit style. Some Javanese priests' and noblemen's homes from the Majapahit era have become temples in Bali.

The Majapahit style was imposed over South Bali, where princely villages such as Klungkung, Sukawati, Kerambitan, Denpasar, Sanur and Kesiman took on the mighty Majapahit mantle, and this is still very visible in the architecture of their temples and palaces today.

The south of Bali adopted brick architecture and the north of Bali seems to have adopted the whimsy in statuary that was a big part of

Majapahit Java. Even Madura Island, in East Java, which is close to the North Bali coast, seems to have exerted an influence on the North Bali style (Wijaya 2014: 263).

Today, contemporary Balinese style is known as one of the most popular Asian tropical architectures, owing largely to the growth of the tourism industry in Bali that has created demand for Balinese-style houses, cottages, villas and hotels. Contemporary Balinese architecture combines traditional aesthetic principles, the island's abundance of natural materials, the famous artistry and craftsmanship of its people, as well as international architecture influences, new techniques and trends.

Conclusion

Majapahit was an Indianized kingdom based in eastern Java from 1293 to around 1500. Its greatest ruler was Hayam Wuruk, whose reign from 1350 to 1389 marked the empire's peak, when it dominated other kingdoms in the southern Malay Peninsula, Borneo, Sumatra, Bali, Kalimantan and eastern Indonesia, and the Philippines.

The Majapahit empire was the last of the major Hindu empires of the Malay archipelago and is considered to be one of the greatest states in Indonesian history.

To an art historian it is obvious that Majapahit had a huge influence on Balinese architecture; but so much ancient Javanese and Hindu-Javanese architectural influence has come to Bali over the centuries that it is hard to identity what is purely Majapahit in origin.

Influences can be recognized where evidence is available. Hinduism was placed as a layer on top of pre-existing variational animist traditions and therefore the resulting outcome of Hinduism differs in the various regions. In fact, on the small island of Bali one can discern an interesting level of variety across the different regions on the island. And in some cases, particularly in East and Central Java, Hinduism became blended with Islamic traditions. Theoretically, Indianization runs for centuries which may lead us to understand that in interpreting it, those who are involved are considering both the foreign values and their local knowledge so that they translate it into all aspects of life: their manners, how they live, how society works and how architecture responds to or suits them.

As a tourist destination, Bali relies on its culture, which includes sociocultural activities and the architectural form of traditional Balinese architecture, inspired also by Hinduism, as the main attraction for tourists.

Exploration of cultural identity within architecture gives much greater sensitivity to local elements (environment, people and society), where architectural identity is a process that operates within the transformation of the environment. Patterns of relationships in the construction of identity and architectural place provide normative guidance that allows intercultural exchange to reconstruct and transform identity.

REFERENCE

Wijaya, Made. 2014. Majapahit Style volume 1. Wijaya Words. Indonesia

PART VI

Evolving Artistic Expressions: From Tradition to Modernity

CHAPTER 17

Natyasastraic Links in Cambodia, Thailand and Indonesia

Padma Subramanyam

INTRODUCTION

This chapter is primarily an expression of the experience gained through my travel, performances and interactions with the artistes of Cambodia, Thailand and Indonesia. For want of space, only these three countries are covered here. Even for an Indian tourist, the imprints of India in these regions are clear. For me, with almost half a century's involvement with an in-depth study of Natyasastra and its connection with sculptures and movements, the presence of the precepts of this encyclopaedic work in Southeast Asia has been an exciting exhilaration. The region used to be referred to as Greater India until the mid-twentieth century, as seen in the monumental pioneering works of Henrich Zimmer and Fobian Bowers.

Bharatamuni's Natyasastra mentions that his work is for Jambudvipa and Bharatavarsha in particular. Hence it is important to understand its geographic significance. The centenarian sage His Holiness Sri Chandrasekarendra Saraswati Swamigal, the sixty-eighth Shankaracharya of Kanchi Kamakoti Peetham, has presented a discourse on the Puranas and thrown

---

P. Subramanyam (✉)
Bharata-Ilanimgo Foundation for Asian
Culture (BIFAC), Chennai, India

© The Author(s) 2018
S. Saran (ed.), *Cultural and Civilisational Links between India and Southeast Asia*, https://doi.org/10.1007/978-981-10-7317-5_17

light on how they are a treasure trove of information on our history and geography. For example, Markandeya Purana (chapters 51–57) has details on geography including descriptions of Jambudvipa and Varshas. From this description we can understand that Jambudvipa is like a lotus with Bhadraashva, Bharata Varsha and others as its petals on four sides (Nileshwari 1968). Jambudvipa is Eurasia with Meru, that is Pamir mountain, in the centre with four Varshas (land masses) like four petals. The petal on the south of Meru is Bharatavarsha, which includes the entire South East Asia region. Bharata Khanda denotes the Indian subcontinent. The civilisational unity of the whole Association of Southeast Asian Nations (ASEAN) region therefore falls into place. It is not surprising that the word 'Bharat' in the Indonesian language means the cardinal direction of west. It is understandable that Thai and Cambodian languages still retain sumptuous Samskrita. Along with our epics, the Natyasastra sailed across the Indian ocean and made a permanent presence. The proof is not taken from mere bookish knowledge; here are some facts revealed through my fieldwork.

Worship of Bharata Muni

Bharata's Natyasastra is the earliest extant literature in the world on performing arts and more. Hence, Bharatamuni is the Ādiguru of the arts in Jambudvipa and Bharatavarsha. He is still worshipped on all Thursdays, Guruvāra, by the dancers in countries such as Thailand and Cambodia. Every training centre and theatre has an altar with the masks of Brahma, Vishnu, Siva and Bharatamuni. They are propitiated by the artistes before their make-up begins. Bharatamuni is referred to as Prot rishi and Khru muni, that is Bharata rishi and Guru muni. He is also called Eisei, the old man of wisdom, Gnani, and he is part of any theatrical production, to be compared with the utterance of Bharatavākya in Sanskrit theatre in India. In India, his voice is represented at the end of the play, but in Southeast Asia he appears as a wise old man at the beginning of the play. It is this representation that we find in the idols and masks symbolising him.

In Thailand, I was fortunate to receive a gift of a miniature mask of Bharatamuni from the Royal Theatre in Bangkok. He is of golden hue with a white beard and a gold crown. In Cambodia, I came across the wooden masks of Bharata as well as his full figure in metal. When I had the honour of meeting Her Royal Highness Princess Bhupa Devi, she directed me to see and photograph the beautiful mask of Bharatamuni in the museum in Phnom Penh, Cambodia. I also saw the standing figure of the sage on the altar in the dance school of the Cambodian choreographer Sopheline Cheam Shapiro. I was pleasantly surprised to come across the miniature of this icon in a wayside street shop when I was climbing Mount Kulen to worship the 1000 Sivalingams constantly anointed by the flowing river on the slope of the hill. Of course I bought it, and the idol has been on our altar ever since. What an irony that Bharatamuni is still worshipped in other parts of Bharatavarsha, whereas he has no shrine in his place of origin. It is not an exaggeration to deem Bharata and his work as a great permanent link between the ASEAN countries.

INFLUENCE OF NATYASASTRA IN CAMBODIA

According to the Natyasastra, the first drama enacted by Bharatamuni and his sons in the presence of Brahma, was 'Amrita Mantana', the Churning of the Milky Ocean. The Natyasastra tells us how the demons were angry to see the enactment of their defeat and hence created hindrances. Indra had to ward off the evil by throwing a part of the stem of his umbrella, to protect the actors. The full figure of Bharata's icon is seen holding a stick, which is like the Danda of the Sūtradhāra in the traditional Kuchipudi drama of Andhra Pradesh. The churning of the milky ocean is the most important panel in Angkor Wat, portraying hundreds of Devas and Dānavas, and Vishnu in his Kūrmāvatāra form. This longest panel is of eternal value in its proclamation of the artistry and authenticity of the portrayal. Bharata says in his Natyasastra that Brahma created the Apsaras to enact the dramas in the graceful Kaisiki Vritti. With thousands of celestial nymphs in Angkor Wat, referred to as Apsaras, the dance of Cambodia has gained the name 'Apsara dance'. Her Royal Highness Princess Bhupa Devi told me that it was to her performance that her mother gave this nomenclature. Even after the tragedy caused by Pol Pot for about four years, when artistes and literati were shot, Cambodia has resurrected the worship of Bharata and kept the flag flying high for Apsara dance all over the world. Toni Shapiro Phim, the dancer—choreographer—ethnologist, opens her project dramatically with the white-haired lady Soth Samon in her seventies on her hospital bed. This great artiste, who survived Pol Pot's killings, taught dance and gave her prized advice to her students, now in a whisper and with a gesture of salutation thus—'Always remember to honour Lok Ta Eisei [the Supreme Spirit or teacher of the arts]' (Burridge 2010). No wonder Bharata's venerable image is in the altar at the dance centre of Sopheline Cheam Shapiro in Phnom Penh.

The Thailand Experience

As far as Thailand is concerned, as early as the 1960s Pūjya Paramāchārya of Kānchi, who was the Centenarian Sage, organised a seminar on Vēda, Āgama and Shilpa, and invited the Venerable Rajaguru from Bangkok, with whom a young dancer came to demonstrate Hanuman's character. Pūjya Āchārya enquired about the Trippēvāi and Triyampēvāi festival in Bangkok, and discovered the link with the Tiruppāvai and Tiruvempāvai religious literary festivals of Tamil Nadu. Much later, in the mid-1990s, I presented the 'Pāvai Nōnbu' dance drama for the India Festival in Bangkok; it was my earnest desire to make it a joint production of Indian and Thai dancers. At my lecture-demonstration in the Department of Dance of Silpakohn University there, the event blossomed into a comparative study of the practical technique of dance based on Bharatamuni's Natyasastra. At the end, Prof. Achan Chaturang Mantri Sart agreed to send six of his students to take part in our dance production. Revered Rājaguru Vamadeva Muni was our Chief Guest. He invited us to the Hindu temple, where I saw the small gold idol of Lord Nataraja which is brought in a procession from the palace to the temple for the Triyampēvāi festival. I also saw the manuscript of this Tamil literature that is preserved there. The pronunciation of the Tamil has, of course, been changed beyond recognition. Still, this cultural link between Tamil Nadu and Thailand is of great significance. Revered Rājaguru traced back the origin of his lineage to priests from Chidambaram in Tamil Nadu, which is the ultimate shrine of the Lord of Dance, where all the 108 Karana sculptures relating to Natyasastra are still intact. It was at the Royal Theatre in Bangkok that I worshipped the mask of Bharatamuni and also offered flowers to the Rangadevata, the goddess of the stage, before going onto the stage. This is the Natyasastraic tradition which Thailand continues to observe. I recited the relevant Sloka from the Natyasastra for them. Incidentally, in our conversation, I discovered that the master choreographer Achan Chaturang Mantri Sart was the young dancer who had demonstrated the Hanuman movements at the seminar convened by Pujya Sankarāchārya of Kānchi in Tamil Nadu a few decades earlier. The gold bracelet that His Holiness awarded to him now adorns Lord Buddha in the altar in his home.

Indonesian Links

Today's Indonesia is mentioned in our epics. Java is Yavadvipa and Sumatra is Suvarnadvipa. In fact, Cambodia or Kampuchea is Kāmbhoja in our Indian texts. Kāmbhoji rāga of Carnatic music are said to have come from there. When I visited Bali to perform my solo Ramayana production, I visited Prambanan monument in Central Java to see the Ramayana sculptures. To my greatest and most pleasant surprise, I came across fifty-two Karana sculptures of dancing Siva in this ninth-century temple. They have now been placed in the balustrade of the Siva temple by the Dutch archaeologists who have been rebuilding that Siva temple that was destroyed in an earthquake in the fifteenth century. The local officials are not aware of its Natyasastra background. I managed to contact them and explain its cultural importance, and requested them to search for the rest of the 108 sculptures; also to rearrange the available Karanas to suit the serial order according to the text. The biggest miracle in my life was that the available sculptures of Prambanan tallied with my designs of a new set of Karana sculptures for the Uttara Chidambaram Nataraja temple in Satara, Maharashtra, built at the behest of the Sage of Kānchi. When I showed him my first six line drawings, he suggested that I should visit Indonesia some day. It was twelve years after that divine order that I went to Prambanan, only to discover that my designs and the Indonesian version projected a profound link beyond time and space. This is the main topic of Dr Alessandra Iyer, the Italian archaeologist, in her book on Prambanan published in Thailand. She uses all my line drawings and compares them with my discovery in Prambanan.

The amazing facts revealed are threefold:

1. The Indonesian version of the Natyasastraic karana sculptures are the earliest available primary source for the study. They belong to the ninth century. The karana sculptures of Thanjavur Brihadeesvara temple come next in chronology, belonging to the early eleventh century.
2. We can recognise the presence of Natyasastra in the Southeast Asian region from remote times.
3. My humble reconstruction of a lost technique of dance has been proved to be truly authentic, throwing light on Marga or the common grammatical path in performing arts based on Natyasastra.

From medieval times, Marga came to mean the common path paved by Bharata; its counterpart is Desi, that is regional observances of the same along with inherited regional taste. If all the neo-classical dance and dance dramas of today in India are understood as respective Desis of the regions, the extension of this concept will be the Desi performing arts of the present day ASEAN countries. All of them have an underlying link with the Marga with or without an awareness about it. This link in performing arts is like the unrecognised link between samskrita and the regional languages coexisting from time immemorial. The Cambodian, Thai and Indonesian Desi dances have unmistakable links with marga: Bhartanatyam, Kathak or Manipuri enjoy this link, both knowingly and unknowingly. The fact is that there is a common root for South East Asian or even Asian performing arts. That unseen deeply buried *beeja* (seed) is natyasastra, which needs nurturing and strengthening for the psychological flowering of the fresh fragrance of harmony.

In my observation, all these three countries have strong links with Natyasastra in their basic structure of dance. The rhombus between the legs in men's dances have their parallels with the sthanas (postures) for men that Natyasastra describes and are still practised in Kathakali, Mohiniattam, Orissi, Bharatanatyam and the like. The sama pada with kunchita janu (bent knees) and lifted heel closely resemble the sthanas for women that Natyasastra prescribes and are still practised in Manipuri. Every action of the dancers in all the three countries has a name in the Natyasastra, and it is imperative that these terms are restated for the protection and progress of art in the region.

Creating an awareness about natyasastra can help in framing a systematic training programme with a common grammar. This will mobilise the revival of forgotten facets and weave the scattered material for the common pooling of artistic values in order to strengthen the common characteristics in Asian style in general and ASEAN countries in particular. After all, Bharata (Eisei) is still honoured as the common Adi Guru. Even a fast bowler takes a few steps backwards to gain a strong forward thrust. The need of the hour is to strengthen the recognition of Natyasastraic links and nurture cultural harmony in the Southeast Asian countries for their joint progress.

References

Nileshwari, Y. Desai (1968) Ancient Indian Society, religion and mythology as depicted in Markandeya Purana (A Critical Study), Baroda University, pp 192–193.

Burridge, Stephanie (series editor) (2010) *Celebrating Dance in Asia and Pacific* (series) – Burridge, Stephanie; Frumberg, Fred (editors), *Beyond The Apsara: Celebrating Dance in Cambodia*

PART VII

Writing Our Own Histories: Changing Methodologies

CHAPTER 18

An Imperial Divorce: The Division of South and Southeast Asia in the Colonial Discourse of the Nineteenth Century

Farish A. Noor

INTRODUCTION

It is commonplace to use terms such as South Asia and Southeast Asia; and the usage of such terms is evident in both academic and non-academic discourse. From international relations to political science to history to the media and popular entertainment, both terms have been in use for decades and have currency of their own. We write and talk about things such as South Asian music and Southeast Asian cuisine, and intuitively we understand what such terms mean, as their meaning has been set in the respective discourses they find themselves in.

Notwithstanding the somewhat mundane and ordinary character of terms such as South Asia and Southeast Asia, we tend to forget the fact that these regions are basically discursive constructs that were invented by people. The World Health Organisation (WHO) once included Afghanistan, India and Sri Lanka in the region of Southeast Asia, but Indonesia, curiously, was seen

F. A. Noor (✉)
S. Rajaratnam School of International Studies (RSIS), Nanyang Technological University (NTU), Singapore, Singapore
e-mail: isbhahmad@ntu.edu.sg

© The Author(s) 2018
S. Saran (ed.), *Cultural and Civilisational Links between India and Southeast Asia*, https://doi.org/10.1007/978-981-10-7317-5_18

as part of the Western Pacific region, closer to Papua New Guinea. Until now, the World Health Organisation's definition of Southeast Asia flies defies everyday understandings of the term—proof that naming and placing have less to do with geography and more with human subjectivity.[1]

The work of K.M. Pannikkar and the Institute of Pacific Relations is often cited as the first instance of the signifier Southeast Asia coming into use,[2] but the reality is that the term was already in circulation in the nineteenth century and can be found in the writings of Western colonial administrators from the Netherlands, Britain, France and America. From the nineteenth century until modern times our understanding of what constitutes Southeast Asia has been set and framed by that prolonged colonial encounter, and along with this has come a sedimentation of what the word means and where the borders of Southeast Asia are set. Along with the fixing of the concept of Southeast Asia has come the assumption that the nation states of the region are equally fixed, and that the states of the region are atomistic, self-defined entities.

This chapter looks at how and why these two parts of Asia were first brought together, and later torn apart, from the eighteenth to the nineteenth centuries. It argues that the designation and naming of regional zones such as South and Southeast Asia has less to do with geography and more to do with the agendas and interests that were at work in the process of coming to know—and thus map, classify and categorise—the whole of Asia. It locates this process of amalgamation and dismemberment in the nineteenth century in particular, when the relationship between the Western powers and the polities of Asia was characterised by the uneven power differentials that were the hallmarks of the age of Empire.

Here we need to take account of one important factor: that by the late eighteenth and early nineteenth century the nature of Western colonialism in Asia was starkly different from that of the earlier encounters between the West and East. This was the era of modern colonial capitalism, driven by militarised companies that were able to project superior military power

---

[1] Among the countries that were defined as 'Southeast Asian' by the World Health Organisation are: Thailand (joined in September 1947), India (July 1948), Sri Lanka (July 1948), Burma (July 1948), Indonesia (May 1950), Nepal (September 1953), Maldives (November 1965), Bangladesh (May 1972), People's Republic of Korea (May 1973), Bhutan (March 1982) and East Timor (September 2002). [See: http://www.searo.who.int/about/history/en/].

[2] Re: Russell H. Fifield, Southeast Asian Studies: Origins, Development, Future, in: *Journal of Southeast Asian Studies*, Vol. 7. No. 2, September 1976.

over long distances and were able to conquer and hold territories far from their home countries.

In terms of the sensibilities, world views and value systems of companies such as the East India Company, the Dutch East Indies Company (VOC) and the French Compagnie des Indes, the men of the East India Company and the VOC were not cut from the same cloth that produced the Spanish and Portuguese missionary-conquistadores who ventured to Southeast Asia centuries before them. While Antonio Pigafetta's account of Magellan's voyage to the Malay Archipelago was glutted with references to the 'Moors' who were the mortal threat to Christendom back home—a term that stuck, and which accounts for the continued use of the word 'Moro' to denote Muslims in Southern Philippines even now—the company men of London and Amsterdam were less concerned with conversion and pious homilies, and more interested in profit. When the Dutch VOC took over the Portuguese bastion of A Famosa in Malacca, they changed the names of the buildings and offices built by the Portuguese according to their own set of market-determined, commercial values. The Portuguese fort that was erected to witness the glory of God was turned into a temple of commerce instead.

The Western companies were also fiercely nationalist, and their operatives and employees were encouraged to remain so while they operated abroad in faraway lands. If Western Europe's sense of collective identity was framed in terms of common Christian brotherhood during the era of the Crusades, that sense of shared religious identity was clearly absent among the company men from England and the Netherlands once they found themselves in the Southeast Asian archipelago in the seventeenth century: The publication of the *True Relation of the Unjust, Cruel and Barbarous Proceedings Against the English in Ambonya* in 1624 shocked England with its grisly details of the torture of English company men at the hands of the Dutch, and showed that once they were out in the East Indies there was no such thing as the bond of Christianity to keep Europeans together.[3]

---

[3] Giles Milton. *Nathaniel's Nutmeg*, 1999, pp. 324–325. Years later the English were to take their revenge against the Dutch for denying them access to the Spice Islands, by invading the territory of New Amsterdam on the east coast of America. The English invaded and captured Manhattan, and renamed it New York; and declared that they had no reason to apologise for the deed for it was 'fair exchange' for their losses in the East Indies.

The companies that operated in Southeast Asia were in fact national concerns, and those who joined them were expected to serve the interest of both the company and their country. So strong was this sense of national pride and obligation that the 1714 East Indies Trade Act which was passed by King George II forbade any Englishman from travelling to the archipelago on non-English ships, or seeking help from other Western nations or companies while there.[4]

The British East India Company established its foothold in Bengal, India; and it was there that the men of the company began to study the lay of the land and its people. These men were fundamentally merchant-conquerors, and many of them had scant knowledge of India, save for what they had learned in England from accounts that had been written by scholars since the days of Ptolemy. It was thus hardly surprising that many of them regarded South and Southeast Asia as a fluid, continuous space— an idea that dated back to the time of Ptolemy when the notion of a 'Greater India' was commonplace and when the region that would later come to be known as Southeast Asia was first referred to as India *Extra Gangem*—India beyond the Ganges.

The company's arrival and eventual consolidation of power in Bengal occurred at a time when the idea of India—as a nation state—was obviously not in use; and the company found itself in the midst of a patchwork of local polities, from the rulers of Bengal to the Rajputs of Rajastan and the Moghuls of Delhi, to the kingdoms of Ava and Siam and the maritime powers of the Southeast Asian archipelago. With the coming of the age of industry came other innovations that would also alter the face of warfare: the gunboat, the rifled musket, the rocket and other modern weapons would come into service in the early nineteenth century, and were initially intended to be used in the Western theatre of war—Napoleon had sought to use them for his invasion of Britain. But such technology would be used with greater effect in Asia and Africa; and with technological and military

---

[4] See: An Act for the Better Securing the Lawful Trade of his Majesty's Subjects To and From the East Indies; and for the more effectual Preventing all his Majesty's Subjects Trading thither under Foreign Commissions, 1714. Act of Parliament during the reign of King George II, London. Printed by John Baskett, Printer to the Kings most Excellent Majesty, and the Assigns of Thomas Newcomb, and Henry Hills. 1719. The Act stated that any English vessel travelling to or returning from the East Indies without the legal permit of the British government would have all its goods confiscated, and brought to land; and that this also included all English vessels that were engaged in trade between the East Indies and Continental Europe.

leverage on their side, the Western powers could finally penetrate, dominate and secure vast areas of space—both terrestrial and maritime—in Asia. With that capability to obtain and hold space came the capability to know, classify and understand the peoples and objects of the region they had been engaging with for so long. The maps that were produced by and for the companies had yet to be festooned with lines that demarcated neat and closed political frontiers; and as the company sought to expand and project its power across both the subcontinent and the archipelago, so did it seek to learn and know more about the nations it was about to confront. Hence from the outset the march of power and epistemology went hand in hand, in tandem with each other.

Projecting India: The Early Studies of Southeast Asia by the Indianists of the Company

Before proceeding any further, I would like to note two important facts. First, in the domain of Southeast Asian studies, works by men such as Stamford Raffles, William Marsden, John Crawfurd, John Anderson and others have come to be regarded as among the pioneering studies of and on Southeast Asia. Even today their writings are found on the reading lists of students and academics who work on Southeast Asia, and yet it should be noted that none of these men were scholars in the strict sense of the word: Marsden, Raffles, Crawfurd and Anderson were all in fact functionaries of the East India Company, and their travels to Southeast Asia had less to do with scholarly interests and more with the needs of the company they served.

Secondly, though the writings of Marsden, Raffles, Crawfurd and Anderson were focused on various parts of Southeast Asia, they all had one thing in common: They were initially schooled in Indian studies and they subsequently viewed all things Southeast Asian from a South Asian perspective.

The perspective bias that Raffles (1817), Anderson (1826), Crawfurd (1820) Marsden (1783) and others had can be traced to one company man in particular: William Marsden. His work *A History of Sumatra* was first published in 1783, and this monumental work set the standard for future writings on Southeast Asia.[5] Marsden's study of Sumatra's land

---

[5] William Marsden, *A History of Sumatra—Containing An Account of the Government, Laws, Customs, and Manners Of the Native Inhabitants, With A Description of the Natural*

and people was certainly the most comprehensive at the time; there was no other account that could match it. But long before he began to look towards Sumatra, Marsden had written about the Indian subcontinent, and it was in South Asia—where he served the East India Company— that his scholarly acumen was honed. Marsden had written on numerous subjects related to India and Indian culture before he began working on Southeast Asia. Invariably much of his later writings on Southeast Asia were done on the basis of his earlier experience in South Asia: In 1790, he published his work *On the Chronology of the Hindoos*, which looked at the chronological systems of the Indian subcontinent, these findings later being shared with members of the Royal Society in London. In his account of the Indian chronology and zodiac, Marsden argued that the same methods of measuring time were used by Southeast Asians, notably the Burmese and Siamese.[6] Again and again, in Marsden's writings South and Southeast Asia were bound together as a contiguous mass, but he also posited the notion that Southeast Asian civilisation was the result of a one-way cultural transmission that came mainly from South Asia.

It was from this period that the notion of India's 'civilising role' came to be first formulated, by Western colonial functionaries who saw the two parts of Asia as one but linked together by a one-way traffic of ideas. For Marsden everything that he saw and found in Sumatra and other parts of Southeast Asia had to come from India (where else?), as he himself was an Indianist. But it also meant that in the colonial and capitalist order of things the peoples and cultures of Asia were not equal: there were those Asiatic races that civilised lesser Asiatic races, and this idea fitted rather neatly within the logic of racialised colonial capitalism that likewise saw the Western presence in Asia as essentially beneficial and benevolent—notwithstanding the occasional use of the gunboat to persuade recalcitrant local rulers to bend to the company's will.

Marsden's theory that Southeast Asia was civilised by South Asia raises a host of questions related to intentionality, purpose and teleology; for it is difficult to ascertain for certain if the merchants from India had intentionally

---

Productions, And A Relation of the Ancient Political State Of that Island. Printed for the Author, London, 1783. [Note: All page references above refer to the 1811 edition of Marsden's work, published by Longman, Hurst and Rees, London.]

[6] See: William Marsden, On the Chronology of the Hindoos, Paper delivered at the Royal Society, The Philosophical Transactions of The Royal Society, London. 24 June 1790. pp. 575–577.

gone to Southeast Asia to civilise their clients rather than to engage in the more mundane and boring task of simply buying and selling goods, as merchants are wont to do anywhere and anytime. Furthermore it begs the question about where local native agency and genius lie, for Marsden seems to be suggesting that Southeast Asians did not even have a chronological system before India introduced it to them—which seems odd at first glance, as if the Siamese and Burmese were walking about not knowing what day it was until a South Asian came along and told them the time.

Yet despite these glaring blind spots in his work, Marsden was eventually elevated to the status of the grand doyen of Southeast Asian studies by other company men who would later follow in his footsteps and venture to mainland and maritime Southeast Asia. Crawfurd (who wrote on maritime Southeast Asia, Ava (Burma), Siam and Tonkin), Raffles (on Java) and Anderson (on Sumatra) all paid homage to their mentor Marsden in their respective works, showering praises upon him and the legacy he left. Like Marsden, these men were men of the East India company, and they shared one common trait: they were for the most part Indianists who served in India and who had studied Indian society first. And like their teacher Marsden, they could only look at Southeast Asia through a South Asian lens.

An Imperial Divorce: The Gradual Dismemberment of South and Southeast Asia in the Nineteenth Century

As an academic who teaches the history, society and politics of Southeast Asia, I often raise a question at the beginning of the course about where Southeast Asia is, and where it begins and ends. The question becomes doubly relevant when we cast a glance at the map, and see the straight vertical line that divides the province of West Papua, Indonesia, from Papua New Guinea; or the lines that demarcate the borders between Burma and India; or Vietnam and China. For indeed why should Southeast Asia suddenly stop a few miles east of Jayapura, West Papua; and how can the rest of that island be regarded as being outside Southeast Asia? And as the field-working scholar walks from Burma and to Bangladesh, he or she is bound to note the similarities and continuities in dress, custom and appearance between the peoples of the two nations—though they have been defined and confined within neat regional blocks.

The division of South and Southeast Asia was a process that took decades, and it occurred on a number of registers: political-economic, administrative and discursive. But it was a process that was engineered and directed not by Asians themselves, but those who had come to know and dominate them. In this section I would like to focus on the experience of one country in particular: Burma.

Though Burma today is seen as a Southeast Asian country and has become a member of the Association of Southeast Asian Nations (ASEAN),[7] few may realise that up until the First World War it was often equally regarded as an extension of the wider Indian world. One of the reasons for this location of Burma within the broader ambit of the Indian universe was that it had come to be known by and to Europeans who were themselves members of the colonial enterprise in India, notably during the era of the East India Company; and that the first instances of contact between Britain and Burma were managed by those company functionaries who were themselves old India hands. Burma's case is of particular interest because of the important role it played in Britain's imperial story in India and Southeast Asia; and in the manner in which it was presented we can see how imperial geographies are themselves hardly fixed or static, and how the placing, naming and knowing of a place and/or a polity was a subjective process determined by calculations of power.

Our entry-point into the story of Burma begins with the work of the Scotsman John Crawfurd, the East India Company functionary who was himself in awe of William Marsden whom we looked at earlier. Crawfurd (1783–1868) joined the East India Company as a surgeon and first served in India, having been posted to Delhi and Agra.[8] He was later posted to

---

[7] Burma became a member of ASEAN in 1997, after Laos and Vietnam. At the time it was given a ranking of 0.524 on the UNDP Human Development Index, making it the lowest in the region. In 2014 Burma/Myanmar finally joined the ASEAN Regional Infrastructure Fund, as the last member of ASEAN to do so.

[8] By the time he was sent on his mission to Ava, John Crawfurd was already an old Indian hand who had served the East India Company in many parts of India and Southeast Asia. He had served as the British Resident at the court of Jogjakarta between 1811 to 1816, and in 1821 Lord Hastings (then Governor-General of India) sent him to a mission to the court of Siam and Cochinchina to ascertain their attitude towards Europeans and the British in particular. Between 1823 to 1826 he was based in Singapore, and though Stamford Raffles is widely regarded (still) as the founder of Singapore, Chew (2002) has argued that 'it was not Raffles but John Crawfurd who made Singapore a British possession. Crawfurd, who had been appointed in April 1823 as second British Resident, arrived in Singapore on 27 May to take charge of the settlement. Raffles left Singapore for good on 9 June' (Ernest Chew, John

Southeast Asia and was a member of the British force that occupied Java under the leadership of Lord Minto.

Three years after Raffles' *The History of Java* (1817) was published, Crawfurd's own work—which was much longer and broader in scope, and which came in three volumes compared with Raffles' two—was published. Crawfurd entitled his mammoth work *A History of the Indian Archipelago* (1820), and in the very title itself we can already see how India loomed large in his world view and calculations, which in turn located the entire archipelago within the wider orbit of Indian civilisation and history.[9] Crawfurd's (1820) work was much grander in scope than Raffles' *The History of Java*, which was focused on that island alone.[10] Casting his net much wider, Crawfurd attempted a history of what would later come to be known as the Southeast Asian or Indonesian archipelago—and in some respects his work anticipated that of Alfred Russel Wallace's (1869), which introduced the term 'The Malay Archipelago' fifty years later.[11] More than a century before the notion of Southeast Asia came into common usage, Crawfurd the roving bookwright had already begun to assemble the parts

---

Crawfurd: The Scotsman Who Made Singapore British, Raffles Town Club, Vol. 8, July–September 2002.) In August 1824 Crawfurd negotiated the treaty between the East India Company and Sultan Hussein Shah and the Temenggung, whereby the British would be given control of Singapore. In the same year the Anglo-Dutch Treaty of 1824 led to the Netherlands giving up all claims to Singapore, thereby affording Crawfurd the time and opportunity to design and build the colony. Crawfurd encouraged further migration into Singapore, and turned it into a free port—which effectively lured more commercial vessels to the island at the expense of Dutch ports such as Batavia. Crawfurd left Singapore in 1826, and was then assigned to Burma on a diplomatic mission for the Anglo-Indian government, to negotiate with King Bagyidaw following the defeat of Burma at the First Anglo-Burmese War.

[9] John Crawfurd, *A History of the Indian Archipelago, containing an Account of the Manners, Arts, Languages, Religions, Institutions and Commerce of its Inhabitants*. Archiband Constable and co. Edinburgh, and Hurst, Robinson and co. London. 1820. From the library of Swinton Colthurst Holland, Royal Navy, Aide de Camp to Queen Victoria (1895) and Commodore-in-Charge of Hong Kong (1896), in the author's private collection.

[10] By the end of his career as a Company functionary Crawfurd would have produced several books on Southeast Asia and also contributed to a three-volume study of China. See: Hugh Murray, John Crawfurd, Thomas Lynn, William Wallace and Gilber Burnet (authors), *A Historical and Descriptive Account of China*, Vols. I–III, Oliver and Boyd, Edinburgh, 1843.

[11] Re: Alfred Russel Wallace. *The Malay Archipelago: The Land of the Orang-Utan and the Bird of Paradise. A Narrative of Travel, with Studies of Man and Nature*; Macmillan and Co., London, 1869.

of the archipelago together into a singular entity that shared common characteristics.[12]

What is interesting about Crawfurd's early attempt to bring together this protean archipelago is that he focused solely on maritime Southeast Asia and disregarded the rest of the region that would later be labelled mainland Southeast Asia. 'The Western boundary of the Archipelago', he wrote, 'is formed by the Malayan Peninsula and Sumatra'—which immediately meant that the kingdoms of Siam and Burma were not seen as part of the Southeast Asian archipelago. So where was the rest of Southeast Asia, and where in particular was Burma?[13]

---

[12] Crawfurd's *History of the Indian Archipelago* (1820) was, at the time of its publication, the most extensive and comprehensive account of the history, geography, culture and languages of maritime Southeast Asia ever written in the English language—far surpassing the works of Marsden (1783) and Raffles (1817). In the introduction to the first volume he outlined the geographical extent of the region he intended to write about, and noted that the Archipelago could be divided into four distinct groups of islands, ranked according to size. The first rank consisted of the larger islands of Borneo (Kalimantan), New Guinea and Sumatra; the second consisted of the islands of Java and (oddly enough) the Malayan Peninsula; the third rank consisted of the islands of Bali, Lombok, Sulawesi (Celebes), the Moluccas and the islands of the Philippines; and the fourth rank consisted of all the other smaller islands of the region (pp. 3–7). Additionally Crawfurd divided the region into five distinct sea zones (p. 5), and introduced an explicit ethnic-cultural hierarchy that distinguished between the 'more civilised' and 'less civilised' natives of the archipelago. He maintained that civilisation had arrived to the region from the West (p. 8) and argued that the spread and development of civilised communities across the region was not equal: The islands of Sumatra and Java, along with the Malayan Peninsula were, for him, the 'most civilised' parts of Southeast Asia then (p. 8), while civilisation had only begun to develop in the second division of the archipelago, in places such as Celebes (Sulawesi) (pp. 8–9). The third division of the archipelago was seen as the least developed and civilised, and whose economy was at the most basic level, focused mainly on the production of cloves and other spices. Conversely the fourth division (which comprised of Sulu and other parts of Southern Philippines) was regarded as being 'more civilised than the third, but less civilised than the first and second' (p. 10). Here it was clear that Crawfurd's history of the archipelago was not merely a recounting of historical data, but he had also introduced a typography that ordered and ranked the communities of Southeast Asia according to a criteria of development and civilisation that was clearly not indigenous. The first volume of the work consisted of four books divided into seventeen chapters, which looked at the physical form of the natives of the archipelago, the manners and customs of the natives, the domestic ceremonies of the natives, the games and amusements of the natives, the manner of foreign settlers, the useful arts of the archipelago, the dress of the native communities, the mode of native warfare, the development of arithmetic among the natives, the calendar and mode of calculating time among the natives, navigation among the native mariners, medicine and local music, husbandry among the native agrarian communities, the materials for food used and consumed by the native communities, standards of luxury among the local communities, items of local manufacture and items made for export beyond the archipelago.

[13] Crawfurd, 1820, p. 5.

The location of Burma—in the wider sense of its geographical placing as well as its ranking in the order of history and societal-civilisational development—was never a given fact that was self evident but rather a process that was contested and impacted upon by a plethora of external variable factors. And this process—of locating, identifying, classifying and subsequently arresting the location of Burma—was never an innocent one either; for it was Burma's misfortune to be where it was, right next to the Bay of Bengal and the centre of the East India Company's growing military-economic complex.

By the nineteenth century Burma was a kingdom that was aware of how precarious its position was. Its geographical location meant that it was at the crossroads between two greater Asian powers—China and India—and it had experienced invasions from the north in the past. To the east Burma was faced with its arch-rival the kingdom of Siam, and the relationship between the two kingdoms was anything but cordial. Successive Burmese rulers had attempted to secure the borders of the Burmese kingdom that was based in the Irrawaddy delta area by first securing the mountainous regions to the west, north and east of the kingdom, which happened to be the highland territories of other ethnic groups such as the Chins, Kachins, Shans and Karen peoples. This, in effect, meant that the Burmese kingdom had long since been in a state of unending conflict with other highland communities who were resentful of Burmese control over their territories. When King Bagyidaw ascended to the throne in 1819 he inherited a kingdom that was already facing the prospect of conflict in Assam and Manipur and ordered his army—led by General Bandula—to regain control of Assam as well as Arakan.[14]

By that time Burma was forced to contend with another greater power that seemed bent on reducing its own: the British. The arrival of the East India Company that was announced in no uncertain terms by the victory of Robert Clive's force against the army of Siraj ud-Daulah at Plassey (Palasi) in Bengal in 1757 meant that Burma was now faced with a more powerful adversary, and as a result the kingdom reasserted itself by attempting to secure the regions adjacent to Bengal.[15] From the Burmese

---

[14] David Joel Steinberg, *In Search of Southeast Asia: A Modern History*. University of Hawaii Press, Hawaii, 1985, pp. 104–105.

[15] The Konbaung dynasty, of which King Bagyidaw was a member of, was in fact started around the same time that the British made their presence felt in India: In 1752 Alaungp'aya rose to power and in 1757 (the same year that Clive triumphed at the Battle of Plassey) he defeated the forces of the Mon-speaking kingdom of Pegu. From 1757 to 1769 Burma was constantly at war, against the Tai-speaking peoples of the Shan plateau region, against invad-

perspective this move was a rational one that sought to protect its frontier and to prevent the British from supporting the neighbouring communities who were seen as hostile to Burmese rule; and King Bagyidaw was merely following the same policy of offensive deterrence that had been pursued by the rulers of the Konbaung dynasty before him, such as Alaungp'aya, Hsinbyushin (r. 1763–1776) and Bodawp'aya (r. 1782–1819). However this proved to be a fateful decision, for Burma's manoeuvres in Assam and Arakan were in turn seen by the British as an act of provocation, and when General Bandula's forces moved on to an island in the middle of the Naaf river, the Rubicon was crossed: It was upon this pretext that the British began to mobilise their forces and the First Anglo-Burmese War was fought in 1824–1826.

The First Anglo-Burmese War ended with a humiliating defeat for the Burmese. Despite the bombast of the Burmese ruler, in reality the power of King Bagyidaw was dispersed throughout the kingdom and was not nearly as centralised as the administrative structure and chain of command of the East India Company. Steinberg (1985) has pointed out that on the ground the provincial government in Burma 'was for the most part hereditary government by a provincial elite that had firm roots in the provinces', and that the Burmese army was made up of peasant levies who would be assembled at the behest of their local feudal lords in times of crisis.[16] (By contrast, the East India Company had by then a private army of more than 260,000 soldiers based across India.)[17]

Though the Burmese army was able to quell the revolts that occurred among the other communities that encircled the Irrawaddy delta, it proved to be no match against the combined arms of the East India Company. Rangoon was overrun by the British in May 1824, and by 1825 the British were on their way to Ava. King Bagyidaw was eventually forced to accept the terms of the Anglo-Burmese Treaty of Peace in February 1826, which stipulated that Burmese forces had to withdraw from Assam and Manipur while also conceding Arakan and Tenasserim to the East India Company.[18]

---

ing Chinese forces from the North, and against the Siamese to the East. Burma reached the peak of its power with the defeat of the Siamese kingdom of Ayudhya in 1767, and the Burmese were ruthless in their military campaign: Ayudhya was sacked and burned to the ground.

[16] Steinberg, 1985, p. 31.

[17] William Dalrymple, *The East India Company: The Original Corporate Raiders*, The Guardian, London, 3 March 2015.

[18] Steinberg, 1985, p. 105.

It was shortly after this debacle that John Crawfurd (then based in Rangoon as its Civil Commissioner after his stint in Singapore) received his orders,[19] on 1 September 1826, to sail up the Irrawaddy River to meet King Bagyidaw and to deliver the terms that had been set by the Anglo-Indian government.[20] Among the results of this mission was the account of the trip to Ava that came in the form of his book, *A Journal of an Embassy to the Court of Ava* (1829).

WEIGHED DOWN BY THE MAUDLIN TYRANT: CRAWFURD'S STATIC BURMA

Published in 1829, John Crawfurd's *Journal of an Embassy to the Court of Ava* was one of the first major works on the kingdom of Burma.[21] It was, like so many of the works on Southeast Asia that were produced during the era of colonial-capitalism, a book that was written primarily for an audience back home in England; and its intended readership included those who held the reins of power in London. Henry Keppel would dedicate his book on Borneo to the Earl of Albermarle, his father; while Rodney Mundy would dedicate his to the Earl of Auckland; but John Crawfurd had raised the bar much higher by dedicating his work on Burma to none other than King George IV himself.

Crawfurd invited King George IV to contemplate 'the unhappy lot of Tyrants, debased and corrupted by absolute power', with the hope that 'your Majesty may see new reason to be gratified that with constitutional exertion of authority by which you redress the grievances of your subjects, and enlarge the fabric of civil and religious liberty, for the preservation of which the illustrious House of Brunswick was called the Throne of Great Britain'.[22] Additionally, Crawfurd stated his hope that his work would be 'sufficient to show the beneficial power of the English Constitution, even in its remote and faint influence; and to awaken sanguine hopes of the blessings of which await your Indian subjects, when the benefits of that Constitution shall be fully and directly imparted to them, under your Majesty's paternal administration'.[23]

---

[19] Crawfurd, 1829, appendix 1, p. 1.
[20] Crawfurd, 1829, p. 1.
[21] John Crawfurd, *Journal of an Embassy from the Governor-General of India to the Court of Ava in the year 1827.* Henry Colburn, New Burlington Street, London. 1829.
[22] Crawfurd, 1829, p. i.
[23] Crawfurd, 1829, p. i.

Here, in Crawfurd's dedication, we can already see the stage-setting and subject-positioning that Kabbabi (1881) alludes to when she notes how such texts written by colonial functionaries of the nineteenth century were self-referential in the manner that they addressed a familiar audience/readership back home; and how—despite the universal claims that were often made—such works were really particular and exclusive in the way that they addressed the fellow countrymen of the respective authors themselves, on terms that were familiar.[24] Crawfurd addresses his ruler while describing another; and alludes to the Empire that he belonged to, served and helped to build. That Empire was in turn (then) centred in India, and his writing on Burma—like his works on Siam, Cochinchina and the Southeast Asian archipelago—would constantly foreground India as the centre of imperial power, second only to London.

The other feature of Crawfurd's work—like his journal of his visit to Siam and Cochinchina—is that it was, fundamentally, a report. And that report was intended for the desks of the colonial governors in India and the East India Company's board of directors, who in turn served the interests of their country and their king. Crawfurd had embarked on his Burmese mission in service of the company, and among the many tasks that were given to him were those of data-collecting and negotiating on their behalf.[25] The Anglo-Indian government in turn wished him 'to regulate (his) discussions with the Court of Ava in the spirit of the Board's observations', cognisant of the fact that Britain then had an enormous advantage over Burma.[26] Crawfurd was directed to press further with Britain's demands, while not making any clear concessions to the Burmese in turn.[27]

---

[24] Rana Kabbani, *Imperial Fictions: Europe's Myths of the Orient*, Pandora-Harper Collins, London. 1988. p. xi.

[25] Crawfurd includes the entire mission statement given to him by the company in the appendices of his work. See: Crawfurd, 1829, Appendix 1, pp. 1–7.

[26] Crawfurd, 1829, Appendix 1, p. 4.

[27] The instructions handed to Crawfurd were about as clear as mud. He was expected to make further demands on the Burmese, but not to the extent of arousing resentment or suspicion at the Court of Ava. At the same time the Company was unwilling to enter into any commercial dealings which might not be of lasting economic value. It was evident that the East India Company and the Colonial government in India did not entertain high hopes of an economically prosperous and rewarding relationship with Burma at any time in the future. And on that somewhat pessimistic note the statement concluded that 'in the existing uncertainty, with regard to the ultimate disposal of our territorial acquisitions on the Martaban and Tennasserim coast, his Lordship in Council would be unwilling to enter into any complex commercial arrangements which, after all, might prove to be of any practical value' (Appendix, p. 4).

Of the Burmese in general, Crawfurd was roundly dismissive. In his work he described their manners as pompous and prone to flattery,[28] rarely punctual,[29] overly formal,[30] and never prepared for discussions.[31] In the art of war they were 'at the very lowest scale' in terms of courage and conduct;[32] their treatment of prisoners was described as cruel and murderous,[33] with their captives universally condemned to slavery.[34] Crawfurd's opinion of the Burman courtiers and officials he met was generally poor, with most of them brushed aside as a lot of fawning lickspittles—though he did regard the Wungyi of Pegu as being more cultivated than the rest, with 'the manners of an Asiatic gentleman'. Upon his arrival at the court of King Bagyidaw, Crawfurd remarked that the rites and rituals of the court were tiresome,[35] and was happy to play the gadfly when he steadfastly refused to perform any gesture of obeisance to anyone save the king himself.[36] Crawfurd was curt in his dealings with the courtiers: He made it clear that 'if any attempt was made to dictate to us' any matters related to court protocol, then he and the entire delegation would immediately up stakes and leave.[37]

The high point of Crawfurd's visit was, as one would expect, his meeting with King Bagyidaw himself—to whom he devoted nine pages in his lengthy and detailed description.[38] In the lead-up to the royal audience Crawfurd had consistently presented the Burmese in disparaging terms. His first description of the king did not veer from the norm he had set, and the ruler of the kingdom is compared somewhat unfavourably to a menial Indian servant;[39] Crawfurd's Anglocentrism and Indiacentrism were both evident here: his *Journal* was, after all, dedicated to none other than King George IV, and here he was describing the monarch of a foreign land to his own. That Crawfurd described King Bagyidaw's fly-whisk in terms that were Anglo-Indian ('what in India is called a Chowrie') and stated that

[28] Crawfurd, 1829, pp. 96, 145.
[29] Crawfurd, 1829, pp. 97, 147, 255, 263.
[30] Crawfurd, 1829, p. 105.
[31] Crawfurd, 1829, pp. 107, 147.
[32] Crawfurd, 1829, pp. 337–338.
[33] Crawfurd, 1829, pp. 244–246.
[34] Crawfurd, 1829, p. 246.
[35] Crawfurd, 1829, p. 130.
[36] Crawfurd, 1829, pp. 129–130.
[37] Crawfurd, 1829, p. 132.
[38] Crawfurd, 1829, pp. 133–141.
[39] Crawfurd, 1829, pp. 133–134.

only a menial servant would carry such a thing in the India that he was familiar with also locates Burma yet again in the wider orbit of the Anglo-Indian Empire.

Crawfurd's relentless assault on the standing of Burma and its king was just one aspect of his *Journal*. Though diminishing the prestige of King Bagyidaw may have been one of his objectives, it has to be remembered that Crawfurd had been sent to the Court of Ava by the Anglo-Indian government and the Company for other reasons too, including finalising the terms of the Treaty of Peace between the two countries. Like John Anderson, the East India Company man whose jaunt through Sumatra was intended to furnish the company with vital economic intelligence, Crawfurd was likewise a Company man who was keenly aware of the economic potential of Burma. In his account of the journey to Ava, he recounted the discoveries that were made along the journey: Dr Wallich had chanced upon a fossil bone that excited much curiosity—though it was admittedly worthless as far as the East India Company was concerned.[40] Crawfurd was, however, more excited by the discovery of petroleum wells near the village of Re-nan K'hyaung,[41] and devoted a substantial part of his second chapter to the subject.[42] Having observed that this petroleum was easily obtained from open wells, and that it was used in almost every household along the Irrawaddy delta, Crawfurd concluded that 'if it were practicable to ascertain the real quantity produced at the wells, we should be possessed of the means of making a tolerable estimate of the inhabitants who use this commodity, constituting the larger part of the population of the kingdom'.[43]

Crawfurd's—and the Company's—desire to know more about the land, people, resources and commodities of Burma was a data-gathering enterprise that was simultaneously linked to the related project of territorial expansion and control; and the more he learned about the Burmese the closer that goal of conquest and eventual colonisation drew. The knowledge that Crawfurd sought and built was comprehensive in its scope. The reader will note the similarities in style and structure that are found in the works of Crawfurd, Raffles, Anderson, Keppel and Mundy. To know Burma was to know it completely; to adopt a panoptic view of

---

[40] Crawfurd, 1829, p. 53.
[41] Crawfurd, 1829, pp. 52–56.
[42] Crawfurd, 1829, p. 55.
[43] Crawfurd, 1829, p. 55.

the land and its people that would in turn present the coloniser's eye with numbers, statistics and raw data that could be fitted together in a vast map of knowledge of the land before him. And having the power to map and know Burma also meant that the Anglo-Indian government and the East India Company had the power to determine where it was.

From South to Southeast Asian: Moving Burma About

Countries do not move, but countries can be placed and relocated discursively, and that was the fate of Burma. In the course of Burma's unequal relationship with the British Empire it had been configured and reconfigured several times, according to the interests and agenda of the latter: Burma was seen as part of 'Greater India', was puffed up as a military threat to British interests when it was labelled 'The Burman Empire', and later brought low when it was reduced to a British colony governed by the Anglo-Indian government. Following the First Anglo-Burmese War Burma's territory was violated again and again, and the waning of Burma's power was partly the result of its proximity to British India and Britain's desire to drag the kingdom closer to its Indian Empire. At the same time Siam's position meant that it would become a buffer state between the ever-expanding spheres of British and French influence, giving the kingdom the breathing space it needed and allowing it to regain some of the power and prestige that it once had. In 1835 Siam was even strong enough to mount an attack on Cochinchina, and its forces besieged the walls of Hanoi.[44]

No such opportunity was ever afforded to Burma, however. King Bagyidaw would later be deposed by King Tharrawaddy, and the latter would up the stakes in the contest between Burma and Britain. The accession of King Pagan Min (in 1846) and then Mindon (1852) did little to alter the balance of power between Burma and its powerful rival. Following the Second Anglo-Burmese War of 1852, Rangoon and the lower Irrawaddy delta were taken by Britain, forcing the Burmese kingdom to retreat further north to Mandalay—which proved to be disastrous as it meant that the Burmese king had lost his main source of revenue that came from the rice-growing fertile lands of the delta.[45] Cut off from the coast and surrounded by hostile highlands and mountains, the Burmese kingdom was no longer able to pay for the modernisation of its state apparatus

---

[44] Report in the *New York Sun*, New York, 9 April 1835, p. 4, column 1.
[45] Steinberg, 1985, p. 108.

and army. King Mindon had sent an emissary to meet Queen Victoria to plead the case of his kingdom, but the meeting was interrupted by the presence of the British Secretary of State for India, implying that Burma was little more than a vassal state of the British Indian government.[46]

The final blow came with the Third Anglo-Burmese War of 1885, which led to the surrender (and eventual exile) of King Thibaw and the forceful annexation of Upper Burma on 1 January 1886, ending the Konbaung dynasty for good.[47] By then the image of the rulers of Burma was decidedly negative in the popular Western imagination, bordering on the grotesque: in the Western press King Thibaw was cast as a bloodthirsty tyrant who sacrificed innocents for the sake of his own health and safety,[48] and his defeat at the hands of the British was depicted in a cartoon carried by Punch with the Burmese ruler in the form of a toad, labelled 'Theebaw the Burmese Toad',[49] booted by a British soldier from the rear. Insult followed insult, and though the history of independent Burma came to its graceless end in 1886 Steinberg (1985) was right when he noted that 'the fate of Burma was actually sealed by the First Anglo-Burmese War' six decades earlier.[50]

Burma would finally become a British colony, governed from India and according to administrative norms that had been developed in the Indian colony earlier.[51] Over the coming decades 'the map of Southeast Asia was

---

[46] Steinberg, 1985, p. 181.

[47] Steinberg, 1985, pp. 182–183.

[48] By the 1880s the news reports that came from Burma had grown more lurid and grisly in form and content: The 13 April 1880 edition of the *St. Louis-Globe Democrat* featured a headline story—taken from British sources—that 700 innocent civilians, including foreigners, had been buried alive in Mandalay in an obscure ritual that was intended to ensure the health and safety of King Thibaw who was said to be ill. [Re. Buried, Not Burned: The Awful Fate of Mandalay's Unfortunates. In: *St. Louis-Globe Democrat*, 13 April 1880, p. 3. column 1.]

[49] *Punch*, 31 October 1885, p. 215.

[50] Steinberg, 1985, p. 110.

[51] Steinberg notes that the administrative and economic systems of British Burma 'developed in the shadow of British Indian practices and were justified in the name of nineteenth-century liberalism' (p. 180). Each region of the British Burman colony was first made a division of the colonial government in India, and in 1862 these were brought together under a Chief Commissioner based in Rangoon. Up to the First World War British Burma was treated and governed as an extension of British India, and during this period the colony witnessed the arrival of large numbers of migrant workers and traders from the Indian subcontinent who were encouraged to relocate to Burma to help develop its economy. The long-term legacy of this policy was the generation of feelings of hostility and suspicion

redrawn to conform with the emerging world political order',[52] and that was an order that was determined and defined by the logic of racialised colonial-capitalism more than anything else. The epistemologies, histories and geographies of the defeated nations of Southeast Asia would be rendered null and void; deemed exotic, quaint and unscientific; and consigned to the museum of Empire or the freak-shows of the colonial metropole. Crawfurd's *Journal* was one of the first works that contributed to the distortion and marginalisation of the native Burmese voice.

Though his mission to the court of Ava may have been unsuccessful, the pen of Crawfurd proved to be more powerful and lasting; and the Burma that the reader is left with is one that was overshadowed by India, dulled by tyranny and rendered exotic. It was only by the first decades of the twentieth century that British Burma came into its own as a colony that could sustain and administer itself, and following the demise of the East India Company (in 1874), Burma and other colonies such as British Malaya and the Straits Settlements would gradually come under control of the imperial mandarins of London. Then by the Second World War the term Southeast Asia came into common use, designating the region as a specific geo-strategic sector and theatre of war against imperial Japan. Then, as before, it was not the peoples of Southeast Asia who determined who they were and where they were, but rather the technocrats and policymakers in centres of power thousands of miles away. Today as we continue to use terms such as South Asia and Southeast Asia, it is important to remember the genesis of such terms and how they were themselves the direct result of calculations of power of the imperial era. The bringing together, and the subsequent separation of, South and Southeast Asia was hardly an accidental or innocent process; and in our understanding of political geography there is the pressing need to appreciate the fact that the epistemology and vocabulary that we use today are themselves the offspring of the age of Empire.

---

between the ethnic groups in Burma, directed towards Indian migrants in particular who were seen by the Burmese as collaborators in the British colonial enterprise. Unsurprisingly, when Burman-Buddhist nationalism began to emerge by the 1930s, among the first groups targeted by the Burman nationalists were the Indian migrants who were regarded as tools of the British Empire.

[52] Steinberg, 1985, p. 175.

Never Having Left the Nineteenth Century: The Challenge of Postcolonial Scholarship Today

That we live in a postcolonial world where the nation state has become the dominant paradigm is undeniable today; as is the salient fact that the world as we know it has been cut up and divided by political frontiers that are, in most cases, fixed and accepted. Scholars such as Davidson (1992) have described this as 'the black man's burden', and have argued that the modern postcolonial nation state has been responsible for perpetuating many of the injuries—political and epistemic—that date back to the colonial era.[53] And yet it seems impossible to ignore the reality of the nation state or to imagine of alternative forms of governance, mobility, connectivity and globalisation that can take place radically outside the model of the state today.

In this chapter I have tried to show how the creation of categories such as 'Greater India', 'The Indian Archipelago', 'South Asia' and 'Southeast Asia' were, from the outset, discursive constructs that were the result of human agency and ideology—the ideology in this case being colonial-capitalism, and how it sought to study an Asia that would later come to be conquered, exposed, rendered vulnerable and thus knowable as well. Knowledge of Asia in the nineteenth century was instrumentalised in many ways, and in the process of learning about India and Southeast Asia the functionaries of the militarised colonial companies also reconstructed the peoples and cultures they studied, ranked them according to a racial hierarchy, and posited the notion of superior cultures and inferior cultures as well. South and Southeast Asia were initially seen as part of the same continuum, but was later split apart according to the necessities of colonial management back in England, as well as in the Netherlands and France, and it was from this prolonged period of uneven contact between West and East that Asia was carved up as we find it today.

By way of a conclusion, I end with three observations that I feel have to be made at this juncture:

The first is that the field of area studies remains one that has its origins in the nineteenth century, and that many of the works that are and have been regarded as their classic foundational texts for area studies were not initially meant to be read as works of anthropology or sociology in the first

---

[53] Basil Davidson, *The Black Man's Burden: Africa and the Curse of the Nation-State*, James Curry, London. 1992.

place. John Bastin (1965) has noted, for instance, that Stamford Raffles' *The History of Java* was destined to be 'one of the classics of Southeast Asian historiography'[54]—despite the fact that the term 'Southeast Asia' had not even been coined then.[55] Bastin is right about the importance of Raffles' work, but may have been wrong to elevate it to the status of a great work on Java or Southeast Asia. For Raffles' work, like Crawfurd's, tells us less about the realities of Java or Burma or Southeast Asia at the time and perhaps reveals more about the mindset of the authors themselves, who were East India Company men who saw the region as an open terrain ripe for conquest and colonisation. In the same way Pigafetta's account of Magellan's voyage to Southeast Asia should not perhaps be read as an accurate account of the people of the Philippines, though it reveals a lot about the values and world view of sixteenth-century European missionaries and conquistadores who viewed the world through the lens of religious conflict and missionary zeal instead. These were works written by Europeans and for Europeans, and in reading them today we learn more about how Europe viewed Asia than about Asia itself.

Secondly, by interrogating the genesis and development of complex ideas such as South Asia and Southeast Asia, we also need to remember that these constructs were invariably linked to interests and power, and that they have less to do with geography per se and more with political and economic interests, both then and now. As mentioned at the outset of this chapter, such categories as South Asia and Southeast Asia abound today and are in common, everyday use. These categories have also become the staple units of disciplines such as international relations and political science, and entire university departments and courses are dedicated to their study. That in itself is not a problem, though we ought to bear in mind that in using these categories today we are also perpetuating the compartmentalising reductivist logic that was at work in the nineteenth century. The prevalence of these categories today, and the manner in which they are used—often uncritically and with little appreciation of their historical provenance—seems to suggest that we still live under the long shadow of the nineteenth century; and that despite the advances that have been made

---

[54] Bastin, 1965, p. vii.
[55] Thomas Stamford Raffles, *The History of Java*, in two volumes. Black, Parbury and Allen, publishers for the Honorable East India Company, Leadenhall Street; and John Murray, Albemarle Street, London. 1817. References to the introductory essay by John Bastin come from the 1965 edition published by Oxford University Press, Oxford and Kuala Lumpur. 1965.

in other areas and disciplines such as critical theory, there remain domains such as international relations where deconstruction has yet to make an imprint. The concern here is twofold: that an epistemology and vocabulary that dates back to the age of Empire is being used in a glib and unreflective manner, and that the other alternative epistemologies, geographies and vocabularies that were erased or sidelined by colonialism are kept silent.

The third and final point I wish to raise is this. Since the end of Empire efforts have been made—some on a grand scale, some piecemeal—by the communities and polities of the post-colonial world to heal the ruptures and divisions that were introduced by the divisive logic of colonialism. From the Bandung conference to present-day efforts of countries such as India and China to reconnect with the rest of Asia—via a revival of the silk route, for instance—Asia seems to be on the move again and eager to revisit and relive a past of an interconnected Asia where boundaries were fluid and the movement of ideas, goods and people was seldom linear or one-directional. Laudable though this effort may be, it has been encumbered and sometimes hindered by the post-colonial epistemology and vocabulary that we still have not been able to overcome.

It has been said that one cannot simply transcend metaphysics, for to transcend metaphysics is itself a metaphysical idea. Likewise, we cannot simply escape from, or wish away, the nation state and modern governmentality from within the framework of the modern state and its attendant conceptual repertoire of citizenship, identity, borders and frontiers. The aim of this chapter was not to suggest that we can escape the legacy of the past, or that we can simply forget or neglect it; but rather to demonstrate that the political categories we have and use today—be they of states or regional blocs—were assembled and constructed, and thus may be reconstructed again. We cannot deny or escape the fact that our concerns today are themselves historical ones, located in the immediate present of a post-colonial modernity, and that we ourselves are modern subjects imbued with a modern sensibility. But awareness of our own entanglement with colonialism's history may be a step towards a more critical, nuanced and complex understanding of how these categories and identities came about, and at the very least may remind us that when we speak of things such as South Asia and Southeast Asia we are treading upon discursive ground that bears the footprints of Empire.

REFERENCES

Bastin, John, Introduction to Thomas Stamford Raffles, The History of Java, in two volumes. Black, Parbury and Allen, publishers for the Honorable East India Company, Leadenhall Street; and John Murray, Albemarle Street, London. 1817. Re-published by Oxford University Press, Oxford and Kuala Lumpur, 1965: page numbers.

Chew, Ernest. John Crawfurd: The Scotsman Who Made Singapore British, Raffles Town Club, Vol. 8, July–September 2002.

Crawfurd, John, A History of the Indian Archipelago, containing an Account of the Manners, Arts, Languages, Religions, Institutions and Commerce of its Inhabitants. Archibald Constable and co. Edinburgh, and Hurst, Robinson and co. London. 1820: page numbers.

Crawfurd, John, Journal of an Embassy from the Governor-General of India to the Court of Ava in the year 1827. Henry Colburn, New Burlington Street, London. 1829.

Crawfurd, John, Hugh Murray, Thomas Lynn, William Wallace and Gilber Burnet (authors), A Historical and Descriptive Account of China, Vols. I-III, Oliver and Boyd, Edinburgh. 1843.

Dalrymple, William, The East India Company: The Original Corporate Raiders, The Guardian, London, 3 March 2015.

Davidson, Basil, The Black Man's Burden: Africa and the Curse of the Nation-State, James Curry, London. 1992.

Fifield, Russell H. Southeast Asian Studies: Origins, Development, Future, in: Journal of Southeast Asian Studies, Vol. 7. No. 2, September 1976.

Kabbani, Rana, Imperial Fictions: Europe's Myths of the Orient, Pandora-Harper Collins, London. 1988.

Marsden, William, A History of Sumatra – Containing An Account of the Government, Laws, Customs, and Manners Of the Native Inhabitants, With A Description of the Natural Productions, And A Relation of the Ancient Political State Of that Island. Printed for the Author, London, 1783.

Marsden, William, On the Chronology of the Hindoos, Paper delivered at the Royal Society, The Philosophical Transactions of The Royal Society, London. 24 June 1790.

Steinberg, David Joel, In Search of Southeast Asia: A Modern History. University of Hawaii Press, Hawaii, 1985.

Wallace, Alfred Russel, The Malay Archipelago: The Land of the Orang-Utan and the Bird of Paradise. A Narrative of Travel, with Studies of Man and Nature; Macmillan and Co., London, 1869.

An Act for the Better Securing the Lawful Trade of his Majesty's Subjects To and From the East Indies; and for the more effectual Preventing all his Majesty's Subjects Trading thither under Foreign Commissions, 1714. Act of Parliament during the reign of King George II, London. Printed by John Baskett, Printer to the Kings most Excellent Majesty, and the Assigns of Thomas Newcomb, and Henry Hills. 1719.

CHAPTER 19

Monuments, Motifs, Myths: Architecture and its Transformations in Early India and Southeast Asia

Parul Pandya Dhar

INTRODUCTION

Since ancient times, India and Southeast Asia have engaged in an intense exchange of ideas, knowledge systems, objects and people traversing vast expanses over land and seas. The historiography of these early interactions has, since the 1950s or so, witnessed an important paradigm shift, with the dominant framework of 'Indianization' yielding to an increased emphasis on 'localization' processes.[1] What is more, notions of homogeneous cultural monoliths have been abandoned in favour of more textured understandings of regional and subregional diversities among the regions belonging to the Indian Ocean zone. More recently, the archaeology of cross-cultural interactions in South and Southeast Asia has

---

[1] See, for example, the idea of Indian colonies in Majumdar (1927).

P. P. Dhar (✉)
Department of History, University of Delhi, New Delhi, India

© The Author(s) 2018
S. Saran (ed.), *Cultural and Civilisational Links between India and Southeast Asia*, https://doi.org/10.1007/978-981-10-7317-5_19

yielded exciting new discoveries about the earliest encounters between the regions.[2]

This chapter looks at select aspects of Indian and Southeast Asian monuments, specifically the processes that shaped early architectural vocabulary and associated imagery in the region. Put differently, it investigates the dynamics of localization of architectural language in early India and Southeast Asia. A close investigation of the architectonics and iconography of these monuments—their underlying concepts and motifs, affiliations and diversities—reveals an intricate web of relationships between the cultural zones of contact and provides significant insights into ancient cosmopolitan circuits of exchange. In a larger context, the chapter highlights key issues for a more nuanced understanding of the networks of exchange between India and Southeast Asia as viewed through the prism of their ancient monumental remains.

EARLY MONUMENTS AND THE TRANSMISSION OF ARCHITECTURAL KNOWLEDGE

By about the seventh century CE, the architectural landscape of a large part of South and Southeast Asia was dotted with religious monuments built in brick and stone. Even earlier, by about the fifth century CE, that is, the period of Gupta dominance in northern India, stone, by virtue of its more enduring or relatively permanent nature, was gradually being preferred over wood and brick for constructing the 'abodes of the gods' or temples. The increasing use of stone as a material for temple-building is evident in several of the well-preserved temples of the Gupta period in India, such as Sanchi Temple 17 (c. 400), Kaṅkālī Devī temple at Tigawa near Jabalpur (c. 425), Pārvatī temple at Nachana-Kuthara in the Satna District (c. late fifth century CE), Śiva temple at Bhumara, also in the Satna District (c. late fifth century CE) and the Viṣṇu temple at Deogarh near Jhansi (c. late fifth–early sixth century CE), to name a few.[3] This is not to suggest that temples in brick were not built during and after this period in India; brick as a medium of construction certainly continued to exert influence. But the surviving examples of brick temples in early medieval India are far fewer than those

---

[2] A useful discussion of the impact of new archaeological discoveries is to be found in Manguin et al. (2011: Introduction).

[3] For further details on the formal logic and historical backdrop of these and other temples of the Gupta period in India, see *EITA* II. 1: *passim*.

built in stone.[4] By the seventh–eighth centuries CE, stone temples were being built across the length and breadth of India, in varied regional and subregional styles and in territories within the control of various early medieval regional dynasties that had gained prominence.

In Southeast Asia, the earliest well-preserved religious structures in situ date from *c.* seventh century CE onwards, although evidence of earlier temples is at times encountered in the shape of fragmentary remains and in other historical sources. At the easternmost extent of mainland Southeast Asia, for example, a fifth-century inscription from ancient Campā (C.72) at the site of present-day Mỹ Sơn in Vietnam speaks of a [wooden] temple dedicated to Śiva as Bhadreśvara, which was consumed by fire.[5] The temples of Campā are built predominantly in brick, with select architectural elements such as altar-pedestals, pillars and tympana being rendered in stone. In fact, brick remained the preferred medium of construction throughout in Campā, with the Chams excelling in brick-building techniques (Fig. 19.1).[6] The structural and ornamental vocabulary of the temples of Campā is a consequence of several factors: the material and mode of construction, cross-cultural contacts with India and other Asian regions, and the local beliefs, predilections and building practices of the people of Campā.

In neighbouring Cambodia, pre-Angkorian temples such as the seventh-century structures from the well-known site of Sambor-Prei-Kuk in the Kampong Thom province were similarly built mainly in brick, although exceptions such as the all-stone flat-roofed structure in the Northern group identified as N 17 are also in evidence (Fig. 19.2). Unlike Campā, however, the medium of construction of temples in Angkorian Cambodia gradually shifted to stone, leading to the construction of grand monumental temple-mountains, the most famous one being the grand Angkor Wat patronized by the Khmer king, Sūryavarman II, during the first half of the twelfth century (Fig. 19.3).[7]

---

[4] See, Hardy (2016), which discusses some important aspects of medieval Central Indian brick temples affiliated to the Pratīhāra period.
[5] For the text and translation of this inscription, see *Études épigraphiques sur le pays Cham* [*EEPC*]: pp. 3–7.
[6] For useful insights into brick-building technology in ancient Campā, see Hardy et al. (2009: 1–13, 260–311).
[7] The significance of the famous temple-mountains of Cambodia will be discussed in the next section of this chapter, titled 'Meru: Mountain and Monument'.

Fig. 19.1 A view of the brick temples of Campā at Mỹ Sơn, Vietnam. Source: Author

Moving to maritime Southeast Asia, Central Java in Indonesia has yielded some of the best-preserved seventh–eighth-century monuments, notably the *Caṇḍi*s Gedong Songo at Mount Ungaran and the remarkable group of *caṇḍi*s located on the picturesque Dieng Plateau. Unlike the earliest temples of Campā-Vietnam and Cambodia, these Indonesian *caṇḍi*s have been built in stone. As a consequence, they are in a relatively better state of preservation than their contemporaneous Cham and Khmer counterparts in Vietnam and Cambodia.

A detailed comparative analysis of the style and architectonics of these seventh–eighth-century religious monuments from Southeast Asia with contemporaneous or earlier examples from India is well beyond the scope of the present chapter. Yet it would be pertinent to mention at least a few of the conclusions arising from such a detailed comparative architectural analyses, as has been attempted by me elsewhere for the early Campā

Fig. 19.2 Flat-roofed structure, N 17, Sambor Prei Kuk, Cambodia. Source: Author

Fig. 19.3 Temple-mountain of Angkor Wat, Cambodia. Source: Author

temples.[8] While the architectural vocabulary of the seventh–eighth-century temples of Southeast Asia reveals close generic links with Indian temples, the details of their form and embellishment clearly indicate that the beginnings of the transmission of architectural ideas and forms between India and Southeast Asia need to be investigated from a period earlier than that of the earliest, well-preserved seventh–eighth-century temples from Southeast Asia. The localization of Indian architectural knowledge systems in the Southeast Asian regions and their assimilation with local predilections and building practices are already in evidence in the earliest preserved Southeast Asian temples.

Although the architectural concepts, plans and elevations of Southeast Asian temples have many obvious commonalities with Indian temples of the Gupta and post-Gupta periods—a fact that has been reiterated in several studies on Southeast Asian architecture—it is equally crucial to understand the processes of localization that render these early monuments distinct from their Indian counterparts.[9] Take, for example, the elevation of Caṇḍi Arjuna situated on the Dieng Plateau in Central Java (Fig. 19.4). This structure rests on a raised platform (*jagati/upapīṭha*) whose mouldings correspond with Indian prototypes. Yet the sequence of the platform mouldings, the particular arrangement of the parts forming the whole and the rhythm of its progressions and recessions are in fact more akin to those seen on image pedestals, especially the bronze images of deities, which, unlike the monuments themselves, were portable and are well known to have been carried across circuitous sea and land routes between South and Southeast Asia since ancient times.

A stairway flanked by banisters (*hastihasta*) leads up to the terrace of the platform of Caṇḍi Arjuna. In India, the *hastihasta* as an architectural member is first noticed in the remains from third-century Nagarjunakonda, then the late fifth-century caves at Ajanta (Cave 20 and 26) in Maharashtra, next in the mid-sixth-century Western Chalukyan caves and seventh-century temples at Badami and Aihole in northern Karnataka, and also in several other southern

---

[8] In Dhar (2016), the present author explores the precise nature of architectural transmission and the localization of architectural knowledge in early Campā (Vietnam) between the seventh and ninth centuries CE.

[9] Early comparisons between early Vietnamese and Cambodian and some Indian monuments are sporadically found in Parmentier (1904, 1909, and 1918). For a recent analysis involving the use of digital technology to interpret the adaptations of Indian 'archetypes' in the case of Southeast Asian temples, see Datta and Benyon (2014).

Indian temples from this period onwards.[10] It is not encountered in the case of northern Indian temples.

The walls of Caṇḍi Arjuna are punctuated by pilasters and spring from a low base (*pīṭha/adhiṣṭhāna*). A central niche (*devakoṣṭha*) is carved on all sides except on the side where the entrance is located. These niches once harboured images of deities, as is known from surviving examples from the site. The pedestals for these images are visible in the accompanying photograph (Fig. 19.4) and reveal an arrangement and character that is

Fig. 19.4 Caṇḍi Arjuna, Dieng Plateau, Central Java, Indonesia. Source: Author

[10] For a clear visual of the *hastihasta* (stairway banister) at the entrance to the early seventh-century Gauḍarguḍi at Aihole, see *EITA* I.2: plate 50.

similar to the platform mouldings of the same structure. This further affirms the connection of the moulding type with portable image-pedestals. Each niche is framed by a *prabhāvalī-toraṇa* (an arched image-frame shaped as an elongated halo), once again an aspect shared with bronze images and image-pedestals.[11] The walls are linked to the upper storeys of Caṇḍi Arjuna by a group of mouldings distantly affiliated to the *varaṇḍikā* (parapet), which connects the wall to the superstructure in northern Indian temple forms. These include the architrave and fillet members topped by curved eave-cornices similar to the *kapotapālikā* (cyma-eave cornice) of the northern Indian type, quite distinct from the *kapota* (roll-cornice) seen at the corresponding level in southern Indian temple types (Fig. 19.5). The eave-cornice of Caṇḍi Arjuna, however, additionally has prominent, upturned corner accents typical of the Javanese *caṇḍi*s. The typical *hāra* (cloistered parapet) seen above the entablature of the Dravidian temples is likewise absent in this case. Miniature aediculae (*karṇakūṭa*s) mark the corners. The *caṇḍi* is four-storeyed, each successive level being a miniaturized model of the lower one, with the whole being topped by a distinctive *stūpī* (finial) of the type which also caps each of the corner aediculae.

The distinctive storeys that make up the superstructure of Caṇḍi Arjuna lend this monument an appearance that is comparable to some seventh-century Western Calukyan temples such as the Upper Śivālaya, Lower Śivālaya and Malegitti Śivālaya at Badami, as well as a few of the Pallavan period monoliths at Mamallapuram, for example the Dharmarāja and Arjuna Rathas (Fig. 19.5). This apparent visual correspondence has led several scholars to look for direct links between the Western Calukyan, Pallavan and Southeast Asian temples. Yet, as has been briefly discussed here, a closer scrutiny of the architecture of Caṇḍi Arjuna reveals a combination of several disparate architectural features—some that correspond to the northern Indian tradition and others to the southern Indian. Several of these, in fact, appear to stem from earlier (prior to the seventh century CE) prototypes of what later came to be distinguished as early medieval northern and southern Indian temple forms. By the late seventh century in Central Java, the specific forms and shapes of some of the architectural mouldings—such as the corner aediculae and the *stūpī*-finial of Caṇḍi Arjuna—reveal a distinctive Javanese character. The formality in structure and logic of Caṇḍi Arjuna certainly reveals Indian influence, but it also indicates processes of localiza-

---

[11] This shall be deliberated upon in the section on 'The Journey of an Architectural Motif' in the latter part of this chapter.

Fig. 19.5 Arjuna Ratha, Mamallapuram, Tamil Nadu, India. Source: Author

tion that had begun to mature into a distinctive architectural language by this time. The missing links need to be more thoroughly investigated in the surviving architectures of the pre-seventh-century CE period.

This pre-seventh-century time-frame, however, is a period from which we have limited surviving examples. Prior to the fourth century CE, apart from the excavated rock-cut caves and the *stūpa*-complexes, the medium of construction, even in India at that time, was largely wood and bricks. What is available in fair measure are the early Indian architectural forms carved in relief sculpture on the *stūpa, toraṇa* and *vedikā* remains from several northern (Bharhut, Sanchi, Mathura) and southern Indian (Amaravati, Nagarjunakonda, Ghantashala, Kanaganahalli) sites.[12] Next in time are the surviving stone (and a few brick) remains of temples built during roughly the fourth to seventh century CE, notably those built during the period of Gupta, Maitraka and Saindhava rule.[13] Further research on the architectural forms prevalent in India during this period is sure to throw new light on the specific nature of architectural dialogue between ancient India and Southeast Asia.

In the case of Southeast Asia, the possibility of arriving at an understanding of earlier architectural forms, that is those built prior to the seventh century CE, is even more remote. The evidence is thus far limited to a few surviving architectural fragments and some important clues that can be gathered from archaeological excavations and inscriptional records.[14] These findings reveal the use of wood, brick, and tile in the making of religious structures. From the seventh century CE, apart from the surviving temple and *stūpa* remains, we also have the representation of architectural forms in relief sculpture. Take, for example, the so-called 'flying palaces' carved on the exterior walls of the brick temples at Sambor-Prei-Kuk (Fig. 19.6). These appear to be representations of earlier building traditions in wood and perhaps also brick.

There is also clear evidence of a rich, intra-Southeast Asian architectural dialogue during this period: the Javanese, the Khmer and the Cham architects and sculptors were also drawing architectural ideas, motifs and forms liberally from each other. The affinities between the architectural forms and motifs of seventh–eighth-century Campā and Cambodia are based on their geographical proximity, a natural circumstance which was further bolstered by marital links between their elites: the Khmer king Īśānavarman and King Prakāśadharman Vikrāntavarman of Campā, who ruled Mỹ Sơn during the second half of the seventh century CE, were related, for example.[15] Links via sea routes with Java are also recorded in the epigraphic

---

[12] A careful analysis of these early Indian architectural types has been made by Ananda K. Coomaraswamy (1992). See also *EITA* II.1: 3–17.

[13] The architectonics of these temples have been discussed most incisively in *EITA* II.1: 19–57, 167–218.

[14] See, for example, the discussion of archaeological findings from Vietnam in Nguyen et al. (2006).

[15] For details, see a discussion on the genealogy of the Campā king, Prakāśadharman Vikrāntavarman in Goodall and Griffiths (2013).

Fig. 19.6 'Flying Palace' on the exterior wall of an octagonal brick temple in the Southern group at Sambor Prei Kuk, Cambodia. Source: Author

corpus. This suggests an intense criss-cross of architectural ideas and forms, and circuitous routes of interface of Southeast Asian with Indian modes and systems of architectural knowledge.

The remaining part of this chapter is devoted to two related aspects that further explicate the ways in which architectural knowledge was transmitted and transformed across India and Southeast Asia. The first of these discusses the shared conceptual underpinnings of some ancient Indian and Southeast

Asian religious structures and the distinctive local element in the translation of these concepts into material manifestations. The second aspect focuses on a shared architectural motif—the *toraṇa*—to highlight processes of selective appropriation and transformation of architectural ideas and motifs in their long and circuitous journey across India and Southeast Asia.

MERU: MOUNTAIN AND MONUMENT

The pervasive concept of 'Meru' or 'Sumeru' and its representation in Indian and Southeast Asian architecture offers an interesting case in point.[16] The symbolism of the mountain of the gods is also known from other cultures such as the Mesopotamian and the Greek. As the writings of Paul Mus (1935), H.G. Quaritch Wales (1953) and F.D.K. Bosch (1960) have shown us, these parallels are important and may reflect earlier connections. Yet, as Ian Mabbett (1983) has convincingly argued, the symbolic content of Meru as a cosmic organizing principle in Indian thought, religions and art is distinct from that of the Mesopotamian or Greek. The motif of Meru as the mountain of gods at the centre of the universe, with its summit being the highest point on earth, is a well-established one not only in Indian cosmography but also as a symbol of Hindu, Buddhist and Jaina cosmology.

Purāṇic literature abounds in descriptive references to the Meru—as the world axis, as the central mountain with four buttress mountains; the navel of the universe encircled by the concentric rings of land and seas (*sapta-saindhavaḥ*); the mountain upon whose summit is the city of gods and beneath which are the netherworlds of demons or *asuras*; the governing principle for the movement of heavenly bodies; and the orienting principle for the directions represented by *dikpālas* or divinities of the directions (Mabbett 1983). In Buddhism too, the concept of the Meru integrates the idea of a vertical spiritual ascent through stages across the worlds of desire (*kāmaloka*), form (*rūpaloka*) and formlessness (*arūpaloka*) (Huntington 2000).

These conceptual underpinnings of the Meru translate into the literature, architecture and epigraphy of South and Southeast Asia. The architectonics and iconography of the Meru signify many levels of meaning—metaphysical, religious and political. The realm of the gods in heaven finds a parallel in the realm of kings who are compared with gods on earth. In poetry too, as in the *Raghuvaṁśa* of Kalidasa, the poet speaks eloquently

[16] See, Vatsyayan (2015).

about kings descended from Raghu, who held sway over the entire earth bounded by oceans (*āsamudrakṣitīśānām*); whose chariots ran unhindered unto the gates of heaven (*ānākarathavartmanām*); who were at the highest point of the earth, being world conquerors and comparable to Meru (*sthitaḥ sarvonnatenorvīṃ krāntvā merurivātmanā*).[17] As is Meru, so is the king: He is unshakeable, of unsurpassable strength, all-transcending lustre and unparalleled stature (*sarvātiriktasāreṇa sarvatejobhibhāvinā*); as *Cakravartin* ruler, he sets the wheel of law in motion. The medieval Indian architectural treatise, the *Samarāṅgaṇasūtradhāra*, mentions that the Meru-prāsāda should be built by a *kṣatrīya*; that is, one belonging to the warrior class (Mabbett 1983). Other Indian architectural treatises also speak of the Meru form of the temple as being the foremost among northern and southern temple types.

While Meru symbolism pervades South and Southeast Asian architecture, one would not hesitate to say that Borobudur in Indonesia in a Buddhist context and Angkor Wat in Cambodia in a Hindu context (Fig. 19.3) are supreme architectural manifestations of the Meru concept. In ancient Cambodia, we find the most magnificent temple-mountains in the image of Meru, on stepped terraces with the abode of god on its summit, and with moats, causeways, barays and dykes around the pyramid-mountain in the image of the continents and seas encircling it. The system of barays and dykes are also believed to have served the important function of channelizing water for irrigation. The Indrataṭāka in Hariharālaya (present-day Rouloh), for example, is among the earlier barays built by the Khmer king Indravarman in the latter part of the ninth century. As the state temples of successive Cambodian kings, the temple-mountains of the Bakong, Bakheng, Koh Ker, Baphuon and Angkor Wat served as ritual centres of the successive capital cities of the kingdom.[18]

The Chinese designation for ancient Cambodia was Funan, a term which the Chinese transliterated as *b'iu-nam*, from *b'nam* or *v'nam*, in modern Khmer *phnom* or *bhnam*, meaning mountain (Coedes 1968: 36; Jessup 1997). Kings were called *kurung bnam* (Sanskrit, Sailaraja), meaning 'king of the mountains'. According to Coedes (1968: 51), who quotes the *History of the Southern Qi*, the Chinese also referred to a sacred mountain in the centre of Funan on which Maheśvara was believed to have

---

[17] The complete text and translations of the verses quoted in this paragraph are given in Devadhar 1993 [1984].

[18] For a lucid survey of the development of Cambodian temple-mountains see Jessup (1997) and Zéphir (1994).

descended. Kurung-bnam in Sanskrit is '*śailarāja*'. The site of the Vat Phu temple in Laos has been identified as Liṅgaparvata (Ling-kia-p'o-p'o in the Chinese records of the Sui dynasty before the year 589), with Śiva-Bhadeśvara as the spirit of the mountain (Bhattacharya 1961).

Meru also finds reference in Cambodian epigraphy: King Udayadityavarman II found it appropriate to have a Meru in the centre of his capital because he was aware that Meru was at the centre of the universe (Mabbett 1983). The iconography of the Cambodian temple-mountains reveals a coming together of the religious, political and economic aspects of ancient Cambodian society. Cambodian artistic genius localizes the Meru symbolism of India within its own belief in the supernatural powers of the mountain, with rituals of kingship and its concerns for water resource management. The mountain as the abode of gods and its connections with *kuruṅg bnam* or the king of the mountains takes the form of the grand temple-mountains of Cambodia. In the process, visualizations of the Meru of Indian textual discourse assumes forms that have no close parallels on Indian soil.

Localization in this case has entailed the appropriation of a concept which took unprecedented forms to serve new contexts and perceptions. Cambodian temple-mountains clearly reveal that the nature of influence in art was not necessarily always based on direct visual prototypes which were replicated in a localized idiom or style. Despite a known shared basis for temple forms in ancient India and Cambodia, the transmission of influence in this case cannot be classified as a formal correspondence. Rather, it reveals transference of an idea or text—a 'mental' image, which journeys across. When translated to materiality, it results in the composition and formalization of a new type of monumental architecture.

The Journey of an Architectural Motif

A persistent architectural motif in ancient and medieval South and Southeast Asian architecture is the *toraṇa*, or the 'festooned archway or entryway' found in association with different types of religious as well as secular structures.[19] During the long course of its journey, one witnesses several visual incarnations of this motif in consonance with changing contexts. Unlike pillars, walls or ceilings, the *toraṇa* does not serve a struc-

---

[19] A detailed discussion of the *toraṇa* and its architectural journey across India and Southeast Asia is to be found in Dhar (2010).

tural or load-bearing function. The rationale for its persistent presence rests in the realm of the aesthetic, symbolic, honorific, didactic and other such purposes. *Toraṇas* are often embellished with other symbolic, hybrid or fantastic motifs such as the *kīrttimukha* (leonine 'face of glory') and *makaras* (imaginary hybrid crocodilian creatures); *garuḍa* (mythical bird) and *nāgas* (serpents); *vyālas* (composite leonine animal), *gajavyālas* (hybrid elephant-lion creature) and *kinnaras* (celestial, hybrid man-bird musician). At times, as was quite often the case during the high medieval period in India, the symbolic potency of such motifs on the *toraṇa* receded and gave way to abstract ornamental patterns. In a different spatio-temporal context, for example, in the different Southeast Asian regions, from about the seventh century onwards, the *toraṇas* took on newer forms and the motifs found on them were selectively assimilated and localized (Dhar 2010: 213–272).

On the Central Javanese *caṇḍis*, for example, the *kāla-makara-toraṇa* became the single most preferred variant (Fig. 19.7).[20] Its crowning motif is called the *kālamukha* or *banaspati*, which is a potent and prominent motif in Javanese art and has strong affinities with the *kīrttimukha* in Indian art (Dhar 2007). On Indian *toraṇas*, the *kīrttimukha*, who signifies 'the devourer', serves an apotropaic function. Though affiliated in form and meaning to the *kīrttimukha* on Indian *toraṇas*, the *kāla-mukha* registers a much stronger presence and differs in terms of its larger proportions and greater status on Javanese *caṇḍis*. Although individual motifs and patterns seen on Javanese *kāla-makara-toraṇas* echo some eastern and southern Indian motifs, the visual details suggest only sporadic borrowings and subsequent assimilations with the local milieu and predilections. The totality of the *kāla-makara-toraṇa* is an essentially Javanese artistic expression.

The most popular *toraṇas* encountered in Java are those framing the entrances (*dvāra-toraṇas*) and wall-niches (*kuḍya-toraṇas*). The earliest are noticed on the *caṇḍis* at Dieng Plateau. These *toraṇas* resemble the *prabhāvalīs* (aureoles) circumscribing bronze images of deities—from Java as well as from eastern and southern India. The Javanese *kāla-makara-toraṇas* which framed the wall-niches also served as aureoles surrounding the images of deities that were housed in the niches. Even the outward-facing *makaras* are in common with some of the bronze *prabhāvalīs*, such

---

[20] For a discussion of the form and significance of *kāla-makara-toraṇas on* Javanese *caṇḍis* see Dhar (2007).

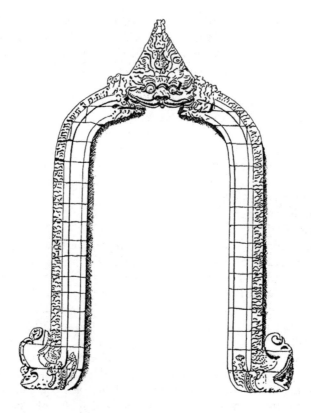

Fig. 19.7 Drawing of *kāla-makara-toraṇa*, Borobudur, Central Java. Source: Author

as the one encompassing Bodhisattva Avalokiteśvara from Sragen in Central Java (Fig. 19.8). When the *kāla-makara-toraṇa*s were placed at entrance doorways, they, in a sense, served as an aureole or halo for the image of the deity in the sanctum, which could be seen through the doorway. Apart from those seen on eastern and southern Indian as well as Javanese bronzes, *prabhāvalī-toraṇa*s are also often noticed on eastern Indian stone sculpture of the Pala-Sena period. Similar comparisons can be made with representations of *toraṇa*s in illustrated manuscripts and those found on Central Javanese monuments—notably Candi Borobudur. Chronologically, of course, we do not have illustrated manuscript representations dating from the time of Borobudur (Dhar 2010: 213–272).

Fig. 19.8 Drawing of *prabhāvalī-toraṇa* framing a bronze image of Bodhisattva Avalokiteśvara from Sragen in Central Java. Source: Author

Some important issues emerge from this brief discussion on *toraṇa*s. It is the *prabhāvalī*s of the portable bronze icons and manuscript illustrations rather than the static architectural forms which seem to have played a greater role in influencing the *toraṇa* forms seen on the doorways and walls of

Javanese *caṇḍi*s. Furthermore, from the range of early *toraṇa* forms it is only the type with the combination of *kālamukha* and *makara* forms that gains currency in Javanese architecture. The significance of the *banaspati* or *kālamukha* in Indonesia seems to be greater than what is seen in India or other parts of Southeast Asia. And finally, the patterns and imagery seen on Javanese *toraṇa*s suggest sporadic borrowings of ideas and motifs, and not complete forms. These shared ideas and motifs may be likened to alphabets and phrases, which led to the creation of a distinctively new language of the *toraṇa* as a symbolic and ornamental motif in Java.

Conclusion

This chapter has drawn attention to several key issues in the transference and translation of architectural ideas, motifs and forms across cultural and political boundaries in the ancient Indian and Southeast Asian regions. The few case studies relating to the transmission of architectural knowledge systems between early India and Southeast Asia discussed here yield a range of meanings in which aesthetic, religious, political and socio-economic aspects are inextricably intertwined. Doubtless, the staggering range of artistic expressions and their varied manifestations are neither possible to comprehensively represent, nor are they likely to subscribe to any overarching theoretical framework. Yet the concerns raised and the representative monuments, motifs and myths taken up for discussion here strongly suggest the necessity to engage with key issues in the interpretation of cultural encounters between pre-modern South and Southeast Asian architectural forms and practices.

A comparative analysis of select architectural types from ancient India, Vietnam, Cambodia and Indonesia indicates the importance of examining the processes of sharing and transference of architectural concepts and forms that appear to have transpired during the period prior to the seventh century CE. Of special importance is the need for a closer investigation of material that could shed greater light on the largely missing links in wood and brick. It is also equally necessary to investigate more closely the intra-Southeast Asian exchanges and the filter of intermediate cultures in the dynamics of cross-cultural architectural exchange. The role of portable architectural models in the transmission of architectural ideas and forms is another important aspect that needs further attention.

Localization of architectural knowledge entailed a selective appropriation and adaptation of forms based on local predilections and needs. As the translation of the Meru concept aptly illustrates, at times shared religious and philosophical concepts created distinct architectural imagery in the different zones of contact. In such cases, the creation of architectural forms proceeded from the transmission of ideas/texts which were translated into the shape of newer imageries and forms. At other times, as in the case of Javanese *caṇḍis*, visual correspondences between Indian and Southeast Asian buildings suggest more direct transmissions and localization processes from an earlier period.

There is much that remains enigmatic. Fresh research is unfolding newer horizons and, more than ever before, it is now gradually becoming possible to track at least some routes and channels of contact with greater precision. This opens up newer frontiers of research and calls for greater collaboration between the archaeologist and the art historian to interpret the newly emerging evidence. Equally crucial and potentially rewarding is the task of fine-tuning the methods and frameworks employed for interpreting intercultural exchange through the lens of the region's rich architectural remains from about the middle centuries of the first millennium onwards. The time is certainly ripe for meaningful collaborations between the Indian, the Cambodian, the Vietnamese, the Indonesian and other South and Southeast Asian scholars to come together and explore their connected histories, for these histories help us better comprehend the present and also perhaps will guide the South and Southeast Asian nations into shaping dialogues for future collaborations.

REFERENCES

Bhattacharya, K. 1961. *Les Religions brahmaniques dans l'ancien Cambodge, d'apres l'epigraphie et l'iconographie*. Paris: EFEO 49.

Bosch, F.D.K. 1960. *The Golden Germ: An Introduction to Indian Symbolism*. The Hague, Netherlands: Mouton & Co.

Coedes, G. 1968, *The Indianized States of Southeast Asia*, ed. WF Vella, Trans. S. Cowing, Hawaii.

Coomaraswamy, Ananda K. 1992. *Essays in Early Indian Architecture*, edited by Michael W. Meister. New Delhi: Indira Gandhi National Centre for the Arts.

Datta, Sambit, and David Benyon. 2014. *Digital Archetypes: Adaptations of Early Architecture in South and Southeast Asia*. England: Ashgate.

Devadhar, C.R., ed. and trans. 1993 [1984]. *Works of Kālidāsa*, vol. II (Poetry), Delhi: Motilal Banarasidass.

Dhar, Parul Pandya. 2007. *Kāla-makara-toraṇas*: Javanese expressions of a Shared Motif. In *Sacred Landscapes in Asia: Shared Traditions, Multiple Histories*, edited by Himanshu Prabha Ray, 257–281. New Delhi: IIC Asia Project and Manohar.

———. 2010. *The Toraṇa in Indian and Southeast Asian Architecture*. Delhi: D.K. Printworld.

———. 2016. "The Early Temples of Campā: Shaping an Architectural Language". In *Temple Architecture and Imagery of South and Southeast Asia. Prāsādanidhi: Papers Presented to Professor M.A. Dhaky*, edited by Parul Pandya Dhar and Gerd J.R. Mevissen, 30–51. Delhi: Aryan Books International.

EITA I.2, 1 and 2. 1986. *Encyclopaedia of Indian Temple Architecture*, vol. I, part 2 (text and plates), *South India, Upper Drāviḍadēśa, Early Phase, A.D. 550–1075*, edited by Michael W. Meister and M.A. Dhaky. New Delhi: American Institute of Indian Studies and Oxford University Press.

EITA II.1, 1 and 2. 1988. *Encyclopaedia of Indian Temple Architecture*, vol. II, part 1 (text and plates), *North India: Foundations of North Indian Style, c. 250 B.C.-A.D. 1100*, edited by Michael W. Meister, M.A. Dhaky, and Krishna Deva. Princeton: Princeton University Press and New Delhi: American Institute of Indian Studies.

Études épigraphiques sur le pays Cham [EEPC]. 1995. de Louis Finot, Edouard Huber, George Coedes et Paul Mus; reunies par Claude Jacques (Reimpression de L'Ecole Francaise d'Extreme-Orient No. 7). Paris: École Français d'Extrême-Orient.

Goodall, Dominic and Arlo Griffiths. 2013. 'Études du Corpus des inscriptions du Campā. V. The Short Foundation Inscriptions of Prakāśadharman-Vikrāntavarman, King of Campā', *Indo-Iranian Journal* 56: 419–440.

Hardy, Adam. 2016. "Brick Infill: Little Known Brick Temples of the Pratīhāra period." In *Temple Architecture and Imagery in South and Southeast Asia. Prāsādanidhi: Papers Presented to Professor M.A. Dhaky*, edited by Parul Pandya Dhar and Gerd J.R. Mevissen, 52–66. Delhi: Aryan Books International.

Hardy, Andrew, Mauro Cucarzi and Patrizia Zolese, eds. 2009. *Champa and the Archaeology of Mỹ Sơn (Vietnam)*. Singapore: NUS Press.

Huntington, John, 2000. "Mount Meru". *Encyclopaedia of Monasticism, vol. 2*, edited by William M. Johnston, 895–901. Chicago and London: Fitzroy Dearborn Publishers.

Jessup, Helen Ibbitson. 1997. Temple-mountains and the Devaraja-cult. In *Sculpture of Angkor and Ancient Cambodia, Millennium of Glory*, edited by Helen Ibbitson Jessup and Thierry Zéphir, 101–116. Washington and Paris: Thames and Hudson.

Mabbett, Ian. 1983. "The Symbolism of Mount Meru", *History of Religions* 23, 1: 64–83.

Majumdar, R.C. 1927. *Ancient Indian Colonies in the Far East, Vol. I: Campā* (Greater India Society Publication No. 1). Lahore: The Punjab Sanskrit Book Depot.

Manguin, Pierre-Yves, A. Mani, and Geoff Wade, eds. 2011. *Early Interactions between South and Southeast Asia: Reflections on Cross-Cultural Exchange.* Singapore: Institute of Southeast Asian Studies and India: Manohar.

Mus, Paul. 1935. *Barabudur.* Arma Artis.

Nguyen, Kim Dung, Ian C. Glover, and Mariko Yamagata. 2006. "Excavations at Trà Kiệu and Go Cam, Quang Nam Province, Central Vietnam." In *Uncovering Southeast Asia's Past,* edited by Elizabeth A. Bacus, Ian C. Glover and Vincent C. Piggot, 216–31. Singapore: NUS Press.

Parmentier, Henri. 1904. "Les monuments du cirque de Mï-Son." *Bulletin de l'Ecole française d'Extrême-Orient* 4: 805–896.

———. 1909. *Inventaire Descriptif Des Monuments Cams De L'Annam, Tome Premier: Description des Monuments* (Text and Plates). Paris: Imprimerie Nationale, Ernest Leroux.

———. 1918. *Inventaire Descriptif Des Monuments Cams De L'Annam, Tome II Etude De L'Art Cham* (Text and Plates). Paris: Editions Ernest Leroux.

Wales, H.G. Quaritch. 1953. *The Mountain of God. A Study in Early Religion and Kingship.* London.

Vatsyayan, Kapila. 2015. "Mountain, Myth, Monument" In *Metaphors of the Indian Arts and Other Essays.* Delhi: D.K. Printworld.

Zéphir, Thierry. 1994. "Khmer Art". In *Art of Southeast Asia* by Maud Girard-Geslan, Marijke J. Klokke, Albert Le Bonheur, Donald M. Stadner, Valérie Zaleski, and Thierry Zéphir. New York: Harry N. Abrams.

Appendix A: Programme of the ASEAN–India Civilizational Links Conference, 23–24 July 2015

© The Author(s) 2018
S. Saran (ed.), *Cultural and Civilisational Links between India and Southeast Asia*, https://doi.org/10.1007/978-981-10-7317-5

Agenda

Day I: 23 July2015	
08.30–09.00	Registration
09.00–10.00	Inaugural Session
	Welcome Address by Prof. Sachin Chaturvedi, Director General, RIS Opening Address by Amb. Shyam Saran, Chairman, RIS Keynote Address by Amb. Anil Wadhwa, Secretary (East), Ministry of External Affairs (MEA), Government of India Inaugural Address by Prof. Lokesh Chandra, President, Indian Council for Cultural Relations (ICCR), New Delhi Vote of Thanks by Prof. Prabir De, Coordinator, ASEAN-India Centre (AIC)
10.00–10.30	Tea/Coffee
10.30–12.30	Session I: Trade and Maritime Links between South and Southeast Asia
	Chair: Dr. Amara Srisuchat Speakers
10.30–10.50	Prof. I Wayan Ardika Early Contacts between India and Bali
10.50–11.10	Dr. Himanshu Prabha Ray Translocality and Mobility across the Bay of Bengal: Nagapattinam in Context
11.10–11.30	Dr. Lotika Varadarajan Indian Patterned Cotton Textiles and Trade with East and Southeast Asia
11.30–12.30	Discussion
12.30–13.30	Lunch
13.30–15.00	Session II: Continuities and Change
	Chair: Amb. Vinod Khanna Speakers
13.30–13.50	Dr. Amara Srisuchat Indigenous Thought on Indian Traditions in Thailand
13.50–14.10	Dr. Joefe B. Santarita Panyupayana: Pre-Islamic Philippines as a Hindu Polity?
14.10–14.30	Dr. Le Thi Lien Indian-Southeast Asian Contacts and Cultural Exchanges: Evidence from Vietnam at One Time
14.30–15.00	Discussion
15.00–15.15	Tea/Coffee
15.15–17.00	Session III: Representations of Religions and Rituals
	Chair: Prof. Sachchidanand Sahai Speakers

APPENDIX A: PROGRAMME OF THE ASEAN–INDIA CIVILIZATIONAL LINKS... 349

15.15–15.35	Dr. Andrea Acri From Śivaśāsana to Agama Hindu Bali: Tracing the Indic Roots of Modern Balinese Hinduism
15.35–15.55	Prof. Madhu Khanna Power, Prestige and Possession: Interwoven Legacies of Ida Pedandas "Priestesses" in Balinese Hinduism
15.55–16.15	Dr. Jasleen Dhamija The Warp and Weft that Linked the World
16.15–17.00	Discussion
19.00	Cultural Programme: Ms. Madhavi Mudgal and Group
20.00	Dinner (Hosted by Secretary (East), MEA) (By invitation)
Day II: 24 July 2015	
09.00–09.30	Special Address by Prof. Lokesh Chandra, President, ICCR, New Delhi
09.30–11.30	Session IV: Textual Traditions and Transmissions
	Chair: Dr. Andrea Acri Speakers
09.30–09.50	Dr. Sudha Gopalakrishnan Transmission of Textual Traditions in South and Southeast Asia: A View from India
09.50–10.10	Dr. Thomas M. Hunter The Bhagavad-Gītā Sections of the Old Javanese *Bhīṣmaparwa*: Text Building and the Formation of the State in Premodern Indonesia
10.10–10.25	Tea/Coffee
10.25–11.30	Session IV Continued...
10.25–10.45	Dr. Ding Choo Ming Reworking of Indian Epics in the Hands of Malay and Javanese Authors in the Past
10.45–11.05	Ms. Malini Saran and Amb. Vinod Khanna Camille Bulcke's *Ramakatha-Utpatti aur Vikas*: an Important Reference Work for Scholars in the Field of Ramayana Studies
11.05–11.30	Discussion
11.30–13.00	**Session V: Sacred Geographies and Localisations of Beliefs**
	Chair: Prof. Himanshu Prabha Ray Speakers
11.30–11.50	Dr. Sachchidanand Sahai Archaeology as Soft Power or Power of Plurality in ASEAN-India Cultural Contexts
11.50–12.10	Dr. John Guy Siva's Land: Understanding the Religious Landscape in Early Southeast Asia

12.10–12.30	Prof. Popo Danes Ancient Architectural Influences between Bali and Majapahit
12.30–13.00	Discussion
13.00–14.00	Lunch
14.00–15.00	Session VI: Evolving Artistic Expressions: From Tradition to Modernity
	Chair: Dr. Sudha Gopalakrishnan Speakers
14.00–14.20	Dr. Padma Subramanyam *Natyashastra*ic Links in Indonesia, Thailand and Cambodia
14.20–14.40	Datuk Ramli Ibrahim Framing Cultural Connections
14.40–15.00	Ms. Pallavi Aiyar Bollywood and Bhima: Historical Resonance and Contemporary Appeal in India-Indonesia Cultural Ties
15.00–15.15	Tea/Coffee
15.15–16.15	Session VII: Writing Our Own Histories: Changing Methodologies
	Chair: Prof. Ding Choo Ming Speakers
15.15–15.35	Prof. Farish Ahmad-Noor An Unwilling Divorce: Colonial-Era Epistemology and the Division of South and Southeast Asia
15.35–15.55	Dr. Parul Pandya Dhar Monuments, Motifs, Myths: Architecture and Its Transformations in India and Southeast Asia
15.55–16.15	Discussion
16.15–16.35	Audio-Visual Presentation on *The Golden Land* by Mr. Vikram Lall
16.35–17.00	Discussion
17.00–17.15	Tea/Coffee
17.15–17.45	Valedictory Address by Dr. Kapila Vatsyayan, Chairperson, IIC-Asia Project
17.45–18.15	Concluding Session: 'Way Forward'
	Chair: Amb. Shyam Saran, Chairman, RIS Vote of Thanks by Prof. Prabir De, Coordinator, AIC
19.30	Dinner (Hosted By Chairman, RIS) (By Invitation)

Appendix B: Keynote Address by Ambassador Anil Wadhwa, Secretary (East), Ministry of External Affairs at the International Conference on 'ASEAN–India Cultural Links: Historical and Contemporary Dimensions' Held at New Delhi on 23 July 2015

Prof. Lokesh Chandra, President ICCR;
Ambassador Shyam Saran, Chairman, RIS;
Prof. Sachin Chaturvedi, DG, RIS;
Dr Prabir De, Coordinator, ASEAN-India Centre;
Distinguished Speakers;

Excellencies;

Ladies and Gentlemen;

1. May I, to begin with, extend a warm welcome to all the eminent speakers who have congregated here today from various parts of Southeast Asia and India for this conference. Some have even come from as far afield as North America! A special welcome also to the galaxy of distinguished observers, ASEAN and other ambassadors in New Delhi, as well as stakeholders involved in various capacities in sustaining and deepening the ASEAN–India relationship.
2. The destinies of Southeast Asia and India have been linked, almost inextricably, for the past two millennia. As the two sides work to bolster their relationship, especially against the backdrop of India's renewed commitment to ASEAN with its action-driven and result-oriented 'Act East Policy', we also wish to concurrently stimulate

intellectual exchange on the historical and contemporary sociocultural linkages that bind us, enabling us to acquire a better understanding of our shared heritage and histories. We recognize that political security and economic cooperation between India and ASEAN must go hand in hand with better understanding between our peoples and deeper integration of our societies.

3. Evidence of the earliest contacts between India and its Southeast Asian neighbours can be traced as far back as the first century CE. Excavations of the Pyu settlements in present-day Myanmar show evidence of the earliest Southeast Asian contacts with India, and one of the sites is called Beikthano, meaning the 'City of Vishnu'. Indian influence is evident in Pyu architecture, coinage, statues of Hindu deities and the Buddha, and other early forms of epigraphy. Pyu coins have been unearthed as far as the Mekong Delta, indicating that trade and culture followed the same route.

4. Besides the famed temples of Cambodia like Angkor Wat and Ta Prohm with distinct Indian connections and influences, another group of sites scattered through central Thailand called Dvaravati, associated with the Mon inhabitants, which flourished from the seventh century CE to the end of the first millennium, also show heavy influence of Indian culture, especially Buddhist influence, in addition to that of Vaishnavite and Shaivaite traditions. The Kingdoms of Cham, which were the southern neighbours of Vietnam, also demonstrated extensive influence of Indian culture, with the famous area of 'My Son' having a complex of temples dedicated to Shiva.

5. The Government of India is today actively involved, along with its ASEAN partners, in efforts to preserve, protect and restore many of these symbols and structures that represent the civilizational bonds between ASEAN and India.

6. In addition to the earliest cultural contacts between our regions, evidence of extensive and dynamic trade between India and Southeast Asia in subsequent centuries has also been found. Under the Gupta Dynasty, which flourished from fourth to sixth century CE, trade links with Kedah on the Malay Peninsula and sea links with the coasts of Vietnam and Thailand were well established. Trade also flourished under the Chola Empire in the ninth century CE, especially between Tamil Nadu and Myanmar.

7. Commerce primarily happened via the seas with the ancient port of Tamralipti at the mouth of the Ganges being one of the earliest

points of embarkation. From there, ships sailed across to the Malay Peninsula, either along the coast of Bengal and Myanmar or through the Bay of Bengal. Later routes diversified, for example, from Tamralipti in Odisha to Sri Lanka and the Nicobar Islands, which would then either go on through the Sunda Straits or the Straits of Malacca. Not only were the trade networks vast but importantly, commerce and exchange was a two-way process, with both Indians and Southeast Asians playing an active role in it.

8. Many centuries have passed since the first signs of the budding commercial relationship between India and Southeast Asia, and while the exchanges have waxed and waned over the centuries, trade between India and Southeast Asia remains an important aspect of our engagement in the twenty-first century, with ASEAN being India's fourth largest trading partner today.

9. Our ancient interactions demonstrate Southeast Asia's widespread religious and political affinities with the Indian sub-continent. Scholars have observed that the Gupta dynasty provided an attractive coherent model of political, social and religious integration for rulers of Southeast Asia, and its success was emulated in Southeast Asia, where Indian constructs such as iconography, the Sanskrit language and religious practices were utilized, often for political ends. Importantly, these constructs spread, not through conquest but essentially through non-political agents such as merchants and religious men, and were an indicator of the 'soft power' that India enjoyed in its extended neighbourhood.

10. Inscriptions reflecting Indian linguistic influence on the kingdoms of Southeast Asia are also present from Vietnam to Indonesia. In the Khorat Plateau of Thailand, there are Sanskrit inscriptions from the sixth century CE. Inscriptions from the same time period are also found in Cambodia where Sanskrit was combined with archaic Khmer, as well as along the coast of Vietnam on the Truong Sane range. Meanwhile, the oldest Sanskrit inscription from Java is estimated to be from the fifth century CE.

11. The adoption of Buddhist architectural styles from southeast India also began around the same time. Many Indian kingdoms sent monks to spread Buddhism in the region. The most famous amongst these was Emperor Ashoka who sent Buddhist emissaries to Myanmar, Thailand, Cambodia, Vietnam as well as the Malay Peninsula. The religious links took with them linguistic, architec-

tural and literary influences. Moreover, the spread of Buddhism to Southeast Asia went beyond the linear path. Contrary to what is traditionally traced from India towards the East, Buddhism instead, once transmitted from India to the East, was localized, recreated and diffused again, through different parts of Asia, including India.

12. With the spread of Hinduism and Buddhism also came the assimilation of Indian mythology and folklore into local mythology of the Southeast Asian region. Even though Hinduism did not take root as a major religion, Hindu texts became part of the historical-cultural DNA of the people across Southeast Asia. The Thai Epic Ramakien is based on the Ramayana, and the city of Ayotthaya was named after Ayodhya. In Lao PDR, the popular version of the Ramayana is called Pha Lak Pha Lam, whilst in the Philippines the folk narrative holds much resemblance to the Ramayana. An adaptation of the Ramayana called the Yama Zatddaw was also introduced as an oral tradition in Myanmar. In Indonesia, the Ramayana is called the Kakawin Ramayana, whilst the Malay version is called the Ramayana Hikayat Seri Rama.

13. Cultural and intellectual exchanges and people-to-people contacts continue to be an important pillar of India–ASEAN relations today, and we aim to expand them through various initiatives, such as through the exchange of artists, students, journalists, farmers and parliamentarians, as well as a multiplicity of think tank initiatives.

14. The ancient socio-cultural relations and linkages have also found contemporary expression in the form of the Mekong Ganga Cooperation, a modern grouping aimed at reviving cooperation between the peoples of the Mekong and Ganga river basins in the fields of tourism, education, culture and people-to-people contacts. An MGC Museum of Asian Textiles has been inaugurated in Siem Reap, Cambodia, last year, not far from the famous Angkor Wat, showcasing affinities in our weaving and textiles.

15. Another major project underway is the reestablishment of the Nalanda University, once a world-renowned knowledge hub where scholars from around the world, including Southeast Asia and India, exchanged knowledge and ideas. We are working to create a similar world class university in the twenty-first century, with the support of our East Asian partners, and have offered scholarships to students from CLMV countries to study there.

16. Connectivity is key to facilitating socio-cultural exchanges and an important priority that we are working on. India shares both a land and maritime boundary with ASEAN. The linkages between ASEAN and India's northeastern states and communities are not just of close geographical proximity but of blood relations. The Tai race from Thailand has its descendants, the Ahoms, living in the northeastern state of Assam. The Khamtis who are descendants of the Tai from Thailand and Myanmar are also found in both Assam and Arunachal Pradesh. Meanwhile, the Khasis in Meghalaya are believed to have ancestral links to Thailand. As connectivity expands, so will the people-to-people exchanges along the border.

17. Moreover, many Indians emigrated to Southeast Asia in the eighteenth and nineteenth centuries, with the British colonial rulers sending hundreds of thousands of Indians to work in plantations and mines in the region. Their descendants today constitute a vibrant community of Indian origin people, contributing actively to their respective countries of adoption. Malaysia alone has nearly 2 million persons of Indian origin, constituting the second largest Indian diaspora abroad, after the United States.

18. During the colonial period, political bonds were also forged between our leaders, who displayed a great sense of hope and unity during our common struggles for independence. For instance, Indian freedom fighters shared close relations with freedom fighters of Myanmar, and Gandhiji visited Yangon thrice, whilst Bal Gangadhar Tilak was deported to Yangon by the British for several years. The Indian National Army under the leadership of Netaji Subhash Chandra Bose recruited Indian personnel from Myanmar and Singapore during the Second World War, making Southeast Asia a theatre of the INA's struggle against British rule. Notably, the last Mughal emperor, Bahadur Shah Zafar, spent his life in exile in Myanmar and lies buried there.

19. India and ASEAN are today at the threshold of a qualitatively more substantive and reinvigorated relationship. As we work to give shape to our Plan of Action for the period 2016 to 2021, setting new goals to move the ASEAN–India Strategic Partnership forward, we not only aim to strengthen the third pillar of our engagement, that is, the socio-cultural pillar, but also wish to bring it to the forefront of our relationship.

20. This conference is a direct outcome of our Prime Minister Narendra Modi's desire to expand our civilizational links with ASEAN countries as well as to document them comprehensively. I would like to thank the ASEAN India Centre at RIS for undertaking this conference at our behest. My special thanks are due to Ambassador Shyam Saran, who already had this idea in his mind and has taken special interest in the conference and invitees. As you have been informed, the idea was born out of the recommendations of the Eminent Persons Group between India and ASEAN, of which he was the chairman. The papers presented at the conference will be published in a book which will be shared with our ASEAN partners.
21. Moreover, this is the first step in our journey to establish research partnerships between universities and academics in India and ASEAN to work on producing high-quality research papers on the entire gamut of the historical and cultural links between India and Southeast Asia. We will also hold a second conference on our historical and cultural linkages in Jakarta in the coming months to take this initiative forward.
22. I would like to conclude by thanking everyone present here for their contribution in making the ASEAN–India relationship richer, fuller and stronger.

Thank you for your attention.

Appendix C: Inaugural Address by Prof. Lokesh Chandra, President, ICCR at the International Conference on 'ASEAN–India Cultural Links: Historical and Contemporary Dimensions', Held at New Delhi on 23 July 2015

The arrival of the Princess of Ayodhya in Korea and her marriage to the Korean King Surowang has to be contextualized in the twin processes of Asian history. One is Sanskritization which includes Buddhism as cultural identity and the concept of *bhumiputra* as political sovereignty, and the other is Sinification with emphasis on assimilation and the contra-image of the barbarian. Both functioned simultaneously and in contradistinction. Every kingdom and people were wide awake to strengthen their original identity in ethnicity, language, value system and polity.

Korea was linked to China by a contiguous land route, without an intervening sea, and was ever in touch with Chinese formulations. It had a distinctive identity that was zealously guarded. So history had to take a new turn. Asoka sent his son and ministers to found the state of Khotan in Central Asia, according to the four accounts of the foundation of Khotan in Tibetan and Chinese. Conflict with the Chinese was resolved by a compromise that a local person would be king. Coexistence of Indian and Chinese in Khotan is indicated by coins from Yotqan with Chinese legends on the obverse and Prakrit in Kharosthi script on the reverse. Thus arose the concept of *bhumiputra* or sovereignty of the sons of the soil. This concept and term is a dynamic political phenomenon in Malaysia and Indonesia of today, where the non-natives are citizens but not *bhumiputra*. In Malaysia every major industrial enterprise has to be headed by a *bhumiputra*. Indian scripts were used for Central Asian languages as they could write their inflections and other grammatical categories. On the other hand, Chinese is a non-inflected language; graphically it cannot express pronunciation and hence it could not be employed to write Central Asian languages. From the very beginning Indian scripts, literature and thought gained a foothold in the kingdoms of Central Asia. Korean and Japanese accepted Chinese characters wholesale, but even they had to develop alphabets on the basis of Sanskrit sound system and symbols. It strengthened their identity and developed their languages to heights of expression and clarity.

In 111 BCE the Han state established four commanderies in four regions of Central Asia to make them its sphere of influence and to diminish the Indic hegemony in its backyard.

Buddhism had become a powerful symbol of identity around the third century BCE when the Yueh-chihs were supplying horses to Ch'ing Shih-huang-ti (r. 221–210). They brought over a hundred Buddhist sutras to his capital to emphasize that they were not 'barbarians' but had a rich literature. They Sanskritized the dynastic name Ch'ing to China (चीन), and taught Sanskrit to a Chinese prince in 1 BCE who had come as an envoy to the Yueh-chih court. The wind has ears. Koreans were close to China in geographic terms and they must have known Buddhism as a feature of contradistinctive identity.

The Korean king was naturally conscious of his contradistinctive identity vis-à-vis the Chinese. To ensure it, he sought a princess of Ayodhya, whose Ikṣvāku dynasty was the prime royal house of India. Lord Rama is its most known scion. Aśvaghoṣa begins the life of Lord Buddha or Buddha-carita by pointing out in the very first stanza that the father of Lord Buddha, Śuddhodana was a descendent of the Ikṣvāku dynasty and his might was invincible like that of the Ikṣvāku (*aikṣvāka Ikṣvāku-sama-prabhāvaḥ*). Because Lord Buddha's father and Lord Buddha himself belonged to the Ikṣvāku dynasty, it was in tune with the political perceptions of the age that the Korean king gets a queen from Ayodhya. There is constant effort in Korean annals to relate themselves to India. The Samguk-yusa says that the kings of the Silla dynasty who united the country are kṣatriyas. The Chinese pilgrim to India Yijing says that the Sanskrit name of Korea is Kukkuteśvara. Li-yen of Kucha also gives the Sanskrit name of Korea in his Chinese-Sanskrit lexicon.

Maitreya cult was practised at the Silla court by young aristocratic warriors who formed a fraternity known as the *Hwarang* 'Perfumed Followers of the Dragon Flower'. This name is an allusion to the nāgapuspa tree under which

Maitreya Bodhisattva will become a Buddha. The Hwarang had a major role in the government both during the Three Kingdoms and the Unified Silla dynasty. They were responsible for national unity. The Buddhist kingdom of Silla accomplished the unification of the Three Kingdoms and consolidated the nation state of Korea for the first time in history. Ever since, Korean Buddhism was the destiny and defence of the land. Monk Wolkwang formulated the 'Five Worldly Commandments' to form the basis of national ethos.

In 776 monk Yulsa erected a 40 ft gilt bronze Maitreya for national unity at the Popchusa monastery. In 1991, Abbot Yu dedicated a 100 ft high image of Maitreya at the same Popchusa monastery to embody the aspirations of the Korean people for national reunification. During the Eye-Opening Ceremony, three rainbows appeared in the clear sky: 'Isn't this a sign that we can even move heaven when we are truly devoted? When we build an image of Maitreya in our hearts too, all lives on earth will turn into lotus flowers, and the very world around us will become a pond of joy' (Chief Abbot Yu).

As part of their national identity the Koreans wanted to have direct relations with India and not exclusively through China. Yijing has written the lives of seven Korean monks who came to Nalanda. A Korean professor, who accompanied me to the archaeological sites in 1981, said that the Koreans went to Nalanda to compare the Chinese translations of Buddhist texts with the Sanskrit originals. Korean has grammar and Sanskrit too has inflections, while Chinese has no grammar. The Koreans could understand Sanskrit texts better because it has inflections. Monk Hyëop compared the Chinese translation of the Vimalakīrti-nirdeśa with the Sanskrit original and made many corrections in the Chinese text, which he left in Nalanda. He says: 'When we compared the Chinese texts with Sanskrit, we made many corrections.' The Vimalakīrti-nirdeśa (VN) was crucial to the importance of the laity vis-à-vis the monastic order. In East Asia, lay Buddhism and monastic Buddhism were contrasted. The monks pointed out the VN as justifying the important role of the laity in the spread of Dharma.

The Korean monk Hyecho came to India around 700 and returned to China in 727. He studied with three Indian masters Śubhākara-siṁha, Vajrabodhi and Amoghavajra in China. Amoghavajra said in his will: 'Hyecho is the second of my six living disciples.' The Korean monks could understand Sanskrit thought more clearly as their language was grammatically richer than Chinese. Hyecho translated the hymn and ritual of Thousand-bowl Mañjuśrī from Sanskrit into Chinese. Mañjuśrī was a symbol of the state in the East

Asian lands. Even Chairman Mao went to the Wu-tai-shan monastic complex for the blessings of Mañjuśrī before taking oath of office in Peking.

In 1941 my father Prof. Raghuvira brought a grammar of Korean written by a European which said that as late as the early twentieth century Korean monks spoke Sanskrit mixed with Korean at the Diamond Mountain. This mountain was dedicated to Esoteric Buddhism or Mantrayāna and its daily prayers, mandala ceremonies and *homa* rituals were conducted in Sanskrit. It had an Aśokan stupa of 84,000 bricks.

In the latter part of the seventh century Shul-ch'ong invented the Yi-do script to denote case-endings in the margin of Chinese texts. It was to aid the reader in Koreanizing the system of the Chinese sentence. At first he composed eight case-endings, that is, nominative, accusative, instrumental, dative, ablative, genitive, locative and vocative. He based them on the Sanskrit case-endings. The book *Kyun yu chun* written in 1075 CE says: 'The Yi-do resembles the Sanskrit in its inflections.' In 1446 the sage-like emperor Seijong invented a new Korean alphabet and moveable printing types. This alphabet continues to this day as the Hangul or 'Proper Writing'. Dr. Kei Won Chung in his dissertation to Princeton University says that the Korean alphabet was composed on the principles of the Sanskrit alphabet. With the new alphabet, learning became accessible to a large mass of people. The birthday of the Hangul script is celebrated in Korea on 9 October.

The last Indian ācārya to visit Korea was Chikong (Dhyānabhadra). He arrived in Korea in the 1340s and established the Juniper Rock Monastery on the pattern of the Nalanda University. Its foundations can be seen near Seoul. He wrote Sanskrit dhāraṅī-mantras on the gigantic Yonboksa Bell for the liberation and peace of the Korean people from Mongol domination. An inscription at the Juniper Rock Monastery dated 1378 records the life and work of Dhyānabhadra and informs us that the king of Kanchi was his nephew. The_ mill for making *sattu* सत्तू still lies at the site of this monastery. A restaurant called Perfume of Grasses recalls the cuisine of Ācārya Dhyānabhadra. It serves 'tea of honey-stick'. Honey-stick is liquorice मधुयष्टि (मुलेठी in hindi).

The rocks of the Juniper Rock monastery were being crushed into cement for construction. India's Ambassador Devare persuaded the Korean government to stop the destruction of this glorious seat of learning whose extensive ruins speak of the vibrant academic traditions of Korea. Built on the pattern of Nalanda it had an area of 33,000 sq m and more than 3000 monks stayed here until the beginning of the Chosun dynasty.

Muhak became a disciple of Dhyānabhadra in 1353 and he played a historic role by suggesting to the Founder King of the Chosun dynasty to move the national capital to Seoul from Kaesung. The King requested Ven Muhak to locate the precise site. The monk took a bow and arrow and said: 'Wherever the arrow falls, that will be the centre of the capital.' A pavilion in Seoul celebrates this site, which I visited in 1981.

I went to see a Zen monastery, atop a high mountain, about 300 years old. I was wearing an Indian dress, which was not comfortable for the steep climb. The monk accompanying me was· in his monastic robes. I asked him, 'From where did this dress come?' He replied, 'This is the Gandharan dress of India.'

When we reached the monastery, we were dead tired. I said 'We can take a round of the monastery before we meet the abbot.' Circumambulating

Sanskrit letters used for writing dhāraṇī-mantras in Korea

7

the monastery, I saw that every frontage of the roof had an *Om*. I asked, 'May I take one?' He said, 'No they are 300 years old. They can't go out of Korea.' I saw the abbot, had a long conversation about Son Buddhism, and, corning out, I asked, 'I would like to have a brick with *Om*.' The monk replied, 'There are monks who do calligraphy of *Om*, and of mantras in the Siddham script.' The accompanying monk took me to a fantastic calligrapher. He calligraphed *Om* about 2 metres high. The day I was to leave Korea, the mounted *Om* came to bless my journey back home. He had a chart of Siddham letters, frayed with the passing of centuries. It is reproduced on the next page. The proximity between our cultures is phenomenal. In the words of our great poet Tagore, Korea is 'The Lamp of the East'.

The journey of the Princess of Ayodhya to Korea reminds us of the political ethos that travelled from Khotan to China along with jade. The concept of the *bhumiputra*, that is territorial identity, emerged from Buddhism. The family of Lord Buddha was of Ikṣvāku lineage according to the opening stanza of Aśvaghosa. Ikṣvāku ruled Ayodhya. King Kim Surowang must have sought the hand of a princess from Ayodhya in his quest of a new and sacred order as he became the first Korean king. The rocks and ruins strewn around Kimhae have come from a foreign land and are the proud heirs of the Indic legacy of the Princess. The tombs of the King and Queen in Hoehyon-dong city are preserved as a historic site by the Government of Korea. The Princess of Ayodhya has been the sense of being of the Korean people and the presence of a profound order as she graces the flowing time mingled in things of the world.

Appendix D: Special Address by Prof. Lokesh Chandra, President, ICCR at the International Conference on 'ASEAN–India Cultural Links: Historical and Contemporary Dimensions', Held at New Delhi on 24 July 2015

Sanskritization and Sinification

Maritime trade was primarily between India and China along the coastline beginning with Kanchi, traversing the shores of Myanmar, Thailand, Malaysia, Cambodia and Champa, reaching Canton. These lands on the long journey were inhabited by tribes who had no script, no state, no agriculture and led a primitive life without fabrics, gathering food and hunting for meat. The historic evolution of language, governance, architecture, art, thought and ethical fabric of the Southeast Asian nations are an outcome of their contacts with Indians for the last 2000 years. From the absence of garb and savage qualities of tribals they came to be endowed with a high mental culture, refinement of civilization, moral responsibility for actions and sustained betterment of life in their contact and marriages with Indian immigrants who became steersmen of a unity, harmony and grandeur never before imagined by the tribal orders. From helpless creatures to agricultural welfare, from skins or leaves to woven fabrics, from huts to constructing houses, appearance of larger communities with the development of trade, system of international commerce leading to choice productions, the unique social and mental attainments gave rise to astounding states like Champa, Cambodia, Laṅkāsukha (in Malaysia), Śrīvijaya and so on. Indian princes, scholars, entrepreneurs, artisans and others developed the whole region as cultural states by the edification of all sectors of life. We shall take five of them.

1. **Social norms**: The yakṣas or nāgas (tribals) were dressed in leaves. As Indians gave them woven fabrics, they had a different self-image. Kauṇḍinya conquered the Nāgī queen of Cambodia, dressed her in a sarong, married her and a new Cambodia was born. Numerous Brahmins accompanied and followed the migrating royal princes and merchant princes. The tribals gave them their daughters who gained in elegance in Indian couture, and their feminine progeny was better equipped to bring up the future generations. In 1967 I was attending a grand ceremony at the residence of the Governor of Bali H.E. Merta. He offered me coconut water, which was really sweet and refreshing. I told him: 'It is far better than the Indian coconuts.' The Governor replied: 'We feed the newly born infants coconut water as sometimes the mothers cannot offer their milk to the new born because of petite breasts.' Marriage of the tribal women and Indian men resulted in eugenic changes, and future generations could be fed on mothers' milk. Ethnic enhancement brought about a constant social merger of the *bhumiputra* and the *kalana* (Old Javanese word for a wandering adventurer of noble birth from abroad). Indians merged themselves into the original population.

2. **Security and state**: Indians sailed with high steeds of Kambuja (Ferghana) to resist the onslaught of the tribals. The Kāraṇḍavyūha narrates that the merchant Siṁhala went to Srilanka with 500 companions and had to flee on the magic horse Balāha when attacked by the demonesses (or aboriginal women). The security role of horses can be seen in the inscription of Mūlavarman whose father was Aśvavarman. Emperor Aśoka gifted a nandyāvarta or six-storeyed palace to the king of Sri Lanka when his son Mahendra went to spread Dharma in the island. A multistoreyed palace was a symbol of the emerging imperial glory. Tribal systems became kingdoms, integrating several tribes by introducing written communications. The rise of kingdoms and nation states with specific names, like Kambujadeśa, was a political innovation leading to a higher civilization.

3. **Script**: Indians raised spoken dialects of the indigenous populations to written languages by introducing a script. Written communications became precision of administration, and large areas could

remain in contact. The outreach and precision of the new system consolidated peoples of similar identity, and gave rise to powerful states. Literature in the local language was written to convey the new values, and the life of the people was filled with the joy of the performing arts which were the 'visual dharma'.

4. **Economy**: Agriculture was introduced on a large scale to develop an economy and to raise the living standards of the people. The inscription of Mūlavarman speaks of his victories, his donations of milch cows and *jaladhenu* (water canals) for the prosperity of the kingdom. Trans-national trade was upgraded by developing ship-building technologies. Naval power was augmented by 'castled ships' which are described in the naval battles with the Chinese.

5. **Dharma** was the value system that united peoples across the long sea-line with community of sacred texts, common forms of worship, similar script systems and similar temples which were divine assurance of safe journeys in the turbulence of waters.

The sea-lanes of Southeast Asia were integrated with Dharma as the Indians merged themselves with the locals in a single generation, and awakened their dormant energy. The foundation and flourishing of Champa on the major marine trade route from Kanchi to Canton, or from the Southeast Asian isles to Canton, was part of a new historic phenomenon of the fast emergence of cultural kingdoms from tribal orders. The new paradigm was the empowerment of the dormant energy of the non-alphabetic tribes by enriching them with a writing system and thinking patterns; establishing kingdoms with a king, ministers, nobility and state functionaries; setting up palaces and temples; the rise of an intellectual class and priestly orders. This sowing of intellectual seeds in the immensity of the regions was the rise of a new order of a spiritual culture and secular civilization in Southeast Asia. The theodiversity, pluralism of lifestyles, along with an organized state, economy and strategic systems of India became the dawn of a new age in the Southeast Asian region. Indian savants, princes and merchants envisioned Suvarṇadvīpa in their quest of affluence of life. Suvarṇadvīpa was a general term for lands in Southeast Asia.

Kauṇḍinya's voyage to Cambodia, his victory over the Nāgī queen and marrying her to found the new kingdom, or the exciting find of a first-century ceramic sherd with Kharosthi characters from the coastal region of Bangkah in Bali, and other happenings evidence the role of India in continuous acculturation of the region as well as the development of trade.

The Chinese concept of 'barbarian' and sinocentrism kept them aloof. The Chinese ideograms could not put their languages into writing and linguistic distance became separative. The concept of China and the ASEAN countries being 'inclusive' is not vindicated by history, nor by their present cultural identities.

Appendix E: Valedictory Address by Dr Kapila Vatsyayan, Chairperson, IIC-Asia Project at the International Conference on 'ASEAN–India Cultural Links: Historical and Contemporary Dimensions', Held at New Delhi on 24 July 2015

Chairman of the RIS, Ambassador Shyam Saran, and distinguished delegates from different parts of Asia:

For the last two days we have been deliberating on ASEAN–India cultural links. To begin with, I think all of us present here have to thank the RIS for this initiative. As Ambassador Shyam Saran said, this conference is a follow up of a series of deliberations which took place in the meetings of the India–ASEAN Eminent Persons Group. Over these two days we have covered a vast area, not only vast geographical area, but also a vast time span, ranging from the prehistoric findings which were brought out by the eminent scholar from Bali, to modern architecture in the papers in the last session.

What does one say in a valedictory address? As they say in Hindi or in Sanskrit, this could be only an 'ashirvachan', a final blessing. However, I do not find myself competent to give such a benediction after such an engaging two-day presentation of papers and discussions. Perhaps it is not necessary for me to make the valedictory address into a rapporteur's address. Nevertheless, I have, as a silent listener registered the important submissions made by the delegates.

Let me make one or two brief remarks in terms of issues which came up repeatedly in the papers that were presented and the discussions that followed.

First and foremost is the question of chronology. Each time an issue was raised or a paper presented there was tension between those who subscribed to an arrow-time linearity and those who saw there was a multilayering of time. One of the facets of this region, called the ASEAN countries, is that no uni-dimensional linear graph could be chalked out. The debate in the first day in terms of what constitutes history, and what constitutes living or living memory, was a feature which was evident in the papers as also the discussions. So, can one really conclude that this region is marked by, negatively speaking, a lack of sense of history or, positively speaking, that it is considerably aware of the multilayering that takes place both in space and time? To mention only one paper, namely that of Himanshu Prabha Ray in respect of Nagapattinam: could one draw a pure linear graph? Yes, there is a linearity and yet there is more to it. Multilinear and multilayering are distinctive. Thus the idea of pure linear time is debatable here. We have to return, just as contrast, to what we call Western culture specially post-renaissance where we can draw linear graphs.

This brings up the question of chronologies. While chronologies can be there, chronology is not something that gives us the answer. So when we speak, I think one of the first things we have to understand is that there is an attitudinal change or distinctiveness in regard to the concept of space as also the concept of time. Space comes multilayered, so also Time is multilayered. So, unless we address the question of what I call the multivolume concept of space and time, we shall not be able to address what we consider to be the characteristics of the region. Naturally, making this statement is different from all that we understand largely from Western culture or European culture. What is the nature of this ambiguity, if we may call it, or lack of clarity, or what one has heard in the Cartesian discourse, of binary opposites?

Let me now turn to something which came up repeatedly in the discussion from different points of view, namely the textual and the oral. There was almost a running theme between the terms textual and oral and the tension between textuality and orality. One has to question here whether orality has a text or does not have a text. Orality certainly has a text, but the tension that we have is really between the oral and the written and not between the textual and the oral. This distinction should always be remembered.

The delegates will remember that the question of the written and the oral, the fixed and the fluid, was repeatedly raised in the context of the many papers presented in this conference. One could elaborate on this from different points of view and from different angles. In the Indian tradition SHRUTI is the articulated word and SMRITI the written word. So, paradoxically, SHRUTI was inviolable and unchangeable; and SMRITI was written but is subject to change, depending upon the time and the space. This has a long history on which there is a body of literature.

In the ASEAN countries the oral enunciated has been given a sacredness throughout. Sometimes it is subject to change or maybe it is not subject to change. This was evident in the brief discussion that we have had on whether manuscripts were important or not. This is an area which requires further investigation and discussion because the characteristics of this region do not place the oral and the written in a hierarchy (not to be confused between our notion of illiteracy or literacy). However, these questions have to be addressed very seriously in terms of transmission of not only knowledge but transmission of value. This is an aspect which we touched upon but it is an aspect of ASEAN cultures which requires much greater sophistication at the level of academic discourse than it has received so far.

This ambivalence that we find between establishment of a hierarchy, between the oral and the written, has to be probed further.

We had a very interesting debate regarding monuments. In this context the most outstanding example is Borobudur. It has been considered a model by scholars of eminence, such as Paul Mus, who have considered Borobudur as a plan of the altars of the vedic Yagna. So, is it the basic model of Yagna and the holding of a Yagna through monumental architecture or is it, as has been largely accepted, a Buddhist stupa? Borobudur is certainly not like the early stupas in India. It is a much more complex structure with multiple meanings, not to speak of the staggering presence of the architectural members of the monument.

What is true of Borobudur is true of many other monuments. What is Angkor Vat? Is it a shaivite temple, is it Buddhist or Vaishnavite? The answer is yes and no.

We have traced Shiva's Feet (Shiva-Pad) in the last session. Can we say Shiva's Feet, at some point, cannot be transformed into Buddha's Feet? Is it possible or is it not possible?

Of course, we also spoke about the Harihar images. The question to be asked is how a culture conceives of multivalence at the conceptual level and then of course in terms of artistic expression? This multivalence is evident not only at the level of artistic creation but penetrates into the creative psyche of the ASEAN cultures.

I do not have to comment on the self-evident phenomena in Thailand where Brahminism and Buddhism have coexisted not only at the level of artistic expressions but also at the level of daily routine. One accepts all this as a matter of course but, on deeper reflection, one is obliged to ask the question, how do these cultures not only accommodate but welcome this multivalence?

Indonesia is a very good example of multilayering and multivalence. In normal discourse one speaks about Java as Muslim Java and Bali as Hindu Bali. While this is true, it is not absolutely true, because everywhere in each of these regions there is coexistence of what we call the Hindu and Islamic traditions.

Now if we look at Java, primarily and rightly known as a Muslim country, how does the Ramayana reverberate there as nowhere else? Once again the question that has to be asked is, how does a text or a tradition primarily considered as Hindu reverberates in all parts of Java and at all levels—be it sculpture, performing arts, Wayang Kulit? Countless instances could be cited. There are specialists on this subject in the audience, so it is not necessary for me to elaborate.

The Wayang Kulit is an excellent example. The Dalangs are mostly Muslims. And what they are performing in the heart of Muslim Java is either texts from the Ramayana or texts from the Mahabharata.

The manner in which the kernel of the Ramayana story is transformed and transmitted in the whole of South East Asia, whether it is Malaysia or Indonesia, or for that matter Thailand, is a story which needs further investigation beyond our talking of the processes of diffusion.

As regards gender issues, which Madhu Khanna brought up: here again there is greater scope for further studies. How are women empowered in the context of Bali? But other instances can be given of women's empowerment in other parts of Java and Sumatra.

Now, finally in the countries of the Asian region there is a very distinctive attitude to the human body. There is no dichotomy between body, mind and soul. The body is sacred and if there is a violation, there is a total disruption in the cultural fabric. This is an area which requires investigation because I think that this body–mind–soul dichotomy, which we have inherited, we have almost refined to the limits of negativity, because attitude to the body is not to be considered marginal. It is central to the world view. The body is not carnal. The body is a vessel of the mind and spirit. This attitude to the body manifests itself in the arts of Asia. This is an area which requires much greater sophistication in the intellectual discourse.

One may say that this is not the occasion to talk about the body despite the reasons emphasized on the body in the Indian art. Further, anyone who has communicated with the arts of Asian countries and has also communicated with empowered women, knows that here is a different attitude. Violations takes place only when there is a change in the attitude to the body found within and without. This is a whole subject which understandably could not be addressed.

I have already said too much and perhaps with a lack of clarity. This is not normal in a formal valedictory address. However, my mind was stimulated after I heard the discussions by the members of this eminent group where engagement was intense and concentrated. I want to compliment Ambassador Shyam Saran, his colleagues and all those who assisted in conceiving and organizing this conference. It has been an educative experience to hear the discussion.

Lastly, where does all this take us? The paper in the final session pertinently brought up the question of categories—of introductory discourse, category of thought and category of critical assessment. This is where we have to address ourselves if we want an authentic and more viable theoretical framework for addressing the cultural fabric of the ASEAN countries. I am not talking about the Indian and ASEAN cultural linkages. I am speaking about the whole of Asian countries including India.

Thank you for your patience.

CPSIA information can be obtained
at www.ICGtesting.com
Printed in the USA
LVHW01*1953240718
584781LV00015B/352/P